BizTalk 2006 Recipes

A Problem-Solution Approach

Mark Beckner, Benjamin Goeltz,
Brandon Gross, Brennan O'Reilly,
Stephen Roger, Mark Smith, Alexander West

Apress®

BizTalk 2006 Recipes: A Problem-Solution Approach

Copyright © 2006 by Mark Beckner, Benjamin Goeltz, Brandon Gross, Brennan O'Reilly, Stephen Roger, Mark Smith, Alexander West

ISBN-13 (pbk): 978-1-59059-711-8

ISBN-10 (pbk): 1-59059-711-7

Printed and bound in the United States of America 9 8 7 6 5 4 3 2

Lead Editor: Jonathan Gennick
Technical Reviewer: Stephen W. Thomas
Editorial Board: Steve Anglin, Ewan Buckingham, Gary Cornell, Jason Gilmore, Jonathan Gennick, Jonathan Hassell, James Huddleston, Chris Mills, Matthew Moodie, Dominic Shakeshaft, Jim Sumser, Keir Thomas, Matt Wade
Project Manager: Tracy Brown Collins
Copy Edit Manager: Nicole LeClerc
Copy Editors: Marilyn Smith, Kim Wimpsett
Assistant Production Director: Kari Brooks-Copony
Production Editor: Ellie Fountain
Compositor: Lynn L'Heureux
Proofreader: Nancy Sixsmith
Indexer: Julie Grady
Cover Designer: Kurt Krames
Manufacturing Director: Tom Debolski

Distributed to the book trade worldwide by Springer-Verlag New York, Inc., 233 Spring Street, 6th Floor, New York, NY 10013. Phone 1-800-SPRINGER, fax 201-348-4505, e-mail orders-ny@springer-sbm.com, or visit http://www.springeronline.com.

For information on translations, please contact Apress directly at 2560 Ninth Street, Suite 219, Berkeley, CA 94710. Phone 510-549-5930, fax 510-549-5939, e-mail info@apress.com, or visit http://www.apress.com.

The source code for this book is available to readers at http://www.apress.com in the Source Code/Download section. You will need to answer questions pertaining to this book in order to successfully download the code.

Contents at a Glance

Contents

Foreword

Everyone will tell you the top concern among CIOs and IT professionals continues to be simplification and optimization of business processes. Couple that with the increasing need to reduce IT operating costs and integrate line-of-business applications and disparate data sources, and you quickly peel back the covers of a complex issue facing mid-market and enterprise customers. This is the challenge many IT staff and system integrators face each day as they attempt to deliver business value to the organizations they serve.

The good news is that more than 1300 professional service firms around the globe have realized Microsoft BizTalk Server is an ideal tool to help address these imperatives. Microsoft BizTalk Server 2006 enables businesses to optimize operations through automation and the exposure of processes and data in real time. It also provides simple yet powerful tools to gain a real-time understanding of business processes. Microsoft BizTalk Server helps you to grow your business and drive efficiency.

With over 15 years combined practical, hands-on customer experience, the authors of *BizTalk 2006 Recipes* have created a powerful reference for realizing the benefits of Microsoft BizTalk Server 2006. Each problem is presented with a practical, proven solution followed by a discussion of alternatives, considerations, and best practices. This book is ideal for consultants and staff who are seeking quicker return on investment and certain business value. Additionally, you will find comprehensive guidance on working through the most complex deployment challenges, including tested, reusable code snippets for use in production, enabling faster deployment and minimal post-implementation engineering support.

Most will agree there is no substitute for training at the school of hard knocks. However, this book should help mitigate and prevent failed deployments. Be sure to apply the lessons learned within its covers every day. Do not leave this in your car, office, or bag.

Robert Bannerman
Partner Strategy Manager
Microsoft Corporation

About the Foreword Author

ROBERT BANNERMAN is a Partner Strategy Manager for the Application Platform Marketing team at Microsoft Corporation. Robert drives worldwide partner strategy, enablement, and sales and marketing support for Microsoft's business process and integration channel. He is responsible for partner relationships and delivery of Microsoft BizTalk Server, Windows Workflow Foundation, and RFID technologies.

Robert grew up in Halifax, Nova Scotia, and holds Master of Business Administration and Master of Information Technology degrees from Bond University in Australia, and a Bachelor of Science degree from Dalhousie University in Canada. Robert lives in Seattle, Washington.

About the Authors

Mark Beckner

After being lost in the desert for a period of years, bearded, unwashed, and resembling a nineteenth century politician, Mark Beckner found himself holding a degree in Computer Science and Information Systems from a small college in southwestern Colorado. Tearfully leaving behind the innocence of his past, he immersed himself in the exotic and adventurous world of enterprise application integration (EAI), .NET development, and Visio diagrams. In a pattern of banality and madness, he frequents airports, hotel rooms, and fast-food joints, sacrificing his free time, health, and youth for the immense satisfaction that comes with increasing the bottom dollar in corporate America.

Benjamin Goeltz

Benjamin Goeltz (benjamin.goeltz@charteris.com) is a consultant specializing in the enterprise application integration (EAI) space, with over six years of experience. Benjamin graduated with a Bachelor of Arts degree in Business Information Systems from the University of Washington. He has designed and implemented solutions for each version of BizTalk Server, deploying solutions integrating both internal (EAI) and external (Business to Business, or B2B) systems to support mission-critical business processes. He has also authored content for white papers, help files, and books related to system integration. He is from Seattle, and currently works for Charteris (www.charteris.com), a business and IT consulting firm with headquarters in London.

I'd like to thank my family and friends, who have been extremely supportive of me reaching for both my professional and personal goals, and helping me remember that the world is at the same time much bigger and smaller than it seems.

Brandon Gross

Brandon Gross is a Managing Consultant with EMC's Microsoft Practice, and is a BizTalk MVP. He received a Bachelor of Arts degree in Business Information Systems and Accounting from the University of Washington. Brandon has worked on Business to Business (B2B) and Application to Application (A2A) solutions for medium-to-large enterprise clients in a wide range of industries, including government, resources, high-tech manufacturing, manufacturing, and software. He has experience in a breadth of Microsoft technologies, including .NET and all versions of

BizTalk. Brandon recently architected an A2A solution that received the 2006 Global Business Process and Integration Technology Innovation Solution of the Year award from Microsoft. Brandon and his coauthors have created a blogging site (`http://biztalk2006recipebook.blogspot.com/`) to discuss concepts from this book.

I would like thank my beautiful wife Cara for sacrificing time with her husband during the writing of this book. I would also like to thank the people at Apress for their support in getting us through the last mile. Finally, I would like to thank the wonderful group of authors and technical reviewers who made producing this book so much fun.

Brennan O'Reilly

Graduating with a Bachelor of Science degree in Psychology and a Bachelor of Arts degree in Drama from the University of Washington, Brennan O'Reilly never dreamed he would be a Managing Consultant with EMC's Microsoft Practice employing those degrees. He has lived in Tashkent, Uzbekistan; San Jose; and Vancouver, Washington, but prefers to call Seattle his home. Brennan has delivered BizTalk and integration-related projects across a wide array of clients and industries, including media/imaging, high-tech manufacturing, seafood processing, and government. Brennan's favorite projects include those with defined requirements, realistic time frames, and easygoing personalities.

I would like to thank my love and best friend Shauna for her support and encouragement through this process.

Stephen Roger

Stephen Roger is a Branch Director with EMC's Microsoft Practice in Seattle, Washington, where he runs the service and operations for EMC's office. He has more than 16 years of experience in developing business applications for customers across numerous industries. Stephen has been involved in integration projects using BizTalk Server since the initial release of the product in December 2000. In addition to delivering solutions on the BizTalk platform, he has coauthored white papers and product help content.

Mark Smith

Mark Smith is the National Integration Practice lead of EMC's Microsoft Practice and member of the Microsoft's global Partner Advisory Council (PAC). His role is to work primarily with enterprise customers within the Application to Application/Business to Business (A2A/B2B) space spanning manufacturing, health care, resources, utilities, and government industries, focusing on lead architect, design, and project management roles. Within the integration practice, his role is to grow a team of integration architects around technology and consulting practices, and to provide primary support to sales, marketing, and delivery functions for Microsoft's integration technologies. He has a Bachelor of Business degree in Information Systems and graduated from Royal Melbourne Institute of Technology in Melbourne, Australia. He has been a consultant for eight years, working with BizTalk and related Microsoft integration and development technologies (COM and .NET).

To my family in Australia and my great friends. I'd especially like to thank my mum, dad, and sisters who always gave me the opportunity. Thanks also to my fellow authors—you are all incredible people! It's been a long road, plenty of early mornings, Dilmah tea, and quiet weekends! Thank you for the support, I owe you all!

Alexander West

Alexander West is an Architect with EMC's Microsoft Practice, where he has been delivering integration solutions based on .NET and the BizTalk integration tool set since 2000. Alexander holds a Bachelor of Science degree in Computational Mathematics and a Bachelor of Arts degree in Business Information Systems from the University of Washington. He delivers integration solutions supporting business process challenges both within and beyond organizational boundaries, to clients in industries such as software, financial services, high-tech manufacturing, law safety and justice, and energy. He is involved in all stages of the project's life cycle, from envisioning and design activities through development, testing, and deployment.

I would like to thank my wife Megan for her love and patience through our engagement and the writing of this book.

About the Technical Reviewer

STEPHEN W. THOMAS has been working with BizTalk Server since early 2001. He has been recognized by Microsoft as a BizTalk Server Most Valuable Professional (MVP) since 2004. He is an active newsgroup participant and blogger. He also runs BizTalkGurus.com, a website focused on BizTalk Server. BizTalkGurus.com has more than 50 samples, labs, and videos written by Stephen, covering both BizTalk 2004 and BizTalk 2006. In his spare time, Stephen enjoys traveling and spending time at home with his wife and two dogs.

Acknowledgments

The author team would like to recognize the key contributions of the following individuals and organizations. Without their tireless efforts and resources, this book would not have been possible.

Individuals:

- The editorial and production teams at Apress

- Robert Bannerman, Microsoft, Partner Strategy Manager

- Stephen Thomas, technical reviewer

- Jeff Pepper, book advisor

Organizations:

- Apress

- Microsoft Product Team

- EMC (formerly Interlink Group)

- Charteris

Introduction

Enterprise integration is a complex problem. Even with an exceptional product like BizTalk Server 2006, many variables and considerations contribute to the enterprise integration puzzle. Each of this book's authors has worked with BizTalk since the product's inception in the early 2000s and has implemented more than ten enterprise integration projects during his IT professional consultant career.

Many books on the market provide solutions without context to the problem. *BizTalk 2006 Recipes: A Problem-Solution Approach* aims to not only give the reader solutions to common BizTalk integration scenarios, but also to provide the reader with information related to the problem at hand. By handpicking the key scenarios, we hope to arm the reader with sufficient information to make the best decision when faced with enterprise integration challenges.

Book Requirements

The recipes in this book are intended to be hands-on exercises, introducing developers and administrators to the different BizTalk Server 2006 components. Given the activity-based nature of this book, it is essential to have a working environment with the following components:

- BizTalk Server 2006 (and all prerequisites; see installation instructions)

- SQL Server 2005 or 2000

- Visual Studio 2005

The majority of developers will be working with BizTalk Server, SQL Server, and Visual Studio on a single platform. Based on this, Microsoft lists the following recommended minimum requirements for the system:

- 1GHz or higher (single processor)

- 1GB of RAM

- 6GB hard disk space

- Super VGA (1024 × 768) resolution monitor

System requirements for BizTalk Server 2006 are highly dependent on the nature of the solutions that will be implemented. For instance, a solution that may be installed on multiple BizTalk and SQL Server database servers could require a substantially different configuration than a single server with both BizTalk and SQL Server installed. Additionally, small solutions with very low processing needs (a few simple orchestrations a day) will require far fewer system resources than a complex solution that is processing large batches throughout the day.

A common approach to setting up enterprise systems is to obtain a server with as much processing power as possible, including multiple CPUs and expansive disk space. However, this paradigm frequently should be altered in the integration space, especially as it relates to BizTalk. Often, the appropriate approach is to decrease the number of CPUs on a single box and spread them across multiple boxes (for example, four BizTalk servers with one CPU each are often preferable to one BizTalk server with four CPUs), increase the RAM, and ignore the disk space (BizTalk solutions are often extremely small). By scaling out instead of scaling up, many BizTalk solutions will operate more efficiently, sharing resources between boxes within a BizTalk group as needed. Additionally, licensing and hardware costs can be reduced.

As you work through the recipes in this book, and begin to build and deploy BizTalk solutions for production environments, you will learn to assess what type of server configurations are most appropriate. Because BizTalk crosses multiple environments, from application servers and Internet Information Services (IIS) servers to SQL database servers, it is important to speak with the administrators of each environment to make sure the systems are set up properly and operating correctly.

Who This Book Is For

The recipes in this book are intended for a diverse audience. Whether you are just picking up the product for the first time and don't know what a schema is or you are a seasoned BizTalk professional looking for the latest patterns, this book has something to offer you. Unlike traditional cover-to-cover books, the recipe format lends itself to problem-solving. Recipes are organized by problem statements that help you quickly identify solutions to common BizTalk scenarios. For this reason, we suggest that you keep a copy of this book next to your workstation as a reference.

How This Book Is Organized

This book is made up of the following ten chapters:

Chapter 1, Document Schemas: The foundations of all BizTalk solutions are schemas—documents that define how messages are structured and accessed within BizTalk Server. Understanding schemas is essential to the successful creation of maps and orchestrations, and the correct routing of messages through the messaging system. Proper design and construction of schemas will reduce the need for substantial rewrites of orchestrations and other dependent components later in the development cycle. The aim of this chapter is to introduce key concepts of working with schemas and to provide the developer with enough information to make the appropriate decisions related to the development of this essential building block.

Chapter 2, Document Mapping: As data is passed between systems, one core need is always present: to define how data maps from one system to the next. BizTalk provides extensive options for mapping, including a graphical user interface to create maps, pre-existing functoids that provide standard mapping functions, the ability to create custom code for advanced mapping requirements, access to pure XSLT for advanced programmers, and powerful XPath functionality for accessing nodes and allowing for alternative mapping methods. This chapter provides numerous recipes to help developers build and test both simple and complex maps.

Chapter 3, Messaging: The BizTalk Server engine is built on messaging—the movement of documents in, through, and out of the system. Messaging allows documents to be routed to subscribers (external systems or internal orchestrations) through ports and pipelines. This chapter describes the methods necessary for routing messages, working with these messages in memory, and performing operations on messages that are outside orchestrations.

Chapter 4, Orchestration: The core of BizTalk processing lies in orchestrations. Multiple thread handling (parallel shapes), synchronous and asynchronous responses (send, receive, and listen shapes), proper exception handling (scope shapes and error-handling patterns), and notifications in the case of failure are highly valuable components of an integration engine, and all of these are available in BizTalk orchestrations. This chapter presents extensive examples for orchestration development and provides detailed discussions to help developers design and build viable solutions.

Chapter 5, Business Rules Framework: Organizations may need to process information differently depending on the data submitted. In the case of BizTalk, information is submitted via a message, and data within that message may require special processing once it has been received by an orchestration. The orchestration must be able to determine what that data is and how to process it. Additionally, rules around how that data is interpreted may change at any given time, even after the solution is in production. For example, a rule may be required that allows processing messages as long as a specific field has a value less than 10, but must stop processing and notify an administrator when this value is equal to or exceeds 10. The ability to store and access such a rule and to make it available for customization through a user-friendly interface is provided by the BizTalk business rules framework.

Chapter 6, Adapters: Adapters are the first point of contact between BizTalk Server and outside systems and provide the functionality necessary to turn incoming data into a message with which the messaging engine can work. Data is often delivered to and from systems in several standard formats, including file transfers, HTTP posts, web services, and SQL calls. BizTalk provides these transport mechanisms through the standard adapters, with interfaces that allow for highly configurable implementations. In situations that require an approach that is not provided for in the standard adapters, custom adapters can be written and deployed. This chapter demonstrates the use of standard adapters for a variety of applications, and introduces the concepts necessary for writing custom adapters when the need arises.

Chapter 7, Deployment: The process of deployment to a production environment can be challenging for any type of solution, but integration solutions are complicated by the number of systems that may be impacted, as well as the number of different components that may be required. BizTalk Server provides a large number of options for deployments, from simple manual installations to all-inclusive MSI packages. This chapter provides recipes that introduce the key tools and concepts used for deploying BizTalk solutions.

Chapter 8, Administration and Operations: Once solutions have been deployed to a production environment, numerous administrative practices are required, including standard maintenance (database backups and data cleanup), issue tracking (determining where a message is in a given process), load considerations (ensuring that the BizTalk Server environment is configured and scaled properly, and that it is using its system resources properly), and other general tasks. This chapter walks through the different tools that are available for administering BizTalk Server and viewing data that is being (or has been) processed.

Chapter 9, Business Activity Monitoring: Once processes are deployed and executing, it is often essential to view statistics about these processes. Business analysts may need to see metrics about how long it takes for a certain orchestration to complete, while a system administrator may need to know the number of instances that occur of a specific orchestration between the hours of 8 AM and 5 PM. Business Activity Monitor (BAM) provides the engine necessary to access this type of information in BizTalk Server and the tools with which to view it. This chapter explores the options available for developing and deploying BAM solutions.

Chapter 10, Encore: BizTalk Server 2006: This chapter provides recipes for additional advanced techniques pertaining to BizTalk Server 2006.

CHAPTER 1

■ ■ ■

Document Schemas

The BizTalk tool set enables exchanging information among computer systems. Each area of BizTalk's rich set of capabilities addresses the common development tasks of building an integration solution. For example, BizTalk has tools for the common task of translating information from a structure understood by a source computer system into a structure understood by a destination computer system. Other BizTalk tools focus on defining integration processes, or patterns of information flows.

This chapter focuses on the capabilities of the BizTalk Editor tool. The BizTalk product team designed the Editor tool specifically for defining the structure of the information that flows through BizTalk. BizTalk calls these definitions *schemas*, and the BizTalk Editor creates them.

For example, suppose a customer message flows through BizTalk. This message may contain customer demographic information such as occupation and gender, logistical information such as address, and information about the particular products of interest to the customer. BizTalk needs to collect and organize this information in a structured format to fully utilize it.

Sometimes BizTalk needs to examine messages to handle them correctly. For example, suppose additional verification steps are needed if a customer's purchase is very expensive and outside his normal buying patterns. A BizTalk schema can promote the purchase amount and make it available throughout BizTalk. BizTalk can examine the purchase amount and take an additional step to send a notification message to the customer's representative. This property promotion process creates a property schema defining information about the message. The BizTalk runtime engine uses property schemas extensively, capturing information such as the location where BizTalk accepts a message or the message's intended destination.

XML standards form the core of BizTalk. At no time is this more evident than when defining messages with the BizTalk Editor development tool. Use the Editor to define the structure of information. For example, you can create a hierarchy in which a customer message contains a demographic section, an address section, and a section for customer preferences. Each of these sections can contain details relevant only to that section.

The XML Schema Definition (XSD) language natively defines message structure to BizTalk. Since the Editor defines messages in XSD by default, any XSD-compliant XML editor can define BizTalk messages. However, the BizTalk Editor supports many of the rich capabilities of XSD, such as importing common schemas to facilitate reuse and consistency across message formats.

In addition to message structure, the BizTalk Editor can also define the data types of specific fields, thus completing the message definition. These data type definitions can be interoperable XSD primitive types, such as `xs:string` or `xs:decimal`, or complex data types.

For example, complex types may require values adhering to regular expressions or a list of enumerated values enforced with the schema.

Finally, while XML standards are the core for BizTalk messages and the Editor, a message structure can extend beyond XML to apply to other formats such as a comma-delimited flat file representation. BizTalk can efficiently parse a diverse population of message formats into XML for processing within the core BizTalk runtime engine. XML must still define the message structure and fields, but a schema can specify additional information defining how the XML message translates to and from the file format.

1-1. Creating Simple Document Schemas

Problem

As part of your business process or messaging solution, you need to create a simple XML schema.

Solution

The following steps outline how to create a simple schema and add it to your BizTalk project.

1. Open an existing project or create a new project in Visual Studio.

2. As shown in Figure 1-1, right-click the project name in the Solution Explorer and select Add ➤ Add New Item (alternatively, select File ➤ Add New Item).

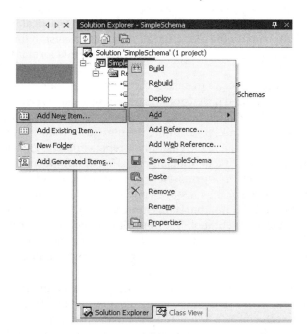

Figure 1-1. *Adding an item from the Solution Explorer*

3. The Add New Item dialog box will appear, as shown in Figure 1-2. Select Schema as the type of item, type in a name for the item, and click OK.

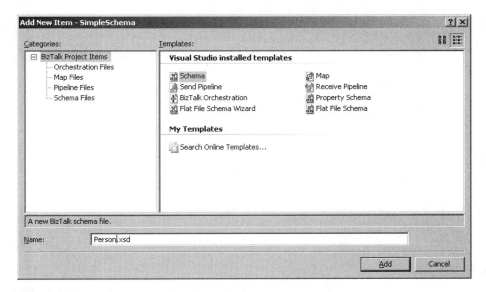

Figure 1-2. *Add New Item dialog box*

4. Right-click the Root node and select Rename. Then change the name of the node.

5. To add nodes, right-click a node and select Insert Schema Nodes. Then select from the following options, as shown in Figure 1-3:

- Child Record, to add a new record node indented one level from the selected node

- Child Field Attribute, to add a new attribute node indented one level from the selected node

- Child Field Element, to add a new element node indented one level from the selected node

- Sibling Record, to add a new record node at the same level of the selected node

- Sibling Field Attribute, to add a new attribute node at the same level of the selected node

- Sibling Field Element, to add a new element node at the same level of the selected node

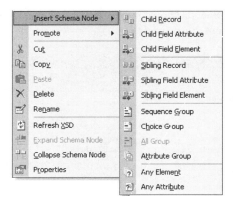

Figure 1-3. *Adding schema nodes*

6. Select a node to view and modify its properties.

7. Build and deploy the solution.

How It Works

XML schemas are the foundation of all scenarios and document exchanges with BizTalk
Server. Once you have created your schema, you can create your scenario. Whether it is a pure
messaging solution or involves business process automation scenarios implemented as
orchestrations (covered in Chapter 4), the schema is available to all other projects and solutions simply by referencing it. Additionally, once you have created your schema, you can
generate instances of the document that will adhere to the schema definition. This feature
makes it very easy to create test data.

To generate a test instance, follow these steps:

1. Open the schema Property Pages dialog box, shown in Figure 1-4, by right-clicking the
schema name in the Solution Explorer and selecting Properties.

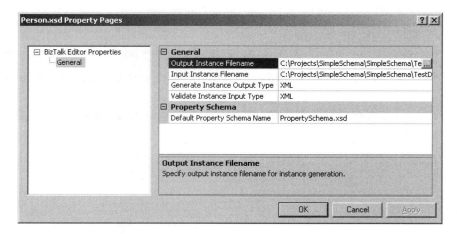

Figure 1-4. *Schema Property Pages dialog box*

2. Type in a path and file name next to `Output Instance Filename`, or select the ellipsis to use the common file dialog box to browse to a file location and name the file. Then click OK.

3. Right-click the schema and select Generate Instance. A test instance of the document will be created, located, and named based on the `Output Instance Filename` property specified.

Similarly, BizTalk Server provides the ability to validate that an instance of a document adheres to a schema definition. To validate an instance, follow these steps:

1. Open the schema Property Pages dialog box by right-clicking the schema name in the Solution Explorer and selecting Properties.

2. Type in a path and file name next to `Input Instance Filename`, or select the ellipsis to use the common file dialog box to browse to a file location and select a file. Then click OK.

3. Right-click the schema and select Validate Instance. The document specified in the `Input Instance Filename` property will be validated against the schema.

1-2. Creating Schema Namespaces

Problem

You have two schemas that need to be represented with the same root node.

Solution

BizTalk Server uses a combination of namespaces and root nodes to resolve schema references. Therefore, it is possible to have two schemas with the same root node as long as their namespace designation is different. By default, the BizTalk Editor will set the namespace of a schema to `http://[solution].[schema]`, where *solution* refers to the name of the solution file and *schema* refers to the name of the schema file. This default namespace designation may be modified as follows:

1. Open the project that contains the schema.

2. Double-click the schema to open it.

3. Select the `<Schema>` node.

4. Right-click and select Properties.

5. Modify the `Target Namespace` property as desired.

When you modify the `Target Namespace` property, BizTalk Server will automatically modify the `Default Namespace` (element name `xmlns`) of the schema to match the `Target Namespace`.

Once the two schemas with the same root node have different namespace designations, they may be used without any conflicts.

How It Works

Namespaces are used to allow elements and attributes from different schemas to share names. For example, two schemas may have an element named FirstName. If the schemas did not have different namespaces, BizTalk Server would not know which FirstName you were referencing.

As well as adopting naming standards and conventions for all BizTalk artifacts, you should adopt a standard for namespaces in schemas. An example of a standard is as follows:

```
http://[Company Name].[Project].BizTalk.Schemas.[Schema].[Version]
```

where Company Name is your company name, Project is the name of the project, Schema is the name of the schema, and Version is the version number of the schema.

In summary, BizTalk Server can accommodate two or more schemas with the same root node as long as the schemas have unique namespace designations.

1-3. Promoting Properties

Problem

You have a scenario where you want to subscribe to a message differently based on the contents or context of the message, and you need to understand how BizTalk Server exposes this metadata.

Solution

In order to promote instance-specific data fields (data that resides in the actual message instances, such as a customer name or the ID of an order), you must create a property schema. You then promote the specific schema elements, attributes, or records you need to subscribe to into the property schema. This task is accomplished in Visual Studio, and can be done in one of two ways: quick promotion and regular promotion. For more information on both of these methods, see Recipe 1-4, which describes how to create a property schema.

In addition to instance-specific data fields, a number of system- or exchange-specific properties are automatically promoted by BizTalk Server. A description of these exchange-specific properties, and the fundamental difference between them and instance-specific properties, is provided in the following "How It Works" section.

All properties that have been promoted, regardless of whether they are associated with a specific instance or the message exchange in general, are available for subscription by other BizTalk Server objects, including send ports, send port groups, and orchestrations. Promoted properties are also available for tracking purposes, which allow them to be used in troubleshooting and reporting.

How It Works

The importance of promoted properties in BizTalk Server's publish/subscribe architecture cannot be overstated. Understanding how they work is absolutely critical when designing and building an integration solution.

From a simplistic perspective, a publish/subscribe integration architecture involves source systems publishing or outputting messages to a centralized hub. After the hub receives these messages, it delivers them to the destination, or subscribing, systems. Within BizTalk

Server, promoted properties are the key data that determine which messages are delivered to subscribing systems or processes. Without promoted properties, messages would be received by BizTalk Server, but they would not be sent out, resulting in a sort of black hole of messages. This would obviously not be a good situation, and BizTalk Server will actually throw an error if a message is received without having a system or process that subscribes to it. This keeps with the theory that it is not a good idea for a publish/subscribe integration hub to accept messages for which it does not have a subscriber.

A term that is commonly used to describe a message's promoted properties is *message context*. Message context includes all the instance-specific and exchange-specific data fields, and essentially is the metadata that the messaging engine of BizTalk Server uses to process messages. As previously noted, instance-specific properties are those that pertain to a specific message instance, and they must be promoted explicitly during development. A common example of this type of property is an XML element containing a unique ID, which may capture an important data field such as an order number. From a message schema, XML elements, attributes, and records may be promoted.

Note In order for an XML record to be promoted, its `ContentType` property must be set to `SimpleContent`. All promoted properties, regardless of whether they are populated by XML elements, attributes, or records, have a maximum length of 255 characters.

Along with being the key data elements allowing message subscription, promoted properties are also commonly used in orchestrations to determine business process. Orchestrations can handle messages dynamically by interrogating promoted properties that hold key metadata elements of a message. For example, sales orders being delivered domestically may need to be handled differently than those being sent overseas. By capturing the destination country of an order in the document schema, and flagging the element as a promoted property, this data element can easily be used as a decision point in the orchestration. Domestic orders could be handled on one branch of decision logic, and international orders handled on another. It is important to note here that as an alternative to using promoted properties, the actual XML message could be interrogated within the orchestration to determine the destination of a sales order. While this method could be used, leveraging promoted properties simplifies programming and has performance benefits, as promoted properties can be accessed directly without incurring the cost of opening the entire XML message.

For additional performance gains, *distinguished fields* can be used as opposed to promoted properties within orchestrations. Distinguished fields provide functionality similar to promoted properties (allowing access to instance- or exchange-specific metadata items on a message), with a few key differences:

- Distinguished fields are available only within a single orchestration instance, and they are not available to other BizTalk Server objects, such as receive locations, send ports, send port groups, and tracking utilities.

- Distinguished fields can be of any length; promoted properties have a maximum length of 255 characters.

- Distinguished fields have less of a performance impact than promoted properties, as they are not persisted to the MessageBox database. Instead, they are essentially XPath aliases, which simply point to the appropriate XML data field. Additionally, adding the `DistinguishedField` attribute to a field on a .NET class allows it to be exposed as a distinguished field.

- Distinguished fields are accessed through a reference to the name of the message, the name of the record structure containing the distinguished field (which could include multiple levels of child records), and the name of the distinguished field, with each named item separated by periods: *MessageName.RecordName.ChildRecordName. DistinguishedFieldName*. Promoted properties, on the other hand, are accessed through a reference to the name of the message, the name of the property schema, and a name of the promoted property, via the following format: *MessageName(PropertySchemaName.PromotedPropertyName)*.

Certain scenarios will call for sensitive information, such as a bank account number, to be used as a promoted property. To allow for enhanced troubleshooting and detailed reporting, promoted properties can be viewed in tools such as Health and Activity Tracking (HAT) and Business Activity Monitor (BAM). Based on privacy regulations, these data fields may need to be hidden from these tools, which can be accomplished by setting the promoted property's `Sensitive Information` property to `True` (this configuration is applied on the property schema).

System- or exchange-specific properties are those that are automatically promoted by BizTalk Server, and allow the successful processing of those documents by the messaging engine. The fundamental difference between the two types of properties is that exchange-specific properties can all be determined without looking into the actual contents, or payload of the message. Instance-specific properties, on the other hand, are all populated with actual values within a message instance.

Exchange-specific properties come in various types. Table 1-1 lists the default exchange-specific property types that come with a complete installation of BizTalk Server. Additional properties may be added as other BizTalk-related items are installed, such as the MQ Series adapter.

Table 1-1. *Default Exchange-Specific Property Types*

Type	Description
BizTalk Framework (BTF2)	Properties that support the BizTalk Framework
BizTalk Server (BTS)	Properties that support core BizTalk Server messaging
Error Reporting (ErrorReport)	Properties that support error reporting and handling
File Adapter (File)	Properties that support the File adapter
FTP Adapter (FTP)	Properties that support the FTP adapter
HTTP Adapter (HTTP)	Properties that support the HTTP adapter
Legacy (LEGACY)	Properties that support BizTalk Server 2002 properties
Message Tracking (MessageTracking)	Properties that support message tracking
HWS (Microsoft.BizTalk.Hws)	Properties that support Human Workflow Services
Orchestration (Microsoft.BizTalk. XLANGs.BTXEngine)	Properties that support the BizTalk Server orchestration engine

Type	Description
MIME (MIME)	Properties that support the processing of MIME-encoded messages
MSMQT Adapter (MSMQT)	Properties that support the MSMQT adapter
POP3 Adapter (POP3)	Properties that support the POP3 adapter
SMTP Adapter (SMTP)	Properties that support the SMTP adapter
SOAP Adapter (SOAP)	Properties that support the SOAP adapter
Windows Sharepoint Services Adapter (WSS)	Properties that support the WSS adapter
XML Document (XMLNorm)	Properties that support the processing of XML documents

BizTalk Server processes promoted properties as messages are received into or sent out of the MessageBox. Specifically, pipelines handle this task. System- or exchange-specific properties are promoted by default, through pipelines such as XML or PassThru (both the receive and send variety). For instance-specific properties to be promoted, a pipeline other than the PassThru must be used, as this pipeline does not attempt to match messages to their associated schemas (and therefore property schemas).

As properties are promoted, their XSD data types are converted to Common Language Runtime (CLR) data types. Table 1-2 shows XSD data types and their associated CLR data types.

Table 1-2. *XSD Data Types and Associated CLR Data Types*

XSD	CLR	XSD	CLR
anyURI	String	Name	String
Boolean	Boolean	NCName	String
byte	sbyte	negativeInteger	Decimal
date	DateTime	NMTOKEN	String
dateTime	DateTime	nonNegativeInteger	Decimal
decimal	Decimal	nonPositiveInteger	Decimal
double	Double	normalizedString	String
ENTITY	String	NOTATION	String
float	Single	positiveInteger	Decimal
gDay	DateTime	QName	String
gMonth	DateTime	short	Int16
gMonthDay	DateTime	string	String
ID	String	time	DateTime
IDREF	String	token	String
int	Int32	unsignedByte	Byte
integer	Decimal	unsignedInt	Uint32
language	String	unsignedShort	Uint16

In addition to pipelines, orchestrations may also be used to explicitly set promoted properties. This is important if your business process requires the copying or creation of messages. Since messages are immutable (meaning once a message has been created, it cannot be modified) in BizTalk Server, a new message must be created prior to any of its promoted properties being set. When a message in constructed in an orchestration as a copy of another message, the message context (its promoted properties), by default, are all copied to the new message. Once this new message is created, its properties may be explicitly set to something different than in the original message. This must be done in the same Message Assignment shape in the orchestration as the duplicate message.

■**Note** When a copy of a message is created in an orchestration, it is important to consider how the properties on the original message are configured. If any of its properties are configured to use `MessageContextPropertyBase` for the `Property Schema Base` (a property of the promoted field found in the property schema), they will not be copied to the new message in the orchestration. By contrast, all those properties that are configured to use the `MessageDataPropertyBase` (the default value) for the `Property Schema Base` will be copied to the new message. For more information about the `Property Schema Base` property, see Recipe 1-4.

1-4. Creating Property Schemas

Problem

You want to subscribe to a message based on the contents of the message.

Solution

Property schemas allow you to promote properties so that they can be used when setting up filter expressions. As long as the PassThruReceive pipeline is not used, these promoted properties are added to the message context during pipeline processing. Once added to the message context, they can be used as filter expressions on send ports. These properties are also available to be evaluated or modified in orchestrations. To create a property schema and promote a property, follow these steps:

1. Open the project that contains the schema.

2. Double-click to open the schema.

3. Select the node that you wish to promote.

4. Right-click and select Promote ➤ Quick Promotion, as shown in Figure 1-5.

Figure 1-5. *Completing a quick promotion of a property*

5. You will be asked if you wish to add the property schema to the project. Click OK. The property schema is created with a reference to the promoted property, as well as a default property of `Property1`. This may be removed from the property schema.

■**Note** You may also add a property schema by highlighting the project in the Solution Explorer and selecting Add ➤ Add New Item ➤ Property Schema. Once the property schema is added to the project, you must associate it with a schema. To do this, select the schema in the Solution Explorer, right-click a node in the schema, and select Promote ➤ Show Promotions. In the dialog box, select the Property Fields tab and click the Folder icon to launch the BizTalk Type Picker dialog box. Browse to the property schema, select it, and click OK.

---

6. To view all promoted properties, select any node in the schema and select Promote ➤ Show Promotions to open the Promote Properties dialog box.

7. Select the Property Fields tab to view all of the promoted properties, as shown in Figure 1-6.

8. You may promote additional fields directly from this dialog box, or repeat steps 3 and 4 to promote other fields.

9. Build and deploy the solution.

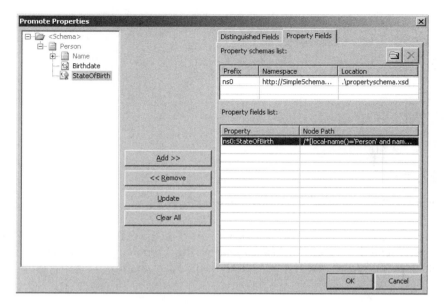

Figure 1-6. *Viewing the promoted properties in the Promote Properties dialog box*

How It Works

Once you have deployed the solution with the promoted properties, they may be used to perform content-based routing on the documents. Following is a simple example of content-based routing. Assume you have the following two documents:

```
<Person>
        <Name>
                <FirstName>John</FirstName>
                <LastName>Doe</LastName>
        </Name>
        <Birthdate>1979-05-31</BirthDate>
        <StateOfBirth>Washington</StateOfBirth>
</Person>

<Person>
        <Name>
                <FirstName>Sam</FirstName>
                <LastName>Evans</LastName>
        </Name>
        <Birthdate>1973-03-15</BirthDate>
        <StateOfBirth>California</StateOfBirth>
</Person>
```

You would like to send each of these documents to a different destination based on the StateOfBirth field. After creating a simple schema to represent these documents, the StateOfBirth element is promoted using the steps outlined in the "Solution" section. Once the project is built and deployed, you are able to reference the promoted property when creating a send port filter expression. In this example, two distinct send ports are created. Figure 1-7 shows the filter expression on the first send port. The subscription is based on the value of the StateOfBirth field being equal to Washington.

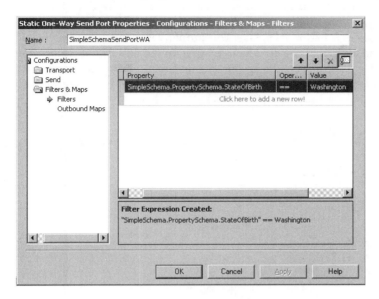

Figure 1-7. *Subscription for Washington*

On the second send port, the subscription is based on the value of the StateOfBirth field being equal to California, as shown in Figure 1-8.

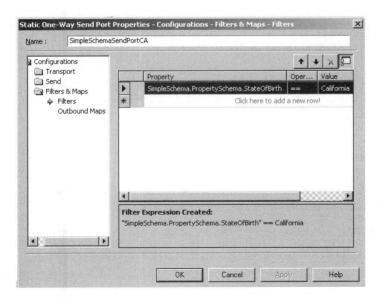

Figure 1-8. *Subscription for California*

Although this example is simple, it is easy to see how you can leverage this feature to create content-based routing scenarios through the use of promoted properties.

It is also possible to create message context properties that do not exist in the message itself, but only in the message context. This may be valuable when you are not allowed to modify the schema, but would like to associate additional information with the document. This may be accomplished by adding a node to a property schema and setting its `Property Schema Base` property to `MessageContextPropertyBase`. This property is then available and can be set in an orchestration, and ultimately the document may be routed based on its value. For example, perhaps you would like to calculate the age for each person processed in the preceding example, but you cannot add an `Age` element to the schema. As opposed to adding a node to the schema, a node is added to the property schema, as shown in Figure 1-9.

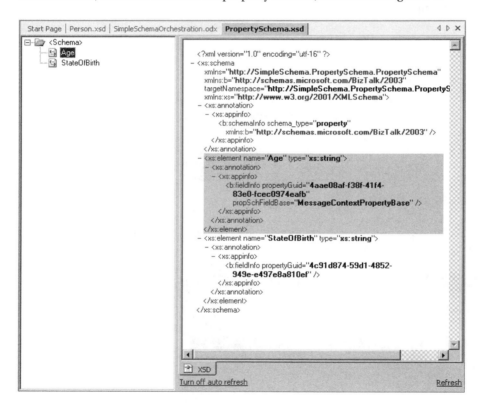

Figure 1-9. *Adding a property to message context*

After building and redeploying the solution, a second property, `Age`, is now available for generating filter expressions. To complete the scenario, you would do the following:

- Create an orchestration that subscribes to all of the documents with no value for `Age`.

- In this orchestration, calculate the `Age` value based on the birth date and set the property accordingly.

- Send the document back into the MessageBox.

- Add a second filter expression to the existing send ports to subscribe based on the StateOfBirth and if the Age value is present.

In summary, content-based routing is a typical scenario, and property schemas are used to extend the message context properties that come with BizTalk Server.

1-5. Importing Schemas

Problem

You would like to import an existing XML schema into another schema.

Solution

You can use the XSD Import method within the BizTalk Editor to reuse an existing common XML object structure within another, as opposed to manually creating an entire schema.

As an example, assume you have two simple XML structures, Customer and Address:

```
<Customer>
  <FirstName> </FirstName>
  <LastName> </LastName>
  <MiddleInit> </MiddleInit>
  <Age></Age>
</Customer>

<Address>
  <AddrLine1> </AddrLine1>
  <AddrLine2> </AddrLine2>
  <AddrLine3> </AddrLine3>
  <Zip> </Zip>
  <State> </State>
  <Country> </Country>
</Address>
```

To use the XSD Import method to allow this scenario within BizTalk, follow these steps:

1. Open the project that contains the schema.

2. Double-click the Customer schema to open it. The schema is shown in Figure 1-10.

3. Click the root node of the Customer schema.

4. In the Properties window, within the Advanced group, click the ellipsis next to Imports to open the Imports dialog box, as shown in Figure 1-11.

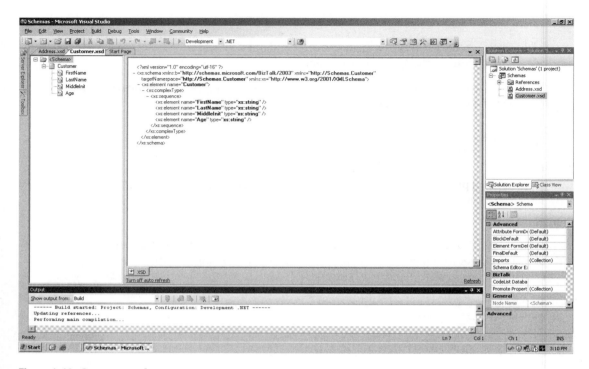

Figure 1-10. *Customer schema*

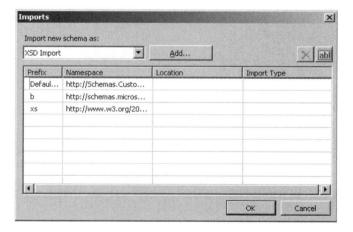

Figure 1-11. *Imports dialog box*

5. Select XSD Import as the import type and click the Add button.

6. In the BizTalk Type Picker dialog box, select the Schemas tree node and select the Address schema, as shown in Figure 1-12.

Note In this example, the Address schema is within the current BizTalk project. If the schema existed outside the BizTalk project, the schema could be imported by selecting the Reference tree node.

The preceding procedure imports the Address schema into the Customer schema. To use the Address schema, follow these steps:

1. Click the Customer node in the Customer schema.

2. Right-click and select Insert Child Record.

3. Click the newly created child record.

4. In the Properties window, within the General group, click the Data Structure Type drop-down list and select the Address reference, as shown in Figure 1-13.

The Customer schema is now referencing and using the Address schema via the Imports schema method within the BizTalk tool set.

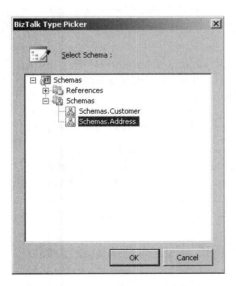

Figure 1-12. *Selecting a schema to import*

Figure 1-13. *Selecting the Address object reference*

How It Works

Within the BizTalk tool set, there are a variety of ways in which you can construct XML schema. The choices revolve around common architecture principles such as reuse, development best practices for schema organization, and fundamental development preferences.

This example illustrated using the Imports method for referencing schema. The Imports dialog box (Figure 1-12) offers three choices for achieving the schema reference activity (step 5 of the recipe):

Include: This method physically includes a schema definition within another. The common usage would be to create a static reference of a schema during the schema build process. This choice could be used to leverage previously defined XSD schema (for example, publicly available schema). The include schema must be the same target namespace of the schema you are including. Alternatively, the target namespace of the include schema can be blank.

Import: The most commonly used import method within BizTalk, the Import option includes XSD Imports statements within the source schema definition. By using this option, namespaces and XSD object structures within the target schema are available for use within the source schema in read-only fashion. The practical application for this choice revolves around common reuse, such as reuse of an existing schema artifact or use of a publicly available XML schema.

Redefine: The least-common import method within BizTalk, the Redefine option, like the Import option, allows namespaces and XSD object references to be used within the source definition. However, the Redefine option allows objects and data structures to be overridden within the source definition. Common uses could be to create an inheritance model or to reuse and customize an existing XSD structure.

This example demonstrated referencing other schemas within the BizTalk tool set. However, while BizTalk provides and implements standard XSD instructions to achieve this functionality, common architecture usage and choices should not be ignored to ensure the correct schema reference method is selected.

1-6. Referencing Schemas

Problem

You would like to reference an XML schema in your BizTalk project, perhaps because you want to reuse an existing BizTalk artifact or prebuilt schema component.

Solution

As an example, assume you have a simple `Customer` XML schema (`CustomerSchema.dll`) stored in an existing BizTalk project:

```
<Customer>
  <FirstName> </FirstName>
  <LastName> </LastName>
  <MiddleInit> </MiddleInit>
  <Age></Age>
</Customer>
```

To reference an existing schema, follow these steps:

1. Open your source project.

2. Within the Solution Explorer, right-click the `References` tree node and select Add Reference.

3. Select the Projects tab in the Add References dialog box.

4. Click the Browse button, navigate to `CustomerSchema.dll`, and then click the Open button.

You now have referenced `CustomerSchema.dll` and can use the inherent BizTalk artifacts in your current project. For example, suppose that you want to use the DLL in a new map within your current project. Follow these steps:

1. Right-click the project and select Add ➤ New Item.

2. In the Add New Item dialog box, double-click Map. This opens a blank map with left and right panes where you can enter the source and destination schema, respectively.

3. Click Open Source Schema in the left pane.

4. In the BizTalk Type Picker dialog box, select the `References` tree node and select the Client Schema reference.

5. Select the `Schemas` node.

6. Select the `Customer` schema, as shown in Figure 1-14.

Figure 1-14. *Selecting a schema to reference*

How It Works

Referencing schemas gives you the ability to reuse and reference existing BizTalk artifacts, as you would normally reference other .NET artifacts. While this can be powerful, you should always keep in mind partitioning and change scenarios. For example, if you were to reference an existing deployed artifact, to make changes to the referenced artifact, you would need to remove the referenced artifact in the dependent project.

This example explored how to reference a schema artifact in another project. BizTalk also gives you the ability to reference schemas in Schema Import tasks. For information on how to import schema references, refer to Recipe 1-5.

1-7. Creating Envelopes

Problem

You are receiving a message that contains multiple records in a batch fashion. In order to import this information into the appropriate systems, each record must be handled individually, as opposed to processing them all in a single batch.

Solution

Envelopes allow you to define a container schema that wraps a number of child schemas or subschemas. By defining which child records it contains, the envelope allows BizTalk Server to access the subrecords individually (a process commonly known as *debatching*) and process them as distinct messages. For this solution, it is assumed that the schema defining the child record has already been created (see Recipe 1-1). To create an envelope schema, follow these steps:

1. Open the project that contains the child record schema.

2. Right-click the project and select Add ➤ Add New Item to open the Add New Item dialog box.

3. Select Schema Files from the BizTalk Project Items category and Schema from the list of templates. Enter a descriptive name for your new schema, as shown in Figure 1-15. Then click Add.

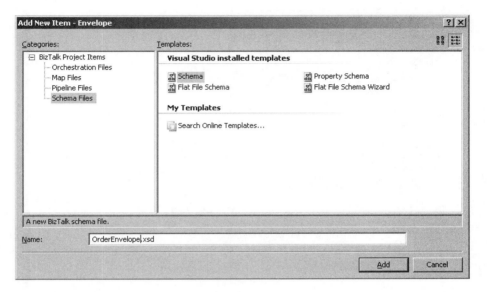

Figure 1-15. *Adding a new schema to a project*

4. Right-click the Root node of the new schema, and change it to the root name of the incoming schema containing the batch of records (OrderEnvelope in this example).

5. Click the Schema node (directly above the newly renamed root node) and change the Envelope property of the schema to Yes (in the Properties window), as shown in Figure 1-16.

6. Right-click the newly renamed root node and select Insert Schema Node ➤ Child Record, Child Field Attribute, or Child Field Element, to add the appropriate envelope elements. In this example, a child field element named BatchID and a child record named Orders, which will contain the child records, are added.

7. Right-click the record that will contain the child records (Orders in this example) and select Insert Schema Node ➤ Child Record to add a container for the child records. In this example, a child record named Order is added.

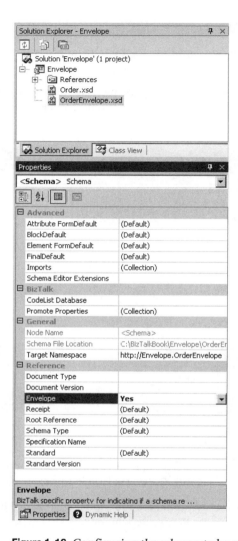

Figure 1-16. *Configuring the schema to be an envelope*

8. Right-click the container child record (Order in this example) and select Insert Schema Node ➤ Any Element to add a placeholder for the child elements. The resulting envelope schema has the structure shown in Figure 1-17.

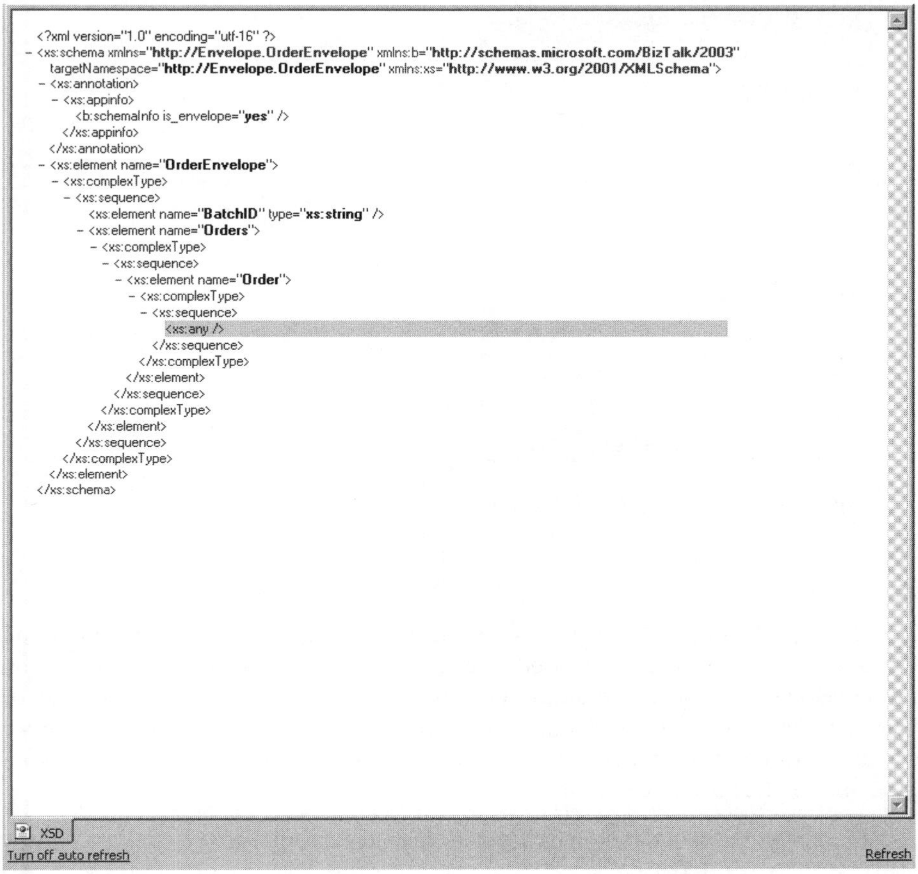

```
<?xml version="1.0" encoding="utf-16" ?>
- <xs:schema xmlns="http://Envelope.OrderEnvelope" xmlns:b="http://schemas.microsoft.com/BizTalk/2003"
    targetNamespace="http://Envelope.OrderEnvelope" xmlns:xs="http://www.w3.org/2001/XMLSchema">
  - <xs:annotation>
    - <xs:appinfo>
        <b:schemaInfo is_envelope="yes" />
      </xs:appinfo>
    </xs:annotation>
  - <xs:element name="OrderEnvelope">
    - <xs:complexType>
      - <xs:sequence>
          <xs:element name="BatchID" type="xs:string" />
        - <xs:element name="Orders">
          - <xs:complexType>
            - <xs:sequence>
              - <xs:element name="Order">
                - <xs:complexType>
                  - <xs:sequence>
                      <xs:any />
                    </xs:sequence>
                  </xs:complexType>
                </xs:element>
              </xs:sequence>
            </xs:complexType>
          </xs:element>
        </xs:sequence>
      </xs:complexType>
    </xs:element>
  </xs:schema>
```

```
XSD
Turn off auto refresh                                                                    Refresh
```

Figure 1-17. *Envelope schema structure*

9. Click the root node (OrderEnvelope in this example) and click the Body XPath property of the schema (in the Properties window), which will open the Body XPath dialog box.

10. Navigate down through the schema structure displayed in the tree view and select the container record for the child records you wish to process individually (the Orders record in this example), as shown in Figure 1-18. Then click OK.

11. Build and deploy the solution.

Figure 1-18. *Specifying a child record*

How It Works

Envelopes provide the means to group multiple messages into one XML document. In the preceding example, the envelope was used to disassemble individual order documents from a single enveloped document containing a batch of orders. Once the envelope and document schemas (OrderEnvelope and Order in the example) have been deployed, BizTalk Server has the ability to leverage the two in message processing. The following XML represents one possible instance of the envelope schema:

```
<ns0:OrderEnvelope xmlns:ns0="http://Envelope.OrderEnvelope">
  <BatchID>BatchID_0</BatchID>
  <Orders>
    <ns0:Order xmlns:ns0="http://Envelope.Order">
      <OrderID>1</OrderID>
      <OrderAmount>1.00</OrderAmount>
    </ns0:Order>
    <ns0:Order xmlns:ns0="http://Envelope.Order">
      <OrderID>2</OrderID>
      <OrderAmount>2.00</OrderAmount>
    </ns0:Order>
  </Orders>
</ns0:OrderEnvelope>
```

When passed through an XML disassembler pipeline component in BizTalk Server, the preceding XML message will produce the following two XML documents, which can be processed individually:

```
<nsO:Order xmlns:nsO="http://Envelope.Order">
  <OrderID>1</OrderID>
  <OrderAmount>1.00</OrderAmount>
</nsO:Order>

<nsO:Order xmlns:nsO="http://Envelope.Order">
  <OrderID>2</OrderID>
  <OrderAmount>2.00</OrderAmount>
</nsO:Order>
```

As these order documents are split up into separate messages within BizTalk Server, they can undergo different forms of business logic or be delivered to a different destination, depending on their properties (see Recipe 1-3 for more information about property-based subscriptions).

The key data element that allows envelope processing in BizTalk server is the Body XPath property. This data element acts as a pointer to the container record that encapsulates or surrounds the child records. On the OrderEnvelope root node, the Body XPath property was set to the Orders record, which contains the individual Order records. In envelope schemas containing a single root node, the Body XPath property must be set to that root node.

For envelope schemas with multiple root nodes, the following apply:

- If the Root Reference property is not set on the envelope schema, the Body XPath property must be set for all root nodes.

- If the Root Reference property is set on the envelope schema, the Body XPath property must be set for the root node configured in the Root Reference property. The Body XPath property can be set for the other root nodes, but it is not required.

- It is not required to set the Root Reference property, but the Body XPath property must always be set on at least one root node.

In addition to encapsulating multiple messages, envelopes can also supply header information that applies to all the records it contains. In the example, the BatchID element is defined once at the envelope level, but applies to all the individual order documents. This functionality of supplementing the individual message data with header data or metadata can be seen in the common example of SOAP envelopes (see Recipe 1-11 for more information about SOAP envelopes).

Within BizTalk Server, envelope processing for received messages occurs in the Disassemble stage of a receive pipeline. The out-of-the-box XML receive pipeline handles the removing and parsing of any envelope data contained within the inbound document. The subschemas are dynamically determined at runtime by the envelope's properties (specifically, the Body XPath), and used to validate the child documents' structure and split each out into an individual message.

A custom receive pipeline can also be used to more precisely process inbound enveloped documents. By leveraging the XML disassembler pipeline component, the envelope and document (child document) schemas can be set explicitly in the properties of the component. All envelope and document schemas explicitly set should have unique target namespaces. (See Recipe 3-8 for more information on custom pipeline components.)

▪Note If envelope or document schemas are explicitly set on an XML disassembler component, only documents matching those schemas will be processed within the pipeline. The order of envelope schemas is enforced based on the configuration within the `Envelope` property on the XML disassembler component. In contrast, the order of the document schemas is not enforced.

After the inbound enveloped document has been debatched into individual messages, the disassembler promotes any properties of the envelope to each individual message. In the example, if the `BatchID` had been configured as a promoted property, it would have been attached to each individual message during disassembly.

Implementing envelopes for outbound messages is also possible within BizTalk Server. This process is handled in the assembling stage of a send pipeline. By leveraging the XML assembler pipeline component in a custom send pipeline, the envelope schemas can explicitly be set in the properties of the component. As it passes through the custom pipeline, the message will be wrapped in the specified envelope(s), and have the appropriate message properties demoted to the envelope. If a batch of outbound messages is sent through the custom send pipeline, the batch of messages will all be combined into a single document and wrapped in the specified envelope.

In addition to having a single envelope, a group of messages can be wrapped in a series of nested envelopes. Using nested envelopes provides a flexible way for transferring message batches that have a complex structure or relationship.

While the preceding solution used BizTalk Server's pipeline capabilities to handle inbound envelope processing, there are other implementation options to consider when designing a solution. A loop can be used within an orchestration to iterate over child records within an enveloped document, splitting out each submessage individually using XPath queries or a node list object. An orchestration can also be used to call out to an external assembly to handle message debatching. When determining which method to use, it is important to consider the following:

- Does the entire batch need to be handled transactionally (for example, if one of the messages fails to process correctly, should the entire batch be canceled)?

- Do the individual records within the batch need to be processed in a specific order (for example, in the same order in which they appear in the original document)?

- Does there need to be any event or notification after all messages in the batch are successfully processed?

- Is business logic (orchestration) implemented on each individual message after it has been debatched?

If your business scenario would lead you to answer yes to any of these questions, using an orchestration to handle the parsing of an enveloped document may be required. The main benefit of using an orchestration is enhanced control over the processing of the individual messages. The order of the messages can be maintained, scopes can be used to implement transactionality across the entire message batch, compensating and error handling are more robust, and it is simple to implement logic required when all messages within a batch have completed processing. The major downsides to using orchestrations for debatching are performance and ease of modification to the solution (as changing the orchestration requires you to redeploy the BizTalk Server solution).

If the requirements of your business scenario allow for envelope processing to be handled via pipelines, you will realize performance gains. Additionally, the solution will be simplified by minimizing the number of implemented artifacts.

1-8. Creating Complex Types

Problem

You would like to create your own data type, by implementing your own complex type.

Solution

You can use XSD complex types within the BizTalk Editor. As an example, assume that you need to create your own complex data type for storing shipping addresses for an Order schema:

```
<Order>
  <CompanyName> </CompanyName>
  <OrderID> </ OrderID>
  <OrderDate> </OrderDate>
  <OrderAmount></ OrderAmount >
  <ShipTo>
        <CompanyID> </CompanyID>
        <AddressLine1> </AddressLine1>
        <AddressLine2> </AddressLine2>
        <AddressLine3> </AddressLine4>
        <Zip> </Zip>
  </ShipTo>
  <ShipFrom>
        <CompanyID> </CompanyID>
        <AddressLine1> </AddressLine1>
        <AddressLine2> </AddressLine2>
        <AddressLine3> </AddressLine4>
        <Zip> </Zip>
  </ShipFrom>
</Order>
```

For this example, the Order schema has been built with Order Header nodes and the <ShipTo> record. The following steps outline how to create a complex type to be the data type for the <ShipTo> and <ShipFrom> addresses. You will model the data type of the existing <ShipTo> record.

1. Open the project that contains the schema.

2. Double-click the schema (the Order schema in this example) to open it, as shown in Figure 1-19.

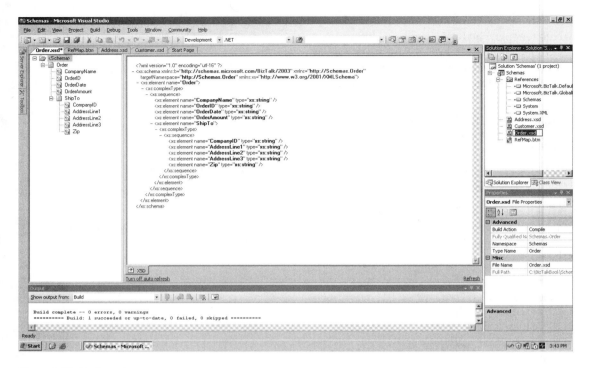

Figure 1-19. *Order schema*

3. Click the existing record on which you want to base the complex type (the `<ShipTo>` record in the `Order` schema in this example).

4. In the Properties window, within the General group, click `Data Structure Type` and type `Address` in the box. This step will now automatically recognize the record as a complex data type.

Now you can reuse the complex type. For example, here are the steps to create a record that uses the sample complex type:

1. Click the `Order` schema node.

2. Right-click and select Insert Child Record. Type in the record name `ShipFrom`.

3. Click the newly created child record.

4. In the Properties window, within the General group, click `Data Structure Type` and select your complex type, `Address`.

This procedure creates the `Address` complex type element structure under the `ShipFrom` record. A sequence instruction is created under both the `ShipFrom` and `ShipTo` records to implement the complex type. Figure 1-20 shows the finished schema.

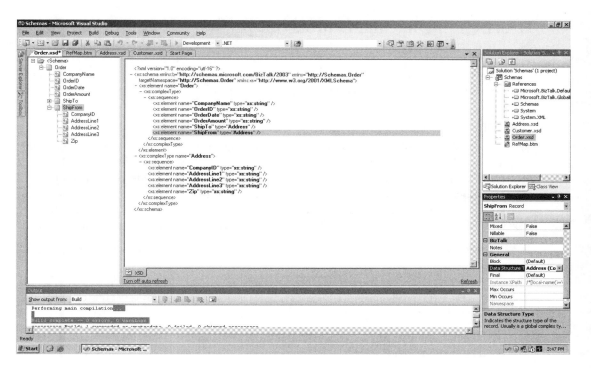

Figure 1-20. *Order schema with the Address complex type*

How It Works

The example demonstrated creating a complex type data type based on an existing schema record within the schema. By XSD definition, a complex type is an element (record) that has child elements or attributes. Complex types can be used to implement custom schema rules and XSD data structure considerations for records, elements, and attributes. For example, you might use complex data types for validation rules via XSD regular expressions, schema cardinality, and order. In addition, you can make data type references to your complex types, allowing you to reuse record structures and XSD implementations.

A complex type is derived from the base data type anyType; that is, in the purest form, a complex type is in essence a stand-alone base type, in which you can define your own XSD structure representation and schema rules.

■**Note** A simple type is an element that in itself is defined and does not have children. For example, you might have a simple type named Order ID, which has a length limit of 6 and must start with an *A* character. In this instance, an XSD length restriction could be defined, along with a regular expression to check that the order starts with the letter *A*: <OrderID> Axxxxx </ OrderID>.

1-9. Defining Regular Expressions

Problem

You have field elements or attributes in your schema for which you want to restrict the valid content beyond data type, enumerations, length, and minimum and maximum values.

Solution

You can use the `Pattern` property of a field element or attribute to place a collection of regular expressions. Regular expressions are used to do pattern matching against the inbound data for the node. If the inbound data adheres to the pattern(s) defined for a node, then the input instance document will pass XML validation. If the inbound data for the node does not match the pattern(s), then the input instance document will fail XML validation. From within the BizTalk Editor, follow these steps to add a regular expression to a field element or an attribute:

1. Select the field element or attribute node to which you wish to add restriction patterns.

2. Right-click and select Properties.

3. Set the `Derived By` property to `Restriction`. This will enable the `Restriction` properties within the Properties window.

4. Select the ellipsis next to the `Pattern` property to launch the Pattern Editor dialog box, as shown in Figure 1-21.

Figure 1-21. *Pattern Editor dialog box*

5. Add one to many valid regular expressions, and then click OK. The BizTalk Editor will add these restriction patterns to the schema definition.

■**Note** Although XSD regular expressions are similar to those in other programming languages that allow for pattern matching, there are some differences. Refer to the W3C specification for the specifics of the regular expression syntax for XSD.

How It Works

More-restrictive validation of the input data may be of value for numerous types of data, such as phone numbers, IP addresses, and Social Security numbers. In these cases, you can use regular expressions to restrict the type of data that will be considered valid.

Once you have created a schema that has nodes with pattern value restrictions, you can use the Generate Instance and Validate Instance capabilities of the BizTalk Editor to test your patterns. See Recipe 1-1 for more information about these two features.

■**Note** If you have pattern restrictions for a node(s) in your schema, the Generate Instance option will not create an instance document with valid data for those nodes. You will need to edit the instance document created. However, the Validate Instance option will validate the schema, including restriction patterns.

At runtime, neither the PassThruReceive nor the XMLReceive pipeline will complete a strict validation of the inbound document against the schema including the pattern matching. To complete a thorough validation of an inbound document, you must create a validation pipeline and add the document schema to the Document Schema property of the XML validator (see Recipe 3-5 for more information about creating validation pipelines). If the document fails schema validation in the pipeline, the instance will terminate and you will see a failure message in Health and Activity Tracking (HAT) that indicates the error that occurred. Figure 1-22 shows an error in HAT when a phone number does not match the restriction pattern defined in the schema.

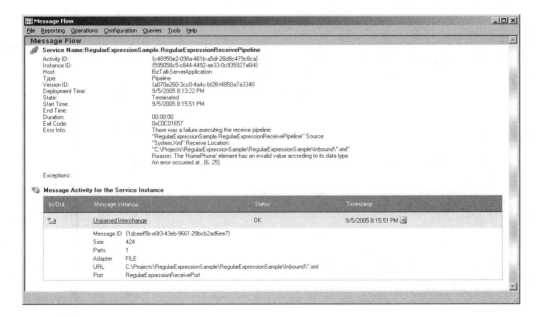

Figure 1-22. *Viewing a message in HAT*

In practice, it may be more beneficial to handle the strict validation of data more gracefully than terminating the instance when the validation fails. This is especially true if the document is coming from an outside source or from a system that is outside your control. However, restriction patterns can be used to safeguard downstream systems and processes from bad data.

1-10. Creating Flat File Schemas

Problem

You are consuming an inbound message in a flat file structure and must represent the data in an XML schema. The inbound flat file contains records that are both positional and delimited.

■**Note** Delimited files contain characters (such as commas) that separate the data. Files that are positional in nature contain data items that are a predefined length within the file. The physical position of the data defines what the data represents.

Solution

The solution outlined in this recipe consumes an inbound flat file schema message that may have a structure similar to the flat file shown in Listing 1-1. Additionally, this recipe outlines the steps required to manually create a schema for a flat file. BizTalk 2006 also includes a Flat File Wizard for creating flat file schemas (see Recipe 10-1)

■**Note** The number bar at the top of Listing 1-1 is included for reference only and is not part of the file content. The number bar is for counting the position of the characters.

Listing 1-1. *CustomerSalesOrder.txt*

```
123456789012345678901234567890123456789012345678912345678901234567890
ORDER2004-10-24
SoldTo Shauna Marie     1223 Buttercup Lane Seattle      WA 98155
ShipTo Jen Schwinn      3030 Moby Road      Kent         WA 98110
ITEMS,ITEM111-AA|Merlot|1|2.00|Bottle of Wine,ITEM111-AB|Cabernet|
1|2.00|Bottle of Wine
```

Additionally, the outbound BizTalk schema may have a structure similar to the XML file shown in Listing 1-2.

Listing 1-2. *CustomerSalesOrder.xml*

```
<ns0:order xmlns:ns0="http://Schema_Chapter_Project.CustomerSalesOrder">
  <date>10/24/2004</date>
  <customerHeader>
    <customerType>SoldTo</customerType>
    <fullName>Shauna Marie</fullName>
    <street>1223 Buttercup Lane</street>
    <city>Seattle</city>
    <state>WA</state>
    <postal>98155</postal>
  </customerHeader>
  <customerHeader>
    <customerType>ShipTo</customerType>
    <fullName>Jen Schwinn</fullName>
    <street>3030 Moby Road</street>
    <city>Kent</city>
    <state>WA</state>
    <postal>98110</postal>
  </customerHeader>
  <items>
    <item>
      <productId>ITEM111-AA</productId>
      <productName>Merlot</productName>
      <quantity>1</quantity>
      <unityPrice>2.00</unityPrice>
      <description>Bottle of Wine</description>
    </item>
    <item>
      <productId>ITEM111-AB</productId>
      <productName>Cabernet</productName>
      <quantity>1</quantity>
      <unityPrice>2.00</unityPrice>
      <description>Bottle of Wine</description>
    </item>
  </items>
</ns0:order>
```

Follow these steps to create the flat file schema:

1. Create a new BizTalk schema and select the Flat File Schema template.

2. Determine the structure and layout of your message schema. The structure and layout of the message schema will largely determine how the inbound document is parsed. In the XML sample in Listing 1-2, all data fields were defined as string elements. The customerHeader, items, and item nodes are defined as records.

3. Select the root node (the orders node in this example) and specify the child delimiter to be a carriage return and a line feed (CRLF). The most straightforward way to set the delimiter to a CRLF is by setting the child delimiter type to be Hexadecimal.

4. Specify the child delimiter to be 0x0D 0x0A.

5. Set the child order to be Infix.

6. Set the tag identifier to read ORDER. The tag identifier tells the schema where the data begins for the message. The children data for the root node of order are delimited by commas that appear in the middle of the data.

7. Based on the fact that there are two instances of customerHeader information, the max cardinality for customerHeader record must be set to 2.

8. Set the structure for the customerHeader to positional since all of the child elements that represent customer information are related in a positional format within the flat file. Each child node that exists under customerHeader must have the position defined for the length of the data and the offset for where that value begins in the file. The way the value is represented starts from the left of the data element. For the length and off-set of each element, see Table 1-3.

9. Set the next node tag value to ITEMS since Items is the next heading in the flat file.

10. Identify the delimiter as a comma and set the child-order to prefix, since each item will be prefixed with a comma to indicate the beginning of that item.

11. Make sure that the child delimiter type is set to character. Select item and make sure the child delimiter is set to the pipe character (|), since the attributes for the items are delimited by the pipe character in the flat file.

12. Set the pipe character to infix, since each line has pipe characters set in between the delimited characteristics. Figure 1-23 shows the CustomerSalesOrder schema in BizTalk.

Table 1-3. *Customer Header Child Elements*

Element	Positional Length	Offset
customerType	7	0
fullName	16	0
street	20	0
city	14	0
state	3	0
postal	5	0

Figure 1-23. *CustomerSalesOrder schema layout*

To test the flat file output of the schema, follow these steps:

1. Verify that `Generate Instance Output Type` on your schema reads `Native`. The `Native` property allows the schema to generate the native file format, which is a flat file, for that schema.

2. Right-click the schema and select Generate Instance. You should see the default generated flat file, as shown in Figure 1-24.

Figure 1-24. *Flat file generated schema*

To test the flat file schema to see the XML generated based on the provided flat file, follow these steps:

1. Verify that `Generate Instance Output Type` on your schema reads `XML`. The `XML` property allows the schema to process the inbound flat file and translate that flat file to an XML representation.

2. Right-click the schema and select Validate Instance. You should see the XML version of the processed flat file, as shown in Figure 1-25.

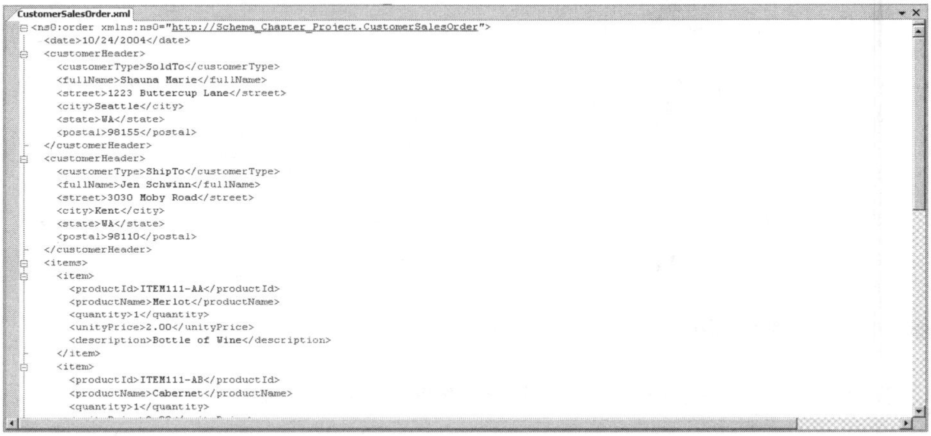

```
CustomerSalesOrder.xml                                                      ▾ ✕
  <ns0:order xmlns:ns0="http://Schema_Chapter_Project.CustomerSalesOrder">
    <date>10/24/2004</date>
    <customerHeader>
      <customerType>SoldTo</customerType>
      <fullName>Shauna Marie</fullName>
      <street>1223 Buttercup Lane</street>
      <city>Seattle</city>
      <state>WA</state>
      <postal>98155</postal>
    </customerHeader>
    <customerHeader>
      <customerType>ShipTo</customerType>
      <fullName>Jen Schwinn</fullName>
      <street>3030 Moby Road</street>
      <city>Kent</city>
      <state>WA</state>
      <postal>98110</postal>
    </customerHeader>
    <items>
      <item>
        <productId>ITEM111-AA</productId>
        <productName>Merlot</productName>
        <quantity>1</quantity>
        <unityPrice>2.00</unityPrice>
        <description>Bottle of Wine</description>
      </item>
      <item>
        <productId>ITEM111-AB</productId>
        <productName>Cabernet</productName>
        <quantity>1</quantity>
```

Figure 1-25. *Validating the flat file schema*

How It Works

BizTalk is capable of processing both positional and delimited data, either in individual files or in a single file. The *child delimiter* is the key concept to keep in mind when creating a flat file schema. Any parent-level record that contains child elements or attributes must define whether the data in the flat file for those child records is delimited or positional and how the data is delimited.

Based on the layout of the destination message schema, you should consider the following when dealing with records versus dealing with child elements and attributes:

Records: If you use records to group child elements or attributes, consider how the child records will be demarcated. Will the child data be delimited or is the child data positional? In the example in Listing 1-1, each line of data is delimited by a CRLF. Knowing that each line of data is delimited by a CRLF aids in determining whether the output schema must support that specific delimiter. The basic line delimiter information points to the need of specifying a delimiter of a CRLF for the parent record of the output schema.

Tag identifiers: Records may contain tag identifiers to distinguish one type of record from another record. A tag value also allows you to identify where data begins in the file.

Positional elements/attributes: In the XML example in Listing 1-2, the customerHeader data is stored in positional format. For each child node, you must provide the offset (where to start reading the data) and the length for that data item. Additionally, the parent record must specify that the child data structure is Positional.

Delimited elements/attributes: The flat file example in Listing 1-1 shows multiple items occurring on the same line delimited by the pipe (|) character. The attributes related to a single item are then further delimited by the comma character. The item's parent record must specify that the child data structure is Delimited. Additionally, the child delimiter for the item's parent record must specify that each item is delimited by a pipe character.

Cardinality for records: By default, BizTalk sets the cardinality field for records and elements/attributes to a default value of 1. The value of 1 means that you expect to receive a maximum and minimum of one instance of that record and associated child values. If you expect an inbound flat file to contain more than a single record instance, you must change the max occurs value to a number equal to unbounded or the number of instances you expect to receive.

Wrap characters: If the incoming data contains characters that have been identified as delimiting characters (for example, commas), those characters can be ignored through the use of wrap characters. For example, if the record contained the name Shauna, Marie and you wanted to have the comma included as part of the name, you could define a wrap character of " (double quote) and enclose the name within the wrap character: "Shauna, Marie". BizTalk will treat any special characters defined within a set of wrap characters as field-level data.

Escape characters: The purpose of escape characters is very similar to that of wrap characters. Escape characters specify the character to be used to escape reserved characters, and then the reserved characters will be treated as literal characters in a message.

If the records are delimited, you must determine how the records are delimited. For managing CRLF type transactions, the child delimiter type is set to hexadecimal and the delimiter is set to 0x0D 0x0A. If the delimiter is a character value like a comma, set the child delimiter type to character. The other key consideration for using delimiters is defining the child-order of the delimiter:

- If the delimiter appears after the set of data, the child-order of the delimiter is postfix.

- If the delimiter appears before the set of data, the delimiter is prefix.

- If the delimiter appears in the middle of the set of data, the delimiter is as infix.

The default child-order for a record is conditional default. The conditional default value means that if a tag value has been set for that record, then the child-order will be prefix. Otherwise, the child-order will be infix.

If the records are positional, you must determine the spacing of the delimited data. In the example, it was assumed that there were no spaces between the data (offsets set to 0) and the beginning of the data fields started at the left of each data value.

Another key consideration to keep in mind is the cardinality of the data groupings. When a BizTalk schema is created, by default, the cardinality is set to 1 (even if no cardinality value is explicitly set for a field). In the example, keeping the cardinality of the items set to the default would have caused some data to be lost when parsing both the customerHeader values and the item values. In the example, the cardinality of the max value was changed to 2 to account for both the shipTo and soldTo values.

1-11. Creating SOAP Header Schemas

Problem

You are using the publish/subscribe method in your orchestration architecture with many different schemas, and there are a number of common fields that need to be passed with all documents delivered to the BizTalk MessageBox (using direct binding on all ports). You want to be able to pass these fields without adding them to all of the individual schemas.

Solution

Assume that you have three schemas as follows:

```
<Person>
  <ID>ID_0</ID>
  <TraceFlag>true</TraceFlag>
  <Name>Name_1</Name>
</Person>

<Company>
  <ID>ID_0</ID>
  <TraceFlag>true</TraceFlag>
  <CompanyName>CompanyName_2</CompanyName>
</Company>

<Address>
  <ID>ID_0</ID>
  <TraceFlag>true</TraceFlag>
  <AddressLine>AddressLine_1</AddressLine>
</Address>
```

Two of the elements are common in all three of the schemas and represent values that are common: ID represents a common tracking ID, and TraceFlag represents whether logging should occur in an orchestration. The elements are not truly part of the description of a Person, Company, or Address, but their values need to be available. Your goal is to move these common fields out of the schemas so that they look as follows:

```
<Person>
  <Name>Name_1</Name>
</Person>
```

```
<Company>
  <CompanyName>CompanyName_2</CompanyName>
</Company>

<Address>
  <AddressLine>AddressLine_1</AddressLine>
</Address>
```

All messages in BizTalk are passed through the MessageBox wrapped in a SOAP Envelope. A SOAP Envelope consists of two sections: the Header and the Body, wrapped in an Envelope, as shown in Listing 1-3. The Header can be common across all schemas, while the Body contains the actual XML instance of any given schema. Adding and accessing fields within orchestrations at the SOAP Header level is made available in a simple and straightforward way. This is a powerful and useful tool that has multiple applications depending on the solution architecture.

Listing 1-3. *Sample SOAP Envelope Structure*

```
<soap:Envelope xmlns:xsi="http://www.w3.org/2001/XMLSchema-instance"
 xmlns:xsd="http://www.w3.org/2001/XMLSchema"
 xmlns:soap="http://schemas.xmlsoap.org/soap/envelope/"
  <soap:Header>
        <MessageId>uuid:bbbb-cccc-dddd-eeee</MessageId>
        <TraceFlag>true</TraceFlag>
  </soap:Header>
  <soap:Body>
        <Person><Name>Name_1</Name></Person>
  </soap:Body>
</soap:Envelope>
```

In Listing 1-3, the Header contains two fields and the Body consists of an XML document that is an instance of the Person schema. This is an actual representation of what a document looks like when placed in the MessageBox by an orchestration when using the SOAPHeader property schema and Person schema described in this recipe.

By default, BizTalk will strip the XML document out of the envelope's Body and deliver it to the appropriate subscribers. These subscribers see the XML document that was originally contained in the Body and do not have context to the Header. However, if a SOAPHeader property schema has been defined, the subscriber will also have access to the envelope's Header information.

The SOAPHeader property schema shows which fields will be promoted and available at the Header level on all schemas within a given project. The SOAPHeader property schema must reference the namespace http://schemas.microsoft.com/BizTalk/2003/SOAPHeader and have each of the elements on it with their Property Schema Base set to MessageContextPropertyBase. The steps for creating a SOAPHeader property schema are as follows:

1. Add a new schema to the project.

2. In the Properties window of the schema, set the Target Namespace to the BizTalk SOAPHeader namespace and the Schema Type to Property, as shown in Figure 1-26.

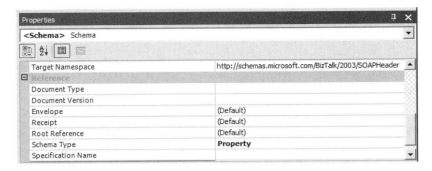

Figure 1-26. *SOAP Header property values*

3. Add the desired elements to the schema. There is no root node on a SOAPHeader property schema; it has only elements. In this example, there would be two elements added to the schema: MessageId and TraceFlag.

4. On each element created, set the Property Schema Base in the Properties window to MessageContextPropertyBase, as shown in Figure 1-27.

Namespace	http://schemas.microsoft.com/BizTalk/2003/SOAPHeader
Node Name	MessageId
Reference	
Property Schema Base	**MessageContextPropertyBase**
RootNodeTypeName	**MessageId**
Sensitive Information	(Default)

Figure 1-27. *Element property values*

5. Build and deploy the solution.

Once compiled, the elements in the SOAPHeader property schema will be available on all messages within an orchestration, and can be accessed and set in Expression shapes and Message Assignment shapes. Listing 1-4 shows how to set these elements.

Listing 1-4. *Setting Properties in a Message Assignment Shape*

```
// populate the SOAP Header information
strMessageId = "111-222-333-444";
blnTraceFlag = true;

msgAddress(SOAPHeader.MessageId) = strMessageId;
msgAddress(SOAPHeader.TraceFlag) = blnTraceFlag;

msgPerson(SOAPHeader.MessageId) = strMessageId;
msgPerson(SOAPHeader.TraceFlag) = blnTraceFlag;

msgCompany(SOAPHeader.MessageId) = strMessageId;
msgCompany(SOAPHeader.TraceFlag) = blnTraceFlag;
```

How It Works

The project accompanying this recipe (SOAPHeader.sln) demonstrates the practical application of the SOAP Header. The basic architecture of the solution is this:

- Primary orchestration receives an incoming document from a file receive location.

- Orchestration sets the promoted SOAP Header properties in a Message Assignment shape.

- Orchestration delivers the message to the BizTalk MessageBox via direct binding on a port.

- A secondary orchestration subscribes to the MessageBox and is instantiated when a document matching the schema it is subscribing to arrives.

- The secondary orchestration reads the values of the SOAP Header and writes them to the Windows event viewer.

Figure 1-28 illustrates the flow of the primary orchestration and the use of a Message Assignment shape to set the SOAP Header properties before delivering to the MessageBox (port_2 is direct binding).

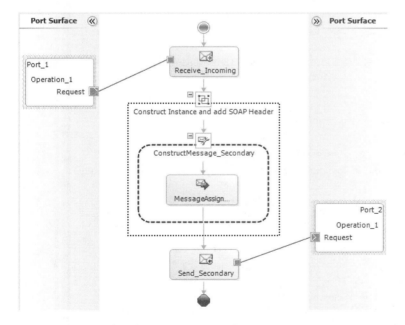

Figure 1-28. *Sample solution primary orchestration*

So, how do you access incoming documents wrapped in SOAP Envelopes? Incoming documents can be wrapped in a SOAP Envelope (by an external client to BizTalk), but by default, only those that are delivered via a SOAP transport receive location will be automatically promoted and made available within an orchestration.

For example, with orchestrations exposed as web services, additional properties can be set at the SOAP Header level using the BizTalk Web Services Publishing Wizard (see Recipe 4-25). These properties are then available to any client who calls the web service, accessible in the same way as all of the standard web methods and properties. However, if the delivery of a message wrapped in a SOAP Envelope via a different transport is required (such as MSMQ or file drop), you need to use a custom pipeline component.

Listing 1-5 demonstrates a process to promote incoming values to the SOAPHeader property schema. This example is a complete custom pipeline intended to be placed on the decode stage of a BizTalk custom pipeline, followed by a standard XML disassembler. It demonstrates how to do the following:

- Load the incoming message stream into an XML document, which can be accessed via the Document Object Model (DOM).

- Load the MessageId value located at the Header level of the incoming SOAP Envelope. The incoming message matches the structure of the document shown in Listing 1-3.

- Promote the field to the SOAP Header and make it available once the document is delivered to the Message Box.

- Return the document within the Body of the SOAP Envelope as a stream.

Listing 1-5. *Pipeline Property Promotion*

```
public IBaseMessage Execute(IPipelineContext pc, IBaseMessage inmsg)
{
        try
        {
                string strMessageId = "";

                // declare XML Document
                System.Xml.XmlDocument xmlDoc = new System.Xml.XmlDocument();

                // prepare the fields to be promoted
                xmlDoc.Load(inmsg.BodyPart.Data);

                // if values are not present, default to empty string
                try
                {
                        strMessageId = xmlDoc.SelectSingleNode
("//*[local-name()='Header'/*[local-name()='MessageID']").
InnerText;
                }
                catch {}
```

```
            // strip off the envelope and return just what is within the Body
            System.IO.MemoryStream ms = new
System.IO.MemoryStream(System.Text.Encoding.UTF8.GetBytes
(xmlDoc.SelectSingleNode("//*[local-name()='Body']").InnerXml));

            inmsg.BodyPart.Data = ms;

            // promote the SOAP Header fields
            inmsg.Context.Promote("MessageId",
"http://schemas.microsoft.com/BizTalk/2003/SOAPHeader"
.ToString(),strMessageId);

            }
            catch (Exception ex)
            {
            throw new Exception("Pipeline component exception - " + ex.Message);
            }
        return inmsg;
}
```

CHAPTER 2

■ ■ ■

Document Mapping

At the core of integration projects is the need to exchange data. When systems are required to pass data, the data must either be in a common format or the systems must have a way in which to map the data from one system to another. Historically, mapping was spread across multiple components and entities, such as the database layer, the data access layer, and even the publishing and consuming systems themselves. When additional systems were added to the integration, or requirements around the mapping logic changed, many systems and components involved in the integration would need to be customized. Integration applications, such as BizTalk Server, offer a centralized and organized platform for handling mapping, and provide tools to aid in the development of these mappings.

Exchanging data requires that all systems have a common way in which data is interpreted or a common way in which data can be mapped from one system to another. BizTalk provides for this through several approaches, the most prominent of which is the BizTalk Mapper (additional approaches include XSLT stylesheets, custom .NET assemblies, message assignment within orchestrations, and other code-driven solutions). The BizTalk Mapper is a graphical interface with which to develop transformations of data between any number of schemas of disparate systems or entities. These maps consist of the business logic necessary to transform the data into the format that the target systems require.

Rather than storing the business logic for transformations across many different components and systems, the rules should be contained in only the integration layer. All that is required of the systems being integrated should be the ability to make available their data (either through the system publishing its data to the integration platform or by the integration hub initiating the request for the data). There is absolutely no need to customize any system based on the way that another system may need to receive the data. If the system data is available, the integration layer will be able to consume and manipulate the data into the needed format. By keeping the business logic needed for transforming data in the integration hub (in this case, BizTalk orchestrations and maps), there is a single, common location for all mapping, and no need to modify individual systems when the mapping requirements change.

When mapping rules change or additional systems are added to an integration solution, one of the greatest objectives is to modify as few components as possible. With a well-organized mapping solution, the only components that will need to be modified, compiled, and redeployed are the map components themselves (mapping assemblies, XSLT, or any other component). None of the individual systems will be affected, none of the business workflows (orchestrations) will be influenced, and none of the schemas will need to be changed. Additional systems should be able to be added to an integration without modifying any of the existing maps for other systems. An intelligently organized mapping solution can eliminate the need for complex modifications across an integration solution.

This chapter will describe how to use BizTalk for data transformation and mapping. As with the rest of the BizTalk platform, there are numerous ways to solve the same problem, and mapping components can range from any variety and combination of traditional BizTalk graphical maps, XSLT, and .NET assemblies. The business requirements should drive the technical solution, and there is no single approach that will suit all situations. The recipes in this chapter introduce the fundamental mapping techniques that will aid in the development of a solid mapping design and architecture, and ultimately in a scalable and configurable integration solution.

2-1. Creating Simple Maps

Problem

You would like to map one XML format to another using the BizTalk tool set. This may be for a variety of reasons, such as application mapping with an internal application, format specifics (such as flat file to database object), or an external business scenario where a business partner requires the core data for a business process in a different format (such as an industry standard) than your schema provides.

Solution

The BizTalk Mapper enables you to perform XML message transformation. The tool is shipped with the core BizTalk product and provides numerous capabilities to support message transformation and translation via straight mapping and functoids, as well as unit test support.

Note The term *functoids* refers to predefined functions within the BizTalk Mapper tool set. Functoids support a number of useful translations and transformations. As a point of interest, *functoid* is a term coined by Microsoft and is commonly described as "functions on steroids."

As an example, suppose that you have the following simple customer schema (Customer):

```
<Customer>
  <FirstName> </FirstName>
  <LastName> </LastName>
  <MiddleInit> </MiddleInit>
  <Age></Age>
  <Address>
  <AddrLine1> </AddrLine1>
  <AddrLine2> </AddrLine2>
  <AddrLine3> </AddrLine3>
  <Zip> </Zip>
  <State> </State>
  <Country></Country>
  </Address>
  </Customer>
```

And you want to map to another customer schema (`CustomerRecord`) that is slightly different in structure and format:

```
<CustomerRecord >
  <Name> </Name>
  <MiddleInit> </MiddleInit>
  <Address> </Address>
  <Zip> </Zip>
  <State> </State>
  <Country> </Country>
  <DateTime> </DateTime>
</CustomerRecord>
```

The example involves mapping values from a source to a destination schema that subsequently demonstrates different structure and invariably, message transformation.

To create the BizTalk map for the example, follow these steps:

1. Open the project that contains the schema.

2. Right-click the project and select Add ➤ New Item.

3. In the Add New Item dialog box, shown in Figure 2-1, double-click Map.

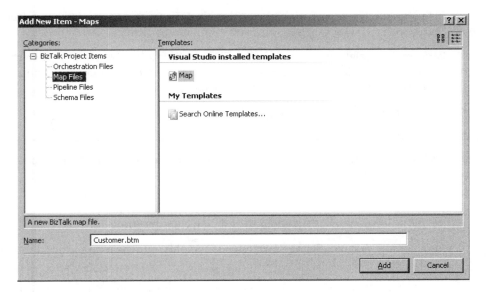

Figure 2-1. *Adding a map*

4. A blank map will now be opened, with left and right panes for the source and destination schema, respectively, as shown in Figure 2-2. Click the Open Source Schema link in the left pane.

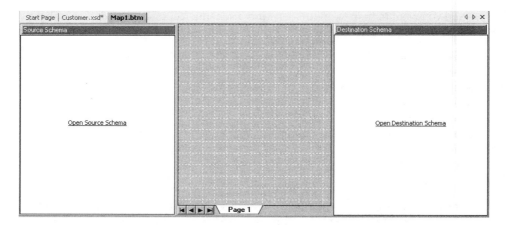

Figure 2-2. *A new blank map*

5. In the BizTalk Type Picker dialog box, select the Schemas tree node, and then select the Customer schema.

6. Click the Open Destination Schema link in the right pane.

7. In the BizTalk Type Picker dialog box, select the Schemas tree node, and then select the CustomerRecord schema. The source and destination schemas will now be displayed.

8. Perform the straight-through mapping. Click the MiddleInit element in the source schema and drag it across to the MiddleInit element in the destination schema. Repeat this for the Zip, State, and Country elements.

9. Perform the concatenation mapping.

■**Note** The term *concatenation mapping* within the BizTalk Mapper refers to the joining of two or more values to form one output value.

---

   a. In the left pane, click the Toolbox, and then click the String Functoids tab.

   b. Click and drag two String Concatenate functoids onto the map surface, as shown in Figure 2-3.

   c. Click the FirstName element in the source schema and drag it across to the left point on the first String Concatenate functoid. Click the right side of the String Concatenate functoid and drag it across to the Name element in the destination schema.

   d. Click the LastName element in the source schema and drag it across to the left point on the first String Concatenate functoid. Click the right side of the String Concatenate functoid and drag it across to the LastName element in the destination schema.

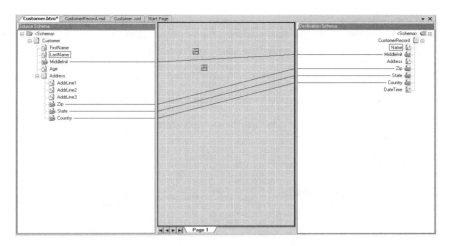

Figure 2-3. *String Concatenate functoids on the design surface*

e. Click the AddrLine1 element in the source schema and drag it across to the left point on the second String Concatenate functoid. Click the right side of the String Concatenate functoid and drag it across to the Address element in the destination schema.

f. Repeat step e for AddrLine2 and AddrLine3. Figure 2-4 shows the completed concatenation mapping.

■**Note** For the purpose of this demonstration, we will not be adding spaces between each element value. This can be done easily though by adding and concatenating a constant functoid with the value ' '.

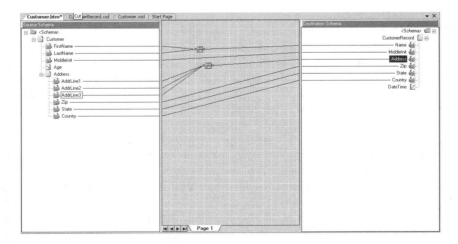

Figure 2-4. *String concatenation mappings*

To demonstrate functoid usage, you will now add a Date and Time functoid to the mapping example. In this instance, the destination schema requires a date/time stamp to be mapped. This value will be generated from the Date and Time functoid, not the source schema.

1. In the left pane, click the Toolbox, and then click the Date/Time Functoids tab.

2. Click and drag a Date and Time functoid onto the map surface.

3. Click the right side of the Date and Time functoid and drag it across to the `DateTime` element in the destination schema.

The map is now complete, as shown in Figure 2-5.

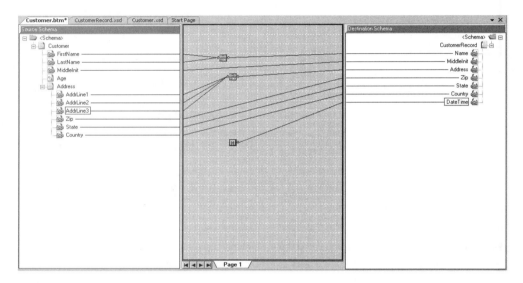

Figure 2-5. *Customer map*

How It Works

The BizTalk Mapper is used to map XML messages (instances of XML schema at runtime) to an alternate format based on transformation and/or translation. It is built on XSLT and shields the user from complex XSLT transformation logic, by providing a GUI environment to facilitate the transformation. The tool comes with numerous functoids and mapping capabilities to support straight-through and deterministic transformation. In addition, the tool gives the built-in ability to perform unit testing (see Recipe 2-24).

The maps created within the BizTalk Mapper environment can be used within other BizTalk runtime environments. For example, they can be used with receive/send ports, for transforming a message to and from application end points. Port mapping might be advantageous when the mapping involves minimal process considerations or the need to apply multiple maps to a given message. Changes to maps on ports can be completed without recompilation of currently deployed BizTalk assemblies. Maps can also be used with transformation shapes, for message transformation within a BizTalk orchestration. Mapping within an orchestration might be preferred when the mapping process involves broad process considerations or process support via robust exception and error handling.

The choices for where and when to map vary depending on a number of factors. A number of these have to do with common development principals (such as consistency and readability) and standards enforced by the environment in which you are operating. However, a few common rules of thumb should be noted:

Keep it simple: Keep maps logically organized. Across maps, ensure that the same look and feel are applied for consistency.

Business rules: Based on the deterministic ability of mapping, be careful or keep in mind the usage of business rules within maps. If you find you are using rules within maps (for example, `If OrderTotal > $1000`), keep in mind maintenance and where in your organization a decision may be made to change this rule. In addition, always consider the right place to maintain rules and context domain knowledge from an operation and support perspective.

Performance considerations: While mapping is powerful, complex and/or large maps can affect performance. As with all common development activities, always ensure that the logic performed is the most efficient and tested for scale in your practical operating conditions and requirements. If you experience performance issues, employ techniques such as revisiting design by exploring the solution breakdown. Consider simplifying the development task at hand.

Like all good development processes, maps should be designed and tested for desired application operation conditions.

The example in this recipe showed a baseline solution of what can be performed with the BizTalk Mapper. Throughout this chapter, other mapping capabilities will be demonstrated, illustrating the use of functoids and mapping techniques for structure and transformation control.

2-2. Organizing Maps

Problem

Maps can become very complex and hence difficult to read and maintain.

Solution

BizTalk Sever provides two main features to aid in the readability and maintainability of maps. One of these features is *grid pages*. BizTalk Server allows you to create, name/rename, and order grid pages. When you create links between source and destination elements, the links will appear on only the selected grid page. Therefore, you can segment groups of links onto different grid pages. By default, a map file is created with one grid page named Page 1. Once you have selected source and destination schemas, you can access the grid page menu by right-clicking the tab at the bottom of the grid page, as shown in Figure 2-6.

Figure 2-6. *Click the tab at the bottom of the grid page to access the grid page menu.*

From this menu, you can perform the following functions:

- Select Add Page to add a new grid page to the map.

- Select Delete Page to delete the selected grid page. (If you delete a grid page, all of the links associated with that grid page will also be removed.)

- Select Rename Page to rename the selected grid page.

- Select Reorder Pages to launch the Reorder Pages dialog box, as shown in Figure 2-7. From this dialog box, you can change the order in which the grid pages appear when viewing the map file.

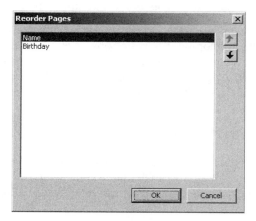

Figure 2-7. *Reorder Pages dialog box*

Another feature provided by BizTalk Server for facilitating the readability and maintainability of maps is the ability to label links. While the labels do not appear on the grid pages, they will be used to designate the input parameters for functoids. By default, a functoid will show the XPath designation if it is linked directly to a source field, or it will show the name of the previous functoid if it is linked from another functoid. However, if the input links to a functoid are labeled, then the Label property of the link will be shown. To label a link, follow these steps:

1. Open the project that contains the map.

2. Open the map file.

3. Select the grid page that contains the link to be labeled.

4. Select the link to be labeled, right-click, and select Properties.

5. Fill in the Label property.

How It Works

There are many ways to segment a map into multiple grid pages. For example, you can create a grid page for each major node in a source schema that requires complex mapping. Regardless of how you divide the map, the goal of using multiple grid pages should be to improve the readability and maintainability of the map.

Figure 2-8 shows a simple map to highlight the use of grid pages and labeling links. Two grid pages were used. The first grid page, Name, holds the links and functoids to map a FirstName and LastName field to a FullName field that is all uppercase. The second grid page, Birthday, holds the link for DateOfBirth to Birthday. To emphasize the use of link labeling, the FirstName field was passed through the Uppercase functoid and the String Concatenate functoid without the use of link labeling. The LastName field was passed through the Uppercase functoid and String Concatenate functoid with the use of link labeling.

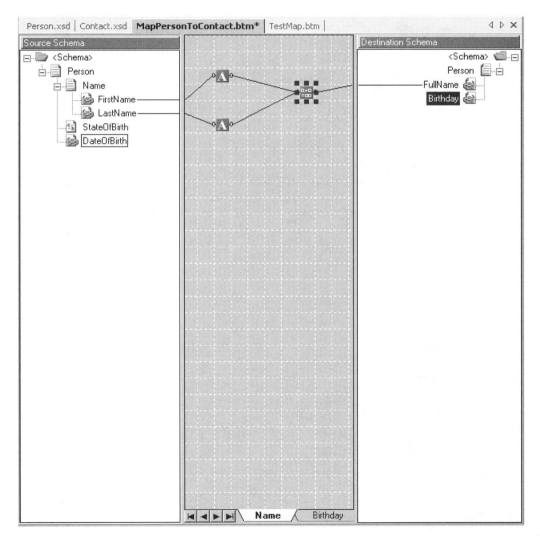

Figure 2-8. *A simple map with grid pages and labeling*

Figure 2-9 shows the input parameter for the Uppercase functoid linked to the `FirstName` field in Figure 2-8. Notice that the input parameter is designated by the XPath query to the `FirstName` field.

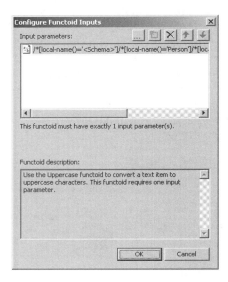

Figure 2-9. *Uppercase functoid input without a link label*

Figure 2-10 shows the Uppercase functoid linked to the `LastName` field in Figure 2-8. However, the link from the `LastName` field to the functoid was labeled with `LastName`. Notice how the input parameter is labeled as `LastName`, as opposed to an XPath query to the `LastName` field.

Figure 2-10. *Uppercase functoid input with a link label*

Figure 2-11 shows the input parameters for the String Concatenate functoid. This functoid takes in the `FirstName`, a constant to add a blank space, and then the `LastName`, and concatenates all three together into a `FullName` field on the destination schema.

Figure 2-11. *String Concatenate functoid input parameters*

Notice how the first input parameter is shown as `Uppercase`, as opposed to anything meaningful. This is simply the name of the functoid previous to the String Concatenate functoid. However, the link between the Uppercase and String Concatenate functoids for `LastName` was labeled as `LastNameAllCaps`. Notice how that label appears as the third input parameter.

2-3. Adding Mapping Constants

Problem

You would like to use constant values within a BizTalk map. This might be because of preset output map values within a destination schema (that do not exist in the source schema), to assist in general programming concepts when using functoids, or for other reasons.

Solution

To demonstrate how to add map constants using the BizTalk Mapper, suppose that you want to use a constant in conjunction with a String Extraction functoid. In this example, you would like to extract a specified number of characters (five) from the left of the source element value. In the source schema, `Customer`, you have `Zip` elements like this:

```
<Zip>98103-00001</Zip>
```

In the destination schema, `CustomerRecord`, you have `Zip` elements like this:

```
<Zip>98103</Zip>
```

To map constants, follow these steps:

1. Set up the BizTalk map with the appropriate source and destination schema (see Recipe 2-1), as shown in Figure 2-12.

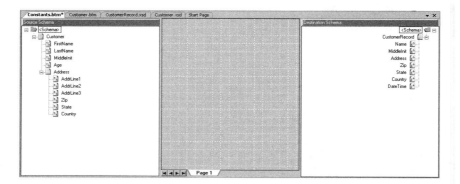

Figure 2-12. *The source and destination schema for the constant mapping example*

2. In the left pane, click the Toolbox, and then click the String Functoids tab.

3. Click and drag a String Left functoid onto the map surface.

4. Double-click the `Zip` element in the source schema and drag it across to the left point of the String Left functoid.

5. Click the String Left functoid on your map surface and select `Input Parameters` in the Properties window. The Configure Functoid Inputs dialog box is now displayed, as shown in Figure 2-13. Notice the first input parameter is the source schema's `Zip` element. This is automatically configured as a result of dragging the source `Zip` element onto the map surface.

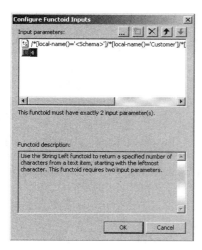

Figure 2-13. *Configure Functoid Inputs dialog box*

6. In the Configure Functoid Inputs dialog box, click the Constant icon.

7. Select the newly created constant, and type in the value 4. As noted, you are extracting five characters for the zip code. Because the functoid is zero-based, the start position will be 0 and the end position will be 4, resulting in five characters.

8. Click OK to complete the functoid configuration.

9. Click on the right side of the String Left functoid and drag it across to the `Zip` element in the destination schema.

This completes the functoid configuration. The finished map is shown in Figure 2-14.

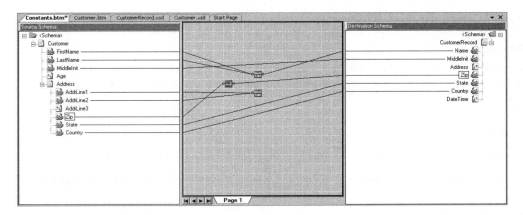

Figure 2-14. *Customer map created with a map constant*

How It Works

You might use constant mapping for the following:

- To support functoid configuration, as in the example in this recipe, which used the String Left functoid.

- For values declared and assigned within a Scripting functoid. In essence, these values can be mapped as output into destination values. Furthermore, they can be declared once, and accessed as global variables within other Scripting functoids in the context of the working BizTalk map.

- With the String Concatenate functoid. Use the input parameter of this functoid as the constant value required. This functoid does not require any input values from the source schema. In this usage, a String Concatenate functoid would simply be mapped through to the desired destination value.

The best use of constant mapping depends on the situation and requirements you are developing against. Examine the likelihood of change within the scenario where you are looking to apply the functoid constant. If there is a high likelihood that values and their application will change, consistency should be the major factor to facilitate maintenance.

If constants are set via deterministic logic or complex or embedded business rules, it might be worth thinking about whether the constant should be applied in the map or applied within a scripting component or upstream/downstream BizTalk artifacts. The key is understanding where rules and deterministic values are set to support the specific situation. Apply the appropriate design principles to ensure the correct constant assignment technique is applied.

You might decide it would be best to map values outside the mapping environment. This could be a result of deterministic logic or business rules being the major requirement in the constants implementation. Furthermore, rules that derive constants may exist outside the BizTalk map. Constants may need to change dynamically, and it may be too cumbersome to perform a recompile/deployment for such changes within a BizTalk map.

2-4. Mapping Any Element Nodes

Problem

You need to create a mapping between two schemas containing elements and attributes that are unknown when building the map, and you must include the unknown schema structures in your mapping.

Solution

You can include unknown schema structures in a map by using the <Any> element.

1. Build a source message schema containing an <Any> element, as shown in Figure 2-15.

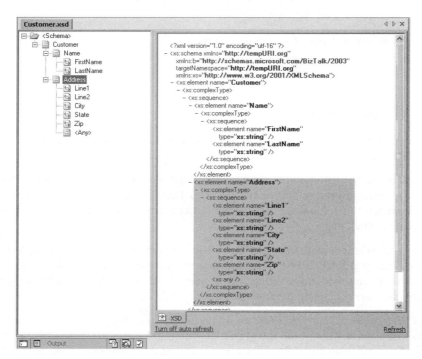

Figure 2-15. *Creating a source message*

2. Build a destination schema containing an <Any> element, as shown in Figure 2-16.

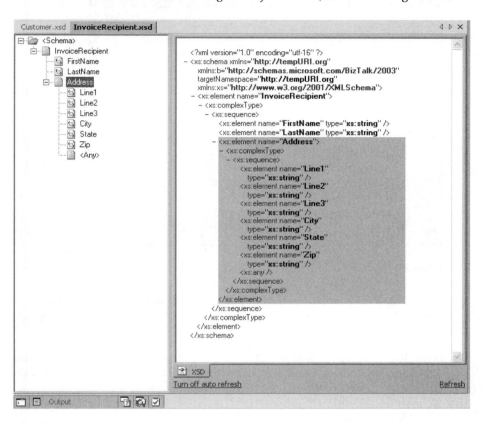

Figure 2-16. *Creating a destination message*

3. Right-click the BizTalk project in the Solution Explorer and select Add ➤ Add New Item to open the Add New Item dialog box.

4. Select the Map template in the right pane, specify the desired name of the BizTalk map that you want to create, as shown in Figure 2-17, and then click Open.

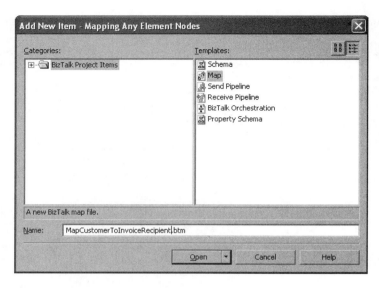

Figure 2-17. *Adding a new map to the BizTalk project*

5. In the empty map created in the development environment, select the Open Source Schema link on the left side. In the BizTalk Type Picker dialog box, select the source schema (Customer in this example), and then click OK.

6. Select the Open Destination Schema link on the right side of the map. In the BizTalk Type Picker dialog box, select the destination schema (InvoiceRecipient in this example), as shown in Figure 2-18, and then click OK.

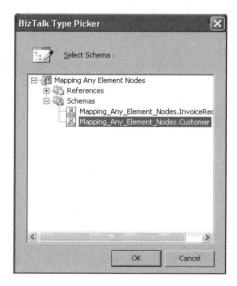

Figure 2-18. *Specifying the destination schema*

7. Click the Toolbox, and then click the Advanced Functoids tab. Drag a Mass Copy functoid onto the map surface. Connect the Address element from the source message to the Mass Copy functoid, and connect the Mass Copy functoid to the Address field of the destination message. (See Recipe 2-6 for details on how to use the Mass Copy functoid.)

8. Create other desired mapping links normally, as shown in Figure 2-19.

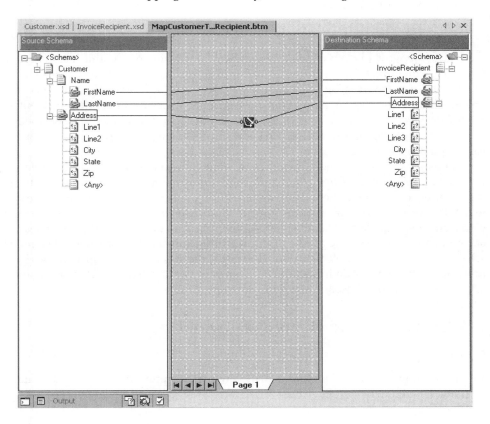

Figure 2-19. *Configuring the Mass Copy functoid*

How It Works

An <Any> element in a schema designates a specific location in the schema where new elements or attributes can be added. When BizTalk uses the schema to process a message containing unknown elements or attributes in the designated location, the schema will still consider the message valid. If this source message is mapped into a different schema that also has a location designated for extensibility with an <Any> element, then the information must be copied to that location with the Mass Copy functoid.

■**Note** By default, BizTalk will examine only the namespace and root node name of a message to identify the schema, and will not detect extra elements in the message body. To perform a deep validation of a message format, create a receive pipeline with the XML disassembler, specify the schema to validate messages against, and set Validate Document Structure to `true`. See Chapter 3 for more information about how to configure receive pipelines.

The contents of an `<Any>` element cannot be mapped with most of the default BizTalk functoids. Other functoids require establishing an explicit link from a source field, and that is not possible if the source field is not known at design time. The Mass Copy functoid can be linked only directly to an ancestor of the `<Any>` element, which may not give the granularity of control desired. Consider using an XSLT script with the Scripting functoid (see Recipe 2-21) to achieve finer control. For example, if you know some element will be present at runtime but cannot predict the element name of its parent, an XSLT script can still perform the mapping.

Sometimes, the BizTalk development environment has difficulty validating schemas containing `<Any>` elements. It can incorrectly determine that elements and attributes appearing in the location designated by the schema should not be there, causing validation for the schema to fail. This complicates schema development because the developer must deploy the schema with a pipeline capable of validating the document structure to check if the schema is correct according to a sample source message. To avoid this deployment effort while developing the schema, wait to add `<Any>` elements until the rest of the schema is developed and verify that those other elements are defined correctly. Then when adding the `<Any>` elements to the schema, there will be a baseline of what is working correctly.

2-5. Using the Value Mapping Functoid

Problem

You need to understand how and when to use the Value Mapping functoid and the Value Mapping (Flattening) functoid.

Solution

BizTalk provides two Value Mapping functoids: Value Mapping and Value Mapping (Flattening). Both will cause a new record to be created in the destination for every record in the source. The Value Mapping (Flattening) functoid is used when the destination document has a flat structure.

Both functoids require two input parameters: a Boolean value and the node that is to be mapped. If the Boolean value is `true`, the value will be mapped; otherwise, it will not be mapped.

The following steps demonstrate the use of the Value Mapping functoid in a map, using the source document shown in Listing 2-1.

Listing 2-1. *Source Document for the Value Mapping Functoid Example*

```
<ns0:NewHireList xmlns:ns0="http://SampleSolution.NewHireList">
  <DateTime>1999-04-05T18:00:00</DateTime>
  <ns1:Person xmlns:ns1="http://SampleSolution.Person">
    <ID>1</ID>
    <Name>C. LaBarge</Name>
    <Role>Consultant</Role>
    <Age>73</Age>
  </ns1:Person>
<ns1:Person xmlns:ns1="http://SampleSolution.Person">
    <ID>2</ID>
    <Name>D. Riggs</Name>
    <Role>Finance</Role>
    <Age>88</Age>
  </ns1:Person>
<ns1:Person xmlns:ns1="http://SampleSolution.Person">
    <ID>3</ID>
    <Name>T. Trucks</Name>
    <Role>Consultant</Role>
    <Age>94</Age>
  </ns1:Person>
</ns0:NewHireList>
```

These steps refer to the Value Mapping functoid, but are identical for the Value Mapping (Flattening) functoid.

1. Click the Toolbox, and then click the Advanced Functoids tab. Drop the Value Mapping functoid on the map surface between the source and destination schemas.

2. The first parameter for the Value Mapping functoid needs to be a Boolean value. For this example, a Not Equal functoid will be used to generate the Boolean value. In the Toolbox, click the Logical Functoids tab, and drop a Not Equal functoid to the left of the Value Mapping functoid. The first input parameter for the Not Equal functoid should be the value from the Role element. The second input parameter should be a constant value. Set this value to Finance. This will ensure that only those records that are not in the Finance role will be mapped across.

3. The second parameter for the Value Mapping functoid in this example is the Name element from the source document. Ensure that a line exists between this node and the functoid.

4. Drop the output line from the Value Mapping functoid on the Company/Employees/ Person/Name node in the destination document, as shown in Figure 2-20.

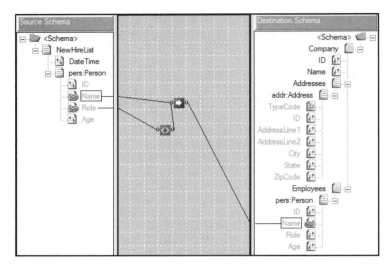

Figure 2-20. *Using the Value Mapping functoid*

At this point, the map can be tested. Using the source document shown in Listing 2-1, output of the map is the document shown in Listing 2-2.

Note If the Value Mapping (Flattening) functoid does not map a value across, the node is not created on the destination schema, whereas if the Value Mapping functoid does not map a value, an empty destination node will be created. To change this behavior, you will need to use additional functoids or scripting.

Listing 2-2. *Output Document Using the Value Mapping Functoid*

```
<nsO:Company xmlns:nsO="http://SampleSolution.Company"
xmlns:addr="http://SampleSolution.Address"
xmlns:pers="http://SampleSolution.Person">
 <Employees>
  <pers:Person>
   <Name>C. LaBarge</Name>
  </pers:Person>
  <pers:Person>
  </pers:Person>
  <pers:Person>
   <Name>T. Trucks</Name>
  </pers:Person>
 </Employees>
</nsO:Company>
```

If the Value Mapping functoid is replaced with the Value Mapping (Flattening) functoid (as shown in Figure 2-21), the document in Listing 2-3 will be output.

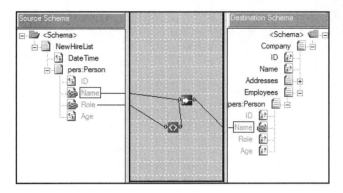

Figure 2-21. *Map with Value Mapping (Flattening) functoid*

Listing 2-3. *Output Document Using the Value Mapping (Flattening) Functoid*

```
<ns0:Company xmlns:ns0="http://SampleSolution.Company"
xmlns:addr="http://SampleSolution.Address"
xmlns:pers="http://SampleSolution.Person">
 <Employees>
 <pers:Person>
  <Name>C. LaBarge</Name>
  <Name>T. Trucks</Name>
 </pers:Person>
</Employees>
</ns0:Company>
```

How It Works

This example showed the default behavior of the Value Mapping functoid. However, the default output of the Value Mapping functoids can be altered through the use of additional functoids and scripting. For example, notice that the output in Listing 2-3 is flat instead of nested (two Person nodes within the Employee node). By adding a Looping functoid (see Recipe 2-13) to the Name element (or any required element in the Person node) in the source document and attaching it to the Person root node in the destination document (see Figure 2-22), you can obtain nested output, as in Listing 2-4. The output is identical to using the Value Mapping functoid as shown in Listing 2-2.

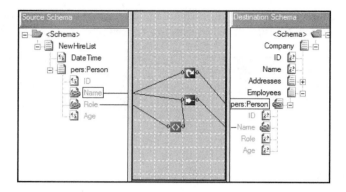

Figure 2-22. *Using the Value Mapping (Flattening) and Looping functoids*

Listing 2-4. *Output Using Value (Mapping) Flattening and Looping Functoids*

```
<ns0:Company xmlns:ns0="http://SampleSolution.Company"
xmlns:addr="http://SampleSolution.Address"
xmlns:pers="http://SampleSolution.Person">
 <Employees>
  <pers:Person>
   <Name>C. LaBarge</Name>
  </pers:Person>
  <pers:Person>
  </pers:Person>
  <pers:Person>
   <Name>T. Trucks</Name>
  </pers:Person>
 </Employees>
</ns0:Company>
```

One of the most common situations in XML document mapping is working with nonexistent elements. By default, if an element does not exist in an incoming document but is mapped to the destination document in a BizTalk map, the node on the destination document will be created with a null value (`<Node/>`). The use of a Value Mapping (Flattening) functoid causes the node to be created in the destination document only if the source node exists in the source document.

2-6. Using the Mass Copy Functoid

Problem

You would like to copy child XML structures from a source to destination schema.

Solution

Using the Mass Copy functoid, a source XML structure can be recursively mapped to a compatible XML structure on the destination schema.

For example, suppose you have the following two schemas:

```
<Person>
  <Hair> </Hair>
  <Eyes> </Eyes>
  <Skin> </Skin>
</Person>

<People>
  <Hair> </Hair>
  <Eyes> </Eyes>
  <Skin> </Skin>
</People>
```

To copy and map the People schema to the Person schema, follow these steps:

1. Set up the BizTalk map with the appropriate source and destination schema, as shown in Figure 2-23.

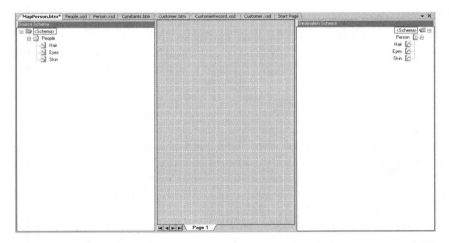

Figure 2-23. *The source and destination schema for the Mass Copy functoid example*

2. In the left pane, click the Toolbox, and then click the Advanced Functoids tab.

3. Click and drag a Mass Copy functoid onto the map surface.

4. Click the Person element in the source schema and drag it across to the left point of the Mass Copy functoid.

5. Click the right point of the Mass Copy functoid and drag it across to the `People` element in the destination schema. The map is now complete, as shown in Figure 2-24.

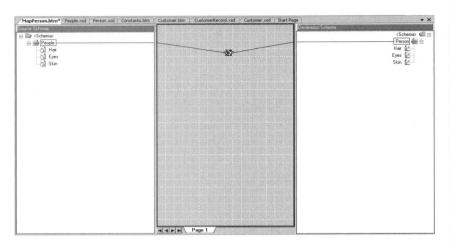

Figure 2-24. *Using the Mass Copy functoid*

How It Works

The Mass Copy functoid allows source records and containing elements and attributes to be copied and mapped across to the destination schema. This in turn, allows large structures to be mapped quickly in design time, without the need of performing 1:1 detailed mapping on all subsequent schema nodes.

The Mass Copy functoid performs the recursive copying by applying a wildcard (/*) XSLT template match on source to destination XML elements. This is of particular benefit when the destination is defined as an `<xs:any>` type.

Consider the scenario where you do not have a preset data structure within your destination schema; for example, communicating an error message with reason code, description, category, and so on, where order and cardinality are not important. By applying the Mass Copy functoid, you could map through the parent element and allow the destination XML object to be determined and derived at runtime.

When mapping from source to destination, only the structure under the destination parent XML record will be copied. This often results in having to re-create the parent record element to allow all subsequent children nodes to be mapped to the destination schema. For example, consider the following two schemas, `Customer` and `Customers`:

```
<Customer>
  <Name> </Name>
  <AccountID> </AccountId>
  <DOB> </DOB>
</Customer>
```

```
<Customers>
  <Customer>
  <Name> </Name>
  <AccountID> </AccountId>
  <DOB> </DOB>
  </Customer>
</Customers>
```

In this instance, the `<Customers>` record cannot be mapped to the `<Customer>` record on the destination schema. A containing element `<Customer>` will need to be defined on the destination schema to enable the correct operation of the Mass Copy functoid mapping.

When mapping source to destination elements, always be cautious of underlying XSD schema rules, such as cardinality, order, and data types. For example, the Mass Copy functoid will "blindly" copy all child elements specified to the destination schema. It will not copy elements out of order or check for required values in the destination schema.

Changes to the source and destination schema may result in the need to update your impacted maps leveraging the Mass Copy functoid. This, in turn, will mandate a recompile and deployment of your BizTalk solution.

Using the Mass Copy functoid within the BizTalk Mapper is one of a variety of ways to recursively copy elements. The following are three key approaches to recursively copy XML structures:

Mass Copy functoid: Creates a wildcard XSLT template match to recursively copy elements. This approach may provide a performance benefit, as each source and destination element does not require a 1:1: XSLT template match. This, in turn, requires fewer XSLT code instructions to be interpreted and executed at runtime.

Recursive mapping: This is achieved by holding down the Shift key and mapping from a source to destination record element. This is a usability design feature that enables a developer to perform recursive mapping via one keystroke. This approach implements 1:1 XSLT template matches on all source and destination elements.

Straight-through mapping: This approach is to manually link all source and associated destination elements within the BizTalk Mapper tool (see Recipe 2-1). This method does 1:1 template matches on all source and destination elements.

2-7. Using the Table Looping Functoid

Problem

You need to create a repeating structure in an output document with no equivalent repeating structure in an input document.

Solution

BizTalk Sever provides two functoids, the Table Looping functoid and the Table Extractor functoid, for creating a repeating node structure from a flattened input structure, from constant values, and from the output of other functoids. The Table Looping functoid is used to create a table of information based on inputs. The functoid will generate output for each row from this table. The Table Extractor functoid is used to direct data from each column in the table to a node in the destination document. Following are the basic steps for configuring these functoids.

1. Click the Toolbox, and then click on the Advanced Functoids tab. Drag the functoid onto the map surface, and create links to the functoid.

   a. Set the first input parameter, which is a link from a node structure in the input document that defines the scope of the table. If this node repeats in the input document, the number of occurrences of this element in the input document will be used to control the number of times the set of Table Extractor functoids will be invoked at runtime.

   b. Set the second input parameter, which is a constant that defines the number of columns for each row in the table.

   c. Set the next input parameters, which define the inputs that will be placed in the table. These inputs can come from the input document, the output from other functoids, constant values, and so on.

2. Configure the table based on inputs for the Table Looping functoid.

   a. Select the ellipsis next to the Table Looping Grid property in the Properties window to launch the Table Looping Configuration dialog box.

   b. For each cell, select a value from the drop-down list. The drop-down list will contain a reference to all of the inputs you defined in step 1.c.

   c. Check or uncheck the Gated check box. If checked, column 1 will be used to determine whether a row in the table should be processed as follows: When the value in column 1 of the row is the output from a logical functoid, if the value is True, the row is processed, and if the value is False, the row is not processed. Similarly, if the value in column 1 of the row is from a field, the presence of data equates to True and the row is processed, and the absence of data equates to False and the row is not processed, and subsequently missing from the output structure.

   d. Select OK to close the dialog box.

3. Configure the outputs for the Table Looping functoid.

   a. Link the Table Looping functoid to the repeating node structure in the output document.

   b. Link the Table Looping functoid to a Table Extractor functoid for each column in the table. The Table Extractor functoid can be found in the Toolbox on the Advanced Functoids tab.

4. Configure the input parameters for each Table Extractor functoid.

   a. Set the first input parameter, which is the output link from the Table Looping functoid.

   b. Set the second input parameter, which is the column number of the data to be extracted from the table.

5. Configure the outputs for each Table Extractor functoid. Link the functoid to a node in the destination schema that is part of a repeating structure.

■Note It is very helpful to label all of the links so that meaningful names are displayed when configuring these functoids. See Recipe 2-2 for more information about linking labels in maps.

How It Works

The Table Looping and Table Extractor functoids are used together. As an example, suppose that you have the sample input document shown in Listing 2-5.

Listing 2-5. *Flattened Input Structure*

```
<AliasesFlat>
    <Names>
        <Alias1FirstName>John</Alias1FirstName>
        <Alias1LastName>Doe</Alias1LastName>
        <Alias2FirstName>Sam</Alias2FirstName>
        <Alias2LastName>Smith</Alias2LastName>
        <Alias3FirstName>James</Alias3FirstName>
        <Alias3LastName>Jones</Alias3LastName>
    </Names>
</AliasesFlat>
```

The goal is to use these two functoids to create an output document of the format shown in Listing 2-6.

Listing 2-6. *Repeating Nested Structure*

```
<AliasesRepeating>
    <AliasNames>
        <FirstName>John</FirstName>
        <LastName>Doe</LastName>
    </AliasNames>
    <AliasNames>
        <FirstName>Sam</FirstName>
        <LastName>Smith</LastName>
    </AliasNames>
    <AliasNames>
        <FirstName>James</FirstName>
        <LastName>Jones</LastName>
    </AliasNames>
</AliasesRepeating>
```

Figure 2-25 shows the configuration for the input parameters for the Table Looping functoid. The first parameter is a reference to the node structure Names in the input schema. The second parameter is a constant value of 2 indicating there will be two columns in the table. The remaining parameters are the first and last name of each alias from the input document.

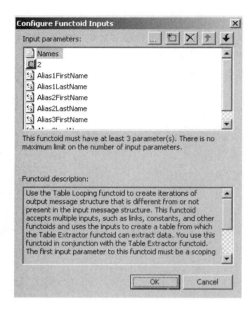

Figure 2-25. *Table Looping input parameters*

Figure 2-26 shows the completed Table Looping Configuration dialog box for the Table Looping functoid. It has been configured so that each row contains an alias first name in column 1 and an alias last name in column 2. There will be three rows in the table to process, one for each alias provided as input.

The output links from the Table Looping functoid are configured as follows:

- An output link to the AliasNames repeating node structure in the destination schema

- An output link to a Table Extractor functoid for processing first names (column 1) from the table

- An output link to a Table Extractor functoid for processing last names (column 2) from the table

Figure 2-27 shows the configuration for the Table Extractor functoid that will process column 1 from the table. The first parameter is a link from the Table Looping functoid, and the second parameter is a constant value of 1, which indicates it will process the first column from each row as it is processed.

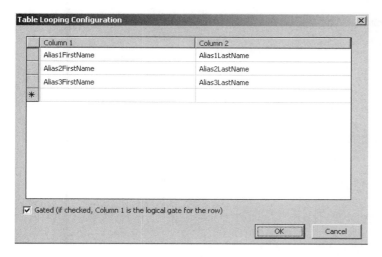

Figure 2-26. *Table Looping Configuration dialog box*

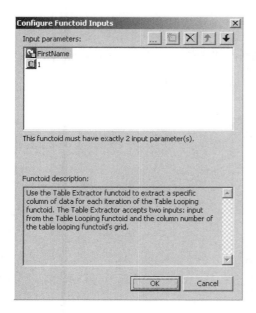

Figure 2-27. *Table Extractor functoid configuration for column 1*

Figure 2-28 shows the configuration for the Table Extractor functoid that will process column 2 from the table. The first parameter is a link from the Table Looping functoid, and the second parameter is a constant value of 2, which indicates it will process the second column from each row as it is processed.

Figure 2-28. *Table Extractor functoid configuration for column 2*

Finally, each Table Extractor functoid must be linked to a node in the destination schema. The complete map is shown in Figure 2-29.

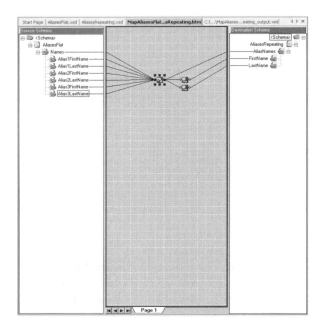

Figure 2-29. *Final map for the Table Looping functoid example*

Here is what the data table will look like when the map is processed:

Column 1	Column 2
John	Doe
Sam	Smith
James	Jones

Once the table is loaded, it will generate three sets of output: one set of output for each row in the table. This, in turn, will create three repetitions of the AliasNames node structure in the destination document: one for each row in the table. A repeating node structure has been created, even though one did not exist in the input document.

2-8. Using the Database Lookup Functoid

Problem

You need to map an incoming node to a database table column to reference a specific set of data via a BizTalk 2006 Server map. Specifically, for an inbound author ID, you need to retrieve the person attributes that are stored in a SQL-based table. Additionally, the data that is stored in the database table is dynamic, and coding the values within the BizTalk map is not possible.

■**Note** The Database Lookup functoid can communicate with any ODBC-compliant data source. For this recipe, SQL Server is the assumed data source.

Solution

BizTalk provides the Database Lookup functoid, which can retrieve a recordset. For example, suppose that the inbound message specifies an author's Social Security number but no personal information. The map must retrieve the author's information and map the information to the outbound message. The Database Lookup functoid can retrieve the information from a specific SQL table using the author's Social Security number as the value for which to search. The inbound XML message may have a format similar to this:

```
<nsO:PersonSearch xmlns:nsO="http://BizTalk_Server_DataBase_Lookup.ID">
  <ID>172-32-1176</ID>
</nsO:PersonSearch>
```

You can use the Database Lookup functoid by taking the following steps:

1. Click the Toolbox, and then click on the Database Functoids tab. On the map surface, in between the source and destination schemas, drag and drop a Database Lookup functoid.

2. Connect the left side of the Database Lookup functoid to the inbound document node that will specify the value used in the search.

3. Configure the input parameters of the Database Lookup functoid, as shown in Figure 2-30. This functoid requires four parameters to be specified either through mapping the inbound source data to the functoid or through setting constants in the functoid.

   a. For the first input parameter, verify that the inbound node, connected in step 2, is the first value in the list of properties. This is a value to be used in the search criteria. It's basically the same as the value used in a SQL WHERE clause.

   b. Set the second parameter, which is the connection string for the database. The connection string must be a full connection string with a provider, machine name, database, and either account/password or a flag indicating the use of Trusted Security mode in SQL. The connection string must include a data provider attribute. A lack of data provider attribute will generate a connection error when the map tries to connect to the database.

   c. Set the third parameter, which is the name of the table used in search.

   d. Set the fourth parameter, which is the name of the column in the table to be used in search.

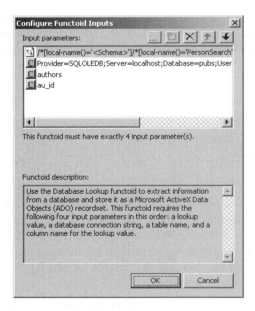

Figure 2-30. *Database Lookup Functoid input parameters dialog box*

4. Again, click the Toolbox, and then click the Database Functoids tab. On the map surface, after the Database Lookup functoid, drag and drop the Error Return functoid.

5. Connect the right side of the Database Lookup functoid to the left side of the Error Return functoid. Connect the right side of the Error Return functoid to the outbound schema node that is a placeholder for error messages.

6. Again, click the Toolbox, and then click the Database Functoids tab. On the map surface, above the Error Return functoid, drag and drop the Value Extractor functoid for each extracted value from the return recordset. For example, if you are returning five values in the recordset, you would need five Value Extractor functoids.

7. For each Value Extractor functoid, connect the left side of the functoid to the right side of the Database Lookup functoid.

8. Configure the properties of each Value Extractor functoid to retrieve the appropriate value by specifying the column name of the extracted value. For example, if the value returned resides in a column named au_fname, you would create a constant in the Value Extractor functoid named au_fname. The Value Extractor functoid's Configure Functoid Inputs dialog box should look similar to Figure 2-31.

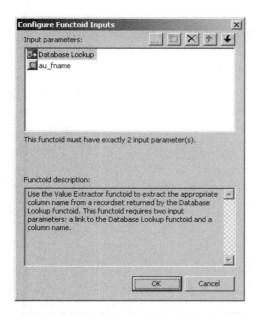

Figure 2-31. *Value Extractor functoid input parameters dialog box*

9. For each Value Extractor functoid, connect the right side of the functoid to the appropriate target schema outbound node. The completed map should look similar to the sample map in Figure 2-32.

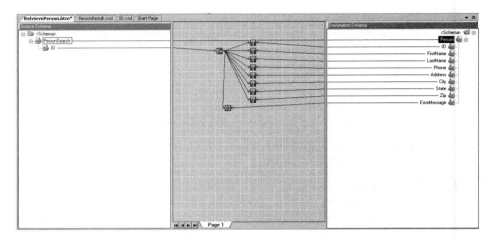

Figure 2-32. *Using the Database Lookup functoid*

Based on the sample XML, the map in Figure 2-32 will produce the XML document shown in Listing 2-7 (assuming that the BizTalk map contains a connection string to the pubs database).

Listing 2-7. *Outbound Retrieve Author Information*

```
<nsO:Person xmlns:nsO="http://BizTalk_Server_DataBase_Lookup.PersonResult">
  <ID>172-32-1176</ID>
  <FirstName>Johnson</FirstName>
  <LastName>White</LastName>
  <Phone>408 496-7223</Phone>
  <Address>10932 Bigge Rd.</Address>
  <City>Menlo Park</City>
  <State>CA</State>
  <Zip>94025</Zip>
  <ErrorMessage />
</nsO:Person>
```

How It Works

The Database Lookup functoid requires four parameters as inputs, and it outputs an ActiveX Data Objects (ADO) recordset. Keep in mind that the recordset returns only the first row of data that matches the specific criteria provided to the Database Lookup functoid.

In addition to the input parameters, the Database Lookup functoid requires two helper functoids for optimal use:

- The Error Return functoid, which returns SQL-related errors or exceptions. The Error Return functoid requires the Database Lookup functoid as the input and a link to an output node in the target schema. To avoid runtime errors, verify that the only inbound connection to the Error Return functoid is that of the Database Lookup functoid and not any other database functoids.

- The Value Extractor functoid, which retrieves a specific column from the returned recordset. The Value Extractor will retrieve the value based on the specific column specified in the input parameters.

Security Considerations

Whenever you use SQL authentication (SQL username and password), there is potential for a security risk. Consider using Trusted Security for access to the database rather than specifying the username and password in the connection string used by the Database Lookup functoid. For example, here is a connection string that uses SQL security:

```
Provider=SQLOLEDB;Server=localhost;Database=pubs;User ID=sa;Password=password;
   Trusted_Connection=False
```

And here is an example of a connection string that uses Trusted Security:

```
Provider=SQLOLEDB;Server=localhost;Database=pubs;Integrated Security=SSPI;
```

Keep in mind that if you choose Trusted Security for authentication, the account under which the BizTalk host instance is running must have appropriate access to the SQL Server, the SQL database, and the table in which the Database Lookup functoid is looking.

Another option to enclosing connection string information within the Database Lookup functoid is to make use of a Universal Data Link (UDL) file. A UDL is simply a text file with the file extension .udl. The connection string is included within the UDL file, and the connection string parameter in the Database Lookup functoid becomes a reference to that file, for example:

```
File Name=c:\BizTalkConfig\ConnectionString.UDL
```

Once the UDL file is created, it can be made available on a secure file share.

■**Note** UDL files are external to the BizTalk map and therefore must be parsed every time a connection to the database is open. The parsing activity will cause some performance degradation.

Additionally consider the use of a SQL view, versus direct table access, and having the Database Lookup functoid point to the database view. A SQL view offers the ability to manage table security permissions or the abstraction of the physical table structure.

Architecture Considerations

The Database Lookup functoid is convenient to implement in mappings. For straightforward data retrieval, this functoid performs adequately. However, the following items should be taken into consideration when evaluating when to use the Database Lookup functoid:

Database availability: If you cannot guarantee that the data source being queried will be available when BizTalk is available, then using the Database Lookup functoid may not make sense.

Error management: Mapping will occur and not trap the SQL errors in the .NET exception style. Errors should be trapped and managed when mapping. When implementing the Database Lookup functoid, consider using the Error Return functoid. Additionally, after the mapping, it would be wise to query the Error Return node for an error message and implement error handling if one exists.

Performance: Evaluate your performance requirements and determine if accessing a SQL database will negatively affect your overall mapping performance. Implementing the Database Lookup functoid may not impact performance greatly, but consider the effect if you must run the Database Lookup functoid multiple times in a single map. Database Lookup functoids that are part of a looping structure will cause a level of performance degradation. Make sure that the latest BizTalk service packs are applied when using the Database Lookup functoid, as they include performance-enhancing features such as caching.

Database support: Evaluate if the database that you must access will support the necessary security requirements and also allow table (or at least view level) access.

Advanced Database Lookup Functoid Usage

The BizTalk map translates the Database Lookup functoid information into a dynamic SQL SELECT statement. If you run a SQL Profiler trace during testing of the BizTalk map, you will see the SELECT call with the dynamic SQL. Knowing that dynamic SQL is created by the Database Lookup functoid allows you to use it to perform some relatively powerful database lookups. The Database Lookup functoid allows only a single value and single column name to be referenced in the query. However, with a bit of extra mapping, you can use this functoid to query against multiple columns. The map in Figure 2-32 generates the following SQL query code:

```
exec sp_executesql N'SELECT * FROM authors WHERE au_id= @P1', N'@P1 nvarchar(11)',
N'172-32-1176'
```

This query performs a SELECT to retrieve all rows from the authors table where the author ID is equal to the value in the inbound XML document (for example, 172-32-1176).

Keep in mind that the Database Lookup functoid returns only the first row that it encounters in the recordset. If multiple authors had the same ID, you would potentially retrieve the incorrect author. For example, if the author ID is the last name of the author, you may retrieve multiple authors that share the same last name. One way to ensure uniqueness, aside from querying on a unique column, is to specify additional columns in the query. The Database Lookup functoid accepts only four parameters, so additional concatenation must occur before submitting the parameters to the Database Lookup functoid. Figure 2-33 shows a sample concatenation of parameters that submitted as a single parameter to the Database Lookup functoid.

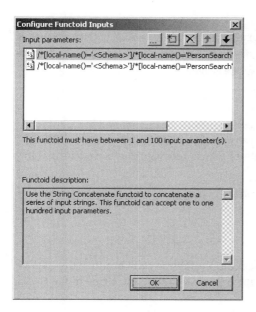

Figure 2-33. *Concatenating Database Lookup functoid input parameters*

After configuring the inbound concatenated value, the next step is to specify multiple column names as the input parameter in the Database Lookup functoid. Figure 2-34 demonstrates
a sample Database Lookup functoid configuration with multiple columns specified. The output
from the Database Lookup functoid to the Value Extractor functoid does not change.

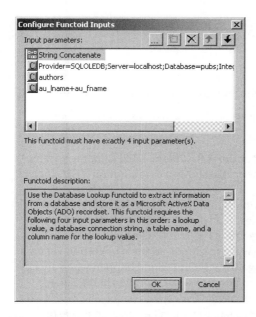

Figure 2-34. *Database Lookup functoid with multiple columns*

■**Note** A plus symbol (+) is used between the column names in the Database Lookup functoid, whereas in the Concatenation functoid, no + is required. If a + is specified in the Concatenation functoid, you will receive incorrect results, as the dynamic SQL statement created will be incorrect.

In this example, the inbound message specifies an author's first name and last name instead of a unique author ID. The map must still retrieve the author's information and map the information to the outbound message. The inbound XML message may have a format to the following message:

```
<ns0:PersonSearch xmlns:ns0="http://BizTalk_Server_DataBase_Lookup.MultipleID">
  <lname>Ringer</lname>
  <fname>Albert</fname>
</ns0:PersonSearch>
```

Based on this source XML, the map specifying multiple columns will produce the following XML document (assuming that the BizTalk map contains a connection string to the pubs database).

```
<ns0:Person xmlns:ns0="http://BizTalk_Server_DataBase_Lookup.PersonResult">
  <ID>998-72-3567</ID>
  <FirstName>Albert</FirstName>
  <LastName>Ringer</LastName>
  <Phone>801 826-0752</Phone>
  <Address>67 Seventh Av.</Address>
  <City>Salt Lake City</City>
  <State>UT</State>
  <Zip>84152</Zip>
  <ErrorMessage />
</ns0:Person>
```

The following is the dynamic SQL created in the map that accepts multiple columns:

```
exec sp_executesql N'SELECT * FROM authors WHERE au_lname+au_fname= @P1', N'@P1
nvarchar(12)', N'RingerAlbert'
```

The dynamic SQL created shows the inbound author's first name and last name parameters as a concatenated parameter. The SQL statement also shows a combination WHERE clause with au_lname + au_fname.

There are some limitations to specifying multiple columns through the concatenation approach. Specifically, string data types are the only data types that work reliably due to the concatenation operation that occurs in SQL. Integer data types may also be used, but in the case of integer (or other numeric data types), SQL will perform an additive operation versus a concatenation operation. Adding two numbers together, as what would happen when specifying numeric data types, and comparing the result to another set of numbers being added together may yield multiple matches and may not achieve the desired results. The mix of varchar and numeric fields will not work with this approach, as you will receive a data casting exception from your data provider.

2-9. Seeding Cross-Reference Tables with ID Cross-References

Problem

You wish to dynamically cross-reference unique identifiers between two or more systems. The reference data already exists, so you wish to load the data into the BizTalk cross-reference tables before you use the cross-reference functoids or Application Programming Interface (API).

Solution

Within an XML configuration file you name `List_Of_App_Type.xml`, insert the XML shown in Listing 2-8, and insert an `appType` node for each system that will have cross-references.

Listing 2-8. *List_Of_App_Type.xml*

```
<?xml version="1.0" encoding="UTF-8"?>
<listOfAppType>
    <appType>
        <name>Oracle</name>
        <description/>
    </appType>
    <appType>
        <name>Siebel</name>
        <description/>
    </appType>
</listOfAppType>
```

■**Note** These node values in Listings 2-8 through 2-11 have been placed in the XML as an example. You should remove them and insert your own.

Within an XML configuration file you name `List_Of_App_Instance.xml`, insert the XML shown in Listing 2-9.

Listing 2-9. *List_Of_App_Instance.xml*

```
<?xml version="1.0" encoding="UTF-8"?>
<listOfAppInstance>
    <appInstance>
        <instance>Oracle_01</instance>
        <type>Oracle</type>
        <description/>
    </appInstance>
    <appInstance>
        <instance>Siebel_01</instance>
        <type>Siebel</type>
        <description/>
```

```
        </appInstance>
        <appInstance>
            <instance>Siebel_12</instance>
            <type>Siebel</type>
            <description/>
        </appInstance>
    </listOfAppInstance>
```

Since unique identifiers are often different for each unique instance of a system, you must create different cross-references for each system. Therefore, you must insert an appInstance node for each instance of an application you will cross-reference, inserting a common type value across instances that are of the same type of system, and which correspond to the appType you created in the List_Of_App_Type.xml configuration file. For instance, you may be running two instances of Siebel, so you would insert two appInstance nodes with a type of Siebel, but give each a unique value in the instance node (for example, Siebel_01 and Siebel_12).

Within an XML configuration file you name List_Of_IdXRef.xml, insert the XML shown in Listing 2-10.

Listing 2-10. *List_Of_IdXRef.xml*

```
<?xml version="1.0" encoding="UTF-8"?>
<listOfIDXRef>
    <idXRef>
        <name>Customer.ID</name>
        <description/>
    </idXRef>
    <idXRef>
        <name>Order.PONumber</name>
        <description/>
    </idXRef>
</listOfIDXRef>
```

For each ID field you plan to cross-reference, insert an idXRef node with a unique name child node. This value will be used to identify the ID field that you are cross-referencing. For instance, if you plan to cross-reference a customer that is in different systems, you would insert an idXRef with a name like Customer.ID.

Within an XML configuration file you name List_Of_IdXRef_Data.xml, insert the XML shown in Listing 2-11.

Listing 2-11. *List_Of_IdXRef_Data.xml*

```
<?xml version="1.0" encoding="UTF-8"?>
<listOfIDXRefData>
    <idXRef name="Customer.ID">
        <appInstance name="Oracle_01">
            <appID commonID="100"> CARA345</appID>
        </appInstance>
```

```
            <appInstance name="Siebel_01">
                <appID commonID="100">99-4D976</appID>
            </appInstance>
            <appInstance name="Siebel_12">
                <appID commonID="100">44OL</appID>
            </appInstance>
        </idXRef>
</listOfIDXRefData>
```

For each field you create in the `List_Of_IdXRef.xml` file, insert an `idXRef` node. For each system you create in the `List_Of_App_Instance.xml` file, insert an `appInstance` node. Insert one or more `appID` nodes for each unique identifier. Insert a `commonID` attribute to store a common identifier, and a set the application-specific value within the node. The common ID will be repeated for each `appID` that is cross-referenced.

Within an XML configuration file you name `Setup-Config.xml`, insert the XML shown in Listing 2-12.

Listing 2-12. *Setup-Config.xml*

```xml
<?xml version="1.0" encoding="UTF-8"?>
<Setup-Files>
    <App_Type_file>C:\List_Of_App_Type.xml</App_Type_file>
    <App_Instance_file>C:\List_Of_App_Instance.xml</App_Instance_file>
    <IDXRef_file>C:\List_Of_IDXRef.xml</IDXRef_file>
    <IDXRef_Data_file>C:\List_Of_IDXRef_Data.xml</IDXRef_Data_file>
</Setup-Files>
```

Each node should point to the physical location where you have created the corresponding XML configuration files.

Seed the BizTalk cross-reference tables by opening a command-line window and running the BizTalk cross-reference import tool, `BTSXRefImport.exe` (found in the BizTalk installation directory), passing in the path to the cross-reference XML file created in Listing 2-12:

```
BTSXRefImport.exe --file=C:\Setup-Config.xml
```

How It Works

During installation of BizTalk, several cross-reference tables are created in the `BizTalkMgmtDb` database. All the cross-reference tables begin with the prefix `xref_`, and the `BTSXRefImport` tool imports the data from the XML files provided into the table structure for access at runtime. It is not necessary to use the `BTSXRefImport.exe` tool to insert data into the cross-reference tables. You may insert data directly into the following tables:

- `xref_AppInstance`
- `xref_IdXRef`
- `xref_IdXRefData`

After running the `BTSXRefImport` tool, and if the data were in a denormalized form, the data would look like this:

AppType	AppInstance	IdXRef	CommonID	Application ID
Oracle	Oracle_01	Customer.ID	100	CARA345
Siebel	Siebel_01	Customer.ID	100	99-4D976
Siebel	Siebel_12	Customer.ID	100	44OL

There are subtle differences between ID and value cross-referencing. Value cross-references, as the name implies, deal with static values, while ID cross-references deal with cross-referencing unique identifiers. Since most value cross-references are not updated at runtime, a functoid and API method are not provided to update the references at runtime. ID cross-references, though, may be updated using the Set Common ID functoid or API method. See Recipe 2-10 for more information about value cross-references.

■**Note** The Set Common ID functoid is poorly named, as it actually sets the `application` ID and the `CommonID`. If a `CommonID` is not provided, the method will return a new `CommonID`.

2-10. Seeding Cross-Reference Tables with Value Cross-References

Problem

You wish to statically cross-reference state values between two or more systems. The reference data already exists, but you must load the data into the BizTalk cross-reference tables before you may use the cross-reference functoids or API.

Solution

Within an XML configuration file you name `List_Of_App_Type.xml`, insert the XML shown in Listing 2-13, and insert an `appType` node for each system that will have static cross-references.

Listing 2-13. *List_Of_App_Type.xml*

```
<?xml version="1.0" encoding="UTF-8"?>
<listOfAppType>
    <appType>
        <name>Oracle</name>
        <description/>
    </appType>
    <appType>
        <name>Siebel</name>
        <description/>
    </appType>
</listOfAppType>
```

■**Note** The node values in Listings 2-13 through 2-15 have been placed in the XML as an example. You should remove them and insert your own.

Within an XML configuration file you name `List_Of_ValueXRef.xml`, insert the XML shown in Listing 2-14.

Listing 2-14. *List_Of_ValueXRef.xml*

```
<?xml version="1.0" encoding="UTF-8"?>
<listOfValueXRef>
    <valueXRef>
        <name>Order.Status</name>
        <description/>
    </valueXRef>
</listOfValueXRef>
```

For each field you plan to statically cross-reference, insert a `valueXRef` node with a unique child node `name`. This value will be used to identify the static field. For instance, if you plan to map between order status codes, you might create a common value of `Order.Status`.

Within an XML configuration file you name `List_Of_ValueXRef_Data.xml`, insert the XML shown in Listing 2-15.

Listing 2-15. *List_Of_ValueXRef_Data.xml*

```
<?xml version="1.0" encoding="UTF-8"?>
<listOfValueXRefData>
<valueXRef name="Order.Status">
    <appType name="Oracle">
        <appValue commonValue="Open">OP</appValue>
        <appValue commonValue="Pending">PD</appValue>
        <appValue commonValue="Closed">CD</appValue>
    </appType>
    <appType name="Siebel">
        <appValue commonValue="Open">1:Open</appValue>
        <appValue commonValue="Pending">2:Pending</appValue>
        <appValue commonValue="Closed">3:Closed</appValue>
    </appType>
</valueXRef>
</listOfValueXRefData>
```

For each static field you create in the `List_Of_ValueXRef.xml` file, insert a `valueXRef` node. For each system you create in the `List_Of_App_Type.xml` file, insert an `appType` node. Insert one or more `appValue` nodes for each value that is permissible for this `valueXRef` field. Insert a `commonValue` attribute to store the common name for the value, and set the application-specific value within the node. The common value will be repeated for each `appType` that is cross-referenced.

Within an XML configuration file you name `Setup-Config.xml`, insert the XML shown in Listing 2-16.

Listing 2-16. *Setup-Config.xml*

```
<?xml version="1.0" encoding="UTF-8"?>
<Setup-Files>
<App_Type_file>c:\List_OF_App_Type.xml</App_Type_file>
<ValueXRef_file>c:\List_Of_ValueXRef.xml</ValueXRef_file>
<ValueXRef_Data_file>c:\List_Of_ValueXRef_Data.xml</ValueXRef_Data_file>
</Setup-Files>
```

Each node should point to the physical location where you have created the corresponding XML configuration files.

Seed the BizTalk cross-reference tables by opening a command-line window and running the BizTalk cross-reference import tool, `BTSXRefImport.exe` (found in the BizTalk installation directory), passing in the path to the `Setup-Config.xml` cross-reference file:

```
BTSXRefImport.exe --file=C:\Setup-Config.xml
```

How It Works

During installation of BizTalk, several static cross-reference tables are created in the `BizTalkMgmtDb` database. All the cross-reference tables begin with the prefix `xref_`, and the `BTSXRefImport` tool imports the data from the XML files provided to the table structure for access at runtime. It is not necessary to use the `BTSXRefImport.exe` tool to insert data into the cross-reference tables. You may insert data directly into the following tables:

- `xref_AppType`

- `xref_ValueXRef`

- `xref_ValueXRefData`

In a denormalized form, the table would look like this after running the `BTSXRefImport` tool:

AppType	ValueXRef	CommonValue	AppValue	AppType
Oracle	Order.Status	Open	OP	Oracle
Siebel	Order.Status	Open	1:Open	Siebel
Oracle	Order.Status	Pending	PD	Oracle
Siebel	Order.Status	Pending	2:Pending	Siebel
Oracle	Order.Status	Closed	CD	Oracle
Siebel	Order.Status	Closed	3:Closed	Siebel

2-11. Using the ID Cross-Reference Functoids

Problem

Within a map, you wish to dynamically cross-reference unique identifiers between two or more systems, and the identifier cross-references have already been loaded into the cross-reference tables. For example, a source system publishes an Account with a unique identifier of 1234, and you want to cross-reference and dynamically translate that identifier to the unique identifier in a destination system of AA3CARA.

Note If you have not already loaded the identifier cross-reference data, see Recipe 2-9 for more information.

Solution

In order to cross-reference the identifiers within a map, take the following steps:

1. Click the Database Functoids tab in the Toolbox.

2. Drag the Get Common ID functoid onto to the map surface.

3. Open the Input Parameters dialog box for the Get Common ID functoid.

4. Add a constant parameter and set the value to the ID type you wish to cross-reference. For instance, you may set the value to something like Customer.ID.

5. Add a second constant parameter to the Get Common ID functoid and set the value to the source system application instance. For instance, you may set the value to something like Siebel_01.

6. Click OK.

7. Connect the unique source identifier node you wish to cross-reference from the source schema to the Get Common ID functoid.

8. Drag the Get Application ID functoid from the Database Functoids tab onto the map surface and place it to the right of the Get Common ID functoid.

9. Open the Input Parameters dialog box for the Get Application ID functoid.

10. Add a constant parameter and set the value to the ID type you wish to receive. For instance, you may set the value to something like Customer.ID.

11. Add a second constant parameter to the Get Common ID functoid and set the value to the destination system application instance. For instance, you may set the value to something like Oracle_01.

12. Click OK.

13. Connect the Get Common ID functoid to the Get Application ID functoid.

14. Connect the functoid to the unique destination identifier node.

15. Save and test the map (see Recipe 2-24 for information about testing maps).

The end result should look like Figure 2-35.

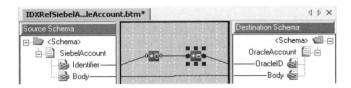

Figure 2-35. *ID cross-reference map*

How It Works

Identifier cross-referencing allows entities to be shared across systems. Although cross-referencing functionality is often not required in small integration projects, as often there is a single system for a given entity type, in larger organizations, it is common to find several systems with the same entities (for example, Account, Order, and Invoice). These entities are often assigned a unique identifier that is internally generated and controlled by the system. In other words, from a business perspective, the entities are the same, but from a systems perspective, they are discrete. Therefore, in order to move an entity from one system to another, you must have a way to create and store the relationship between the unique identifiers, and to discover the relationships at runtime.

BizTalk Server provides this functionality through cached cross-referencing tables, API, an import tool, and functoids. Using the import tool, you can load information about systems, instances of those systems, the entities within those systems you wish to cross-reference, and the actual cross-reference data into a set of cross-reference tables that are installed with BizTalk in the BizTalkMgmtDb database. Then, using the functoids or API at runtime, you access the tables to convert an identifier from one recognized value to another. The basic steps for converting from one system to another are as follows:

1. Using the source identifier, source instance, and source entity type, retrieve the common identifier by calling the Get Common ID functoid.

■**Note** The common identifier is commonly not stored in any system. It is an identifier used to associate one or more identifiers.

---

2. Using the common identifier, destination system instance, and destination entity type, retrieve the destination identifier by calling the Get Application ID functoid.

This recipe has focused on accessing identifier cross-referencing functionality through BizTalk functoids, but an API is also available. The cross-referencing class may be found in the Microsoft.Biztalk.CrossRreferencing.dll, within the namespace Microsoft.BizTalk.CrossReferencing. This class has several members that facilitate storing and retrieving identifier cross referencing relationships, as listed in Table 2-1.

Table 2-1. *ID Cross-Referencing API*

Member	Description
GetCommonID	With an application instance, entity/id type, and application identifier value, retrieves a common identifier. If a cross-reference does not exist, a blank will be returned. If the application instance or entity/id type does not exist, an exception will be thrown.
GetAppID	With a common identifier, application instance, and entity/id type, retrieves the application identifier value. If a cross-reference does not exist, a blank will be returned. If the application instance or entity/id type does not exist, an exception will be thrown.
SetCommonID*	With an application instance, entity/id type, application identifier value, and optionally a common identifier, create a relationship in the cross-referencing tables. If a common identifier is not passed to the method, one will be created and returned. If the application instance or entity/id type does not exist, an exception will be thrown.

* *The* SetCommonID *method does set the common identifier, and will create one if not passed to the method, but more important, it creates the relationship between the application-specific identifier and the common identifier. Perhaps a better name would have been* SetIDCrossReference.

2-12. Using the Value Cross-Reference Functoids

Problem

Within a map, you wish to statically cross-reference state values between two or more systems, and the value cross-references have already been loaded into the cross-reference tables. For example, a source system publishes an Order with a status of 1:Open, and you want to cross-reference and translate the static state value to the static value in a destination system of OP.

> ■**Note** If you have not already loaded the value cross-reference data, see Recipe 2-10 for more information.

Solution

In order to cross-reference the static values within a map, take the following steps:

1. Click the Database Functoids tab in the Toolbox.

2. Drag the Get Common Value functoid to the map surface.

3. Open the Input Parameters dialog box for the Get Common Value functoid.

4. Add a constant parameter and set the value to the static value type you wish to cross-reference. For instance, you may set the value to something like Order.Status.

5. Add a second constant parameter to the Get Common Value functoid and set the value to the source system application type. For instance, you may set the value to something like `Siebel`.

6. Click OK.

7. Connect the state value source node you wish to cross-reference from the source schema to the Get Common Value functoid.

8. Drag the Get Application Value functoid from the Database Functoids tab to the map surface and place it to the right of the Get Common Value functoid.

9. Open the Input Parameters dialog box for the Get Application Value functoid.

10. Add a constant parameter and set the value to the static value type you wish to cross-reference. For instance, you may set the value to something like `Order.Status`.

11. Add a second constant parameter to the Get Common Value functoid and set the value to the destination system application type. For instance, you may set the value to something like `Oracle`.

12. Click OK.

13. Connect the Get Common Value functoid to the Get Application Value functoid.

14. Connect the functoid to the unique destination state value node.

15. Save and test the map (see Recipe 2-24 for information on testing maps).

The end result should look like Figure 2-36.

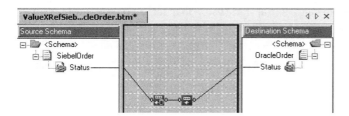

Figure 2-36. *Value cross-reference map*

How It Works

Identifier and value cross-referencing are similar in concept, with the following differences:

- Value cross-referencing is commonly between enumeration fields. Identifier cross-referencing is commonly between entity unique identifiers.

- Value cross-referencing occurs between system types. Identifier cross-referencing occurs between instances of system types.

- Identifier cross-references may be set at runtime. Value cross-references are static and may be loaded only through the import tool or direct table manipulation.

■**Note** For a conceptual overview of the cross-referencing functionality provided by BizTalk, see Recipe 2-9.

The basic steps for converting from one system to another are as follows:

1. Using the source application type, source application static value, and source entity value type, retrieve the common value by calling the Get Common Value functoid.

■**Note** The common value is commonly not stored in any system. It is a value used to associate multiple values.

2. Using the common static value, destination system type, and destination entity value type, retrieve the destination static value by calling the Get Application Value functoid.

This recipe has focused on accessing value cross-referencing functionality through BizTalk functoids, but an API is also available. The cross-referencing class may be found in the `Microsoft.Biztalk.CrossRreferencing.dll`, within the namespace `Microsoft.BizTalk.CrossReferencing`. This class has several members that facilitate storing and retrieving value cross-referencing relationships, as listed in Table 2-2.

Table 2-2. *Value Cross-Referencing API*

Member	Description
GetCommonValue	With an application type, entity/node value type, and application value, retrieves a common value. If a cross-reference does not exist, a blank will be returned. If the application type or entity/node value type does not exist, an exception will be thrown.
GetAppValue	With a common value, application type, and entity/node type, retrieves the application value. If a cross-reference does not exist, a blank will be returned. If the application type or entity/node value type does not exist, an exception will be thrown

2-13. Using the Looping Functoid

Problem

The structure of a message from a source system you are integrating with contains multiple repeating record types. You must map each of these record types into one record type in the destination system. In order for the message to be imported into the destination system, a transformation must be applied to the source document to consolidate, or standardize, the message structure.

Solution

Create a map that utilizes the BizTalk Server Looping functoid, by taking the following steps:

1. Click the Toolbox, and then click the Advanced Functoids tab. On the map surface, in between the source and destination schemas, drag and drop a Looping functoid. This functoid accepts 1 to 100 repeating source records (or data elements) as its input parameters. The return value is a reference to a single repeating record or data element in the destination schema.

2. Connect the left side of the Looping functoid to the multiple repeating source data elements that need to be consolidated.

3. Connect the right side of the Looping functoid to the repeating destination data element that contains the standardized data structure.

How It Works

An example of a map that uses the Looping functoid is shown in Figure 2-37.

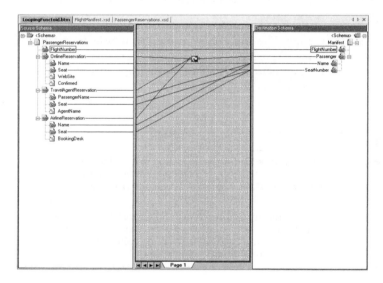

Figure 2-37. *Using the Looping functoid*

In this example, multiple types of plane flight reservations are consolidated into a single list of records capturing passengers and their associated seats. The XML snippet in Listing 2-17 represents one possible instance of the source schema.

Listing 2-17. *Source Schema Instance for the Looping Functoid Example*

```
<ns0:PassengerReservations xmlns:ns0="http://tempURI.org ">
  <FlightNumber>123</FlightNumber>
  <OnlineReservation>
    <Name>Ben Lange</Name>
    <Seat>5A</Seat>
    <WebSite>QuickTravel</WebSite>
```

```
    <Confirmed>True</Confirmed>
  </OnlineReservation>
  <OnlineReservation>
    <Name>Lauren Jones</Name>
    <Seat>5B</Seat>
    <WebSite>QuickTravel</WebSite>
    <Confirmed>False</Confirmed>
  </OnlineReservation>
  <TravelAgentReservation>
    <PassengerName>Meghan Stone</PassengerName>
    <Seat>25E</Seat>
    <AgentName>Josh HecK</AgentName>
  </TravelAgentReservation>
  <AirlineReservation>
    <Name>Sydney Oniel</Name>
    <Seat>12B</Seat>
    <BookingDesk>Heathrow</BookingDesk>
  </AirlineReservation>
</nsO:PassengerReservations>
```

Based on this source XML, the looping map displayed in Figure 2-37 will produce the XML document shown in Listing 2-18, containing a single passenger seat assignment list.

Listing 2-18. *Destination Schema Instance for the Looping Functoid Example*

```
<nsO:Manifest xmlns:nsO="http://tempURI.org">
    <Passenger Name="Ben Lange" SeatNumber="5A"></Passenger>
    <Passenger Name="Lauren Jones" SeatNumber="5B"></Passenger>
    <Passenger Name="Meghan Stone" SeatNumber="25E"></Passenger>
    <Passenger Name="Sydney Oniel" SeatNumber="12B"></Passenger>
</nsO:Manifest>
```

This example displays a simplistic but useful scenario in which the Looping functoid can be used. Essentially, this functoid iterates over the specified repeating source records (all those with a link to the left side of the functoid), similar to the For...Each structure in coding languages, and maps the desired elements to a single repeating record type in the destination schema.

■**Note** The four source records in the XML instance (the two OnlineReservations records, the one TravelAgentReservation record, and the one AirlineReservation record) produced four records in the output XML. If the source instance had contained five records, the resulting output XML document would also contain five records.

Based on this simple principle, you can develop much more complex mappings via the Looping functoid. One example of a more advanced use of the Looping functoid is conditional looping. This technique involves filtering which source records actually create destination records in the resulting XML document. The filtering is done by adding a logical functoid to the map, which produces a `true` or `false` Boolean value based on the logic. Common examples of filtering are based on elements that indicate a certain type of source record, or numeric elements that posses a certain minimum or maximum value.

The previous flight reservation example can be extended to implement conditional looping, in order to map only those online reservations that have been confirmed. This can be accomplished via the following steps:

1. Click the Toolbox, and then click the Logical Functoids tab. On the map surface, in between the source and destination schemas, drag and drop a logical Equal functoid. This functoid accepts two input parameters, which are checked for equality. The return value is a Boolean `true` or `false`.

2. Specify the second input parameter for the logical Equal functoid as a constant, with a value of `true`.

3. Connect the left side of the logical Equal functoid to the data element whose value is the key input for the required decision (equality, in this case) logic.

4. Connect the right side of the logical Equal functoid to the element in the destination schema containing the repeating destination data element that contains the standardized data structure.

An example of the enhanced map is shown in Figure 2-38.

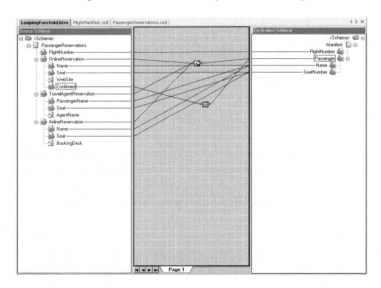

Figure 2-38. *Conditional looping*

Based on the same source XML outlined earlier in Listing 2-17, the looping map displayed in Figure 2-38 will produce the following XML document, containing a single passenger seat assignment list with only three passengers (Lauren Jone's reservation, which was not confirmed, is filtered out by the conditional looping logic):

```
<ns0:Manifest xmlns:ns0="http://tempURI.org">
    <Passenger Name="Ben Lange" SeatNumber="5A"></Passenger>
    <Passenger Name="Meghan Stone" SeatNumber="25E"></Passenger>
    <Passenger Name="Sydney Oniel" SeatNumber="12B"></Passenger>
</ns0:Manifest>
```

■**Note** Due to the fact that the `Confirmation` element is not being mapped over to the destination schema, the output of the logical Equal functoid is tied to the `Passenger` record. If the logical Equal functoid were being applied to an element that is being mapped to the destination schema, such as the `Seat` element, the output of the Equal functoid could be tied directly to the `SeatNumber` element in the destination schema.

In this example of conditional looping, the second input parameter of the logical Equal functoid is a hard-coded constant set to `true`. In real-world scenarios, it may not be ideal for this value to be hard-coded. You may prefer to have it driven off a configurable value. Several alternatives exist:

- Implement a Scripting functoid to the map, which passes the name of a configuration value to an external assembly. This external assembly would then handle the "look up" of the actual configuration value. (See Recipe 2-18 for information about calling compiled assemblies from a map.)

- Implement a Database Lookup functoid, which as the name implies, would look up the appropriate configuration value from a database table. (See Recipe 2-8 for information about using the Database Lookup functoid.)

- Use a custom functoid, written in any .NET-compliant language. This option is similar to the external assembly route, except that it is implemented specifically as a functoid as opposed to a general .NET assembly. (See Recipe 2-15 for more information about creating a custom functoid.)

When implementing a map that uses the Looping functoid, it is important to understand how BizTalk Server inherently handles repeating records in the source schema. If a record in the source schema has a `Max Occurs` property set to greater than 1, BizTalk Server handles the record via a loop. No Looping functoid is required in order for the map to process all appropriate source records. A Looping functoid is needed only to consolidate multiple repeating source records into a single repeating destination record.

2-14. Using the Iteration Functoid

Problem

You need to implement a map that handles certain records within a repeating series in an intelligent fashion. The map must be able to determine the sequential order, or index, of each repeating record, and perform customized logic based on that index.

Solution

Develop a BizTalk Server map, and leverage the Iteration functoid by taking the following steps.

1. Click the Toolbox, and then click the Advanced Functoids tab. On the map surface, in between the source and destination schemas, drag and drop an Iteration functoid. This functoid accepts a repeating source record (or data element) as its one input parameter. The return value is the currently processed index of a specific instance document (for a source record which repeated five times, it would return 1, 2, 3, 4, and 5 in succession as it looped through the repeating records).

2. Connect the left side of the Iteration functoid to the repeating source record (or data element) whose index is the key input for the required decision logic.

3. Connect the right side of the Iteration functoid to the additional functoids used to implement the required business logic.

How It Works

An example of a map that uses the Iteration functoid is shown in Figure 2-39.

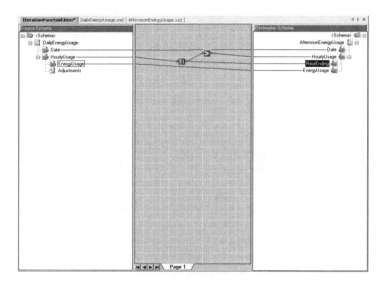

Figure 2-39. *Using the Iteration functoid*

In this example, all the afternoon hourly energy values from the source XML are mapped over to the destination XML. The Iteration functoid is used to determine the index of each HourlyUsage record, with those having an index value of 13 or higher being flagged as afternoon hours. Additionally, the output from the Iteration functoid is also used to create the HourEnding element in the destination XML, defining to which hour the energy reading pertains. The XML snippet in Listing 2-19 represents one possible document instance of the source schema (the first 12 HourlyUsage XML records have been omitted for simplicity).

Listing 2-19. *Sample Source Instance for the Iteration Functoid Example*

```
<ns0:DailyEnergyUsage xmlns:ns0="http://Mapping.DailyEnergyUsage">
  <Date>05/21/2006</Date>
    ...
    12 HourlyUsage records omitted
    ...
  <HourlyUsage>
    <EnergyUsage>2.4</EnergyUsage>
    <Adjustments>0</Adjustments>
  </HourlyUsage>
  <HourlyUsage>
    <EnergyUsage>2.5</EnergyUsage>
    <Adjustments>0</Adjustments>
  </HourlyUsage>
  <HourlyUsage>
    <EnergyUsage>2.8</EnergyUsage>
    <Adjustments>0</Adjustments>
  </HourlyUsage>
  <HourlyUsage>
    <EnergyUsage>3.0</EnergyUsage>
    <Adjustments>0</Adjustments>
  </HourlyUsage>
  <HourlyUsage>
    <EnergyUsage>2.9</EnergyUsage>
    <Adjustments>0</Adjustments>
  </HourlyUsage>
  <HourlyUsage>
    <EnergyUsage>2.8</EnergyUsage>
    <Adjustments>0</Adjustments>
  </HourlyUsage>
  <HourlyUsage>
    <EnergyUsage>2.5</EnergyUsage>
    <Adjustments>0</Adjustments>
  </HourlyUsage>
  <HourlyUsage>
    <EnergyUsage>2.3</EnergyUsage>
    <Adjustments>0</Adjustments>
  </HourlyUsage>
  <HourlyUsage>
    <EnergyUsage>2.3</EnergyUsage>
    <Adjustments>0</Adjustments>
  </HourlyUsage>
  <HourlyUsage>
    <EnergyUsage>2.0</EnergyUsage>
    <Adjustments>0</Adjustments>
  </HourlyUsage>
```

```
<HourlyUsage>
  <EnergyUsage>1.7</EnergyUsage>
  <Adjustments>0</Adjustments>
</HourlyUsage>
<HourlyUsage>
  <EnergyUsage>1.5</EnergyUsage>
  <Adjustments>0</Adjustments>
</HourlyUsage>
</ns0:DailyEnergyUsage>
```

When passed through the map displayed in Figure 2-39, this XML will produce the XML document shown in Listing 2-20, containing all the afternoon hourly energy usage values with their associated HourEnding value.

Listing 2-20. *Sample Destination Instance for the Iteration Functoid Example*

```
<ns0:AfternoonEnergyUsage xmlns:ns0="http://Mapping.AfternoonEnergyUsage">
  <Date>05/21/2006</Date>
  <HourlyUsage>
    <HourEnding>13</HourEnding>
    <EnergyUsage>2.4</EnergyUsage>
  </HourlyUsage>
  <HourlyUsage>
    <HourEnding>14</HourEnding>
    <EnergyUsage>2.5</EnergyUsage>
  </HourlyUsage>
  <HourlyUsage>
    <HourEnding>15</HourEnding>
    <EnergyUsage>2.8</EnergyUsage>
  </HourlyUsage>
  <HourlyUsage>
    <HourEnding>16</HourEnding>
    <EnergyUsage>3.0</EnergyUsage>
  </HourlyUsage>
  <HourlyUsage>
    <HourEnding>17</HourEnding>
    <EnergyUsage>2.9</EnergyUsage>
  </HourlyUsage>
  <HourlyUsage>
    <HourEnding>18</HourEnding>
    <EnergyUsage>2.8</EnergyUsage>
  </HourlyUsage>
  <HourlyUsage>
    <HourEnding>19</HourEnding>
    <EnergyUsage>2.5</EnergyUsage>
  </HourlyUsage>
```

```
<HourlyUsage>
  <HourEnding>20</HourEnding>
  <EnergyUsage>2.3</EnergyUsage>
</HourlyUsage>
<HourlyUsage>
  <HourEnding>21</HourEnding>
  <EnergyUsage>2.3</EnergyUsage>
</HourlyUsage>
<HourlyUsage>
  <HourEnding>22</HourEnding>
  <EnergyUsage>2.0</EnergyUsage>
</HourlyUsage>
<HourlyUsage>
  <HourEnding>23</HourEnding>
  <EnergyUsage>1.7</EnergyUsage>
</HourlyUsage>
<HourlyUsage>
  <HourEnding>24</HourEnding>
  <EnergyUsage>1.5</EnergyUsage>
</HourlyUsage>
</ns0:AfternoonEnergyUsage>
```

The Iteration functoid can be a crucial tool for those business scenarios that require the current index number of a looping structure within a map to be known. In the energy usage example, it allows a generic list of chronological usage values to be mapped to a document containing only those values that occur in the afternoon, along with adding an element describing to which hour that usage pertains. As the map processes the repeating HourlyUsage records in the source XML in a sequential fashion, the index from the Iteration functoid is passed to the logical Greater Than functoid, which compares the index with a hard-coded value of 12. If the index value is 13 or greater, the element is created in the destination XML, and its hour ending value is set.

This example works well for the purposes of our simple scenario, but those who have dealt with hourly values of any kind know that days on which daylight saving time (DST) falls need to be handled carefully. Since the time change associated with DST actually occurs early in the morning, there are 13 morning (pre-afternoon) hourly values in the fall occurrence of DST, and 11 morning hourly values in the spring occurrence.

The map in Figure 2-39 can easily be enhanced to account for this by adding logic based on the record count of hourly values in the source XML document. You can accomplish this via the following steps:

1. Click the Toolbox, and then click the Advanced Functoids tab. On the map surface, in between the source and destination schemas, drag and drop a Record Count functoid. This functoid accepts a repeating source record (or data element) as its one input parameter. The return value is the count of repeating source records contained in a specific instance document.

2. Connect the left side of the Record Count functoid to the repeating source record (or data element) whose index is the key input for the required decision logic.

3. Drag and drop a Subtraction functoid from the Mathematical Functoids tab onto the map surface, positioning it to the right of the Record Count functoid. This functoid accepts a minimum of 2 and a maximum of 99 input parameters. The first is a numeric value, from which all other numeric input values (the second input parameter to the last) are subtracted. The return value is a numeric value equaling the first input having all other inputs subtracted from it.

4. Connect the right side of the Record Count functoid to the left side of the Subtraction functoid.

5. Specify the second input parameter for the Subtraction functoid as a constant, with a value of 12.

6. Connect the right side of the Subtraction functoid to the left side of the Greater Than functoid. Ensure that this input to the Greater Than functoid is the second input parameter.

Figure 2-40 shows an example of this enhanced map.

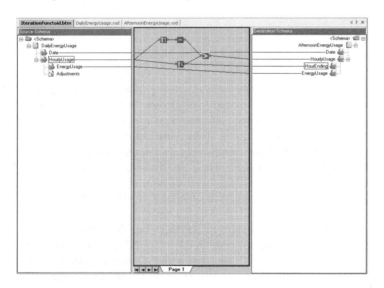

Figure 2-40. *DST map*

In this modified example, the repeating source record's count has 12 subtracted from it to adjust for the two DST days of the year (this works since we are interested in only the afternoon energy usage values, which are always the final 12 readings for a day). This adjusted value is then passed through the same logical Greater Than functoid as in the previous example, and the DST issue is effectively handled.

The use of the Iteration functoid is common in a number of other scenarios. One such scenario is when dealing with a document formatted with comma-separated values (CSV). Often, the first row in a CSV document contains column header information, as opposed to actual record values. The following flat file snippet shows one possible representation of energy usage values in CSV format:

```
EnergyUsage,Adjustments
2.4,0
2.5,0
2.8,0
```

In cases like these, it is likely that you do not want to map the column headers to the destination XML document. You can use an Iteration functoid to skip the first record of a CSV document. The index from the Iteration functoid is passed to a logical Not Equal functoid, which compares the index with a hard-coded value of 1. If the index is anything other than 1 (the record at index 1 contains the column header information), the values are mapped to the destination XML. See Recipe 1-10 for more information about CSV files.

■**Note** You can also strip out column headers by using envelope schemas. See Recipe 1-7 for more information.

Another common use of the Iteration functoid is to allow the interrogation of records preceding or following the currently processed record. This can be helpful when mapping elements in a repeating record in the source schema that require knowledge of the next or previous record.

2-15. Creating a Custom Functoid

Problem

You have a mapping need that requires the repeated use of complex functionality.

Solution

Rather than writing the same inline code (C#, XSLT, and so on) and pasting it in multiple shapes, or using a combination of multiple existing functoids, you can develop your own custom functoid.

As an example, we'll describe the process to develop, deploy, and use a custom functoid that replaces the ampersand (&), greater than (>), and less than (<) symbols with their HTML/XML equivalents. The functoid will have one input parameter and one output parameter, representing the string on which to run the replacement. This functoid would be used primarily with XML that may be returned from an external source, such as a .NET assembly, where the XML may not have been validated and contains characters that must be escaped.

Use the following steps to create, deploy, and use a custom functoid. Refer to the sample solution `SampleCustomFunctoid.sln` included with this book.

1. Create a new Class Library .NET project. Functoids can be coded in any .NET language. This example is implemented in C#.

2. Add a reference to the `Microsoft.BizTalk.BaseFunctoids.dll` assembly located in the `%\Program Files\Microsoft BizTalk Server 2006\Developer Tools` directory.

3. Create a resource file (`resx`) to store the functoid configuration parameters. The name of the file and the parameters should match what is shown in Listing 2-21.

■**Note** Adding a bitmap (or any file) to a resource file may require using a third-party application. You can download such applications freely from the Internet.

---

   4. Code the functoid. The functoid code should match that shown in Listing 2-21. This is
       a complete C# class library and will compile into a deployable functoid.

Listing 2-21. *Custom Functoid Class Library*

```
using System;
using Microsoft.BizTalk.BaseFunctoids;
using System.Reflection;

namespace SampleCustomFunctoid
{
    /// <summary>
    /// See sample solution (SampleCustomFunctoid.sln)
    /// which accompanies this recipe
    /// </summary>
    [Serializable]
    public class EncodeFunctoid : BaseFunctoid
    {
        public EncodeFunctoid() : base()
        {
            //Custom functoids should begin with 6000 or higher
            this.ID = 6667;

            // resource assembly reference
            SetupResourceAssembly
                ("SampleCustomFunctoid.SampleCustomFunctoidResource",
                Assembly.GetExecutingAssembly());

            //Set the properties for this functoid
            SetName("SAMPLECUSTOMFUNCTOID_NAME");
            SetTooltip("SAMPLECUSTOMFUNCTOID_TOOLTIP");
            SetDescription("SAMPLECUSTOMFUNCTOID_DESCRIPTION");
            SetBitmap("SAMPLECUSTOMFUNCTOID_BITMAP");

            // one parameter in, one parameter out
            this.SetMinParams(1);
            this.SetMaxParams(1);
```

```
            //Function code below
            SetExternalFunctionName(GetType().Assembly.FullName,
             "SampleCustomFunctoid.EncodeFunctoid", "EncodeChars");

            //Category in Toolbox where this functoid will appear
            this.Category = FunctoidCategory.String;

             //output of functoid can go to all nodes indicated
            this.OutputConnectionType = ConnectionType.All;

            // add one of the following lines of code for every input
            // parameter. All lines would be identical.
            AddInputConnectionType(ConnectionType.All);
        }


        // Actual function which does the replacement of symbols
        public string EncodeChars(String strInputValue)
        {
            strInputValue = strInputValue.Replace("&","&amp;");
            strInputValue = strInputValue.Replace("<","&lt;");
            strInputValue = strInputValue.Replace(">","&gt;");

            return strInputValue;
        }
    }
}
```

5. Add a strong name key and build the project.

6. Place a copy of the assembly in the following directory: `%\Program Files\Microsoft BizTalk Server 2006\Developer Tools\Mapper Extensions`.

7. To add the functoid to the Toolbox, on the window toolbar, click Tools ➤ Add/Remove Toolbox Items. In the Customize Toolbox dialog box, click the Functoids tab. Click the Browse button and select the functoid DLL from step 5, as shown in Figure 2-41. Then click OK.

8. Add the functoid to the Global Assembly Cache (GAC).

■**Note** Functoids can be tested in maps without deploying to the GAC.

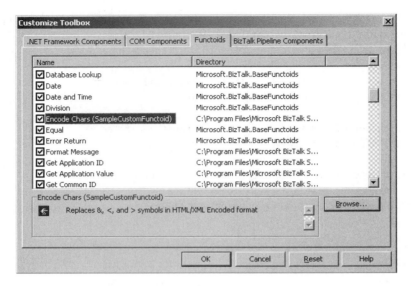

Figure 2-41. *Adding a custom functoid to the Toolbox*

This completes the steps for creating a custom functoid. You can now add the functoid to a BizTalk map and test it (see Recipe 2-24 for details on testing maps). When a map is ready for deployment, the functoid will need to be copied to the `Mapper Extensions` folder (see step 6) and the GAC on the production server.

How It Works

One of the biggest benefits to using custom functoids is that you have full access to the .NET libraries. Inline code within maps gives only limited access to libraries, and coding is often primitive. Custom functoids are created as .NET class libraries, and they have all of the related coding benefits.

The example shown in this recipe is very simple. Custom functoids do not have to be limited to the two functions shown in the code. For example, assume that you need a functoid that does some sort of interaction with a database. You may need to include an `Init()` function and a deconstructor to terminate a connection, all of which can be included in the class library.

Additionally, you may need multiple input parameters for your functoid. Additional parameters can be added very easily. See Listing 2-22 for an example of a functoid with three input parameters.

Listing 2-22. *Multiple Input Parameters for a Custom Functoid*

```
SEE CODE FROM Listing 2-21.

// three parameters in, one parameter out
this.SetMinParams(3);
this.SetMaxParams(3);

...
```

```
            // add one of the following lines of code for every input
            // parameter. All lines would be identical.
            AddInputConnectionType(ConnectionType.All); // input parameter 1
            AddInputConnectionType(ConnectionType.All); // input parameter 2
            AddInputConnectionType(ConnectionType.All); // input parameter 3

    }

    // Actual function which does the replacement of symbols
    public string EncodeChars(String strInputValue, strReplace1, strReplace2)
    {
        strInputValue = strInputValue.Replace("&",strReplace1);
        strInputValue = strInputValue.Replace("<",strReplace2);

        return strInputValue;
    }
```

2-16. Using the Date and Time Functoids

Problem

You are mapping a message in BizTalk Server, and need to manipulate date and time fields. Specifically, you must use the current date in order to determine a required date and time in the future, which is added to the outbound message during mapping. Additionally, you must apply the processing time for each document during mapping.

Solution

Within a map, use the Date and Time functoids provided with BizTalk Server. In order to apply the current processing time to the outbound document within the map, take the following steps:

1. Click the Toolbox, and then click the Date and Time Functoids tab. On the map surface, in between the source and destination schemas, drag and drop a Date and Time functoid. Since this functoid simply outputs the current date and time, it requires no input values.

2. Connect the right side of the Date and Time functoid to the element in the destination schema containing the date and time the message is processed.

In order to determine a future date based on the current date, take the following steps:

1. Drag and drop a Date functoid from the Date and Time Functoids tab of the Toolbox onto the map surface. This functoid is similar to the Date and Time functoid, but returns only the current date, as opposed to the current date and time. It also requires no input values.

2. Drag and drop an Add Days functoid from the Date and Time Functoids tab onto the map surface, positioning it to the right of the Date functoid. This functoid accepts two input parameters: a date or datetime value, and a numeric value indicating the number of days to add to the date supplied in the first input parameter. The return value is the date with the specified amount of days added.

3. Connect the right side of the Date functoid to the Add Days functoid.

4. Specify the second input parameter for the Add Days functoid as a constant with a value of 1.

5. Connect the right side of the Add Days functoid to the element in the destination schema containing the future date.

How It Works

An example of a map that uses the Date and Time functoids is shown in Figure 2-42.

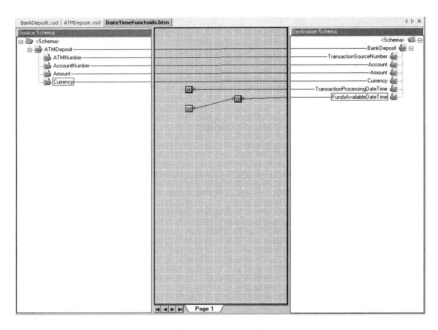

Figure 2-42. *Using the Date and Time Functoids*

This example captures the current date and time in the TransactionProcessingDateTime element, which is supplied by the Date and Time functoid. The format of the date and time produced by the Date and Time functoid is *YYYY-MM-DDThh:mm:ss*, which is ISO 8601-compliant. The time values are notated in 24-hour format.

The future date that the deposited funds will be available is captured in the FundsAvailableDateTime element. This value is based off the current date, supplied by the Date functoid, with a single day added to it to provide tomorrow's date, which is supplied by the Add Days functoid. The format of the Date functoid's output is *YYYY-MM-DD*, while the Add Days functoid accepts dates formatted as *YYYY-MM-DD* or *YYYY-MM-DDThh:mm:ss*. The format of the Add Days functoid's output is *YYYY-MM-DD*. All date formats used by these two functoids are ISO 8601–compliant. The time values are notated in 24-hour format.

The XML in Listing 2-23 represents one possible instance of the source schema.

Listing 2-23. *Sample Source Instance for the Date/Time Functoid Example*

```
<nsO:ATMDeposit xmlns:nsO="http://Mapping.ATMDeposit">
  <ATMNumber>00111</ATMNumber>
  <AccountNumber>123456</AccountNumber>
  <Amount>100.00</Amount>
  <Currency>USD</Currency>
</nsO:ATMDeposit>
```

When passed to the map in Figure 2-42, this XML message will produce the outbound XML document shown in Listing 2-24.

Listing 2-24. *Sample Output Instance for the Date/Time Functoid Example*

```
<nsO:BankDeposit xmlns:nsO="http://Mapping.BankDeposit">
  <TransactionSourceNumber>00111</TransactionSourceNumber>
  <Account>123456</Account>
  <Amount>100.00</Amount>
  <Currency>USD</Currency>
  <TransactionProcessingDateTime>2006-08-06T12:34:05</TransactionProcessingDateTime>
  <FundsAvailableDateTime>2006-08-07</FundsAvailableDateTime>
</nsO:BankDeposit>
```

The Date and Time functoids provide a baseline set of functionality when needing to interrogate and manipulate date and time values. In the bank account example, the Date and Time functoid provides the current date and time, allowing a timestamp to be applied to the outbound document, indicating the time that the message was processed. Often, messages include an element or elements detailing the time that the message pertains to, or the time at which a message was created. The Date and Time functoid is useful when the actual processing time (in this example, the time a deposit is processed within a bank's integration system) is required, which will likely be different from any time value embedded in the source document. The difference between date and time values within a source instance message and the actual processing time of the message can be particularly important when dealing with batched or time-delayed processes.

This example also shows how you can use the Date and Add Days functoids in conjunction to calculate a future date based on the day a message is processed. The current date is provided by the Date functoid, which is used by the Add Days functoid in order to come up with a date that is a specified number of days in the future. In the bank account scenario, this functionality is used to determine the day on which deposited funds are available. Business rules like this can be common among financial institutions, as validation procedures are often required when dealing with monetary transactions.

■**Note** You can also use a negative numeric value with the Add Days functoid, resulting in a date that is the specified number of days in the past. For this example, the Date and Time functoid (substituting for the Date functoid) could have been used as the first input parameter for the Add Days function, and the map would be functionally equivalent. This is due to the fact that the Add Days functoid can accept either date or datetime values, and in either case, produces only a value indicating a date (excluding a time element).

This bank account example can be extended to illustrate how the Time functoid can be used to add a time component to the data capturing the date at which deposited funds are available. Currently, the example simply calculates a date for this value, but it is likely that a financial institution would additionally need to know the time at which deposited funds should be made available for use. Since the Add Days functoid produces only date values (without a time component), you must use a Time functoid, in addition to a String Concatenate functoid. In order to implement this enhancement, take the following steps:

1. On the mapping grid, in between the source and destination schemas, drag and drop a Time functoid. Since this functoid simply outputs the current time, it requires no input values.

2. Drag and drop a String Concatenate functoid onto the mapping grid. This functoid allows multiple string values to be concatenated, or added, together.

3. Delete the current connection between the Add Days functoid and the element in the destination schema containing the future date that the deposited funds will be available in the bank account.

4. Connect the right side of the Add Days functoid to the String Concatenate functoid.

5. Specify the second input parameter for the String Concatenate functoid as a constant, with a value of T. This value is required in between the date and time portions of a datetime value for ISO 8601–compliant values.

6. Connect the right side of the Time functoid to the String Concatenate functoid.

7. Connect the right side of the String Concatenate functoid to the element in the destination schema containing the future date that the deposited funds will be available in the bank account.

Figure 2-43 shows an example of a map implementing these changes.

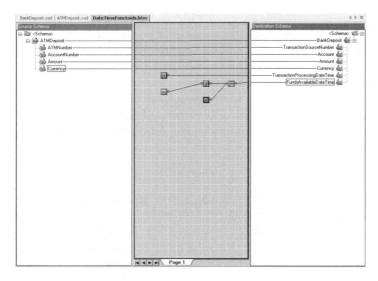

Figure 2-43. *Using the Time functoid*

Based on the same source XML used in the preceding example, the map in Figure 2-43 will produce the XML document shown in Listing 2-25, with a time component included in the FundsAvailableDateTime element.

Listing 2-25. *Sample Output Instance for the Time Functoid Example*

```
<nsO:BankDeposit xmlns:nsO="http://Mapping.BankDeposit">
  <TransactionSourceNumber>00111</TransactionSourceNumber>
  <Account>123456</Account>
  <Amount>100.00</Amount>
  <Currency>USD</Currency>
  <TransactionProcessingDateTime>2006-08-06T12:34:05</TransactionProcessingDateTime>
  <FundsAvailableDateTime>2006-08-07T12:34:05</FundsAvailableDateTime>
</nsO:BankDeposit>
```

One common challenge when dealing with datetime values is standardizing on a common format. This issue can be seen with dates adhering to the *MM-DD-YYYY* (common in the United States) or *DD-MM-YYYY* (common in Europe and other areas) format. Unfortunately, BizTalk Server does not have any Date and Time functoids that do complex datetime formatting. There are a number of ways to handle this issue. The simplest way is to use string functoids provided with BizTalk Server to manipulate and standardize the order of year, month, and day values. Specifically, you can use String Extract functoids to pull out values within a date (in this scenario, you would pull out the *DD*, *MM*, and *YYYY* values in three separate String Extract functoids), and then a String Concatenate functoid to combine the individual values in the correct format (in this scenario, you would append the three values in an order of *YYYY-MM-DD*).

There are also more robust ways of implementing complex date/time formatting. One option is to use the Scripting functoid, which provides access to the libraries of C#, VB .NET, and JScript .NET (either via inline code embedded in the map, or by referencing external assemblies written in one of the .NET-compliant languages). See Recipe 2-18 for information about calling compiled assemblies from a map, and Recipe 2-19 for information about using inline C# in a map. Additionally, you could use a custom functoid (which would leverage the datetime functionality of a .NET language). See Recipe 2-15 for information about creating a custom functoid.

2-17. Creating Functoid If-Then-Else Logic

Problem

You need to map values from the source to the destination message depending on whether a logical condition evaluates to true or false.

Solution

Define the logical condition that the mapping actions should be based on by dragging logical functoids from the Toolbox onto the map surface. Any functoid or combination of functoids that returns a Boolean value can establish the logical condition, but these functoids can return only true or false.

In this example, the logical condition will check whether the amount of a sale is greater that 1,000, as shown in Figure 2-44.

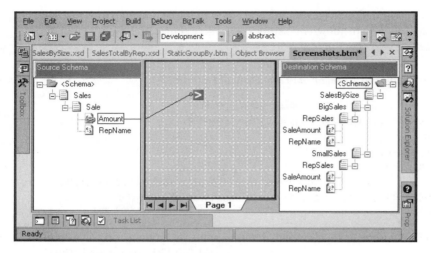

Figure 2-44. *Creating the logical operator*

Only large sales should appear under the <BigSales> element in the destination message, so the logical condition will check if the Amount in the source message is greater than 1,000.

1. Drag a Greater Than functoid from the Logical Functoids tab of the Toolbox onto the map surface.

2. Select the Amount field of the input message. Drag the cursor over the Greater Than functoid while pressing the mouse button to establish the first comparison value.

3. Right-click the functoid on the map surface and select Properties.

4. In the Properties window, click the Configure Functoid Inputs field, and then select the ellipsis that appears.

5. Define the constant value in the Configure Functoid Inputs dialog box by selecting the second button from the left at the top of the window.

These steps define the logical operation that determines mapping actions, as shown in Figure 2-45.

Next, define the mapping actions that depend on the evaluation of the logical condition. In this example, the contents of the <Sales> elements should map to different parts of the destination message, so the map must use the Boolean outcome of the logical comparison as input to a Value Mapping functoid.

1. Drag a Value Mapping functoid from the Advanced Functoids tab of the Toolbox to the right and below the Greater Than functoid.

2. Create a link from the Greater Than functoid to the Value Mapping functoid.

3. Create a link from the Amount field of the input message to the Value Mapping functoid to determine the value mapped when the logical condition is true.

4. Create a link from the Value Mapping functoid to the SaleAmount field appearing under the BigSales record to define where the large value will occur in the destination message.

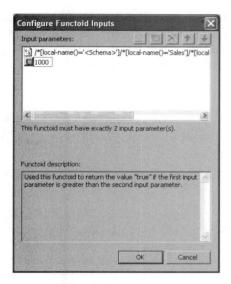

Figure 2-45. *Defining the comparison value*

The Value Mapping functoid defines the action the map should take when the logical condition evaluates to true. Both the amount of the big sale and the name of the sales representative must appear in the destination message in this example, so the map must use two Value Mapping functoids, as shown in Figure 2-46.

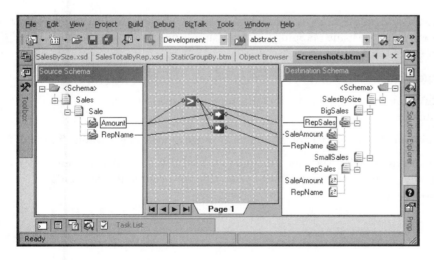

Figure 2-46. *Defining conditional mapping actions*

BizTalk must also know that it should create only the <RepSales> element in the destination message when the amount is greater that 1,000. Establishing a link from the logical operator to the RepSales element will ensure that BizTalk creates this parent to the actual values mapped.

When the logical condition evaluates to `false`, BizTalk should map the sale to the `<SmallSales>` part of the destination message. The map can check this directly by placing a Not Equal functoid on the mapping surface and comparing to the result of the logical comparison established earlier with a constant value equal to `true`, as shown in Figure 2-47.

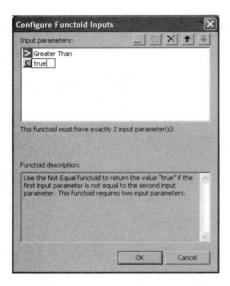

Figure 2-47. *Defining the else condition*

Finally, define the mapping actions that BizTalk should take when the logical comparison is not true. In this example, the Value Mapping functoids simply need to map under the `<SmallSales>` element in the destination message.

1. Drag a Value Mapping functoid onto the map surface.

2. Create a link from the Not Equal functoid that represents the else case to the Value Mapping functoid.

3. Create a link from the Amount field of the source message to the Value Mapping functoid.

4. Create a link from the Value Mapping functoid to the SaleAmount field appearing under the SmallSales record to define where the small value will occur in the destination message, as shown in Figure 2-48.

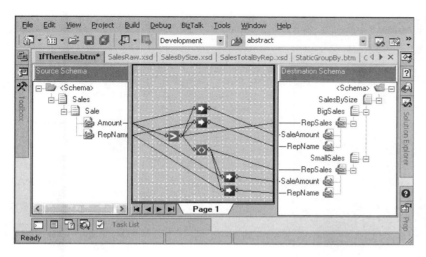

Figure 2-48. *Completed If . . . Then . . . Else map*

How It Works

Working with the BizTalk Mapper can be an unfamiliar process, even to experienced programmers. Business rules defined in source code can be procedural and explicit, but the graphical depiction of a BizTalk map can abstract the runtime behavior.

The link to the logical condition defines the information on which the map will perform the logical operation. BizTalk will evaluate the logical condition for each occurrence of the information in the source message, and remember the context of the logical condition when performing the output actions dependent on it. This means that the Value Mapping functoid will automatically know the right Amount and RepName values to map when the map executes.

The order of the Value Mapping functoid inputs is critical. The first input parameter must be either true or false. The second input parameter specifies the value that the functoid will return when the first parameter is true. While the order is established based on the order in which the inputs are connected to the Value Mapping functoid, sometimes the order can get mixed up when modifying the functoid links. There is no indication of the input parameter order on the mapping surface, but fortunately, it is easy to check. Open the Configure Functoid Inputs window, and the Boolean value should appear first in the list. Modify the order here by selecting one of the input parameters and clicking the up and down arrows, as shown in Figure 2-49.

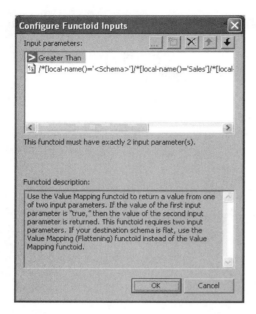

Figure 2-49. *Checking the parameter order*

This example establishes a logical condition, and defines mutually exclusive mapping actions that are directly determined from the evaluation of the logical conditions. Alternatively, a map can define separate logical conditions independently. With this alternative approach, the developer must carefully define the logical conditions to ensure that every input message will map to some outcome, and never both. This becomes an increasingly important consideration as the logical comparison becomes more and more complex.

When there are more than two mutually exclusive outcomes, the Not Equal functoid in this example can be combined with additional logical comparisons by linking its result to the Logical AND functoid. The result of the Logical AND functoid also evaluates to true or false, and the developer can define actions to take based on this result, as with any other logical operator.

2-18. Calling Compiled Assemblies

Problem

You need to access logic contained within an external assembly while transforming a message via a BizTalk Server map. The logic contained within the assembly cannot and should not be embedded within the map.

Solution

Create a map that uses the BizTalk Server Scripting functoid's ability to call external assemblies. The following steps outline the procedure.

1. Click the Toolbox, and then click the Advanced Functoids tab. On the map surface, in between the source and destination schemas, drag and drop a Scripting functoid. This functoid's input and output values are dependent on the logic contained within the Scripting functoid.

2. Connect the left side of the Scripting functoid to the appropriate source data elements or records. In this solution, no source data elements are used.

3. Configure the Scripting functoid.

   a. While the Scripting functoid is highlighted on the mapping grid, click the ellipsis to the right of the `Script` item in the Properties window.

   b. In the Configure Functoid Script dialog box, select External Assembly for Script Type, and the appropriate assembly, class, and method for Script Assembly, Script Class, and Script Method, as shown in Figure 2-50. Then click OK.

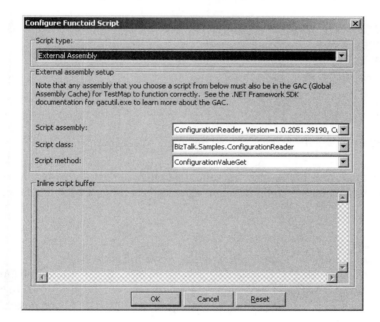

Figure 2-50. *Configuring a Scripting functoid*

■**Note** You must add a reference to the external assembly to the Visual Studio project containing the map for it to be available in the Configure Functoid Script dialog box. The external assembly must also be placed in the GAC.

---

    c. Click the ellipsis to the right of Input Parameters in the Properties window.

    d. In the Configure Functoid Inputs dialog box, create or order the appropriate input parameters for the method specified in step 2, as shown in Figure 2-51, and then click OK.

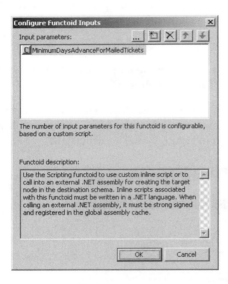

Figure 2-51. *Configuring the Scripting functoid's input parameters*

4. Connect the right side of the Scripting functoid to the appropriate destination data element or additional functoid (if further logic needs to be applied to the data).

How It Works

An example of a map that uses a Scripting functoid is shown in Figure 2-52.

    In this example, ticket request documents are translated into ticket orders. The functoids in the map determine whether there is enough time before the event for the tickets to be mailed to the purchaser. The XML snippet shown in Listing 2-26 represents one possible instance of the source schema.

Listing 2-26. *Sample Source Instance for the Scripting Functoid Example*

```
<nsO:TicketRequest xmlns:nsO="http://Mapping.TicketRequest">
  <EventName>Chelsea vs. Arsenal</EventName>
  <EventDate>08/06/2006</EventDate>
  <Venue>Stamford Bridge</Venue>
  <NumberOfTickets>2</NumberOfTickets>
  <PurchasedBy>George Murphy</PurchasedBy>
  <MailTicketFlag>True</MailTicketFlag>
</nsO:TicketRequest>
```

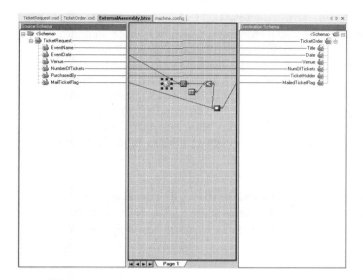

Figure 2-52. *Using a Scripting functoid*

Based on this source XML, the map shown in Figure 2-52 will produce the XML document (assuming that the current date is prior to August 4, 2006) shown in Listing 2-27, with the `MailedTicketFlag` appropriately set.

Listing 2-27. *Sample Output Instance for the Scripting Functoid Example*

```
<nsO:TicketOrder xmlns:nsO="http://Mapping.TicketOrder">
  <Title>Chelsea vs. Arsenal</Title>
  <Date>08/06/2006</Date>
  <Venue>Stamford Bridge</Venue>
  <NumOfTickets>2</NumOfTickets>
  <TicketHolder>George Murphy</TicketHolder>
  <MailedTicketFlag>True</MailedTicketFlag>
</nsO:TicketOrder>
```

This example demonstrates one of the many reasons why external assemblies may need to be called from a BizTalk Server map. Here, the external assembly provides access to a configuration value. This value is held in a configuration file (but alternatively could be held in a database or other data store), which is updated over time by system administrators and business analysts. For the purposes of this example, the following configuration value was used.

```
<add key="MinimumDaysAdvanceForMailedTickets" value="-2" />
```

The value of `-2`, which represents the minimum number of days required to mail tickets to a purchaser, is added to the `EventDate` element (by the Add Days functoid), resulting in a date value two days prior to the event (08/04/2006 in this example). The current date (supplied by the Date functoid) is then compared to the calculated date value (by the Less Than logical functoid) to determine if there is enough time to mail the purchased tickets. Finally, if there is ample time to mail the tickets, and the source document indicates the purchaser requested tickets to be mailed, the `MailedTicketFlag` element in the destination message is set to `true`.

The benefit of having the MinimumDaysAdvanceForMailedTickets value stored in a file external to BizTalk, as opposed to being hard-coded within the actual map, is that a change to the value does not require a redeployment of BizTalk Server artifacts for the modification to be applied. Additionally, by encapsulating the custom logic in an external assembly, any changes to that logic will require only that the external assembly is rebuilt and redeployed to the GAC. No changes to the BizTalk Server environment (aside from a BizTalk service restart to immediately apply the changes in the redeployed custom assembly) are required. Implementing this logic in an external assembly has the additional benefits of allowing reuse of the logic, minimizing code maintenance, and providing access to the debugging utilities within Visual Studio.

■**Note** You can step into the external assembly in debug mode by: running the external assembly solution in Visual Studio in debug mode, attaching to the process of the Visual Studio solution containing the BizTalk Server map, and testing the map. See Recipe 2-24 for information about testing a map from within Visual Studio.

In addition to using a generic external assembly, a custom functoid could also have been used to implement the configuration value retrieval logic (see Recipe 2-15). It is important to consider the differences between the two options prior to selecting your design. The main benefit of using a custom functoid is that the assembly is hosted within the BizTalk Server environment. The actual assembly file is located within the BizTalk Server program file directory, and the functoid can be added to the Functoid Toolbox within the development environment. Using generic external assemblies is sometimes a requirement, however, such as when the existing logic contained within them needs to be accessed directly (without modification to the source code or assembly location). This may be the case when using third-party or proprietary assemblies, where you do not have access to the source code.

Other common examples of logic contained in external assemblies are complex database-retrieval mechanisms, calculations above and beyond what is possible with the out-of-the-box mathematical functoids, and complex date and string formatting.

■**Caution** Care should be taken with regard to data types for values passed into and out of external assemblies. For example, if a source document element having a data type of xs:int is used as an input parameter for a method contained in an external assembly, it will be passed as an integer. Likewise, if the output from an external assembly is used to populate a destination document element having a data type of xs:int, it should be returned as an integer.

2-19. Using Inline C#

Problem

You are mapping a message in BizTalk Server, and must implement custom logic via an inline C# code snippet. The custom logic should be embedded within the map.

Solution

Create a map that uses the BizTalk Server Scripting functoid's ability to call inline C#. The following steps outline the procedure.

1. Click the Toolbox, and then click the Advanced Functoids tab. On the map surface, in between the source and destination schemas, drag and drop a Scripting functoid. This functoid's input and output values are dependent on the logic contained within the Scripting functoid.

2. Connect the left side of the Scripting functoid to the appropriate source data elements or records. This specifies the order and location of the Scripting functoid's input parameters.

3. Configure the Scripting functoid.

   a. While the Scripting functoid is highlighted on the mapping grid, click the ellipsis to the right of the `Script` item in the Properties window.

   b. In the Configure Functoid Script dialog box, select Inline C# for Script Type, choose the appropriate assembly, and enter your custom C# logic in the Inline Script Buffer text box, as shown in Figure 2-53. Then click OK.

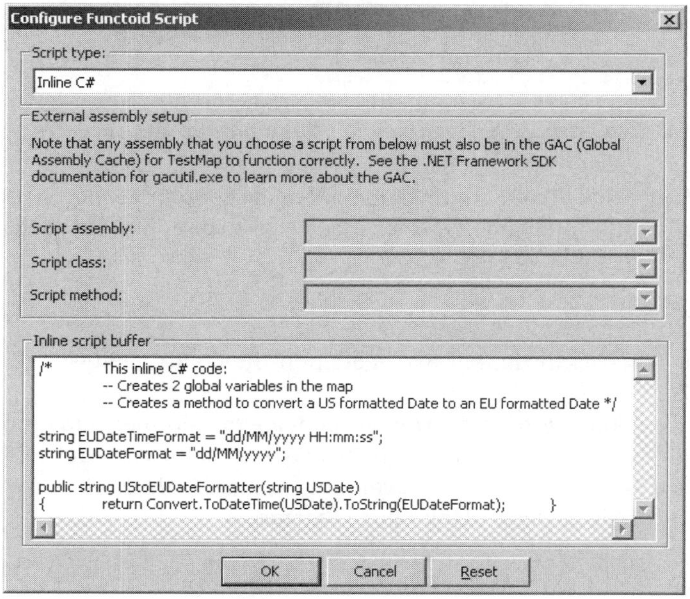

Figure 2-53. *Configuring a Script functoid to call inline C#*

■**Note** You can add tab characters within the Inline Script Buffer text box by pressing Ctrl+Tab. If you just press Tab while typing in the Inline Script Buffer text box, it changes the focus to the OK button.

c. Click the ellipsis to the right of `Input Parameters` in the Properties window.

d. In the Configure Functoid Inputs dialog box, create or order the appropriate input parameters for the method specified in step 2, as shown in Figure 2-54. Then click OK.

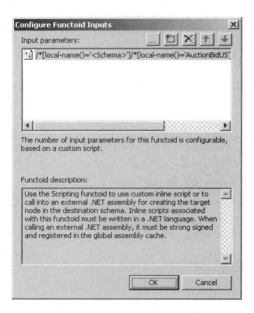

Figure 2-54. *Configuring a Script functoid's input parameters*

4. Connect the right side of the Scripting functoid to the appropriate destination data element or additional functoid (if further logic needs to be applied to the data).

How It Works

An example of a map that uses the BizTalk Server Scripting functoid's ability to call inline C# is shown in Figure 2-55.

In this example, auction bids from the United States are transformed into European Union (EU) bids. The Scripting functoids used in the map format the date and datetime values common in the United States to those that are common in the EU. The XML snippet in Listing 2-28 represents one possible instance of the source schema.

Listing 2-28. *Sample Source Instance for the Inline C# Example*

```
<ns0:AuctionBidUS xmlns:ns0="http://Mapping.AuctionBidUS">
  <BidID>12345</BidID>
  <LotID>123-456</LotID>
  <BidDate>09/25/2006</BidDate>
  <LotCloseDateTime>09/18/2006 23:59:59</LotCloseDateTime>
</ns0:AuctionBidUS>
```

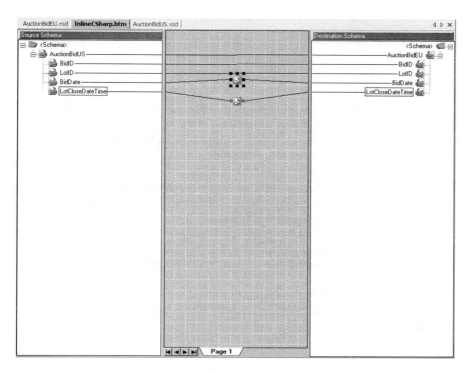

Figure 2-55. *Using the Scripting functoid to call inline C#*

Based on this XML snippet, the map displayed will produce the XML document shown in Listing 2-29. Notice that the format of the BidDate and LotClosedDateTime values have been changed from *MM/DD/YYYY* and *MM/DD/YYYY hh:mm:ss* format to *DD/MM/YYYY* and *DD/MM/YYYY hh:mm:ss* format, respectively.

Listing 2-29. *Sample Output Instance for the Inline C# Example*

```
<ns0:AuctionBidEU xmlns:ns0="http://Mapping.AuctionBidEU">
  <BidID>12345</BidID>
  <LotID>123-456</LotID>
  <BidDate>25/09/2006</BidDate>
  <LotCloseDateTime>18/09/2006 23:59:59</LotCloseDateTime>
</ns0:AuctionBidEU>
```

Date formatting like this is one of countless examples where custom logic could be needed within a BizTalk Server map. In the auction bid example, date and datetime values were formatted with inline C# to account for regional differences. Additionally, in the first Scripting functoid, two variables were defined that specify the date and datetime format for the EU. This illustrates another helpful use of Scripting functoids: the ability to create global variables that can be used by any other functoid within the map. In the example, the UStoEUDateFormatter method in the second Scripting functoid referenced the EUDateTimeFormat variable that was defined in the first Scripting functoid.

■Note All methods defined in inline Scripting functoids should have unique names. This is important to avoid naming conflicts, as all inline script is embedded within the map inside CDATA tags.

You can format dates in a number of different ways within a BizTalk Server map. In our example, we used inline C#, but we could have used either of the other available script languages (VB .NET or JScript .NET), an external assembly, or a custom functoid.

Inline scripting is a good option when a simple implementation of custom logic is needed, and the logic is unlikely to be leveraged outside the map. It is important to recognize a key limitation of inline scripting: debugging utilities. Because the inline script is embedded into the map's XSLT, stepping into the code at runtime is not possible. One possible way to allow easier debugging of an inline script is to first create and test it in a separate executable or harness. This will allow you to use the robust debugging utilities of Visual Studio. Once the code has been fully tested, it can be placed into a Scripting functoid. See Recipe 2-18 for more information about calling external assemblies from a map and Recipe 2-15 for more information about custom functoids.

The fact that the inline script is saved in the XSLT of the map has another important consequence: only those libraries available to XSLT stylesheet scripts may be leveraged. The following are available namespaces:

- System: The system class

- System.Collection: The collection classes

- System.Text: The text classes

- System.Text.RegularExpressions: The regular expression classes

- System.Xml: The XML classes

- System.Xml.Xsl: The XSLT classes

- System.Xml.Xpath: The XPath classes

- Microsoft.VisualBasic: The Visual Basic script classes

2-20. Passing Orchestration Variables into Maps

Problem

You need to include information from variables in an orchestration in the destination message of a BizTalk mapping.

Solution

Begin by creating a new message schema with fields for capturing the information from the orchestration, as shown in Figure 2-56. The information from the orchestration variables must be set in a separate message from the input message, referred to here as a *context message*. In this recipe, the mapping will transform a customer purchase message for the customer support department, and the orchestration will define the support information with the business process. BizTalk will use the new message schema to capture the support information.

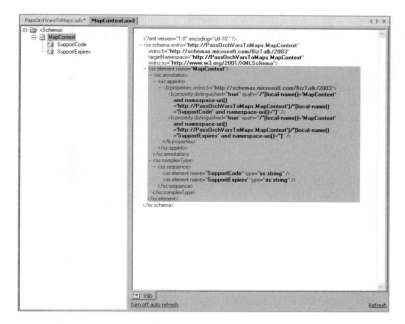

Figure 2-56. *Defining the context message schema*

Follow these steps to set up the orchestration (see Chapter 4 for more information about setting up orchestrations).

1. To access the fields of this message easily from within the orchestration, define them as distinguished fields. Right-click the context message schema tree and select Promote ➤ Show Promotions. In the Promote Properties dialog box, select each field in the left window and click the Add button, as shown in Figure 2-57. Then click OK.

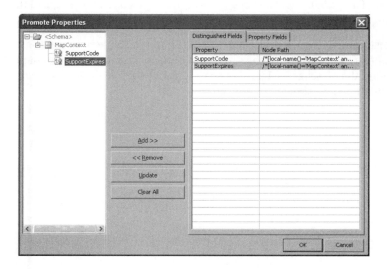

Figure 2-57. *Designating the distinguished fields*

2. Define a message with the type set to this new schema in the orchestration, as shown in Figure 2-58. This message passes the information from the orchestration into the map.

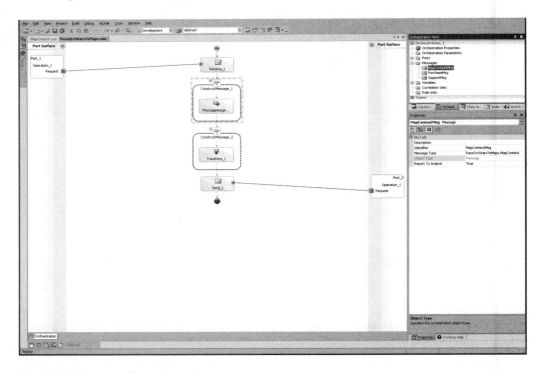

Figure 2-58. *Creating the context message*

3. Define a variable in the orchestration with type System.Xml.XmlDocument, as shown in Figure 2-59. This variable will be used to instantiate the context message in the orchestration.

4. In the Orchestration Designer, drag a Message Assignment shape from the Toolbox onto the orchestration surface. In the properties of the Construct Message shape that appears around the Message Assignment shape, specify MapContextMsg as the only message constructed, as shown Figure 2-60.

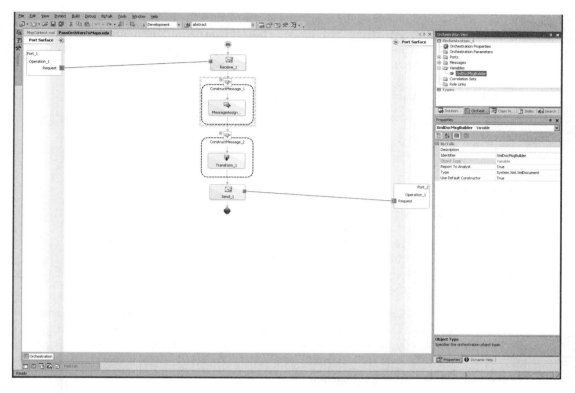

Figure 2-59. *Creating an XmlDocument*

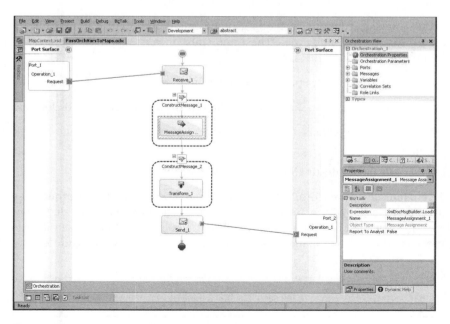

Figure 2-60. *Constructing the context message*

5. Double-click the Message Assignment shape to open the BizTalk Expression Editor window. Load an XML string conforming to the schema of the context message into the `XmlDocMsgBuilder` variable. Then create the `MapContextMsg` message by assigning the loaded `XmlDocument` variable to it. This example uses the code shown in Listing 2-30.

■**Note** Obtain a sample XML string by right-clicking the schema in the Solution Explorer and selecting Generate Instance.

Listing 2-30. *Build the Context Message*

```
XmlDocMsgBuilder.LoadXml("<ns0:MapContextxmlns:ns0=
'http://PassOrchVarsToMaps.MapContext'>
<SupportCode>SupportCode_0</SupportCode>
<SupportExpires>SupportExpires_0</SupportExpires>
</ns0:MapContext>");
MapContextMsg = XmlDocMsgBuilder;
```

Once instantiated, the values in `MapContextMsg` can be set anywhere in the orchestration. For simplicity in this example, they are created and set in the same Message Assignment shape, and the expiration is the same day that the context message is created, as shown in Listing 2-31.

Listing 2-31. *Set the Values in the Orchestration*

```
MapContextMsg.SupportCode = "R-2";
MapContextMsg.SupportExpires = System.DateTime.Now.ToString("yyyy-MM-dd");
```

Once the context message contains the required orchestration information, the BizTalk orchestration must create the mapping. The orchestration must create mappings that have more than one source or destination message.

1. Drag a Transform shape (see Recipe 4-12) onto the Orchestration Designer surface.

2. Double-click the new Transform shape to open the Transform Configuration dialog box.

3. Specify the source messages to be the `PurchaseMsg` and `MapContextMsg` messages, as shown in Figure 2-61.

4. Specify `SupportMsg` for the destination message, and then click OK.

BizTalk will generate a new transformation with two input messages and one output message. One of the input messages will be the `MapContextMsg` message containing the values from the orchestration. The developer can choose to either drive mapping logic from these values, or map them directly to the destination message as in this example, as shown in Figure 2-62.

■**Caution** BizTalk may not be able to recognize the second schema if the project name begins with a number.

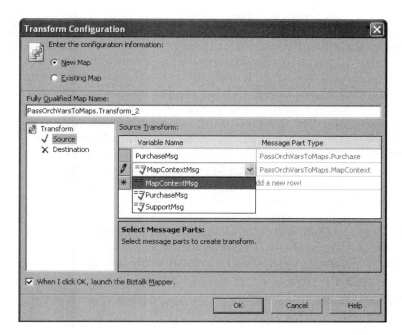

Figure 2-61. *Configuring map source messages*

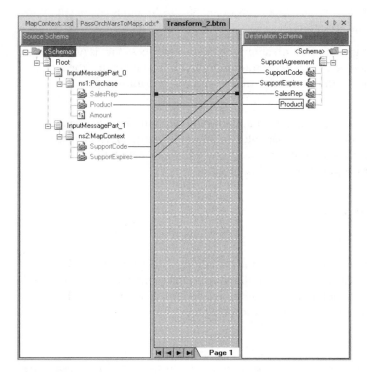

Figure 2-62. *Defining mapping logic from the source messages*

How It Works

BizTalk developers often think about translation among message types when defining integration processes in an orchestration. They can place a Transform shape directly within an orchestration to transform a message into different formats, so it seems that the transformation and orchestration are integral to each other. However, BizTalk Mapper cannot directly access the contextual information of the business process and the logic existing in the orchestration.

The BizTalk Mapper can natively access many resources outside the map with the default functoids. For example, the Database Lookup functoid can access records in a database, and the Scripting functoid can invoke an external assembly. However, the most direct way to access information about the context of the business process is by creating a message specifically for capturing the state of the business process. Add the information required in the mapping to this additional message, and then add the context message as an additional input message to the map.

The possible reasons for passing information from an orchestration into a mapping with a second message are as varied as the capabilities of BizTalk orchestrations. However, in all cases, the mapping destination message must contain information that cannot or should not be added to the schema of the input message. Here are some examples:

- A standards body such as RosettaNet sets the source message schema, and it should not change.

- The mapping must access message context properties. A map cannot access these values. For example, if the SMTP adapter is used, an orchestration can access the sender with the SMTP.From property but not directly from the BizTalk Mapper. The destination message may need this information.

- The mapping must include information about the business process that is not known until runtime and is required in the orchestration. Rather than duplicating the logical definitions, define it once within the orchestration and pass the information to the mapping.

- BizTalk must be capable of modifying the mapped values without redeploying the BizTalk artifacts. For example, the BizTalk rules engine (see Chapter 5) can be easily invoked from within an orchestration, and facilitates additional capabilities like rule versioning and seamless deployment.

2-21. Using Inline XSLT

Problem

You need to map an incoming document with a node containing a document that matches exactly the destination schema. All of the nodes in the source document need to be mapped in their entirety to the destination document. Both the source and the destination schemas have target namespaces, and the namespaces must be preserved.

Solution

By using inline XSLT within a Scripting functoid, you can create the target document with the appropriate nodes and the correct namespace. Listing 2-32 shows a sample input document.

Listing 2-32. *Sample Input Document for the Inline XSLT Example*

```
<ns0:SampleSource xmlns:ns0="http://Sample.Source">
  <ID>ID_0</ID>
  <Payload>
    <SampleDestination>
      <Name>Name_0</Name>
      <Address>Address_0</Address>
      <Company>Company_0</Company>
    </SampleDestination>
  </Payload>
</ns0:SampleSource>
```

Figure 2-63 depicts the source and target schemas with a Scripting functoid in place.

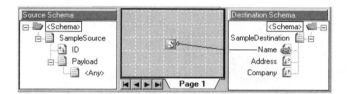

Figure 2-63. *Using the Scripting functoid and schemas*

The inline XSLT is written to parse the incoming document as a whole; there is no need to have an input to the Scripting functoid. The output of the Scripting functoid occurs under the node that the output is tied to—in this case, the XSLT output will be directly below the SampleDestination element. When XML documents contain namespaces, use the local-name() qualifier to reference a specific node by name. Because of the requirement that the namespaces be preserved, it is necessary to copy each of the nodes in the source document's Payload node (which consists of an Any element that can contain any XML structure) separately to the destination document.

Figure 2-64 shows the configuration for the Scripting functoid with the inline XSLT for the <Name> element. Additional nodes (such as Address and Company) can be added using the same code pattern.

This XSLT script will produce the desired XML document on output, as shown in Listing 2-33.

Listing 2-33. *Sample Output Document for the Inline XSLT Example*

```
<ns0:SampleDestination xmlns:ns0="http://Sample.Dest">
  <Name>Name_0</Name>
  <Address>Address_0</Address>
  <Company>Company_0</Company>
</ns0:SampleDestination>
```

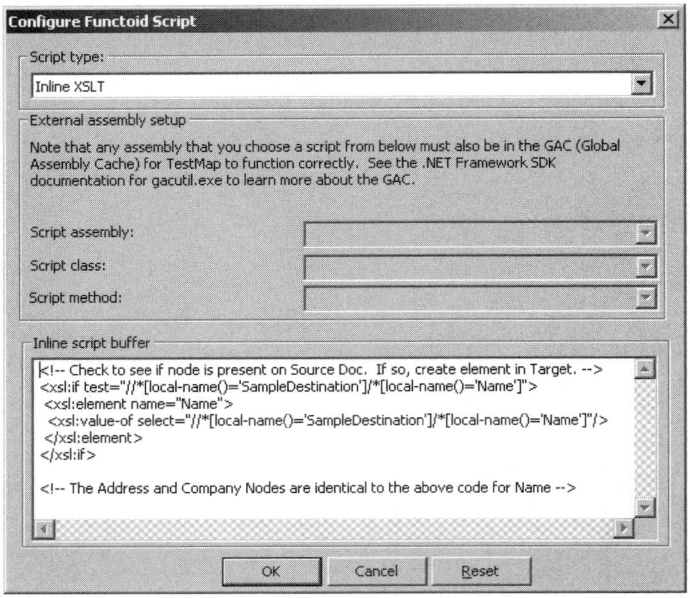

Figure 2-64. *Configuring the Scripting functoid to use inline XSLT*

How It Works

The negative aspect of using the given solution is that the inline XSLT can become quite long for larger documents with many elements. The two expected solutions to this, the Mass Copy functoid or the `<xsl:copy-of>` function, both end up requiring additional logic and code outside the map due to the presence of the namespaces. These can be solved in orchestration mapping, but not in maps outside orchestrations. An additional approach would be to reference an external XSLT file where more complex functions are available.

The Mass Copy functoid, designed specifically to copy entire documents to a destination node, is a graphic representation of the XSLT `<xsl:copy-of>` function. Both of these copy the entire source document to the destination document. The problem is that the source document namespace will be copied to the target document, regardless of the node level being copied. There is no simple way in XSLT to remove the source document namespace. For instance, if in the given solution for this recipe, the inline XSLT was changed to simply read:

```
<xsl:copy-of select="//*[local-name()='Payload']"/>
```

The following document would be created on output of the map (note that the root node contains the namespace of the source schema):

```
<Payload xmlns:ns0="Sample.Source">
  <SampleDestination>
    <Name>Name_0</Name>
    <Address>Address_0</Address>
    <Company>Company_0</Company>
  </SampleDestination>
</Payload>
```

If a Mass Copy functoid (see Recipe 2-6) were used on the Payload node, the following document would be produced (note that the root node repeats itself and that it contains the namespace of the source schema):

```
<ns0:SampleDestination xmlns:ns0="http://Sample.Dest">
  <SampleDestination xmlns:ns0="http://Sample.Source">
    <Name>Name_0</Name>
    <Address>Address_0</Address>
    <Company>Company_0</Company>
  </SampleDestination>
</ns0:SampleDestination>
```

The output document for both of these approaches is not the desired outcome. However, if the mapping is being done in an orchestration, the output document will be in a message that can now be accessed and corrected in a Message Assignment shape, using the code in Listing 2-34.

Listing 2-34. *Message Assignment*

```
// xmlDoc is a variable of type System.Xml.XmlDocument()
// msgSampleDestination contains the output of the map

// xpath will access the contents of the SampleDestination node
xmlDoc = xpath(msgSampleDestination, "/*/*");

// populate the message
msgSampleDestination = xmlDoc;
```

Figure 2-65 shows using a Message Assignment shape to correct the mapping.

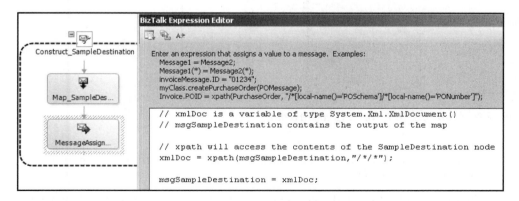

Figure 2-65. *Using message assignment to correct copy-of mapping*

Another option would be to move the entire solution to an external XSLT document, where more complex functions such as templates are available, and reference it in the map directly rather than using the mapping functions. This can be done by selecting properties on the map being developed and indicating the path to the XSLT file in the Custom XSLT Path property.

In summary, there are a number of approaches that can be taken to map an incoming document with a node containing a document that matches exactly the destination schema. The cleanest and most viable approach is described in this recipe's solution. Quicker and more convoluted solutions involve using the Mass Copy functoid and <xsl:copy-of> function. An additional approach is to move the mapping completely out of the map into a separate XSLT document. The appropriate solution must be decided by the developer.

2-22. Using Call Templates

Problem

You want to use the inline XSLT call template functionality within the Scripting functoid and understand the difference between inline XSLT and an inline XSLT call template.

Solution

Use the following steps to add an inline XSLT functoid call to a map. The steps assume the schemas shown in Figure 2-66 are being used.

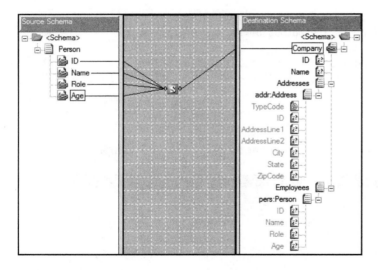

Figure 2-66. *Scripting/XSLT call template in a map*

1. Click the Toolbox, and then click the Advanced Functoids tab. Drop a Scripting functoid onto the map surface.

2. While the Scripting functoid is highlighted on the mapping grid, click the ellipsis to the right of the Script item in the Properties window. In the Configure Functoid Script dialog box, select Inline XSLT for Script Type, place the code shown in Listing 2-35 into the Inline Script Buffer text box, and then click OK.

Listing 2-35. *Template Code*

```
<xsl:template name="CreateCompanySchema">
<xsl:param name="ID" />
<xsl:param name="Name" />
<xsl:param name="Role" />
<xsl:param name="Age" />
<xsl:element name="Company">
 <xsl:element name="ID">Default Company ID</xsl:element>
 <xsl:element name="Name">Default Company Name</xsl:element>
 <xsl:element name="Employees">
  <xsl:element name="Person">
   <xsl:element name="ID"><xsl:value-of select="$ID" /></xsl:element>
   <xsl:element name="Name"><xsl:value-of select="$Name" /></xsl:element>
   <xsl:element name="Role"><xsl:value-of select="$Role" /></xsl:element>
   <xsl:element name="Age"><xsl:value-of select="$Age" /></xsl:element>
  </xsl:element>
 </xsl:element>
</xsl:element>
</xsl:template>
```

3. Create four input parameters by dropping each of the four nodes (ID, Name, Role, and Age) in the source document onto the Scripting functoid.

4. Drop the output of the functoid onto the root node (Company) of the destination schema.

5. Test the map (see Recipe 2-24 for details on testing maps). Assuming that the input document that is shown in Listing 2-36 is used as input, the document shown in Listing 2-37 will be output.

Listing 2-36. *Input Document for the Call Template Example*

```
<ns0:Person xmlns:ns0="http://SampleSolution.Person">
  <ID>1</ID>
  <Name>S. Brekalo</Name>
  <Role>Acupuncturist</Role>
  <Age>29</Age>
</ns0:Person>
```

Listing 2-37. *Output Document for the Call Template Example*

```
<Company>
 <ID>Default Company ID</ID>
 <Name>Default Company Name</Name>
 <Employees>
```

```
<Person>
 <ID>1</ID>
 <Name>S. Brekalo</Name>
 <Role>Acupuncturist</Role>
 <Age>29</Age>
</Person>
</Employees>
</Company>
```

How It Works

Calling an XSLT template is very similar to using inline XSLT (see Recipe 2-21). The main difference is the way in which values within the source document are passed and accessed. With inline XSLT, node values in the source document are accessed through XSL methods, whereas with called XSLT templates, the values are passed in as parameters.

In the case where code may need to be reused for multiple nodes, it may be more advantageous to create a template that can be reused without modifying the code. Templates will also allow for more traditional programming techniques, such as setting and updating variables dynamically within the template (for example, the ability to update a variable to store the number of loops that have occurred within a for-each).

Listing 2-38 demonstrates the use of inline XSLT rather than a called XSLT template. The output of Listing 2-38 will produce the same output as that of the XSLT template code shown earlier in Listing 2-35.

Listing 2-38. *Inline XSLT for Comparison*

```
<xsl:element name="Company">
 <xsl:element name="ID">Default Company ID</xsl:element>
 <xsl:element name="Name">Default Company Name</xsl:element>
 <xsl:element name="Employees">
  <xsl:element name="Person">
   <xsl:element name="ID">
    <xsl:value-of select="//*[local-name()='ID']" />
   </xsl:element>
   <xsl:element name="Name">
    <xsl:value-of select="//*[local-name()='Name']" />
   </xsl:element>
   <xsl:element name="Role">
    <xsl:value-of select="//*[local-name()='Role']" />
   </xsl:element>
   <xsl:element name="Age">
    <xsl:value-of select="//*[local-name()='Age']" /></xsl:element>
   </xsl:element>
  </xsl:element>
 </xsl:element>
</xsl:element>
```

2-23. Using XSLT Group-By

Problem

You need to define mapping from an input message with a flat structure to an output message grouping elements by the values of fields in the input message.

Solution

The input message must have records containing a field on which the grouping should be performed, as well as the information that needs to be grouped together. The output message needs to define records for each group and a field containing the aggregated information. The input message may have a structure similar to the XML in Listing 2-39.

Listing 2-39. *Sample Source Message for the XSLT Group-By Example*

```
<ns0:Sales xmlns:ns0="http://tempURI.org">
  <Sale>
    <Amount>100.01</Amount>
    <RepName>Megan</RepName>
  </Sale>
  <Sale>
    <Amount>200.01</Amount>
    <RepName>Megan</RepName>
  </Sale>
  <Sale>
    <Amount>10.10</Amount>
    <RepName>Leah</RepName>
  </Sale>
  <Sale>
    <Amount>2000</Amount>
    <RepName>Misti</RepName>
  </Sale>
  <Sale>
    <Amount>50.10</Amount>
    <RepName>Leah</RepName>
  </Sale>
</ns0:Sales>
```

To create the mapping, follow these steps:

1. Click the Toolbox and then click the Advanced Functoids tab. Place a Scripting functoid on the map surface and connect it to the record that will contain each group in the destination message.

2. While the Scripting functoid is highlighted on the map surface, click the ellipsis to the right of the Script item in the Properties window. In the Configure Functoid Script dialog box, select Inline XSLT for Script Type, and then click OK.

3. Create an `xsl:for-each` element in the inline XSLT script, and define the groups to create in the output message by selecting the unique values of the grouping field. This statement will loop through each unique value appearing in the input message.

4. Inside the `xsl:for-each` element, create the record that should contain the group and the field containing the value that must be aggregated for the group. The `current()` function obtains the current iteration value of the `xsl:for-each` element's select statement. Listing 2-40 shows the inline XSLT.

Listing 2-40. *Inline XSLT Group-By Script*

```
<xsl:for-each select="//Sale[not(RepName=preceding-sibling::Sale/RepName)]/RepName">
  <RepSales>
    <RepTotalAmount>
        <xsl:value-of select="sum(//Sale[RepName=current()]/Amount)"/>
    </RepTotalAmount>
    <RepName>
        <xsl:value-of select="current()"/>
    </RepName>
  </RepSales>
</xsl:for-each>
```

This XSLT script will produce the XML message shown in Listing 2-41, containing one RepSales element for each sales representative with the total sales and name of the representative.

Listing 2-41. *Sample Destination Message for the XSLT Group-By Example*

```
<ns0:SalesByRep xmlns:ns0="http://tempURI.org">
  <RepSales>
    <RepTotalAmount>300.02</RepTotalAmount>
    <RepName>Megan</RepName>
  </RepSales>
  <RepSales>
    <RepTotalAmount>60.2</RepTotalAmount>
    <RepName>Leah</RepName>
  </RepSales>
  <RepSales>
    <RepTotalAmount>2000</RepTotalAmount>
    <RepName>Misti</RepName>
  </RepSales>
</ns0:SalesByRep>
```

How It Works

The key feature of this inline XSLT example is the `select` statement appearing in the `xsl:for-each` element. This statement will create a list of values to create a group for, containing the distinct values of RepName in our example. Each RepName is located at `//Sale/RepName` in the input message. However, the select statement should obtain only the first occurrence of each distinct group value. This inline example achieves this by adding the filter [not(RepName=preceding-sibling::Sale/RepName)] to the select statement. The xsl:for-each element will loop through the first occurrence of each unique grouping value, and the value can be obtained within the xsl:for-each element with the current() function.

When the filter expression evaluates a Sale element, the condition RepName= preceding-sibling::Sale/RepName is true whenever there is an element appearing before it with the same RepName value. Placing the condition inside the not() function makes it true only when there are no preceding elements with the same RepName value, so it is only true for the first occurrence of each distinct RepName value.

The inline XSLT script in Listing 2-40 calculates the total sales of each representative and creates one record in the output message containing the total sales and the sales representative's name.

In addition to grouping fields in the output message, the map may need to perform aggregations for the groups of input message values. Perhaps BizTalk cannot determine the specific groupings that the map needs to perform until runtime, or static links may not be practical because of a large number of possible groups.

When inline XSLT performs the grouping, BizTalk applies the filter expression to the //Sale statement, which means BizTalk applies the filter expression to every Sale element in the input message. For each input message, the expression checks the value of every preceding-sibling, and returns true when none of the preceding-sibling elements has the same RepName value. This algorithm is not efficient for large messages.

There is a generally more efficient alternative XSLT approach to the group by problem. This alternative approach is the Muenchian method. The Muenchian method is generally more efficient than the inline solution presented here, but the default BizTalk functoids cannot implement it. The Muenchian method declares an xsl:key element at the top level of the XSLT stylesheet. The map directly obtains a node set for each distinct RepName with an xsl:key, eliminating the computational cost of checking every preceding sibling incurred with inline XSLT. However, since the top level of the xsl:stylesheet element must declare the xsl:key element, inline XSLT cannot implement it. Only a separate stylesheet file can implement the Muenchian method. Place the XSLT stylesheet in Listing 2-42 in a separate file for this example.

Listing 2-42. *Sample Group-By Stylesheet*

```
<?xml version="1.0"?>
<xsl:stylesheet xmlns:xsl="http://www.w3.org/1999/XSL/Transform" version="1.0">
    <xsl:key name="SalesByRepKey" match="Sale" use="RepName"/>
    <xsl:template match="/">
        <nsO:SalesByRep xmlns:nsO='http://tempURI.org'>
<xsl:apply-templates select="//Sale[generate-id()=
generate-id(key('SalesByRepKey', RepName)[1])]"/>
        </nsO:SalesByRep>
    </xsl:template>
    <xsl:template match="Sale">
        <RepSales>
            <RepTotalAmount>
```

```
<xsl:value-of select="sum(key('SalesByRepKey', RepName)/Amount)" />
          </RepTotalAmount>
          <RepName>
<xsl:value-of select="RepName" />
          </RepName>
      </RepSales>
   </xsl:template>
</xsl:stylesheet>
```

Specify the external XSLT file used by a BizTalk map with the following steps.

1. Right-click the map surface and select Properties.

2. Click the ellipsis next to the Custom XSLT Path property, and open the file containing the custom XSLT.

3. Compile the map. The XSLT file is included in the BizTalk assembly and does not need to be deployed separately.

2-24. Testing Maps

Problems

You have developed a map and are ready to test and view its output.

Solution

For the purposes of testing, there are two basic types of maps:

- Simple maps, which consist of a single source schema and single destination schema

- Complex maps, which consist of two or more source schemas and/or two or more destination schemas

This solution will work through both types, illustrating several techniques for creating the necessary input documents and obtaining the test results. Figure 2-67 shows a simple map, with a Company schema being mapped from a combination of a Person schema and hard-coded values in two String Concatenate functoids.

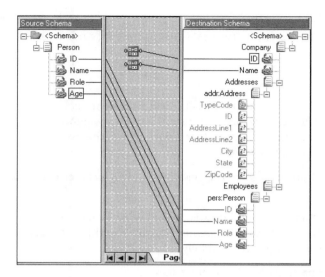

Figure 2-67. *A simple map*

Use the following steps to test a simple map:

1. In the Solution Explorer, right-click the map to test and select Properties. The Property Pages dialog box contains the properties listed in Table 2-3.

Table 2-3. *Map Properties*

Property	Description
Validate TestMap Input	Boolean value indicating whether the source document will be validated against the source schema.
Validate TestMap Output	Boolean value indicating whether the output document should be validated against the destination schema.
TestMap Input Instance	Path to the file that contains an instance of the source schema. Used when the TestMap Input property is not set to Generate Instance.
TestMap Input	Indicates the origin of the source document. If set to Generate Instance, BizTalk will generate an instance in memory that contains values for all attributes and elements in the source schema. If set to XML or Native, BizTalk will look for an instance of the document in the location specified in the TestMap Input Instance property. Native indicates a non-XML file, such as a flat file.
TestMap Output	Indicates the format of the output document. The document will be output to a file stored in a temporary directory on Windows and accessible through Visual Studio.

■**Note** All map files are stored in the following directory: `$\Documents and Settings\[current user]`
`\Local Settings\Temp\_MapData`.

---

2. If testing with the `TestMap Input` property set to `Generate Instance`, right-click the map and select Test Map. This will cause BizTalk to write to the Output window in Visual Studio and display any errors that may exist. If no errors exist in the map, a link to the test's output XML file will be made available.

3. If testing with the `TestMap Input` property set to `XML` or `Native`, and no instance currently exists, follow these steps:

   a. Right-click the source schema in the Solution Explorer and select Properties. Set the path to where an instance of the output document should be written to. Click OK when the properties have been set appropriately.

   b. Right-click the source schema and select Generate Instance.

   c. Open the document created in the previous step. BizTalk will give default values to all of the elements and attributes in the schema. Edit these with appropriate values for your testing needs. When generating instances from schemas, all `Any` elements and `Any` attributes will be created. These will fail validation when a map is tested. Either delete these from the generated instance or replace them with a value that would be expected.

   d. Right-click the map in the Solution Explorer and select Properties.

   e. Set the `TestMap Input Instance` property to the path of the instance created in step 3.c. Set the `Test Map Input` property to the appropriate type. Click OK.

   f. Right-click the map and select Test Map. This will produce an output document that can be validated for accuracy. Check the Output window in Visual Studio for details in case of failure.

Testing complex maps requires several more steps to create a valid input instance. The main difference in testing the two types of maps lies in how the input instances are generated.

When a map has multiple source schemas, they are wrapped in a hierarchy created by BizTalk. This hierarchy must be matched if using anything other than `Generate Instance` for the `TestMap Input`. In cases where nodes such as `Any` elements or `Any` attributes exist in the source documents, generated instances will fail during testing. It then becomes a requirement to create by hand an instance of the multipart input document.

Figure 2-68 shows a complex map with a `Company` schema being mapped from a combination of two source schemas, `Person` and `Address`, and hard-coded values in String Concatenate functoids.

There is never a time in which multiple native instances can be set as source, since the only place that a map with multiple source schemas can be created is in a Transform shape within an orchestration. Therefore, the following steps are specific to creating XML instances that match the multipart input instance needed, and can be taken to aid in producing a valid source instance.

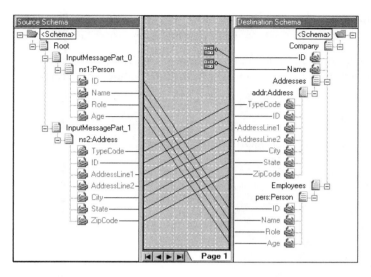

Figure 2-68. *A complex map*

1. To generate an instance of the source schema, create a temporary map that is the inverse
of what you are trying to produce. In the case of the example shown in Figure 2-68, the
map would consist of the Company schema being the single source schema, with the
Person and Address being the two destination schemas. The intention is to have BizTalk
generate an output message that closely resembles the needed input instance. When
namespaces are involved, this is all the more important, as prefixes will be added by
BizTalk when creating the multipart message. Figure 2-69 illustrates the inverse mapping.

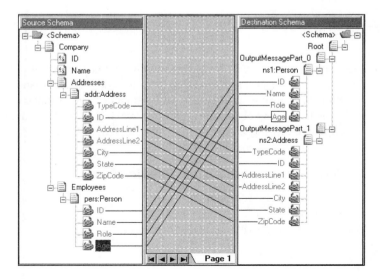

Figure 2-69. *Inverse complex map used to generate an input instance*

2. Once a temporary map has been created, right-click the map in the Solution Explorer and select Properties. Check that the `TestMap Input` property is set to `Generate Instance`.

3. Right-click the map in the Solution Explorer and select Test Map. This will produce an output document. The output of the map shown in Figure 2-69 is shown in Listing 2-43.

Listing 2-43. *Output of Map*

```
<ns0:Root xmlns:ns2="http://SampleSolution.Address"
xmlns:ns1="http://SampleSolution.Person"
xmlns:ns0="http://schemas.microsoft.com/
BizTalk/2003/aggschema">
 <OutputMessagePart_0>
  <ns1:Person>
   <ID>ID_0</ID>
   <Name>Name_0</Name>
   <Role>Role_0</Role>
   <Age>Age_0</Age>
  </ns1:Person>
 </OutputMessagePart_0>
 <OutputMessagePart_1>
  <ns2:Address TypeCode="TypeCode_0">
   <ID>ID_0</ID>
   <AddressLine1>AddressLine1_0</AddressLine1>
   <AddressLine2>AddressLine2_0</AddressLine2>
   <City>City_0</City>
   <State>State_0</State>
   <ZipCode>ZipCode_0</ZipCode>
  </ns2:Address>
 </OutputMessagePart_1>
</ns0:Root>
```

4. Copy the output document into a text editor and manually change the names of the `OutputMessage` nodes to `InputMessage` nodes so that the outcome is a valid instance of the input document for the true map. In this case, you want a document that can be used as the input for the map shown in Figure 2-68, as shown in Listing 2-44. The bold elements in the example are the only elements that need to be modified.

Listing 2-44. *Input Instance Produced by Modifying Output from Listing 2-43*

```
<ns0:Root xmlns:ns2="http://SampleSolution.Address"
xmlns:ns1="http://SampleSolution.Person"
xmlns:ns0="http://schemas.microsoft.com/BizTalk/2003/aggschema">
 <InputMessagePart_0>
  <ns1:Person>
   <ID>ID_0</ID>
   <Name>Name_0</Name>
```

```
     <Role>Role_0</Role>
     <Age>Age_0</Age>
    </ns1:Person>
  </InputMessagePart_0>
  <InputMessagePart_1>
   <ns2:Address TypeCode="TypeCode_0">
    <ID>ID_0</ID>
    <AddressLine1>AddressLine1_0</AddressLine1>
    <AddressLine2>AddressLine2_0</AddressLine2>
    <City>City_0</City>
    <State>State_0</State>
    <ZipCode>ZipCode_0</ZipCode>
   </ns2:Address>
  </InputMessagePart_1>
</ns0:Root>
```

5. Once the modifications have been made to the document, save it to a file. This document can now be used as a valid input instance for the valid map (you can delete the temporary map at this time). Right-click the valid map in the Solution Explorer and select Properties. Set the TestMap Input property to XML and the TestMap Input Instance to the file that you just created.

6. Right-click the map in the Solution Explorer and select Test Map. This will produce an output document that can be validated for accuracy. Check the Output window in Visual Studio for details in case of failure.

How It Works

The difficulty in testing maps lies in the creation of the source schema instances. There are a number of ways in which these instances can be created. The objective of this solution was to provide the steps necessary for creating documents that would allow for the testing of both simple maps and complex maps. Additionally, the steps necessary for producing the test output were described.

CHAPTER 3

■ ■ ■

Messaging

Messaging is the core functionality provided within BizTalk Server. On a very basic level, it is the "plumbing" that moves messages from one location to another. A number of different parts or objects make up this plumbing, taking actions at each step of a message's path through BizTalk Server. Generally speaking, messaging objects can be split into two categories: receive and send. Figure 3-1 outlines the stages a message goes through as it is processed.

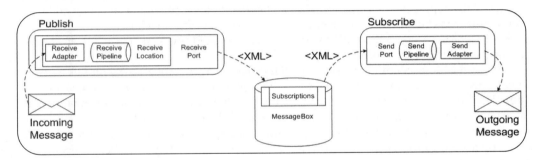

Figure 3-1. *BizTalk messaging architecture*

The receive objects are what enable the publishing side of BizTalk Server's publish/subscribe architecture. They publish messages into the MessageBox database, the central repository for all messages handled by BizTalk Server. The following objects are involved with receiving messages:

- *Receive location*: Handles the actual retrieval of messages from a specified location. The following are the main objects included within receive locations:

  - The *receive adapter* defines the location and method (file, MSMQ, SQL, and so on) to retrieve messages.

  - The *receive pipeline* allows decoding, decryption, disassembling, and validating messages against a schema. Receive pipelines also enable party resolution. A custom pipeline component can implement custom logic.

- *Receive port*: Groups one to many receive locations, and defines any transformation (or mapping) that occurs on messages being received by the receive port.

The send objects enable the subscribing side of BizTalk Server's publish/subscribe architecture. They subscribe to messages in the MessageBox database and deliver the messages onward to destination locations. The following objects are involved with sending messages:

- *Send port*: Handles the actual delivery of messages to a specified location. The following are the main objects included within send ports:

  - A *filter* defines the subscriptions for the send port. *Promoted properties* define these subscriptions, and determine which messages the send port will handle. (See Recipe 1-3 for details on promoted properties.)

  - A *map* defines any transformation occurring on messages sent through the send port. (See Chapter 2 for details on document mapping.)

  - The *send pipeline* allows assembling, validating against a schema, encoding, and encrypting messages. A customer pipeline component can also implement custom logic.

- *Send port group*: Groups one to many send ports and defines the filter(s) used to determine the messages handled by the send ports.

As the MessageBox database receives a message, BizTalk Server checks to see what active subscriptions (send port filters, for example) there are for that message and routes the message to each of the appropriate subscribers. This publish/subscribe architecture facilitates adding new consumers of information, making it easy to deliver messages to additional systems if needed. Once the MessageBox database receives a message, BizTalk can deliver it to any number of subscribing destination systems.

While the MessageBox database holds all messages that are processed by BizTalk Server, messaging objects (receive ports, receive locations, send ports, and send port groups) are stored in the Management database. In BizTalk Server 2006, messaging objects can be associated with an *application*, which is a logical grouping of all objects related to a specific application or solution (including messaging objects, orchestrations, schemas, and so on). The application concept facilitates the management of a wide variety of BizTalk objects that are essentially part of one unit of work (see Recipe 8-4 for details on BizTalk applications).

Messaging objects are created and managed through either the BizTalk Administration Console or the BizTalk Explorer view within Visual Studio. A number of other tools are also available for managing messaging objects. This chapter focuses on using the tools provided with BizTalk Server to "lay the pipes" for your integration solutions.

■**Note** Some messaging object configuration can be done only in the BizTalk Administration Console. For example, managing applications and configuring routing for failed messages can be done only in the Administration Console.

3-1. Configuring Receive Ports and Locations

Problem

You have messages from an external application or system that you want to receive into BizTalk Server.

Solution

In BizTalk, receive ports and receive locations are configured to receive data from other applications, systems, or processes. As an example, this solution describes the procedure for configuring a one-way receive port and a location to receive data from another application via a file input.

1. Open your source project.

2. Within the Solution Explorer, locate the BizTalk Explorer and navigate to the Receive Ports node.

3. Right-click and select Add Receive Port. The Create New Receive Port dialog box will appear.

4. Select One-Way as the port type. The One-Way Receive Port Properties dialog box will appear, as shown in Figure 3-2.

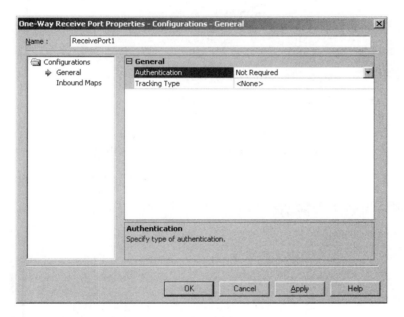

Figure 3-2. *One-Way Receive Port Properties dialog box*

5. In the Name text box, name the receive port (rprtSampleReceive in our example). Then click OK.

6. In BizTalk Explorer, right-click the Receive Locations node under the newly created receive port rprtSampleReceive. Select Add Receive Location. The Receive Location Properties dialog box will appear, as shown in Figure 3-3.

7. In the Name text box, enter a name for this location (rlocSampleReceive in this example).

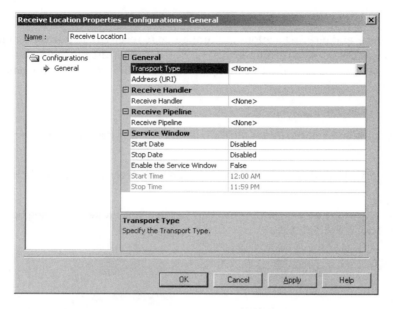

Figure 3-3. *Receive Location Properties dialog box*

8. Set the properties as follows (see Figure 3-4), and then click OK.

   • Transport Type: FILE

   • Address (URI): Click the ellipsis and navigate to or enter the path C:\data\in

   • Receive Pipeline: Microsoft.BizTalk.DefaultPipelines.XMLReceive pipeline

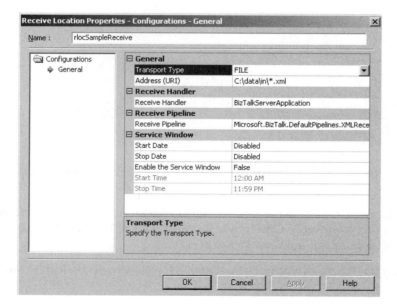

Figure 3-4. *Configured receive port item*

How It Works

Receive ports and receive locations are used in tandem to receive data into the BizTalk environment. This could be from an internal application or an external entity across the Internet, for instance. Receive locations are tied to a receive port; however, there can be many receive locations per port.

There are two types of receive ports:

- *Static one-way*: A port defined to receive data into BizTalk.

- *Request response port*: A port that is used to receive data, but then submit a response back to the sending entity. An example of this could be a web service or HTTP request (request/response-based transport).

Within the receive port configuration, an XML message can be transformed via inbound maps (see Recipe 3-3 for details on configuring port maps).

Associated with a receive port are one to many receive locations. Receive locations are the physical entry point into the BizTalk MessageBox. The following receive location options can be configured:

- *General*: Configure the transport type and location. The transport type includes all BizTalk out-of-the-box adapters (for example, FILE, MSMQ, SQL, HTTP, and so on). The location includes the physical location, input masking, authentication, and batching options based on the transport type.

- *Receive handler*: The physical BizTalk host the receive location is to run under.

- *Receive pipeline*: Receive pipelines are BizTalk components that support various types of message construction. In addition, pipelines can be extended via .NET code through the BizTalk interface iComponent. Common uses of pipelines are to enable message transformation for non-XML messages, such as a flat file format or a recordset from a database. In addition, receive pipelines can also be specified for well-formed XML messages.

- *Service window*: Service window properties enable constraints on when a receive location is active by date and time filters. This might be useful when dealing with cost-prohibitive communication entities or nondedicated transport.

3-2. Configuring Send Ports

Problem

You have a document that you would like to send to a downstream application, partner, or process.

Solution

You use a send port to send documents from the BizTalk Server platform to other applications, partners, or processes. Send ports are configured using the BizTalk Explorer or BizTalk Server 2006 Administration Console and can be used in a pure messaging scenario (no orchestration) or from an orchestration.

■Note You will see a slightly different set of properties to configure if you're creating the send port in the BizTalk Explorer versus the BizTalk 2006 Administration Console.

The steps for creating and configuring a send port are as follows:

1. From the BizTalk Explorer, right-click Send Ports and select Add Send Port. The Create New Send Port dialog box will appear.

2. Select the type of send port to be created, as shown in Figure 3-5, and then click OK. The choices are as follows:

   - Static One-Way Port: Static indicates that the properties are fixed and set at design time. One-way indicates that there will be no response back to BizTalk after the message is sent.

   - Static Solicit-Response Port: Static indicates that the properties are fixed and set at design time. Solicit-response indicates that there will be a response back to BizTalk after the message is sent.

   - Dynamic One-Way Port: Dynamic indicates that properties will be set at runtime to define the ultimate destination of the message. One-way indicates that there will be no response back to BizTalk after the message is sent.

   - Dynamic Solicit-Response Port: Dynamic indicates that properties will be set at runtime to define the ultimate destination of the message. Solicit-response indicates that there will be a response back to BizTalk after the message is sent.

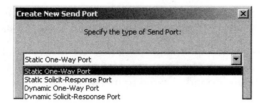

Figure 3-5. *Selecting a send port type*

3. The Send Port Properties dialog box will appear. Send port configurations are divided into three main categories: Transport, Send, and Filters & Maps properties, as shown in Figures 3-6, 3-7, 3-8, and 3-9. Set the properties as required (see the "How It Works" section). Then click OK to save the configurations and create the send port.

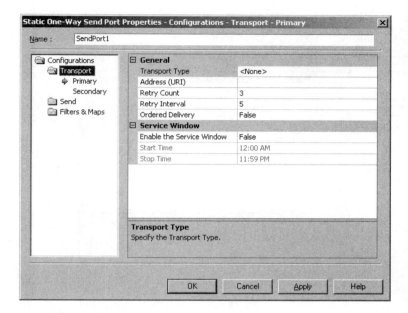

Figure 3-6. *Send port transport properties*

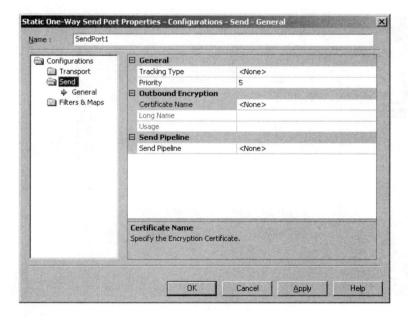

Figure 3-7. *Send port send properties*

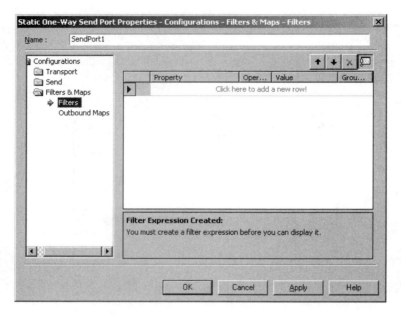

Figure 3-8. *Send port filters*

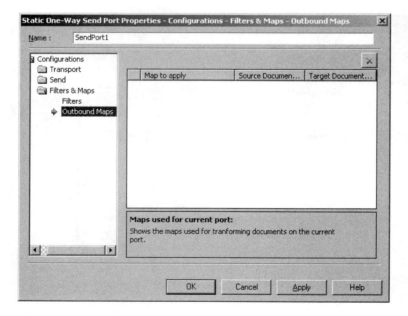

Figure 3-9. *Send port maps*

How It Works

Send ports are one of the fundamental BizTalk artifacts and are used to send any types of messages or data from the BizTalk platform to physical locations, systems, or processes. Determining the type of send port to create is important when constructing a solution. You may use send ports in pure messaging or orchestration-based solutions.

You can configure various properties for send ports. Transport properties are available only for static port types (one-way or solicit-response). Both a primary and a secondary transport can be defined. The secondary transport will take effect if an error is encountered sending to the primary transport and all retries as defined by the primary transport Retry Count setting were also attempted. Table 3-1 describes the Transport properties.

Table 3-1. *Send Port Transport Properties*

Property	Description
Transport Type	The type of adapter. If you chose a solicit-response port type, only those adapters that support solicit-response, such as HTTP and SOAP, will be available in the drop-down list.
Address (URI)	Click the ellipsis to launch a window for configuring the properties specific to the adapter chosen as the transport type. (See Chapter 6 for more information about adapter properties.)
Retry Count	Represents the number of times BizTalk Server will retry sending the message if there is a problem during transmission.
Retry Interval	Represents the number of minutes between retry intervals.
Ordered Delivery	When set to True, BizTalk will guarantee the ordered delivery of messages.
Enable the Service Window	When set to False, BizTalk will send messages at any time of day. When set to True, BizTalk will send messages only within the Start Time and Stop Time settings.
Start Time	Indicates when BizTalk will start sending messages if Enable the Service Window is set to True. Time is represented as *HH:MM* AM/PM.
Stop Time	Indicates when BizTalk will stop sending messages if Enable the Service Window is set to True. Time is represented as *HH:MM* AM/PM.

Send properties are the general properties that apply to all send ports. Table 3-2 describes the send properties.

Table 3-2. *Send Port Send Properties*

Property	Description
Tracking Type	Sets how messages will be tracked. To allow message tracking before sending a message, check the Before Send check box. To allow message tracking after sending a message, check the After Send check box. For solicit-response send ports, you can also check the Before Receive check box to allow message tracking before receiving a message or check the After Receive check box to allow message tracking after receiving a message.
Priority	Sets the delivery priority for the port, where 1 is the highest priority and 10 is the lowest priority. The default value is 5.

continued

Table 3-2. *Continued*

Property	Description
Certificate Name	A drop-down list of all certificates installed and available for use on the send port.
Long Name	The certificate's long name, which will fill in automatically if a certificate name is selected.
Usage	The certificate usage, which will fill in automatically if a certificate name is selected.
Send Pipeline	A drop-down list of the send pipelines available. You can select a pipeline for processing messages sent over this send port.
Receive Pipeline	A drop-down list of the receive pipelines available. For solicit-response send ports, you can select a pipeline for processing the responses received over this port.

Filters are used to create subscriptions when orchestrations are not part of the scenario. From the Filters dialog box, you can create one or more filter expressions, which are used to filter messages to the send port. There is a set of BizTalk properties for use in filtering, and promoted message properties can be used for filtering as well. If you bind a send port directly to an orchestration port, the filters do not apply. Maps are used to transform the document being sent. You may edit one or more maps to the collection, but there may only be one map with a given source schema. Only maps deployed in assemblies are available for selection.

Send ports have few requirements for basic operation. For example, you must specify the transport mechanism, the transport location (such as the HTTP URL), and the BizTalk pipeline that will process the message outbound from BizTalk.

3-3. Configuring Port Maps

Problem

Before receiving an XML message, you would like to transform a message into a predetermined XML format.

Solution

Within BizTalk, you can map source messages into a destination format. You can map with a receive port, an orchestration, or send port. Here, we will outline the steps for mapping to a receive port.

1. Open your source project.

2. Within the Solution Explorer, locate the BizTalk Explorer and navigate to the Receive Ports node.

3. Right-click and select Add Receive Port. The Create New Receive Port dialog box will appear.

4. Select One-Way Port. The One-Way Receive Port Properties dialog box will appear.

5. In the Name text box, enter a name for the receive port (rprtSampleMapReceive in this example).

6. Under Configurations in the left pane, click Inbound Maps. The center pane now has a drop-down list from which you can choose the maps you would like to apply to the receive port.

7. From the drop-down list under Map to Apply, select a map that is applicable for your receive port, as shown in Figure 3-10. The maps that are available for use are those that are deployed to the BizTalk Management database. Click OK after selecting a map.

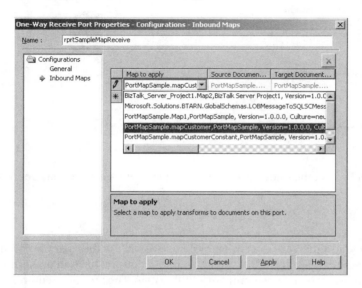

Figure 3-10. *Selecting a map for a port map*

How It Works

This recipe's solution described how to configure a receive port to perform inbound mapping transformation. Remember that when using a receive port, the inbound message must be in an XML format. If inbound mapping is configured, the message must also conform to the schema of that specified in the inbound format of the map in question. If the message does not match, the message will fail in the map, and the message interchange will be marked for exception processing.

Another key concept to keep in mind when configuring receive port maps is that more than one map can be specified on a receive port. Multiple XML schema can be accepted by the receive port; it is not tied to one specific schema. For example, if you have three purchase order document formats arriving from external entities, you could transform each format to a common (canonical) format via port maps on the receive port. This process is commonly referred to as *document normalization*. In this instance, you could have three maps to support each format and a single receive port to satisfy the solution. This scenario is demonstrated in Figure 3-11.

A key consideration when applying receive port maps is how you plan to handle exceptions, such as an XML message that does not conform to a map, invalid XML received, and data enrichment required during or before transformation. All of these exceptions could be handled within a port map or receive location, or with downstream BizTalk orchestration functionality.

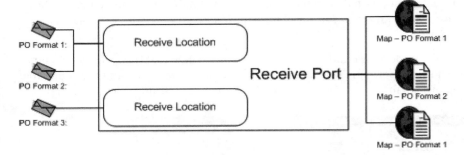

Figure 3-11. *Document normalization*

3-4. Using Send Port Groups

Problem

You want BizTalk Server to send the same message to multiple downstream systems for further processing.

Solution

To demonstrate how to send a message to multiple systems, we will use the example of sending data to an enterprise resource planning (ERP) system. Suppose that you have an orchestration that sends sales order information to your company's ERP system. The business requires sales order information to be available to other departments in your company that do not have access to the ERP system. The business would like to see the data available via the internal data warehouse. Additionally, the business requires minimal downtime for the existing deployed solution due to the need to process orders 24 hours a day, 7 days a week.

The solution is to create a send port to the data warehouse and create a send port group that will manage sending messages from the orchestration to the existing ERP send port as well as the new data warehouse send port. This recipe assumes that the orchestration already exists.

1. Create a new Static-One Way send port, to represent the communication port to the data warehouse, using the BizTalk Explorer. Choose the desired transport type desired. (See Recipe 3-2 for details on how to create a send port.)

2. To create the new send port group, in the BizTalk Explorer, right-click Send Port Groups and select Add Send Port Group.

3. In the Send Port Group Properties dialog box, add the two existing send ports, as shown in Figure 3-12.

4. Update the send port binding of the deployed orchestration (see Recipe 4-4 for details on binding orchestrations) and choose the send port group, as shown in Figure 3-13. Your completed orchestration binding will resemble Figure 3-14.

5. Verify the send port group and referenced send ports are enlisted and started before testing the updated orchestration binding.

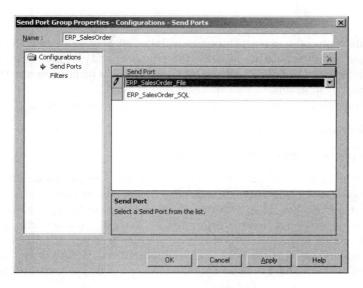

Figure 3-12. *Adding send ports to a send port group*

Figure 3-13. *Updating your orchestration binding*

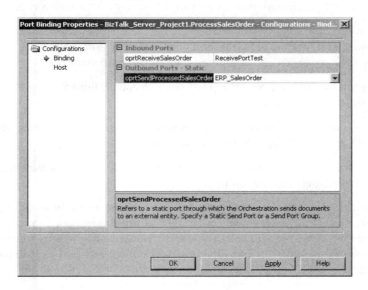

Figure 3-14. *Completed orchestration binding*

How It Works

Send port groups are collections of send ports through which BizTalk Server can publish the same message to multiple destinations using a single configuration. Send port groups are similar to send ports in their ability to be bound to orchestrations, as well as be implemented in pure messaging scenarios (via filter subscriptions).

Send ports that are included in a send port group process messages in two ways:

- As a participant in a send port group

- As a direct recipient of messages routed from BizTalk

Send port groups are incredibly useful in the situations where multiple parties are subscribing to the same message using different messaging protocols or different message formats. For example, one subscriber could receive an XML version of a message, and a separate subscriber could receive a flat file version of that same message, without extra coding or changes to the orchestration that produced the message. Another good use for a send port group is to keep backup files of the transactions sent from BizTalk to external subscribers. Without changing the existing orchestration and with little effort, you can implement a new send port and send port group that creates a backup of the existing message.

Send ports that are included in a send port group operate differently from send ports operating independently. Keep the following considerations in mind when using send port groups:

Filters: Filters on send port groups do not override filters on individual send ports. Filters used on both send ports and a send port group operate in a cumulative nature. If the same filter is used on a send port group as well as the individual send ports within the group, it's likely that duplicate messages will be sent. Special care must be given if filters are implemented on both send ports and send port groups.

One-way static ports: Send port groups can use only static one-way send ports. The strength of send port groups is the ability to send the same message to multiple subscribers. However, one limitation of send port groups is that they can include only static one-way send ports.

Operating states: The operating state between send ports and send port groups is independent. The states between send ports and send port groups are identical:

- *Bound*: The send port or send port group has been physically linked to an orchestration.

- *Enlisted*: The send port or send port group has been associated with the message to which it will be subscribing from the MessageBox.

- *Started*: The send port or send port group is ready to process messages matching the appropriate message subscription.

Enlisted ports: You must verify that both send ports and their parent send port groups have been enlisted and started before messages will be sent. Additionally, send ports must be enlisted or started before a send port group can be started. However, a send port group can be enlisted, regardless of the state of the individual send ports it references. The send port group must be stopped before all of the individual send ports can be unenlisted. See Recipe 7-4 for details on enlisting and starting send ports.

Table 3-3 shows how state affects the behavior of message processing.

Table 3-3. *Send Port and Send Port Group States*

Message Published	Send Port Group State	Send Port State	Description
Send port	Any state	Started	Message processed
Send port	Any state	Stopped	Message suspended
Send port group	Started	Started	Message processed
Send port group	Any state	Stopped	Message suspended
Send port group	Stopped	Any state	Message suspended

Send port groups are a powerful tool for allowing multiple subscribers to subscribe to the same message. Individual mappings for each subscriber can be maintained and implemented without affecting other subscribers. Additionally, send port groups allow the ability to resubmit suspended messages, if there is a communication problem, to a single system without having to resubmit to other systems in the send port group. (See Recipe 8-3 for details on resubmitting messages.)

3-5. Creating Validation Pipelines

Problem

You have an inbound or outbound document that requires validation beyond checking for well-formed XML.

Solution

You can use a send or receive pipeline to perform a strict validation of an instance of an XML document by providing validation against an XSD schema. BizTalk Server provides an XML Validator pipeline component for validating XML (schema) documents. If the inbound or outbound document is not XML, it must be converted to XML prior to validation. The following steps define how to create a receive pipeline that can be used to validate an XML document. The steps are similar to those for configuring a send pipeline.

1. Open the project that will contain the pipeline.

2. Right-click the project and select Add ➤ Add New Item.

3. In the Add New Item dialog box, select Receive Pipeline and provide a name. Then click Add.

4. Drag the XML Validator component from the BizTalk Pipeline Components section of the Toolbox to the Drop Here location under the Validate label, as shown in Figure 3-15.

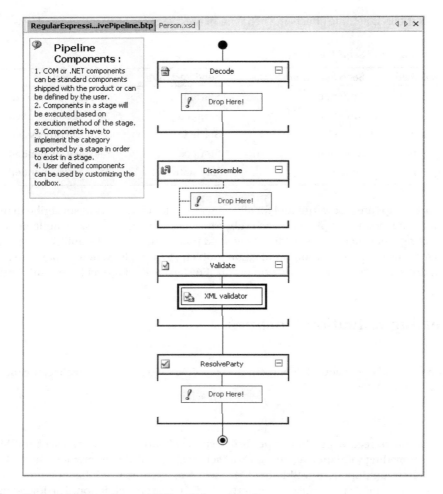

Figure 3-15. *Creating an XML validator pipeline*

5. Select the ellipsis next to the Document Schemas property for the XML Validator component (in the Properties window) to launch the Schema Collection Property Editor
   dialog box, as shown in Figure 3-16.

6. Use the Schema Collection Property Editor to add schemas to the collection, and then
   click OK.

7. Build and deploy the project.

Now that you have created the validation pipeline, when configuring the Receive
Pipeline property of a receive location (see Recipe 3-1), select the pipeline from the list of
available receive pipelines.

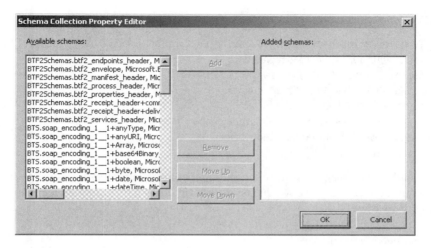

Figure 3-16. *Schema Collection Property Editor dialog box*

How It Works

Strict validation of an XML document is achieved with the use of a validation pipeline. The XMLReceive receive pipeline and XMLTransmit send pipeline that come with BizTalk Server will validate only that an XML document is well formed. It will not perform strict validation of the document, including data types and restriction values (length, enumerations, patterns, and so on).

You use the XML Validator pipeline component to validate the instance document. This component may be placed in any pipeline stage, except the Disassemble or Assemble stages. If you do not add a schema using the Schema Collection Property Editor dialog box for the component, the component will attempt to locate an appropriate schema to validate against based on the namespace and root node of the document. If no schema is found to validate against, or the document fails validation, an error will occur, and the instance will be terminated.

3-6. Creating Encryption Pipelines

Problem

You need to guarantee that only the intended recipient of a message can understand it by encrypting the message. The recipient needs to verify the message sender by checking a digital signature included with the message.

Solution

You can implement an encryption mechanism for outgoing messages, as well as a decryption mechanism for the inbound messages. As an example, suppose that you need BizTalk to send this message shown in Listing 3-1 across the Internet to move the requested amount of money between the specified accounts. This message contains sensitive information, including bank account numbers and a Social Security number.

Listing 3-1. *Sensitive Information*

```
<ns0:MoneyTransfer xmlns:ns0="http://Creating_EncryptionPipelines.Confidential">
    <TransferAmount>108.37</TransferAmount>
    <TransferInitDate>2005-09-30</TransferInitDate>
    <FromAccount>0987-654-321</FromAccount>
    <ToAccount>1234-567-890</ToAccount>
    <RequestedBySSN>123-45-6789</RequestedBySSN>
    <RequestedByName>StacyR</RequestedByName>
</ns0:MoneyTransfer>
```

BizTalk sends the message with the encryption pipeline constructed in this recipe. The message becomes encrypted, as shown in Listing 3-2. No one but the intended recipient can understand the message.

Listing 3-2. *Encrypted Message*

```
Content-ID: {51572541-E6CE-4DD6-913C-B7C7558D2269}
Content-Description: body
Bcc:
MIME-Version: 1.0
Content-type: application/x-pkcs7-mime; smime-type=enveloped-data; name="smime.p7m"
Content-Transfer-Encoding: base64
```

MIAGCSqGSIb3DQEHA6CAMIACAQAxgbwwgbkCAQAwIjAUMRIwEAYDVQQDEwlkZXZvbmx5Y2ECCmEI
BAMAAAAAAIwDQYJKoZIhvcNAQEBBQAEgYAH+kU66z4r4lZYzq1eOKNfoYt1HVMBaYL61W5wrTPt
...
qQ+ubHBbgHMXyJl/SPylOtSN9XeQGZgBGKb2j+MeBONEjHlRE22aDnazailnmgu2x588820wnQAA
AAAAAAAAAA=

The message recipient decrypts the message with the decryption pipeline constructed in this recipe, obtaining the same message as before encryption (Listing 3-1).

The following sections show how to enable message encryption and decryption.

Send an Encrypted Message

To implement an encryption mechanism for outgoing message, follow these steps on the BizTalk Server responsible for encrypting the message and sending it:

1. Obtain the public key certificate from the party that will securely receive the message, and install it in the Local Computer\Other People\Certificates folder, as shown in Figure 3-17.

■**Note** BizTalk provides native support for MIME encryption decryption using X.509 version 3 certificates. Microsoft Certificate Services can generate the certificates used by BizTalk.

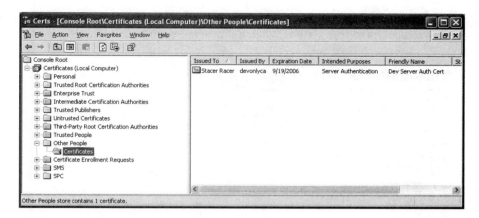

Figure 3-17. *Installing the public key of the receiver*

2. Create an empty BizTalk solution and add a new send pipeline to the solution (right-click the project, select Add New Item, and select Send Pipeline from the Add New Item dialog box).

3. Drag the MIME/SMIME Encoder component from the BizTalk Pipeline Components section of the Toolbox to the Encode stage of the send pipeline, as shown in Figure 3-18.

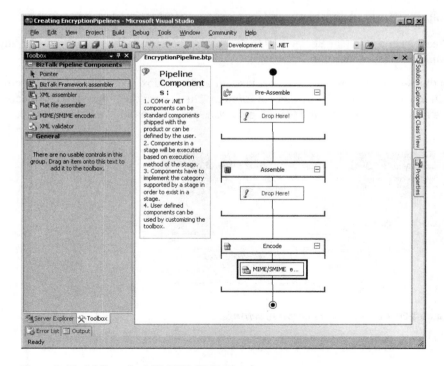

Figure 3-18. *Adding the MIME/SMIME encoder*

4. Right-click the encoder in the pipeline and select Properties. Change the value of the
Enable encryption property to True, as shown in Figure 3-19.

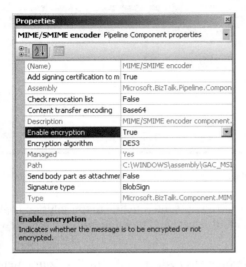

Figure 3-19. *Enabling pipeline encryption*

5. Build and deploy the BizTalk project containing the send pipeline.

6. Create a send port (see Recipe 3-2) to deliver the message to the recipient, using any
transport adapter desired.

7. In the Send section of the Send Port Properties dialog box, select the send pipeline
with the MIME/SMIME encoder component. Then select the public-key certificate of
the message receiver for the Certificate Name property, as shown in Figure 3-20.

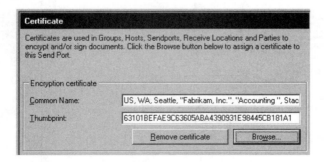

Figure 3-20. *Configuring encryption settings*

Receive an Encrypted Message

To configure a decryption mechanism for an incoming message, follow these steps on the BizTalk Server responsible for decrypting the message upon receipt:

1. Obtain a certificate from a Certification Authority (CA) containing a private key.

2. Log in to the BizTalk Server with the BizTalk service account credentials. Open the certificate file containing the private key, and install it into the `Current User\ Personal\Certificates` folder of the BizTalk service account. When properly configured, the certificate should appear as shown in Figure 3-21.

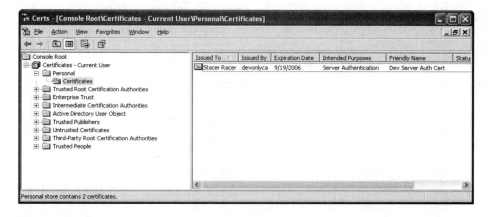

Figure 3-21. *Private key certificate in the personal store*

3. Create an empty BizTalk solution and add a new receive pipeline to the solution (right-click the project, select Add New Item, and select Receive Pipeline from the Add New Item dialog box).

4. Drag the MIME/SMIME Decoder component from the BizTalk Pipeline Components section of the Toolbox to the Decode stage of the receive pipeline, as shown in Figure 3-22.

5. Build and deploy the BizTalk project containing the receive pipeline.

6. Create a receive port and a receive location to accept the encrypted message from the sender, using any desired transport adapter (see Recipe 3-2).

7. In the Receive Location Properties dialog box, specify the receive pipeline with the MIME/SMIME decoder, as shown in Figure 3-23.

8. Open the BizTalk Administration Console by selecting Start ➤ All Programs ➤ BizTalk Server 2006 ➤ BizTalk Server Administration.

9. Right-click the BizTalk host that will receive the encrypted message and select Properties.

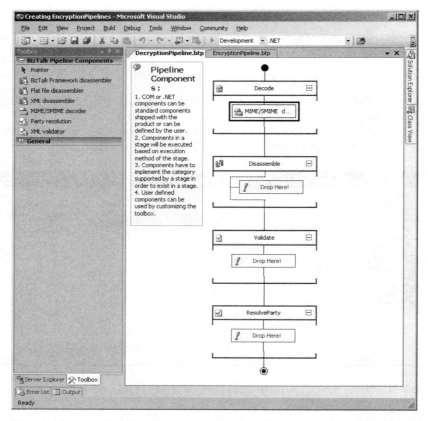

Figure 3-22. *Adding the MIME/SMIME decoder*

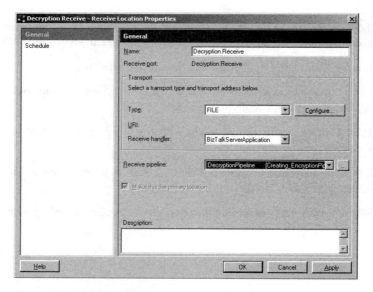

Figure 3-23. *Configuring the decryption pipeline*

10. Specify the decryption certificate BizTalk will use to receive messages. Secure messages by pasting the thumbprint of the certificate containing the private key into the Thumbprint field in the Certificates section of the Host Properties dialog box, as shown in Figure 3-24.

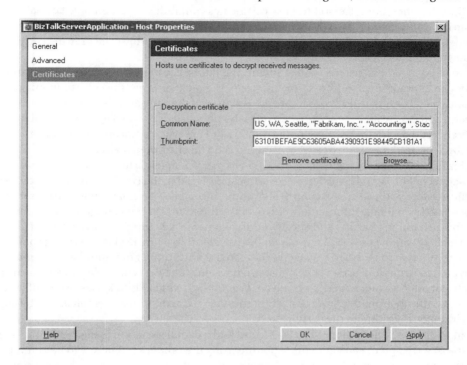

Figure 3-24. *Specifying the decryption certificate*

How It Works

Organizations often deal with confidential information that only the message sender and recipient should understand. For example, financial information may contain sensitive information such as Social Security or bank account numbers. Medical information may contain private information protected by law. Use the encryption capabilities of BizTalk to protect the confidentiality of sensitive information, while still allowing two parties to share it easily.

BizTalk can transmit encrypted information across a network securely. This is particularly important when transmitting messages over a public network, such as the Internet. If the two parties must keep the message confidential, then encryption can ensure only the intended recipient can understand it.

One option for ensuring the confidentiality of messages is to use a secure transport like HTTPS. Securing the message transport can be effective, but the transport generally secures only communication directly between two machines on a network. When a message has several network hops before it arrives at the final destination, each hop must be secured individually, providing multiple chances for a configuration error to expose the sensitive information. For example, HTTPS may securely transmit a message to a trading partner, but then be transmitted without encryption over an insecure transport within the trading partner's internal network. To ensure a higher level of confidentiality, you should encrypt the contents of the message, rather than depend on the communication protocol. Message content encryption provides confidentiality over any transport, including transports or BizTalk adapters that cannot support encryption, such as the FTP and SMTP adapters.

BizTalk's encryption capabilities use certificates containing cryptographic key pairs of a public key and a private key. The owner of a certificate can share the public key freely with anyone who wants to send the owner confidential information. However, only the certificate's owner should know its private key.

To encrypt a message, the sender obtains the public key of the message recipient and applies an encryption algorithm to the message. The recipient uses the corresponding private key and the same algorithm to decrypt and understand the message. Certificate owners must fiercely protect private keys because anyone who possesses a private key can decrypt messages encrypted with the corresponding public key. However, certificate owners must distribute public keys to anyone who wishes to send an encrypted message.

BizTalk can securely transmit information to many recipients, using a different certificate for each recipient. BizTalk will detect all certificates placed in the Local Computer\Other People certificate store of the local machine. For example, if you have several trading partners that you must securely exchange information with over the Internet, you can configure a different send port for each trading partner and specify a different public key certificate in each send port.

The decryption certificate must be in the private store of the BizTalk service account receiving encrypted messages. While BizTalk can use any number of public keys to send encrypted information, each BizTalk host can have only one decryption certificate. Each certificate contains a unique identifier called a *thumbprint*, which BizTalk uses to identify the correct certificate from this store to decrypt messages. The thumbprint is calculated by applying a hashing algorithm to the certificate.

In addition to encryption, BizTalk can also add a digital signature to encrypted messages. The message recipient can verify the signature using the sender's public key to be guaranteed that the message originated with the original sender and was not modified while in transit. To enable message signing, set the Signature type property of the MIME/SMIME encoder component, as shown in Figure 3-25.

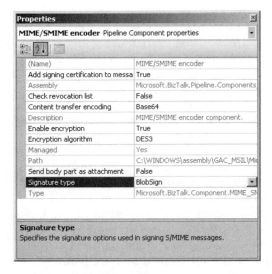

Figure 3-25. *Enabling message signing*

While each BizTalk host can have a unique decryption certificate, an entire BizTalk group can have only one signing certificate. Specify the signing certificate by entering the thumbprint of the certificate in the Group Properties dialog box for the BizTalk group, as shown in Figure 3-26.

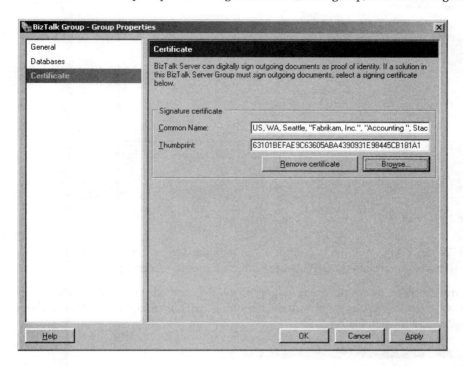

Figure 3-26. *Specifying the signing certificate*

3-7. Creating Flat File Send and Receive Pipelines

Problem

You are integrating two systems that can communicate only via flat file messages, and must provide the mechanisms for receiving and sending the messages within BizTalk Server.

Solution

Create a flat file receive and send pipeline, as follows (these steps assume that a flat file schema has already been created; see Recipe 1-10):

1. Open the project that contains the flat file schema.

2. Right-click the project and select Add ➤ New Item.

3. In the Add New Item dialog box, select Pipeline Files from the BizTalk Project Items category, and then choose Receive Pipeline from the list of templates. Give a descriptive name to your new pipeline, as shown in Figure 3-27, and then click Add.

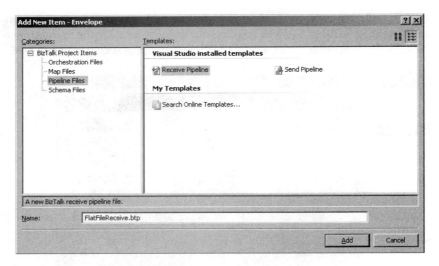

Figure 3-27. *Adding a new receive pipeline to a project*

4. From the Pipeline Components section of the Toolbox, drag and drop a Flat File Disassembler component into the Disassemble stage of the receive pipeline.

5. With the Flat File Disassembler component highlighted, set the `Document schema` property in the Properties window to the appropriate flat file schema (`FlatFile` in the example), as shown in Figure 3-28.

Figure 3-28. *Configuring a receive pipeline for a flat file schema*

■**Note** Setting the Document schema property is required when using the Flat File Disassembler component. All other properties are optional.

6. Save the receive pipeline.

7. Right-click the project and select Add ➤ Add New Item.

8. In the Add New Item dialog box, select Pipeline Files from the BizTalk Project Items category, and then choose Send Pipeline from the list of templates. Give a descriptive name to your new pipeline, as shown in Figure 3-29, and then click Add.

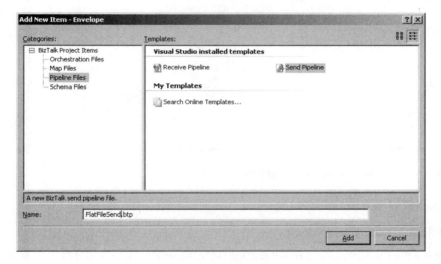

Figure 3-29. *Adding a new send pipeline to a project*

9. From the Pipeline Components section of the Toolbox, drag and drop a Flat File Assembler component into the Assemble stage of the send pipeline.

10. With the Flat File Assembler component highlighted, set the Document schema property in the Properties window to the appropriate flat file schema (FlatFile, in this example), as shown in Figure 3-30.

■**Note** If the Document schema property is not specified, runtime schema discovery will be attempted. During schema discovery, BizTalk Server attempts to determine the correct flat file schema to assemble the message with, based on the namespace and root node of the message.

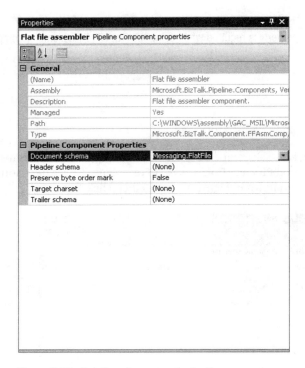

Figure 3-30. *Configuring a send pipeline*

11. Save the send pipeline.

12. Build and deploy the solution.

Once the flat file schema and pipelines (FlatFile, FlatFileReceive, and FlatFileSend in this example) have been deployed, BizTalk Server can use them in message processing.

How It Works

Many systems in use today were designed and engineered prior to the advent of XML. In order to communicate with these systems, it is often necessary to use flat file formats such as positional, delimited, or a combination of the two. In our example, a simple positional flat file message is parsed into XML as BizTalk Server receives the document. BizTalk Server then assembles the XML back into its correct flat file format when sending the message to the appropriate subscribers.

More specifically, the custom receive pipeline created in the example (FlatFileReceive) is used in a receive location that retrieves inbound flat file messages. This receive pipeline disassembles the flat file message into an XML document by leveraging the out-of-the-box Flat File Disassembler pipeline component. By setting the Document schema property on the Flat File Disassembler component, BizTalk Server is instructed to apply the correct schema to inbound documents, thereby producing the appropriate XML representation of the original flat file.

The following flat file represents one possible instance of the inbound flat file document (braces have been added to the beginning and end of the flat file for clarity):

```
[Cust12345Johnathan O'Brien    ]
```

When passed through the `FlatFileReceive` pipeline created in the solution (which can be implemented via a receive location), BizTalk Server disassembles the flat file into the following XML message, based on the details defined within the `FlatFile.xsd` schema:

```
<Customer xmlns="http://Messaging.FlatFile">
  <RecordType xmlns="">Cust</RecordType>
  <ID xmlns="">12345</ID>
  <FirstName xmlns="">Johnathan</FirstName>
  <LastName xmlns="">O'Brien</LastName>
</Customer>
```

The `FlatFile.xsd` schema defines the following positional data elements:

- `RecordType`: position 0–3

- `ID`: position 4–9

- `FirstName`: position 10–19

- `LastName`: position 20–29

Since the `FlatFileSend` pipeline (which can be implemented via a send port) is configured to assemble instances of the `FlatFile.xsd` message type back into flat file format, the following flat file document would be output (again, braces have been added to the beginning and end of the flat file for clarity):

```
[Cust12345Johnathan O'Brien    ]
```

As well as the required `Document schema` property, you can configure other optional properties for the Flat File Disassembler component, as shown in Table 3-4.

Table 3-4. *Flat File Disassembler Optional Properties*

Property	Description
Header schema	Defines the schema to apply to any header included in the flat file message.
Preserve header	Specifies if the flat file header should be stored in the message context (properties). The message context contains metadata about the message and is attached to the message throughout its lifetime in BizTalk Server.
Recoverable interchange processing	Specifies if the flat file disassembler should attempt to recover from errors occurring during message processing.
Trailer schema	Defines the schema to apply to any trailer included in the flat file message.
Validate Document Structure	Specifies if the configured schemas (document, header, and trailer schemas) should be used to validate their respective message parts (document, header, and trailer, respectively).

The custom send pipeline created is then used in a send port to deliver flat file messages to subscribers. This send pipeline assembles the XML messages back into flat file format by using the Flat File Assembler pipeline component provided with BizTalk Server. By setting the Document schema property on the Flat File Assembler component, BizTalk Server is instructed to apply the correct schema to outbound documents, thereby producing the appropriate flat file representations of the original XML document.

Along with the required Document schema property, you can set the optional properties listed in Table 3-5 for the Flat File Assembler component.

Table 3-5. *Flat File Assembler Optional Properties*

Property	Description
Header schema	Defines the schema to apply to the header portion of the flat file message. If a header schema is defined on an instance message via the XMLNORM. HeaderSpecName context property, it will override this property setting.
Preserve byte order mark	Specifies if a byte order mark (BOM) should be added to messages passing through the pipeline.
Target charset	Specifies the target character set, which is used as the outbound message is encoded.
Trailer schema	Defines the schema to apply to the trailer portion of the flat file message.

You can configure encoding of outbound messages in a number of different locations, and you should understand the logic BizTalk Server uses to determine which to use if there are discrepancies. Table 3-6 lists the methods that can be used to specify message encoding, ordered to reflect their precedence. If none of the methods listed in Table 3-6 is used to configure message encoding, UTF-8 is used.

Table 3-6. *Methods for Encoding Outbound Messages*

Method	Description
Message- XMLNORM.TargetCharset	This message context property takes precedence over all other encoding configurations, and will be used if its value is set.
Component- Target Charset	This Flat File Assembler pipeline component property will be used if its value is set, and none of the higher precedence (XMLNORM.TargetCharset) values are set.
Schema- CodePage	This schema property will be used if its value is set, and none of the higher precedence values (Target Charset or XMLNORM.TargetCharset) are set.
Message- XMLNORM.SourceCharset	This message context property will be used if its value is set, and none of the higher precedence values (CodePage, Target Charset, or XMLNORM.TargetCharset) are set.

You can also configure flat files through their message headers. In addition to configuring the header schema via the Flat File Disassembler or Flat File Assembler pipeline components, you can use the XMLNORM.HeaderSpecName message context property.

One common challenge encountered when receiving flat file messages from source systems is determining which schema to apply to different messages. This is particularly important when multiple message types (for example, customer and order message types) are received from the same location. Since flat file messages are not inherently self-describing, as XML messages are, it can be difficult to determine which flat file message schema to apply to the inbound messages.

In these scenarios, you can use a solution similar to the Schema Resolver Component SDK example that comes with BizTalk Server. This example shows how to implement a custom Flat File Disassembler pipeline component to dynamically associate message types to inbound instances based on an identifier contained in each instance message.

Finally, to assist in testing the assembling and disassembling of flat file messages, the `FFAsm.exe` and `FFDasm.exe` tools are provided with BizTalk Server. These tools allow you to run the flat file assembler and disassembler directly against instance messages. These tools can be particularly useful and time-saving when working with large or complex flat file schemas.

3-8. Creating Custom Pipeline Components

Problem

You need to create a context property to assist in the routing of the inbound message.

Solution

The BizTalk custom pipeline component promotes a context property of an inbound message. The component does not alter the content of the original message, but rather creates a property and promotes the property to the message context.

As an example of implementing a custom pipeline, we will use the code shown in Listing 3-3, which is a complete C# class library that will compile into a complete custom pipeline assembly.

Listing 3-3. *Sample Pipeline Assembly Class Library*

```
//----------------------------------------------------------------------
// File: SamplePromotionPipelineComponent.cs
//
// Summary: A sample of how to write a pipeline component that
//          creates a context property.
//----------------------------------------------------------------------

using System;
using System.IO;
using System.Collections;
using System.ComponentModel;
using System.Resources;
using System.Reflection;
// BizTalk classes
using Microsoft.BizTalk.Message.Interop;
using Microsoft.BizTalk.Component.Interop;

namespace SampleCustomPipelineComponent
{
    /// <summary>
    /// BizTalk Server custom pipeline component that creates
    /// a custom context property for the inbound message.
```

```
/// </summary>
///
// Attribute declarations to identify this class is a pipeline component
// and that the assembly can be used in any pipeline stage
[ComponentCategory(CategoryTypes.CATID_PipelineComponent)]
[ComponentCategory(CategoryTypes.CATID_Any)]
[System.Runtime.InteropServices.Guid("63ed4b26-63cd-4d29-9661-f584c94cf858")]
public class SampleCustomPipelineComponent :
    Microsoft.BizTalk.Component.Interop.IBaseComponent
    , Microsoft.BizTalk.Component.Interop.IComponent
    , Microsoft.BizTalk.Component.Interop.IComponentUI
    , Microsoft.BizTalk.Component.Interop.IPersistPropertyBag
{
    //Key for storage on property bag:
    private string m_propbagkey_customproprop
            = "SAMPLECUSTOMPROPROP";
    private string m_propbagkey_custompropropnamespace
            = "SAMPLECUSTOMPROPROPNAMESPACE";

    //Var to store design time value
    private string m_propname = "";
    private string m_propnamespace = "";

    static ResourceManager resManager = new ResourceManager("SampleCustom
PipelineComponent.SampleCustomPipelineComponent", Assembly.GetExecutingAssembly());

    public SampleCustomPipelineComponent()
    {
        // Default constructor logic
    }

    #region Public Properties
    // Display the following public properties for design time
    public string CustomContextPropertyName
    {
        get {    return m_propname;}
        set {    m_propname = value;}
    }

    // Display the following public properties for design time
    public string CustomContextPropertyNamespace
    {
        get {    return m_propnamespace;}
        set {    m_propnamespace = value;}
    }
    #endregion
```

```csharp
#region IBaseComponent members defines Description, Name, and Version
public string Description
{
    get
    {
        return "Sample Custom Pipeline Component";
    }
}

public string Name
{
    get
    {
        return "Sample Custom Pipeline Component";
    }
}

public string Version
{
    get
    {
        return "1.0";
    }
}
#endregion

#region IComponent members contains the main implementation
public IBaseMessage Execute(IPipelineContext pContext
                        , IBaseMessage pInMsg)
{
    // Create custom context property on message
    pInMsg.Context.Promote(m_propname, m_propnamespace, string.Empty);
    return pInMsg;
}
#endregion

#region IComponentUI members contains design time information
// Include a validate method used by BizTalk
public IEnumerator Validate(object obj)
{
    IEnumerator enumerator = null;
    // Return a null
        return enumerator;
}
// We do not have an icon for this custom component
[Browsable(false)]
public System.IntPtr Icon
```

```csharp
{
    get
    {
        // No icon associated with this pipeline component
        return  IntPtr.Zero;
    }
}
#endregion

#region IPersistPropertyBag members contains placeholders
public void GetClassID(out Guid classid)
{
    // Return class ID of this component for usage from unmanaged code.
    classid = new System.Guid("63ed4b26-63cd-4d29-9661-f584c94cf858");
}

public void InitNew()
{
    // Initialization not implemented
}

public void Load(IPropertyBag propertyBag, Int32 errorlog)
{
    // Load configuration property for component.
    string val = (string)ReadPropertyBag(propertyBag,
            m_propbagkey_customproprop);

    if (val != null)
        m_propname = val;

    val = (string)ReadPropertyBag(propertyBag,
            m_propbagkey_custompropropnamespace);
    if (val != null)
        m_propnamespace = val;
}

public void Save(IPropertyBag propertyBag
        , Boolean clearDirty, Boolean saveAllProperties)
{
    // Saves the current component configuration into the property bag.
    object val = (object)m_propname;
    WritePropertyBag(propertyBag,
        m_propbagkey_customproprop, val);

    val = (object)m_propnamespace;
    WritePropertyBag(propertyBag,
        m_propbagkey_custompropropnamespace, val);
}
```

```
        private static object ReadPropertyBag(IPropertyBag propertyBag
                , string propertyName)
        {
            // Reads property value from property bag.
            object val = null;
            try
            {
                propertyBag.Read(propertyName, out val, 0);
            }
            catch(ArgumentException)
            {
                return val;
            }
            catch(Exception ex)
            {
                throw new ApplicationException(ex.Message);
            }
            return val;
        }

        private static void WritePropertyBag(IPropertyBag propertyBag
                , string propertyName, object val)
        {
            // Writes property values into a property bag.
            try
            {
                propertyBag.Write(propertyName, ref val);
            }
            catch(Exception ex)
            {
                throw new ApplicationException(ex.Message);
            }
        }
        #endregion
    }
}
```

Use the following steps to create, install, and implement a custom pipeline component.

1. Create a new Class Library .NET project. Custom pipeline components can be coded in any .NET language. This example is implemented in C#.

2. Add a reference to the `Microsoft.BizTalk.Pipeline.dll` assembly located in the `%\Program Files\Microsoft BizTalk Server 2006` directory.

3. Develop the custom component code, which should match that shown in Listing 3-3.

4. Build the component and place a copy of the assembly in the pipeline components folder located where BizTalk is installed (for example, `C:\Program Files\Microsoft BizTalk Server 2006\Pipeline Components`).

5. To add the pipeline component to the Visual Studio Toolbox, select Tools ➤ Choose Toolbox Items. In the dialog box, select the BizTalk Pipeline Components tab, and then select the pipeline assembly created in step 4. The component should appear in your Toolbox, as shown in Figure 3-31.

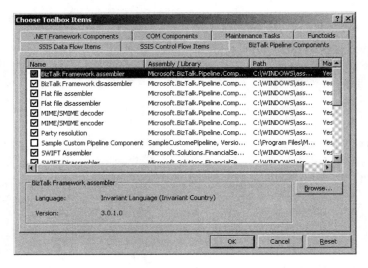

Figure 3-31. *Adding a custom pipeline component to the Toolbox*

■**Note** Loading the Choose Toolbox Items dialog box may take some time.

---

6. To add and configure the custom component as a receive pipeline, create a new BizTalk solution with the following items:

- Schema containing the message to be received (see Recipe 1-1).

- A property schema containing the context property implemented in the solution (see Recipe 1-4). For this example, create a property schema that contains a string element named Routing.

- A receive pipeline that implements the custom pipeline component (see Recipe 3-1).

How It Works

BizTalk includes out-of-the-box functionality for processing messages within receive and send pipelines. However, situations may arise where custom processing of messages is required. For example, you may need custom message validation, processing of flat files, or formatting of messages to HTML that BizTalk does not natively support. Custom pipeline components offer incredible flexibility for preprocessing or postprocessing messages via send and receive pipelines. Additionally, custom pipeline components can coexist with native BizTalk pipeline components in the same pipeline.

In BizTalk solutions where message content or context determines routing, you may need to route messages based on the lack of existence of a property. BizTalk does not have the ability to route on the lack of property existence. However, you can use a custom pipeline component to create a property that is always part of a message. Rather than check for the existence of the property, you can check whether the property contains an empty string value. The solution that accompanies this recipe creates a custom pipeline component that creates a context property for every message that is processed by the component.

Creating custom pipeline components may seem like an extensive task due to the code required for hosting the component in a BizTalk pipeline, as well as setting the design-time properties. In actuality, there is a single method that contains the processing logic, and the remainder of the code supports the component design-time properties.

Your first task in creating a custom pipeline component is to create a project reference to the Microsoft.BizTalk.Pipeline.dll file contained in the main BizTalk installation folder. After you have added the appropriate project reference, you must consider the implementation of the custom pipeline component. There are three logical areas to a custom pipeline component to consider:

- Attributes and class declaration

- Design-time properties

- Implementation of the four pipeline interfaces: IBaseComponent, IComponentUI, IPersistPropertyBag, and IComponent

The following sections describe each of these areas in more detail.

Attributes and Class Declaration

Consider how you plan on using the custom component, such as in a send or receive pipeline. Additionally, consider the pipeline stage in which you plan on implementing the custom component. The attributes and class declaration indicate to Visual Studio that the assembly is a custom pipeline component. If you do not properly identify that you are creating a BizTalk custom pipeline component, you will not be able to add the component to the Visual Studio Toolbox or be able to add the component to a pipeline stage. Here is the header section from the sample code in Listing 3-3:

```
[ComponentCategory(CategoryTypes.CATID_PipelineComponent)]
    [ComponentCategory(CategoryTypes.CATID_Any)]
    [System.Runtime.InteropServices.Guid("63ed4b26-63cd-4d29-9661-f584c94cf858")]
    public class SampleCustomPipelineComponent :
        Microsoft.BizTalk.Component.Interop.IBaseComponent
        , Microsoft.BizTalk.Component.Interop.IComponent
        , Microsoft.BizTalk.Component.Interop.IComponentUI
        , Microsoft.BizTalk.Component.Interop.IPersistPropertyBag
```

The sample custom component is identified, via the ComponentCategory attributes, as a pipeline component for use in any pipeline stage. Additionally, the class declaration specifies that four interfaces (IBaseComponent, IComponent, IComponentUI, and IPersistPropertyBag) will be implemented within the class. The GUID is required for use in COM interop with unmanaged code.

Design-Time Properties

Custom component design-time properties are exposed via public declarations and appropriate get/set methods. The following is the section of Listing 3-3 that demonstrates how two design-time properties are exposed.

```
#region Public Properties
        // Display the following public properties for design time
        public string CustomContextPropertyName
        {
            get {    return m_propname;}
            set {    m_propname = value;}
        }

        // Display the following public properties for design time
        public string CustomContextPropertyNamespace
        {
            get {    return m_propnamespace;}
            set {    m_propnamespace = value;}
        }
#endregion
```

Implementation of the Four Pipeline Interfaces

The final logical area required in the creation of a custom pipeline component is the implementation of four interfaces, as summarized in Table 3-7. The four interfaces provide the design-time and runtime implementations for the custom component and serve as a guide. Not all of the interfaces must contain code, and the IComponent interface contains the function that performs the message processing.

■**Note** If the custom component is to reside in either the Assemble or Disassemble pipeline stages, then the component must also implement the appropriate assemble/disassemble interface.

Table 3-7. *Interface Implementation*

Interface	Description	Implementation Notes
IBaseComponent	Properties related to the basic information about the custom component.	Contains three properties that enable the engine to retrieve the component name, version, and description.
IComponentUI	Defines the properties for displaying the custom component in the design-time user interface as well as the validation rules for design-time properties.	Contains two methods: one that allows the validation of the component's configuration and another that provides a pointer reference to the icon that will be displayed in the development tool set for the custom component. If null is set for the pointer, then the default icon will be used.

Interface	Description	Implementation Notes
IPersistPropertyBag	Custom pipeline properties that are displayed at runtime when using the custom assembly in a pipeline.	Enables a component to store and receive its configuration information.
IComponent	Defines the method used by all pipeline components. Assembler/ disassembler custom components implement their own interface.	Contains the main function that performs the heavy lifting and processing of the inbound/outbound message. This method takes as parameters the pipeline context and incoming message.

IBaseComponent

IBaseComponent contains three read-only properties that return the description, version, and name of the component to the design-time environment and other tools interested in basic component information. Implementing the IBaseComponent is straightforward and requires implementing only the three read-only properties. Here is the section of the code in Listing 3-3 that demonstrates the implementation of the three properties.

```csharp
#region IBaseComponent members defines Description, Name, and Version
    public string Description
    {
        get
        {
            return "Sample Custom Pipeline Component";
        }
    }

    public string Name
    {
        get
        {
            return "Sample Custom Pipeline Component";
        }
    }

    public string Version
    {
        get
        {
            return "1.0";
        }
    }
#endregion
```

IComponentUI

IComponentUI serves to present the component icon in the design-time tool set. The two methods implemented in the IComponentUI are Icon and Validate. The Icon method provides a pointer to the graphic icon displayed in the design-time user interface. If no icon is specified, Visual Studio will display the default icon in the BizTalk Pipeline Components section of the Toolbox. The Validate method allows processing of any design-time properties. For example, if you have a custom design-time property that requires information, you can include validation rules within the Validate method to verify the design-time information entered.

The following portion of Listing 3-3 shows both the Validate and Icon methods. In the solution example included with this recipe, the default Visual Studio icon will be used, and no special validation rules are required for the specified user data.

```
#region IComponentUI members contains design time information
        // Include a validate method used by BizTalk
        public IEnumerator Validate(object obj)
        {
            IEnumerator enumerator = null;
            // Return a null
                return enumerator;
        }
        // We do not have an icon for this custom component
        [Browsable(false)]
        public System.IntPtr Icon
        {
            get
            {
                // No icon associated with this pipeline component
                return  IntPtr.Zero;
            }
        }
}
        #endregion
```

IPersistPropertyBag

The purpose of the IPersistPropertyBag interface is to provide access to your object to unmanaged code. If you are familiar with .NET, then you may have used property bags in other projects. IPersistPropertyBag also allows access to design-time configuration values. There are four public methods that exist in the IPersistPropertyBag interface: GetClassID, initNew, Load, and Save. The GetClassID function must return a unique ID that represents the component. The initNew function can be used to establish structures (data, caching, and memory) used by the other IPersistPropertyBag methods. The final functions facilitate the loading and saving of property values. In the solution example accompanying this recipe, two additional methods were created to wrap the actual read/write functions of the property bag; however, the read and write functions could also be called directly from the Load and Save functions.

The following portion of the code from Listing 3-3 demonstrates the implementation of the four IPersistPropertyBag functions as well as the two helper functions.

```
#region IPersistPropertyBag members contains placeholders
        public void GetClassID(out Guid classid)
        {
            // Return class ID of this component for usage from unmanaged code.
            classid = new System.Guid("63ed4b26-63cd-4d29-9661-f584c94cf858");
        }

        public void InitNew()
        {
            // Initialization not implemented
        }

        public void Load(IPropertyBag propertyBag, Int32 errorlog)
        {
            // Load configuration property for component.
            string val = (string)ReadPropertyBag(propertyBag,
                    m_propbagkey_customproprop);

            if (val != null)
                m_propname = val;

            val = (string)ReadPropertyBag(propertyBag,
                    m_propbagkey_custompropropnamespace);
            if (val != null)
                m_propnamespace = val;
        }

        public void Save(IPropertyBag propertyBag
                , Boolean clearDirty, Boolean saveAllProperties)
        {
            // Saves the current component configuration into the property bag.
            object val = (object)m_propname;
            WritePropertyBag(propertyBag,
                m_propbagkey_customproprop, val);

            val = (object)m_propnamespace;
            WritePropertyBag(propertyBag,
                m_propbagkey_custompropropnamespace, val);
        }

        private static object ReadPropertyBag(IPropertyBag propertyBag
                , string propertyName)
        {
            // Reads property value from property bag.
            object val = null;
```

```
            try
            {
                propertyBag.Read(propertyName, out val, 0);
            }
            catch(ArgumentException)
            {
                return val;
            }
            catch(Exception ex)
            {
                throw new ApplicationException(ex.Message);
            }
            return val;
        }

        private static void WritePropertyBag(IPropertyBag propertyBag
                , string propertyName, object val)
        {
            // Writes property values into a property bag.
            try
            {
                propertyBag.Write(propertyName, ref val);
            }
            catch(Exception ex)
            {
                throw new ApplicationException(ex.Message);
            }
        }
    }
    #endregion
```

IComponent

IComponent is the most important interface in the component, as it contains the processing logic for messages. This interface contains a single method, Execute, which takes two parameters. BizTalk calls the Execute method to process the message, and then passes the message and the context of the message as the two parameters. The following outlines the Execute method declaration and the two required parameters in Listing 3-3.

```
#region IComponent members contains the main implementation
        public IBaseMessage Execute(IPipelineContext pContext
                                , IBaseMessage pInMsg)
        {
            // Create custom context property on message
            pInMsg.Context.Promote(m_propname, m_propnamespace, string.Empty);
            return pInMsg;
        }
#endregion
```

The IPipelineContext parameter refers to the environment in which the component is running. For example, the IPipelineContext object contains pipeline property information, including the pipeline stage in which the component is running. The IPipelineContext object also contains a resource tracker, which cleans up objects. The IBaseMessage object contains the inbound message. The main purpose of the custom component is to perform some level of processing on the inbound message object.

The Execute method returns the IBaseMessage object, which represents all parts of the processed message (such as the message content and context). You may perform any type of message or context processing if you return the IBaseMessage object at the end of the function. When BizTalk processes messages through pipelines, it streams the messages, rather than passing the whole messages. Additionally, the message passed through the pipeline is a read-only data object. The solution example accompanying this recipe demonstrates only adding a context property and does not demonstrate updating the content of the message. You must perform the following steps if you plan to alter the message content:

1. Create a memory stream object to hold the contents on the updated message or a copy of the inbound message. Remember that an inbound message is read-only, and you need a new container to perform updates to the inbound message. The new memory stream object is a container for the updated message.

2. Process the inbound message stream. The easiest way of processing the inbound message is to copy the stream to a string and load the message into an XMLDocument. However, using an XMLDocument object does not perform well and is not recommended for a production-type solution. A better method involves using a stream reader to manipulate the inbound stream. Consider the following approaches for manipulating the inbound memory stream:

   • Use Stream.Read() as the primary mechanism for dealing with message content.

   • Use XMLReader.Read() as the secondary mechanism for dealing with message content.

   • Use the XML message in the DOM as a last resort option due to the performance hit. Specifically, if you're dealing with large messages, do not load the entire message into the DOM for processing.

3. Set the message body part. After processing the message, you must return the updated message. If you used a memory stream object, you can set the return IBaseMessage. Data object to the memory stream object. Remember to rewind the updated memory stream object so you are passing the whole message and not the end of the memory stream. The pipeline processor will not attempt to rewind the stream, and you will receive a pipeline if the stream is not rewound.

4. Add the memory stream to the resource tracker. If you used a new memory stream object, make sure to add the memory stream object to the IPipelineContext.Resource tracker for cleanup.

Pipelines are the first line of processing before a message is received by the BizTalk MessageBox or before the message is received by a target system. Out-of-the-box functionality supports the ability to perform straightforward processing of messages. There may be situations that require more complex processing, data validation, or interaction with .NET objects.

In those situations, implementing a custom pipeline component offers the flexibility of adding processing logic within the BizTalk framework.

The main function required for implementing a custom pipeline component is the Execute function in the IComponent interface. The other interfaces serve for design-time and component interactions with the runtime engine.

Manipulation of the inbound message requires making a copy of the inbound message stream, as the inbound message stream is read-only. Before a memory stream can be returned to the IBaseMessage.Data object, it must be rewound, as the BizTalk pipeline engine does not perform this function. You should also clean up memory stream objects by adding the object to the pipeline resource tracker.

■**Note** An alternative to creating a custom pipeline component from scratch would be to use the Pipeline Component Wizard available from GotDotNet.

3-9. Handling Pipeline Errors

Problem

You need to implement custom logic within a pipeline for an integration solution you are building. Based on the solution's requirements, message delivery must be guaranteed, with no messages being lost once they are received by BizTalk Server. Any errors within the custom pipeline must result in a notification e-mail being sent to the appropriate system administrators.

Solution

How you trap and handle pipeline errors depends on whether you are running BizTalk Server 2004 or BizTalk Server 2006. BizTalk Server 2006 introduces some very convenient, easy-to-use error-handling functionality.

Handle Pipeline Errors in BizTalk Server 2006

BizTalk Server 2006 introduces new functionality called *error reporting*, which enables simplified handling of pipeline (and other) errors. Error reporting is specified on receive and send ports within the BizTalk Administration Console, as shown in Figure 3-32 (see Recipe 3-2 for details on configuring send ports using the BizTalk Administration Console).

By enabling this feature on a port, you instruct BizTalk Server 2006 to take a number of steps in the event an error is encountered during message processing (which includes adapter, pipeline, mapping, and routing processing). Specifically, a clone of the errored message is created, with all the original promoted properties demoted. The message does, however, have the appropriate error reporting properties promoted, such as the failure code and receive port/send port name. This message is then delivered to the MessageBox, and can be subscribed to by an SMTP send port via the error reporting promoted properties. This SMTP send port can be configured to deliver notification messages to a system administrator.

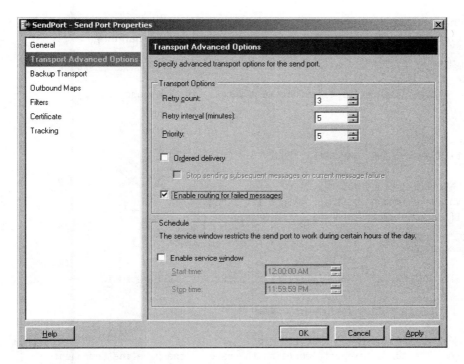

Figure 3-32. *Configuring error reporting on a send port*

■**Note** If error reporting is enabled, and an error occurs when BizTalk Server 2006 attempts to deliver the cloned message to the MessageBox, the original message is placed in the suspended queue.

Handle Pipeline Errors in BizTalk Server 2004

Implementing pipeline error handling in BizTalk Server 2004 is a manual task, involving three basic steps:

1. Implement the required logic in a custom pipeline component. Wrap this logic inside a `try` block. See Recipe 3-8 for details on creating pipeline components.

2. Implement the appropriate error-trapping logic in the custom pipeline component. Wrap this logic inside a `catch` block.

3. Build or configure the component(s) necessary for handling pipeline errors.

One common scenario requiring pipeline error handling is document validation. By default, the XML validation pipeline component provided with BizTalk Server handles errors by suspending messages that cannot be validated against a known schema and writing errors to the event log. In some situations, a more robust error-handling mechanism may be desired when document validation fails. This can be achieved by writing a custom validation pipeline component that contains the enhanced exception-handling logic. The following stubbed-out code snippet represents one possible implementation of pipeline error handling:

```
// Implement custom pipeline logic in the Execute method of the IBaseMessage
// interface
public IBaseMessage Execute(IPipelineContext pContext, IBaseMessage pInMsg)
{
    try
    {
        // STEP NUMBER ONE: IMPLEMENT REQUIRED / CUSTOM LOGIC

        // Retrieve inbound message
        // Validate inbound message against its schema
        // If successful, return validated message
    }
    catch (Exception e)
    {
        // STEP NUMBER TWO: IMPLEMENT PIPELINE EXCEPTION HANDLING LOGIC

        // Option 1: Default BizTalk Exception Handling

            // Set the exception's source property:
            //  The source property contains the name of the pipeline component
            //  which threw the exception, and will be displayed in the Event Log
            //  error written by BizTalk Server
            e.Source = "ExceptionHandlingPipeline";

            // Throwing the exception results in the default error handling of
            //  BizTalk Server, which is to suspend the message and write Event
            //  Log errors
            throw (e);

        // Option 2: Custom Exception Handling

            // Create an error message

            // Return Error Message:
            //  By returning a message (in this case, a message describing the
            //  error) via a return statement, BizTalk server will deliver the
            //  message to the MessageBox database
    }
}
```

With the appropriate document validation and error-handling logic implemented in a custom pipeline component, the component is leveraged in the Validate stage of a custom receive pipeline. A receive port and receive location are then created, with the receive location using the custom receive pipeline to validate inbound messages.

Lastly, the exception-handling process is implemented. In our scenario, this involves sending a notification e-mail with the error message included in the e-mail body. Option 2 from the previous code snippet is used, which creates an error message (including the original inbound document that could not be validated) and delivers it to the MessageBox database. The error message schema essentially acts as an envelope, wrapping the original inbound message in the following fashion:

```
<PipelineErrorEnvelope>
  <MessageInstanceID />
  <SourcePipeline />
  <PipelineErrors>
    <Any>
  </PipelineErrors>
</PipelineErrorEnvelope>
```

Create a send port, and configure its filter properties to subscribe to the error message schema created by the custom pipeline component. Configure the send port to use the SMTP adapter, which sends notification e-mail messages to the appropriate address. For more information about configuring the SMTP adapter, see Recipe 6-3.

How It Works

The following subsections describe the solutions for BizTalk Server 2006 and BizTalk Server 2004.

Pipeline Errors in BizTalk Server 2006

Pipeline error handling has been significantly improved in BizTalk Server 2006 with the new error-reporting functionality. Error reporting allows a variety of receive/send port errors to be trapped and managed. The details of the error are promoted as properties on a copy of the original message, which is sent to the MessageBox database. This allows you to handle error messages just like any other message: via subscriptions. You can define error-handling mechanisms specific to a single integration point, an application, or an entire BizTalk environment. Your error-handling mechanisms can be a simple notification e-mail (as shown in this solution), or a complex set of processes implemented as orchestrations.

Table 3-8 shows the error-reporting properties promoted on errored messages.

Table 3-8. *Error-Reporting Properties Promoted on Errored Messages*

Property	Description
FailureCode	The code identifying the error.
FailureCategory	The category of the failure.
MessageType	The BizTalk message type of the failed message. This property may be empty if BizTalk Server could not determine the type of message.
ReceivePortName	The name of the receive port where the failure occurred. This property is populated and promoted only if the failure occurred on a receive port.
InboundTransportLocation	The URI of the receive location where the failure occurred. This property is populated and promoted only if the failure occurred on a receive port.

continued

Table 3-8. *Continued*

Property	Description
SendPortName	The name of the send port where the failure occurred. This property is populated and promoted only if the failure occurred on a send port.
OutboundTransportLocation	The URI of the send port where the failure occurred. This property is populated and promoted only if the failure occurred on a send port.
ErrorType	The type of message that the error report contains.
RoutingFailureReportID	The ID of the related routing failure report message in the Message-Box. The routing failure report message contains the properties (context) of the original message, and can be queried to provide additional information about the errored message.

Pipeline Errors in BizTalk Server 2004

BizTalk Server 2004, by default, does not allow the implementation of custom pipeline exception handling. Instead, BizTalk Server handles pipeline errors consistently, by writing errors to the event log and suspending the message. In those scenarios requiring custom error handling, a custom pipeline component must include the exception logic. The solution described previously catches document validation errors, delivering notification e-mail messages as a means of enhanced exception handling. You can extend this approach of trapping exceptions in custom pipeline components for a number of other scenarios, such as message decoding and encoding, or message disassembling or assembling.

Once you have implemented the custom pipeline logic, a number of options exist for handling exceptions. On a general level, you can handle exceptions within the custom pipeline component itself, or alternatively by objects outside the BizTalk pipeline.

The pipeline component's catch block can write custom errors to the event log or modify BizTalk objects, either by Windows Management Instrumentation (WMI) or BizTalk Object Model method calls. For example, you can disable a receive location to stop a certain integration point in the event an exception is encountered. These types of tasks can either be done directly in the pipeline component or split out into a separate assembly that is called from the pipeline component.

Common error-handling methods via external objects include writing error messages to a log folder or creating a robust error-handling business process. You can implement each of these methods by extending the previous example. Based on BizTalk Server's publish/subscribe architecture, you can set up new subscribers to enable folder logging (via a file adapter send port) or more complex processes for exception handling (via an orchestration).

CHAPTER 4

■ ■ ■

Orchestration

If publish/subscribe messaging capabilities are at the heart of BizTalk, then process orchestration capabilities are BizTalk's brain. A BizTalk orchestration can define a complex integration process, coordinating the flow of information when simple data synchronization will not suffice. BizTalk provides a graphical design tool for defining these integration processes. These orchestration capabilities build upon the foundational publish/subscribe architecture of the BizTalk messaging runtime.

In the simplest cases, integration is strictly about receiving information from one system and delivering it to another. Accordingly, a BizTalk orchestration receives and sends messages through orchestration ports. However, many real-world situations require more than simple message delivery. With an orchestration, the BizTalk developer can graphically define additional processing steps in Visual Studio. For example, these processing steps may involve examining a message or invoking a .NET assembly and deciding on the appropriate actions to take. An orchestration can define an integration process with sequential processing steps or perform independent activities simultaneously. Define higher-level integration services in an orchestration by composing the messaging capabilities of BizTalk with additional integration processing logic. Future integration requirements can reuse the higher-level integration services to reduce implementation effort and enable greater agility.

BizTalk orchestrations support many of the capabilities needed to compose integration activities together, as follows:

- Atomic and long-running transactions help ensure that all systems involved in an integration process come to a consistent result.

- Transformations convert from a format understood by a source system to a format understood by a destination system.

- Orchestrations can invoke an external .NET assembly or use expressions defined with custom code.

- Exceptions can be handled by defining the scope of integration activities.

BizTalk orchestrations also provide terrific support for interacting with services defined by interoperable contracts. With BizTalk 2006, an orchestration can directly consume ASMX .NET web services, exposing the service operations within the graphical orchestration design environment. The BizTalk developer can also expose an orchestration as a web service, which any service consumer can invoke without having to know that BizTalk technology implements the service. As future services technologies like the Windows Communication Framework integrate further into the Microsoft .NET platform, expect BizTalk to take full advantage of the platform's capabilities.

4-1. Receiving Messages

Problem

You are building a solution that requires the implementation of a business process. You must configure an orchestration to receive messages, which begins the business process.

Solution

BizTalk Server orchestrations receive messages either through a Receive shape or directly from another orchestration as an orchestration input parameter. A Receive shape allows messages to be routed from the MessageBox to the orchestration, as demonstrated in this solution.

To create an orchestration that receives messages via a Receive shape, follow these steps:

1. Open the project that contains the schema (see Chapter 1 for details on creating schemas).

2. Right-click the project and select Add ➤ New Item.

3. In the Add New Item dialog box, select Orchestration Files from the Categories list, choose the BizTalk Orchestration template, and give a descriptive name to your new orchestration, as shown in Figure 4-1. In our example, the orchestration is named ReceiveShapeOrchestration. Then click Add.

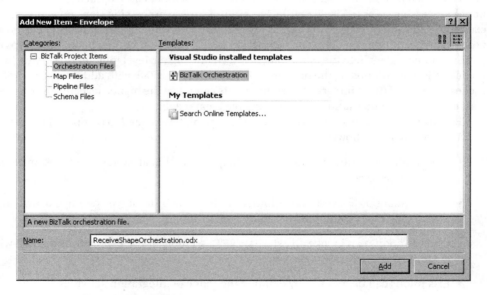

Figure 4-1. *Adding a new orchestration to a project*

4. In the Orchestration View window, expand the top node of the tree view (this node will have the same name as the orchestration), so that the Messages folder is visible. (If the Orchestration View window is not visible, select View ➤ Other Windows ➤ Orchestration View.)

5. Right-click the Messages folder and select New Message, which creates a message.

6. Click the new message, and give it a descriptive name in the Properties window. In our example, the message is named msgCustomerMessage.

7. Click the Message Type property in the Properties window and select the appropriate type to associate with the message, as shown in Figure 4-2. In our example, we select the CustomerSchema message type.

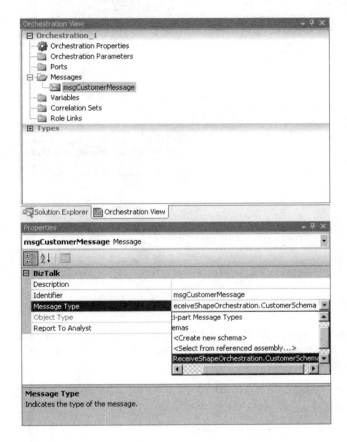

Figure 4-2. *Creating a message*

8. From the Toolbox, drag a Receive shape onto the orchestration directly beneath the green circle at the top of the design surface.

Note In addition to dragging and dropping shapes from the Toolbox, you can also add shapes to an orchestration by right-clicking a section of the vertical process flow arrow and selecting Insert Shape.

---

9. With the Receive shape selected, specify the shape's `Name`, `Message`, and `Activate` properties, as shown in Figure 4-3. The `Message` property is set via a drop-down list, which is populated with all the messages that are in scope for the Receive shape. The `Active` property is also set via a drop-down list, with the choices `True` or `False`. In our example, we use `ReceiveCustomerMessage`, `msgCustomerMessage` (created in step 6), and `True`, respectively.

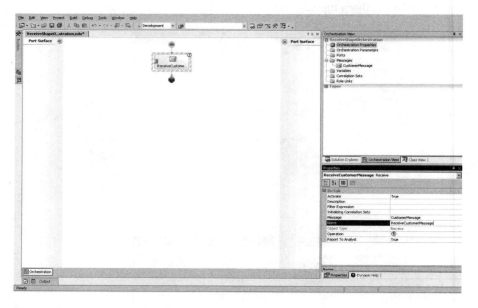

Figure 4-3. *Adding a Receive shape*

10. To configure a port and port type for the orchestration to use to receive a message, right-click the Port Surface area and select New Configured Port. This will start the Port Configuration Wizard.

11. Step through the Port Configuration Wizard, specifying the following items (accept all other defaulted values):

   - Port Name: `oprtReceiveCustomerMessagePort`.

   - New Port Type Name: `oprtTypeCustomerMessagePortType`.

   - Port Binding: Select Specify Now, and configure the appropriate receive adapter to consume inbound messages, as shown in Figure 4-4. In this example, we configure the port to use the FILE adapter, which receives XML messages from the `C:\ReceiveShapeOrchestration\In` folder.

■**Caution** Using Specify Now as your method of port binding can make your development and deployment process easier, but be careful when using this feature. It is not the recommended method for production code, as you should not embed port bindings inside an orchestration. A better approach is to use a binding file.

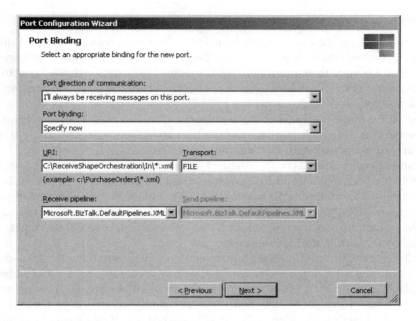

Figure 4-4. *Configuring an orchestration port for receiving messages*

12. Connect the orchestration port's Request operation to the Receive shape, as shown in Figure 4-5.

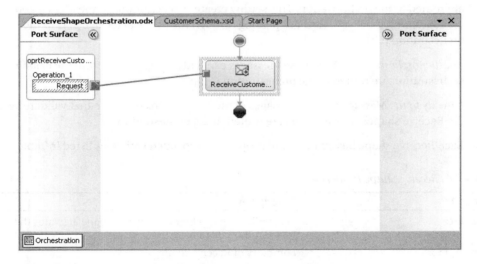

Figure 4-5. *Connecting an orchestration port to a Receive shape*

How It Works

Understanding how messages are received into orchestrations is critical when designing and implementing orchestrations in BizTalk Server. Receive shapes are the most common method used to deliver messages to orchestrations. In this recipe's solution, we showed how to add a Receive shape to an orchestration, configure the Receive shape's `Message Type` and `Activate` properties, and connect it to a receive port.

If the Receive shape is the first shape in the orchestration, it must have its `Activate` property set to `True`. If an orchestration does not have an activating Receive shape, it must be called or started (instantiated) from another orchestration.

The data a Receive shape accepts is defined by its `Message` property, which relates to a message that has been defined within the orchestration. All messages in BizTalk are bound to a specific type, which can be an XSD schema or a .NET class. This allows orchestrations to receive instances of XSD schemas or .NET classes as inputs. While our example used a single Receive shape, orchestrations can use many Receive shapes to accept different types of messages at different points in the business logic.

Each Receive shape must be bound to an operation, or orchestration port. An orchestration port is the interface through which messages pass on their way into or out of orchestration instances. Orchestration ports define the direction messages flow (receiving into an orchestration, sending from an orchestration, or both), and are bound to a physical port, another orchestration, or directly to the MessageBox database. The topic of binding orchestrations is covered in more detail in Recipe 4-4, but it is important to understand the methods by which orchestration ports can be bound and how they affect the way messages are received into an orchestration:

Physical receive port: All messages that are consumed by the specified receive port are routed to the orchestration. This setting creates subscriptions in the MessageBox database, which deliver messages passing through the physical receive port to the orchestration port.

Another orchestration: Only those messages explicitly being passed from the calling orchestration are routed to the orchestration.

Directly to the MessageBox: All messages in the MessageBox database that validate against the Receive shape's message type are routed to the orchestration.

Each Receive shape has a number of properties associated with it, as listed in Table 4-1.

Table 4-1. *Receive Shape Properties*

Property	Description
Activate	Flag indicating whether the Receive shape activates the orchestration instance.
Description	Summary of Receive shape.
Filter Expression	A filter that is applied to all messages being received via the Receive shape.
Initializing Correlation Sets	A list of correlation sets that are initialized as messages pass through the Receive shape (see Recipes 4-14, 4-15, and 4-16 for more information).

Property	Description
Following Correlation Sets	A list of correlation sets that are followed as messages pass through the Receive shape. This property is not available on the first Receive shape of an orchestration.
Message	The message that will be created when a document is passed through the Receive shape. A message with a message type of XmlDocument can be used to receive a generic XML message, without limiting documents to a specific XSD schema.
Name	Name of the Receive shape.
Object Type	Name of the object type (read-only, automatically set to Receive).
Operation	Specifies through which orchestration port operation the Receive shape receives its message.
Report To Analyst	Flag indicating whether the message part should be exposed via the Visual Business Analyst Tool.

The Filter Expression property allows you to be a bit more specific about which messages make it into your orchestration. Clicking the ellipsis in the input box for the Filter Expression property launches the Filter Expression dialog box. This dialog box allows you to create specific filters, which include one to many logical expressions that must be met in order for a message to be received into the orchestration. These logical expressions are based on a property, an operator, and a value, and can be grouped by using the And and Or keywords. Figure 4-6 demonstrates the use of a filter expression, which allows only those customer messages that are in the Europe or Asia region to be routed to the orchestration. A customer message that has North America defined in the region element would not be received into this orchestration.

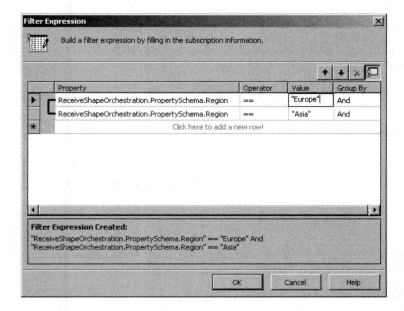

Figure 4-6. *Adding a filter expression*

A filter expression can be set on only a Receive shape that has its `Activate` property set to `True`. When the value portion of the filter expression is a string, you must put double quotes around the actual value for the expression to work properly, as shown in Figure 4-6.

The `Initializing Correlation Sets` and `Following Correlation Sets` properties specify which correlation is followed when messages are received on the Receive shape. Generally speaking, correlation sets allow you to send and receive messages in and out of orchestrations that directly relate to one another. Correlation is covered in Recipes 4-14, 4-15, and 4-16.

4-2. Sending Messages

Problem

You want to send messages from within a BizTalk orchestration for processing by other orchestrations.

Solution

Within a BizTalk orchestration, messages are sent using the Send shape. To use the Send shape, follow these steps:

1. Open the BizTalk project that contains the orchestration with the messages you want to send.

2. Drag a Send shape from the Toolbox. Place the shape underneath the orchestration Receive shape.

3. In the Orchestration View window, expand the top node of the tree view so that the `Messages` folder is visible.

4. Right-click the `Messages` folder and select New Message, which creates a message.

5. Click the new message and give it a descriptive name in the Properties window (`msgCustomer` in our example).

6. Click the `Message Type` property in the Properties window, select the `.Schema` node, and select the `Orchestration Customer` schema.

7. Select the Send shape, and in the Properties window, assign the message to `msgCustomer`.

■**Note** The port and type you are creating is not a physical BizTalk port. This is an orchestration port that will be bound later to the physical port.

---

8. To configure a port and port type for the orchestration to use to send a message, right-click the Port Surface and click New Port, as shown in Figure 4-7.

9. Click the exclamation mark (tool tip) and select "No port type has been specified." This starts the Port Configuration Wizard.

10. On the Select a Port Type page, name the port `oprtSendCustomer` and click Next.

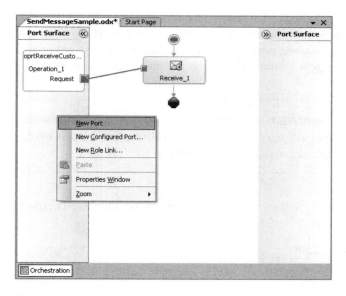

Figure 4-7. *Creating a new port*

11. On the Configure Port page, enter the following details, as shown in Figure 4-8, and
then click Next:

- Select the Create a New Port Type radio button.

- Name the port type oprtTypeSendCustomer.

- Select the One-Way radio button under Communication Pattern.

- Select the Internal - Limited to This Project radio button under Access Restrictions.

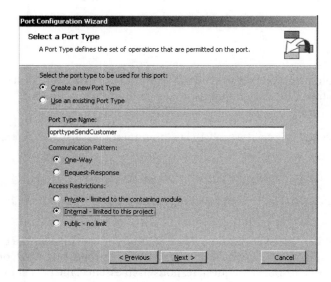

Figure 4-8. *Configuring an orchestration port for sending messages*

12. On the Port Binding page, select "I'll always be sending messages on this port" for the port direction of communication. For port binding, select Direct, and select the first radio button. Routing between ports will be defined by filter expressions on incoming messages in the MessageBox database. Click Finish after making your selections.

■**Note** In this example, we are implementing a standard publish/subscribe model; that is, the message implementation does not need to be physically specified. The BizTalk MessageBox database will be responsible for initializing one or more downstream messaging subscriptions.

---

13. From the port on the Port Surface area, click the green pixel and drag it to the Send shape on the orchestration design surface, as shown in Figure 4-9.

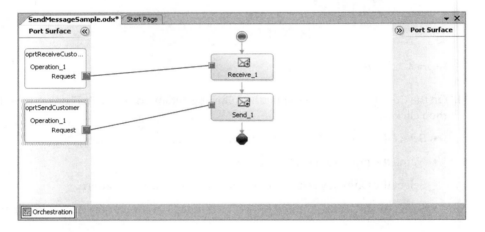

Figure 4-9. *Send message configuration*

How It Works

In this recipe's solution, we demonstrated how to send messages out of an orchestration to BizTalk messaging and downstream BizTalk endpoints. To review, the following are the key steps to perform to send a message:

1. Identify a message to send. This can be a .NET class, multipart message, web reference message, or schema.

2. Create an orchestration port. Specify the port type and access restrictions.

3. Set port binding. Set the port direction and binding (dynamic or direct) to BizTalk messaging artifacts.

When sending messages out of an orchestration, it is also important to consider the type of request you would like to implement. Should the message not be returned (one-way), or should the orchestration wait for a response (request/response)? In essence, the port choice should support the type of communication being implemented.

Another important consideration is the message context. Within the orchestration, is the message its own instance or should it be aware of correlation implications? Within the Send shape, you have the ability to address correlation message context by setting the `Following Correlation Sets` or `Initializing Correlation Sets` property.

4-3. Creating Multipart Messages

Problem

You are building an integration solution, and receive multiple documents that together form a single logical message in your back-end system. You must group these documents into one message by using a multipart message in BizTalk Server.

Solution

Multipart messages are created in BizTalk Server orchestrations, as opposed to being created as schemas. Multipart messages are a collection of message parts, with each part having a specific type. Message part types can be defined by an XSD schema or a .NET class. This solution describes how to use XSD schemas to define each of the message parts.

To create an orchestration and a multipart message, follow these steps:

1. Open the project that contains the schemas (see Chapter 1 for details on creating schemas).

2. Right-click the project and select Add ➤ New Item.

3. In the Add New Item dialog box, select Orchestration Files from the Categories list, BizTalk Orchestration as the template, and give a descriptive name to your new orchestration, as shown in Figure 4-10. In our example, the orchestration is named `MultiPartMessageOrchestration`. Then click Add.

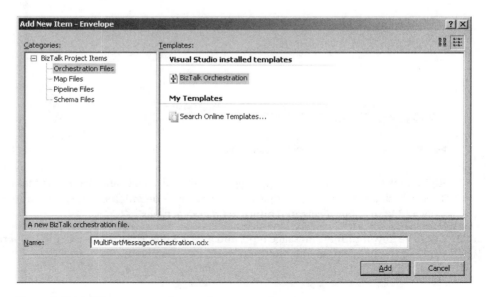

Figure 4-10. *Adding a new orchestration to a project*

4. In the Orchestration View window, expand the Types node of the tree view so that the Multi-part Message Types folder is visible, as shown in Figure 4-11. (If the Orchestration View window is not visible, select View ➤ Other Windows ➤ Orchestration View.)

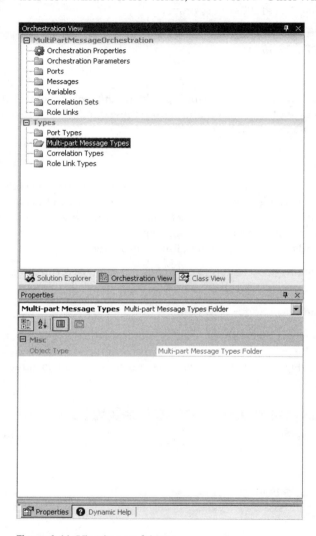

Figure 4-11. *Viewing multipart message types*

5. Right-click the Multi-part Message Types folder and select New Multi-part Message Type, which creates a new multipart message type. A default message part is automatically added to all newly created multipart message types.

6. Click the new multipart message type, and give it a descriptive name in the Properties window. In our example, the multipart message is named Order.

7. Expand the new multipart message type, click the default message part, and give it a descriptive name in the Properties window. In our example, the message part is named Header. Note that the Message Body Part property is set to True.

8. Click the Type property in the Properties window and select the appropriate schema to associate with the message part, as shown in Figure 4-12. In our example, the schema is named Orchestration.OrderHeader.

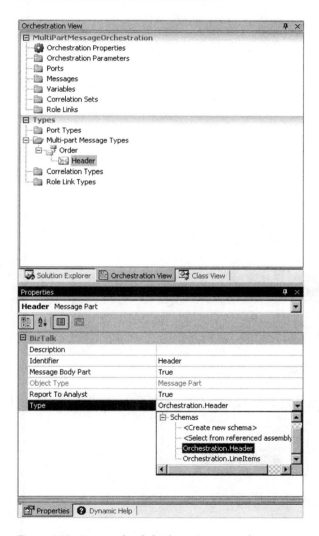

Figure 4-12. *Setting the default message part's type*

9. Right-click the Order multipart message type and select New Message Part, which creates a new message part.

10. Click the new message part and give it a descriptive name in the Properties window. In our example, the message part is named `LineItems`. Note that the `Message Body Part` property is set to `False`.

11. Click the `Type` property in the Properties window and select the appropriate schema to associate with the message part, as shown in Figure 4-13. In our example, the schema is named `Orchestration.LineItems`.

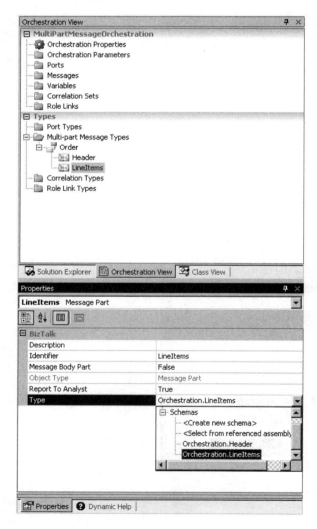

Figure 4-13. *Setting an additional message part's type*

12. In the Orchestration View window, expand the top node of the tree view so that the `Messages` folder is visible.

13. Right-click the `Messages` folder and select New Message, which creates a message.

14. Click the new message and give it a descriptive name in the Properties window. In our example, the message is named `MultiPartOrderMessage`.

15. Click the `Message Type` property in the Properties window and select the appropriate type to associate with the message, as shown in Figure 4-14. In our example, we select the `Orchestration.Order` multipart message type.

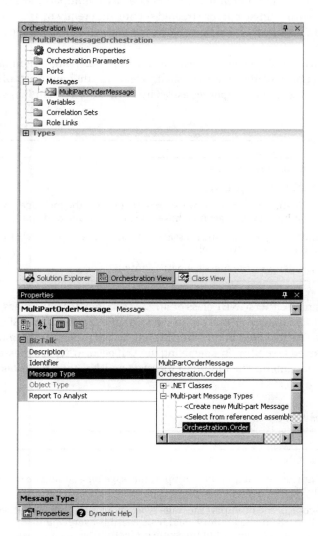

Figure 4-14. *Creating a multipart message*

How It Works

Multipart messages allow for the grouping of multiple parts into a single message. In our solution, we group an order header document and an order line item document into a single order message.

All messages within BizTalk Server are multipart messages, although most of them just have a single part (the message body), and therefore are not created as a multipart message within orchestrations. Messages with a single part are treated slightly differently by BizTalk Server, as the single part is not displayed when referring to the message and the message is referred to directly.

The concept of messages having multiple parts is easier to grasp after creating a multipart message type within an orchestration, where you must explicitly create the different parts of a message. Each message part has a number of properties associated with it, as listed in Table 4-2.

Table 4-2. *Message Part Properties*

Property	Part
Description	Summary of message part
Identifier	Name of the message part
Message Body Part	Flag indicating whether the message part contains the message body (every multipart message must have one and only one body part)
Report To Analyst	Flag indicating whether the message part should be exposed via the Visual Business Analyst Tool
Type	The type defining the message part's content

The type of message part can be either a .NET class or an XSD schema. If a .NET class is specified, the class must be XML-serializable or support custom serialization. If an XSD schema is used, the schema must be included in the same BizTalk Server project as the multipart message type or in a referenced assembly. By specifying the XmlDocument type, a message part can contain any valid XML document. The multipart message type has the properties listed in Table 4-3 associated with it.

Table 4-3. *Multipart Message Type Properties*

Property	Part
Identifier	Name of the multipart message type
Report To Analyst	Flag indicating whether the multipart message type should be exposed via the Visual Business Analyst Tool
Type Modifier	The scope of the multipart message type; choices are Private (accessible within the orchestration), Public (accessible everywhere), or Internal (accessible within the same project)

Once you have defined your multipart message types, you can create and access message instances of those types within the orchestration. Figure 4-15 illustrates how you can assign the Header and LineItems message parts of the Order message. In this example, the OrderHeaderMessage and OrderLineItemsMessage messages are instances of the Header and LineItems schemas.

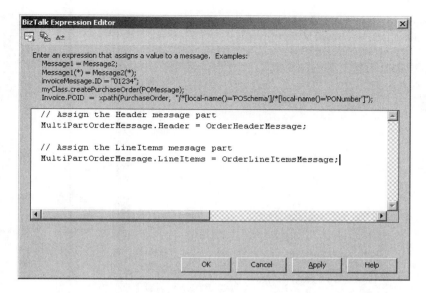

Figure 4-15. *Assigning message parts*

Some common uses of multipart messages in BizTalk Server are when you are consuming a web service or processing e-mail messages within orchestrations. When you add a web reference to an orchestration, a multipart message type is generated automatically, with one part created for each message part defined in the web service's WSDL file. For those scenarios where e-mail messages are being processed, it is common to use multipart message types to handle MIME multipart messages; the body message part would contain the body of the e-mail, and subsequent parts could contain e-mail document attachments.

4-4. Binding Orchestrations

Problem

You need to bind an orchestration to a physical port, in order to associate a process with a BizTalk messaging port, and consequently, a downstream BizTalk process.

Solution

Binding orchestrations to physical ports is the activity that enables defined processes (orchestration) to be associated with physical connectivity and communication, such as file, HTTPS, or web service. BizTalk enables two methods of binding orchestrations. You can choose to specify the binding immediately, within the BizTalk Orchestration Designer (by choosing the Specify Now option during the port binding process), or later using the BizTalk Explorer (by choosing Specify Later). When you choose Specify Later, this indicates that binding information will not be determined at design time. This recipe demonstrates using the Specify Later option.

1. Deploy an orchestration and choose the Specify Later method during the port binding process.

2. Open the BizTalk Explorer and under the `Orchestrations` tree, locate your orchestration.

3. Right-click the orchestration and select the Bind option. The Port Bindings Properties dialog box will appear, as shown in Figure 4-16.

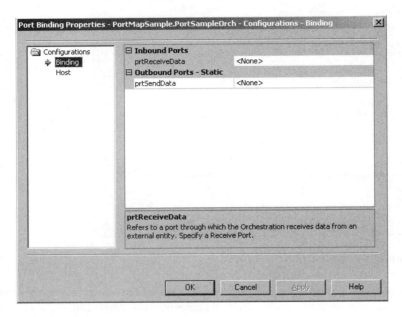

Figure 4-16. *Port Bindings Properties dialog box*

4. For each orchestration port, select the desired BizTalk messaging port. The port choices available for selection will be filtered based on the port type (send or receive).

How It Works

Binding orchestrations enables processes to be associated with BizTalk messaging ports and consequently, downstream BizTalk processes and artifacts.

Binding can be completed within the BizTalk Orchestration Designer (when you choose Specify Now) or within the BizTalk Explorer (when you choose Specify Later). The two binding choices allow for separation between process and configuration activities for both task and environment orientation.

Consider the separation of roles between a developer and administrator. The developer would be responsible for development activities within BizTalk, whereas the administrator would be responsible for deployment activities. These activities can be abstracted to allow for environment-specific configuration, without development involvement or consideration. To illustrate this point, consider testing and production BizTalk environments, and how the specification of port values (such as URLs, file locations, and so on) and physical receive locations can be achieved via this abstraction.

4-5. Configuring a Send Port at Runtime

Problem

You need to send a message from BizTalk Server, but will not have all of the required information to do so until the orchestration is executing.

Solution

To be able to configure a send port at runtime, you create a dynamic send port within the orchestration. This recipe demonstrates how to configure the outbound dynamic send port in the Message Construct shape. The first step is to copy the contents of the inbound message to the outbound message. Listing 4-1 shows an example of a dynamic XML message.

Listing 4-1. *Sample Dynamic XML Message*

```
<nsO:DynamicMessage xmlns:nsO="http://DynamicSendPortProject.xsdDynamicMessage">
  <Header>
    <FTPServer>myFTPServer.com</FTPServer>
    <FTPUserName>FTPUserName</FTPUserName>
    <FTPPassword>FTPPassword</FTPPassword>
    <Retry>3</Retry>
    <RetryInterval>5</RetryInterval>
    <FileName>FileName.xml</FileName>
  </Header>
  <Body>
    <Content>This is a test message.</Content>
  </Body>
</nsO:DynamicMessage>
```

Next, configure the address that BizTalk will use to communicate the message. The address uses the same format as a standard URL. In this example, we specify `ftp://` to transmit the file via FTP. The FTP transport protocol requires additional properties to be specified (such as the username and password). Listing 4-2 shows an example of a construct message configuration.

The following steps outline the procedure:

1. Open the project containing the orchestration that will be processing the inbound message and sending that message via a dynamic send port.

2. Create a new orchestration send port with a port binding that is dynamic (named `oprtSendDynamic` in this example). See Recipe 4-2 for details on creating an orchestration send port.

■Note You will be required to choose a send pipeline when configuring the send port. You can choose from any deployed send pipeline, any send pipeline referenced by your project, or any send pipeline that is part of your existing solution.

---

3. Verify that you have a message that contains all of the properties required for configuring the send port and that the properties are promoted or distinguished. Your message may look similar to the message shown earlier in Listing 4-1.

4. Select the Message Assignment shape from the BizTalk Orchestrations section of the Toolbox and drag it to the appropriate location within the orchestration.

5. Select the Message Assignment shape and update the properties.

   - Change the default name if desired.

   - Add a description if desired.

   - Identify the output message(s) constructed.

   - Set the Report To Analyst property. Leave the property as True if you would like the shape to be visible to the Visual Business Analyst Tool.

6. Update the Message Assignment shape to contain the information that constructs the outbound message as well as configures the properties on the outbound dynamic send port. Your construct message may look similar to the one shown earlier in Listing 4-2.

Listing 4-2. *Sample Message Assignment Code*

```
// Construct Message
msgDynamicOut = msgDynamicIn;

// Set the FTP properties based on message content.
// Reference the send port to set properties.
oprtSendDynamic(Microsoft.XLANGs.BaseTypes.Address) =
    "ftp://" + msgDynamicIn.Header.FTPServer + "/"
    + msgDynamicIn.Header.FileName;

// Set message context properties for ftp.
msgDynamicOut(FTP.UserName) = msgDynamicIn.Header.FTPUserName;
msgDynamicOut(FTP.Password) = msgDynamicIn.Header.FTPPassword;
msgDynamicOut(BTS.RetryCount) =
                System.Convert.ToInt32(msgDynamicIn.Header.Retry);
msgDynamicOut(BTS.RetryInterval) =
                System.Convert.ToInt32(msgDynamicIn.Header.RetryInterval);
```

7. Complete the orchestration. Your completed orchestration may look similar to Figure 4-17.

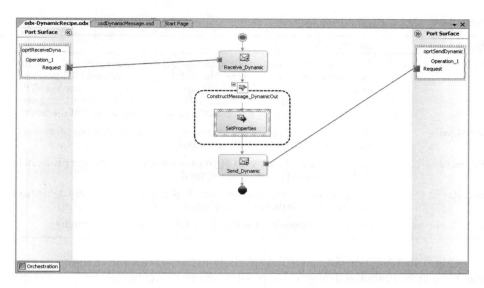

Figure 4-17. *Completed dynamic send port orchestration*

How It Works

Dynamic ports allow the physical location of a physical send port (one-way or solicit-response) to be determined at runtime. The only requirement for a dynamic port is setting a pipeline at design time. The ability to specify the transport protocol and address at runtime allows for the flexibility of routing messages based solely on message content or on the output of message processing in an orchestration.

For example, implementing the SMTP send adapter to send an e-mail from BizTalk requires configuration information (SMTP server, e-mail recipient, and subject). Rather than specifying the configuration information at design time, you can use a dynamic port, which allows you to configure the information programmatically and modify it based on the message content or processing. Additionally, dynamic send ports can be set via content returned from the Business Rule Engine.

This recipe's solution demonstrated setting up a dynamic send port to send a message via FTP. The inbound message contains the message content as well as the configuration information for transmitting the message to the FTP recipient. The properties of the message are distinguished fields and are therefore easily referenced. Depending on the transport protocol being specified for the dynamic port, different properties will be required and optional.

■**Caution** If you attempt to set the `Microsoft.XLANGs.BaseTypes.Address` field with an orchestration port that is not a dynamic port in BizTalk, you will receive a compile-time error.

Table 4-4 shows the required and optional properties for configuring the dynamic send port communicating via FTP.

Table 4-4. *Dynamic Send Port Properties*

Name	Description
Address	A required property that contains the location and possibly the file name of the output message to create. The Address property uses URL prefixes to indicate how to transmit the message. To transmit a message via FTP, the address must begin with the prefix ftp://. If the message is being sent via FTP or FILE, then a file name attribute is required as part of the address.
UserName	Specifies the FTP username. If you are specifying a different protocol in the URL, a username may not be required.
Password	Specifies the FTP password. If you are specifying a different protocol in the URL, a password may not be required.
RetryCount	An optional property that specifies how many times to retry delivery of the message, in case there is a problem transmitting the message.
RetryInterval	An optional property that specifies the retry interval in minutes.

This recipe's solution demonstrated creating a dynamic send port in the orchestration. When the orchestration is deployed, the physical send port will be created, and specific binding of the orchestration to a physical send port is already done. In addition to creating dynamic send ports as part of an orchestration, you can also create them via BizTalk Explorer.

4-6. Creating Branching Logic in an Orchestration

Problem

From within an orchestration, you would like to execute different processing based on the evaluation of available information.

Solution

A Decide shape is the equivalent of an If...Then...Else statement in standard programming. It allows you to direct different processing at runtime based on the evaluation of information. The following steps outline how to add a Decide shape to an orchestration and configure it.

1. Open the project containing the orchestration.

2. Open the orchestration.

3. Select the Decide shape from the Toolbox and drag it to the appropriate location within the orchestration.

4. Select the Decide shape and update its properties.

   - Change the default name if desired.

   - Add a description if desired.

   - Set the Report To Analyst property. Leave the property as True if you would like the shape to be visible to the Visual Business Analyst Tool.

5. Select the rule branch named `Rule_1` and update its properties (click it and set its properties in the Properties window).

- Change the default name if desired.

- Add a description if desired.

- Set the `Report To Analyst` property. Leave the property as `True` if you would like the shape to be visible to the Visual Business Analyst Tool.

- Right-click the ellipsis next to the `Expression` property and enter a valid Boolean expression for the rule.

6. To add an additional rule, right-click the Decide shape and select New Rule Branch.

■**Note** To delete a branch, right-click the branch and select Delete. To delete the Decide shape, right-click the shape and select Delete.

How It Works

Decide shapes can be used to complete different processing based on information available at runtime. The following is a simple example of using and configuring the Decide shape from within an orchestration. Assume you have a document as follows:

```
<Employee>
    <FirstName>John</FirstName>
    <LastName>Doe</LastName>
    <SSN>111-22-3333</SSN>
    <State>Washington</State>
    <HireDate>1999-05-31</HireDate>
</Employee>
```

From within an orchestration, you would like to complete different processing under the following scenarios:

- The State is "Washington" and an SSN is provided.

- The State is "Washington" and no SSN is provided.

- The State is not "Washington".

To set up this different processing based on these three scenarios, you add a Decide shape to the orchestration and configure two rule branches and the else branch. For the first rule branch, define the expression to ensure the state is Washington and that a Social Security number was provided, as shown in Figure 4-18.

■**Note** To access schema nodes from within an orchestration, you must set the nodes as distinguished fields from within the schema editor.

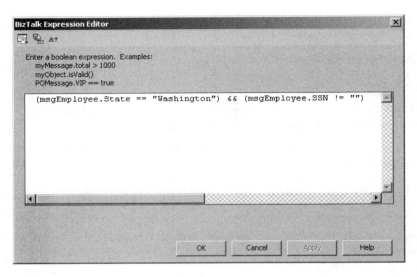

Figure 4-18. *First rule branch*

For the second rule branch, configure the expression to ensure the state is Washington and that no Social Security number was provided, as shown in Figure 4-19.

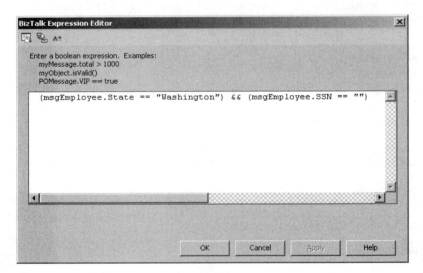

Figure 4-19. *Second rule branch*

■**Note** Refer to the BizTalk help file for a complete list of valid operators in orchestration expressions.

The else branch will accommodate all other inbound documents where the state is not Washington. Figure 4-20 shows a completed orchestration with a Decide shape configured as described in this example. In this example, a document will be sent to different locations depending on whether the State is "Washington" and whether or not the document contains an SSN. If the State is not "Washington", then no document will be sent. It is not required that the branch of a Decide shape contain any actions.

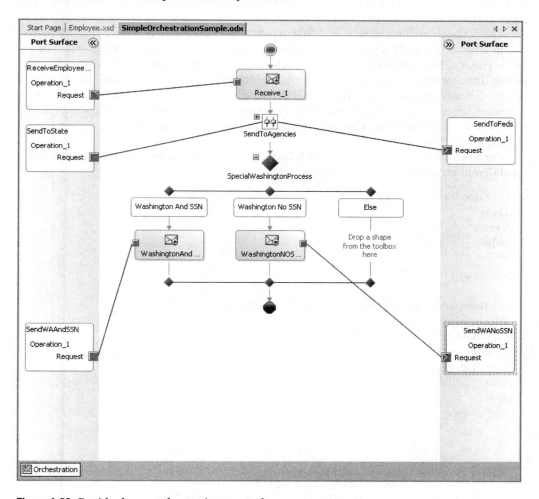

Figure 4-20. *Decide shape orchestration example*

4-7. Receiving Multiple Message Formats in a Single Orchestration

Problem

You need to execute the same orchestration logic for two or more different schemas.

Solution

Instead of creating separate orchestrations with identical logic, you can have one orchestration that uses the Listen shape and multiple Receive shapes. The Listen shape enables an orchestration to listen for any messages matching the schemas of any Receive shapes within the Listen shape. A Listen shape can contain multiple Receive shapes, all listening for different messages. In this solution, we will look at how to create an orchestration that listens for either of two messages to arrive.

The first step in the process is to define two different schemas to represent the different documents for which the orchestration will be listening. A typical example of this would be two versions of the same schema, where the elements defined differ enough to warrant a completely different schema. For instance, several required nodes on version 1 may not exist on version 2. Another example would be two different schemas representing similar data (such as customer, order, and so on) from two different legacy systems. In both cases, you would need to have both of the documents instantiate the same orchestration and be subject to the same rules and workflow.

For this solution, we will assume the following two documents are being used, representing different versions of the Person schema.

```
<ns0:Person xmlns:ns0="http://SampleListenShape.Person.V2">
  <ID/>
  <Name/>
  <Role/>
  <Age/>
</ns0:Person>

<ns0:Person xmlns:ns0="http://SampleSolution.Person">
  <ID/>
  <FirstName/>
  <MiddleName/>
  <LastName/>
  <Role/>
  <Age/>
</ns0:Person>
```

1. In an empty orchestration, drop a Listen shape onto the design surface.

2. Add two Receive shapes within the Listen shape.

   a. Set the Activate property on both Receive shapes to True.

   b. Rename the Receive shapes to Receive_Ver_1 and Receive_Ver_2. This is for reference purposes only.

   c. Create two message variables in the orchestration (click the Orchestration tab, right-click Messages, and select New Message), named msgVer1 and msgVer2, pointing them to the appropriate schema.

   d. Set the message type of Receive_Ver_1 to msgVer1 and Receive_Ver_2 to msgVer2.

3. Add a new port to the Port Surface with the following properties (using the Port Configuration Wizard).

   - Name the new port `Port_Receive_Incoming`.

   - Create a new port type of `PortType_ReceiveIncoming`.

   - Select "I'll always receive messages on this port."

   - Set the port binding to Specify Later or give a file path and set it to Specify Now.

4. Create two operations on the port (there will be one created automatically). Right-click the port, name the operation `Operation_VI`, and set the Message Type to `msgVer1`. Repeat this to add `Operation_V2` with the Message Type set to `msgVer2`.

5. Add a map to transform the version 1 documents into version 2. This will allow the orchestration to work with one message type throughout.

   a. Add a construct message with a Transform shape under the `Receive_Ver_1` shape.

   b. Create a new map.

   c. Set the source schema to `msgVer1` and the destination schema to `msgVer2`. The orchestration will resemble Figure 4-21.

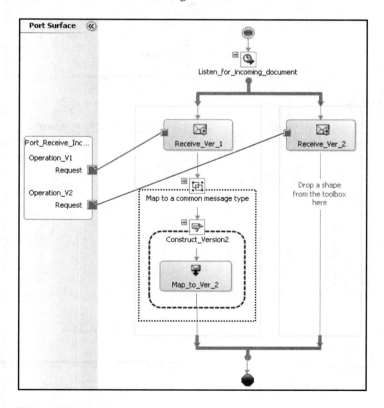

Figure 4-21. *Orchestration with Listen shape*

At this point, the orchestration can be deployed, bound to a receive port, and started. If either version of the Person schema is dropped on the MessageBox (via a port or directly bound), the orchestration will instantiate.

How It Works

This recipe demonstrated how to uses the Listen shape with multiple Receive shapes. There are alternative ways to use the Listen shape. One of the most common is a combination of a Receive shape and a Delay shape. This can be used for polling behavior in a long-running orchestration. For example, an orchestration could be set up to listen for a document to be dropped on a file directory. If a file is not dropped within a certain amount of time (as specified in the Delay shape), a series of steps could take place (such as notifying an administrator). By adding a Loop shape, the orchestration could return to listening for the document to arrive. An example of this is shown in Figure 4-22.

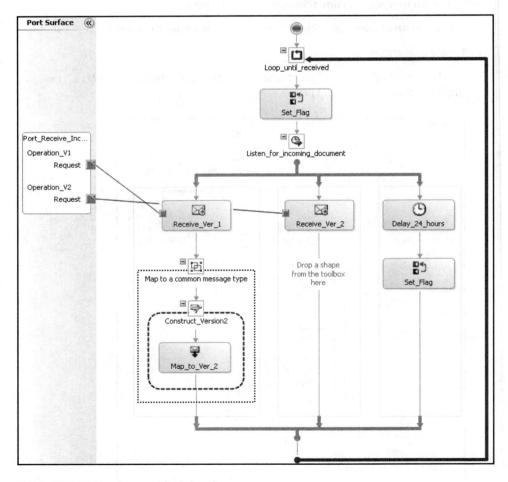

Figure 4-22. *Listen shape with Delay shape*

4-8. Calling External Assemblies

Problem

You need to call a method contained in a .NET class library assembly. You want to understand how to reference this assembly within your BizTalk project and how to call it from an Expression shape.

Solution

This solution will walk you through referencing an external assembly and calling the assembly from code within an Expression shape. Assume that the assembly is called SampleClass.dll, which contains a class called Helper. The Helper class has a function to set a string of characters to uppercase. Use the following steps to reference the assembly.

1. Open a BizTalk project in Visual Studio.

2. In the Solution Explorer, right-click References under the project header and select Add Reference.

3. In the Add Reference dialog box, click the Browse tab, find the SampleClass.dll assembly, and then click OK.

4. Now that the assembly is available in the BizTalk project, create a new orchestration variable. With an orchestration open, click the Orchestration View window. Right-click the Variables folder and select New Variable from the drop-down menu.

5. In the Properties window of the variable, set the following properties (see Figure 4-23):

   • Name the variable objSample.

   • Add a description, such as Demonstration Object.

   • Specify the variable's .NET type by clicking the drop-down box for the Type property and selecting <.NET Class>. In the Select Artifact Type dialog box, select the SampleClass.Helper class, as shown in Figure 4-24.

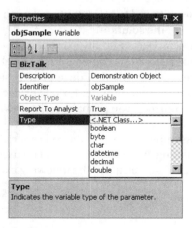

Figure 4-23. *Variable Properties window*

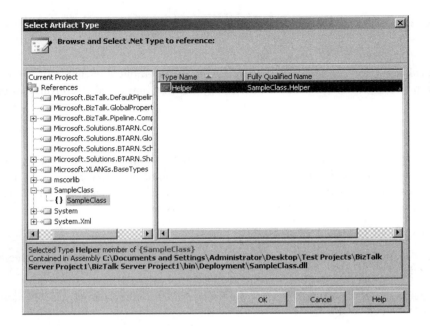

Figure 4-24. *Selecting the artifact type*

6. Drop an Expression shape in the orchestration and enter the following code to invoke the external assembly.

```
objSample = new SampleClass.Helper();
strOutput = objSample.strToUpperCase("abc");
```

How It Works

When creating a .NET class variable in BizTalk, an option exists to Use Default Constructor. This property causes an instance of the object to be constructed when the orchestration instantiates. If this property is set to False, the variable will need to be instantiated in an Expression shape through the new keyword (as in step 6 of the solution).

Another property that should be noted is on the referenced assembly itself: Copy Local. This property indicates whether the assembly referenced should be copied into the local bin directory when a project is built. Several factors will help decide whether the assembly should be copied locally; if a reference is to a dynamic assembly (such as another BizTalk project that is built at the same time as the project in which it is referenced), you probably will not want to copy the assembly locally.

It is important to note that when calling a .NET assembly that is not marked as serializable, it must be called from an atomic scope. When creating an assembly that will be used primarily by BizTalk, it is appropriate to mark all classes as serializable. The following example demonstrates doing this in C#.

```
[Serializable]
public class Example { }
```

4-9. Receiving Untyped Messages

Problem

You have messages that conform to several different schema types. You wish to create a single orchestration to consume the messages and process them in a generic fashion.

Solution

BizTalk orchestrations deal with messages that are strongly typed. A strongly typed message conforms to a selected BizTalk schema or .NET class, and the message inherits its properties from this schema or class. An untyped message is configured to use `System.Xml.XmlDocument` as the message type, and is not tied to a specific schema.

For example, a large business may receive purchase orders from several different systems, and each message must follow the same processing steps. Although the messages are similar, they differ in minor details, and are strongly typed to different schemas. In order to process the messages from these disparate systems using the same process, you may wish to define a process with an untyped message to receive the different purchase order schemas into the same receive port.

■Note It is important that you have a basic understanding of receiving messages prior to implementing untyped messages. See Recipe 4-1 for more information.

To create an untyped message and use it within an orchestration, take the following steps:

1. In the Orchestration View window, expand the top node of the tree view (this node will have the same type name as the orchestration) so that the `Messages` folder is visible.

2. Right-click the `Messages` folder and select New Message, which creates a message.

3. Click the new message and give it a descriptive name in the Properties window. In this example, the message is named `incomingOrder`.

4. Click the `Message Type` property in the Properties window and select the .NET type `System.Xml.XmlDocument`.

5. From the Toolbox, drag a Receive shape onto the orchestration directly beneath the green circle at the top of the design surface.

6. With the Receive shape selected, specify the shape's `Name`, `Message`, and `Activate` properties. In our example, we use `ReceiveOrder`, `incomingOrder` (created in step 3), and `True`, respectively.

■Note All message types will be received by an untyped port. Therefore, if you directly bind your port to the MessageBox, you will receive every message received into the MessageBox. This could create unintended behavior down the road.

---

7. Right-click one of the Port Surface areas and select New Configured Port. This will open the Port Configuration Wizard.

8. Step through the Port Configuration Wizard, specifying the following items (accept all other default values):

- Port Name: `ReceiveOrderPort`

- New Port Type Name: `ReceiveOrderPortType`

- Port Binding: Specify Later

- Connect the orchestration port's Request operation to the Receive shape

How It Works

Untyped messages are a deceptively complex and powerful BizTalk feature. Untyped messages are powerful because they allow for abstracted processes. For instance, rather than create three processes for three different purchase orders that your company receives from trading partners, you could create a single process that handles the different messages in the same process. Although the single process may increase in complexity, it reduces the amount of maintainable code.

When implementing untyped messages, pay attention to the following areas:

Direct binding: Creating an untyped message that is directly bound to the MessageBox is not a best practice. All schema-based messages within BizTalk have a base type of `System.Xml.XmlDocument`. The implication of this fact is that using a message variable that is typed as `System.Xml.XmlDocument` will set up a receive subscription for all messages that are received into the MessageBox through the directly bound port. Since, in almost every case, this is not the desired functionality, take caution when implementing this type of scenario.

Casting: Creating an untyped message will negate many of the common operations available for that schema type. For instance, accessing common promoted properties (`MessageDataBaseProperties`) and using Transform shapes are not supported with untyped messages. It is possible, though, to cast between an untyped message and a typed message. To cast a message, create an instance of the typed message in a Construct/Assignment shape, and assign the untyped message to the typed message. You now have the ability to use the typed message with all associated orchestration functionality.

Promoted properties: Although it is not possible to access common promoted properties (`MessageDataBaseProperties`) for an untyped message, it is possible to create and access a type of promoted property known as a `MessageContextPropertyBase` property for an untyped message. Refer to the BizTalk help file for more information about how to create this type of context property within your property schema. Setting the `MessageContextPropertyBase` property is done in the same manner as setting other promoted properties.

■**Note** MessageContextPropertyBase properties of untyped messages may be set within the orchestration, but the context property cannot be filtered on within other services unless a correlation set containing the MessageContextPropertyBase property is first initialized. In addition, it is not possible to map on a send port, because the MessageType property, which is required to match a message to a map, is not promoted for untyped messages.

By considering direct binding, casting, and promoted properties, you can safeguard your solution from complex bugs that are difficult to identify and triage.

4-10. Using the Parallel Action Shape

Problem

From within an orchestration, you would like to complete numerous activities at the same time and independently of one another.

Solution

A Parallel Action shape may be added to an orchestration to implement the concurrent processing of all parallel branches when the orchestration executes. Processing beyond the parallel branches will not occur until all branches of the Parallel Action shape have completed. The following steps outline how to add a Parallel Action shape to your orchestration.

1. Open the project containing the orchestration.

2. Open the orchestration.

3. Select the Parallel Action shape from the Toolbox and drag it to the appropriate location within the orchestration.

4. Select the Parallel Action shape and update its properties.

   - Change the default name if desired.

   - Add a description if desired.

   - Set the Report To Analyst property. Leave the property as True if you would like the shape to be visible to the Visual Business Analyst Tool.

5. To add an additional branch, right-click the Parallel Action shape and select New Parallel Branch.

■**Note** To delete a branch, right-click the branch and select Delete. To delete the Parallel Action shape, right-click the shape and select Delete.

How It Works

You can use the Parallel Action shape within an orchestration to create concurrent processing. Care should be taken when accessing data from within parallel actions to avoid contention or deadlock situations. This can also be avoided by using synchronized scopes in conjunction with parallel actions. Additionally, if an orchestration is terminated from within a branch of a Parallel Action shape, the process will terminate regardless of the status of the processing within the other parallel branches.

4-11. Using the Loop Shape

Problem

You need to repeat a series of steps in an orchestration until a certain condition is met.

Solution

You can use the Loop shape in a BizTalk orchestration, in a manner similar to using a loop in any programming language, such as this looping logic:

```
int a = 0;
while(a < 3)
{
  System.Console.WriteLine(a);
  a = a + 1;
}
```

As an example, the following steps show how to implement a loop that terminates after a counter variable has been incremented to a certain value. The orchestration will loop three times, logging its progress to the Windows Event Viewer.

■**Note** The example demonstrates a complete orchestration that could be called from another orchestration using the Call or Start Orchestration shape. To make this a stand-alone orchestration, simply add a Receive shape as the first step and bind it to a port.

---

1. In an empty orchestration, create a new variable called `intCount`. Make it of type `Int32`. This will represent the loop counter.

2. Drop an Expression shape on the design surface. Rename this shape to `Init_Count`. Then double-click the shape and type in the following code:

   ```
   //initialize counter
   intCount = 0;
   ```

3. Drop a Loop shape below the Init_Count shape. Double-click the Loop shape and enter the following code (note there is no semicolon):

```
//loop while count is less than 3
intCount < 3
```

4. Drop another Expression shape inside the Loop shape and rename it Increase_Count. Enter the following code:

```
//increase counter
intCount = intCount + 1;
//log to the event viewer
System.Diagnostics.EventLog.WriteEntry("Count",
System.Convert.ToString(intCount));
```

The orchestration is shown in Figure 4-25.

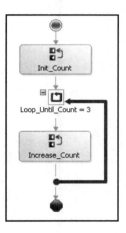

Figure 4-25. *Loop shape with counter*

How It Works

The Loop shape has many applications, from looping through XML documents to supplementing the Listen shape, exception handling routines, and so on. Orchestrations can mimic the behavior of long-running Windows services with the proper placement of a Loop shape. For example, if you need to poll for data on a timed interval, you could set up an orchestration to do this. An initial Receive shape would instantiate the orchestration and immediately enter a loop. Once in the loop, it would never exit, looping every [x] number of minutes to reexecute a series of steps. The orchestration would be long-running, and would never end until terminated manually. An example of this type of orchestration is shown in Figure 4-26.

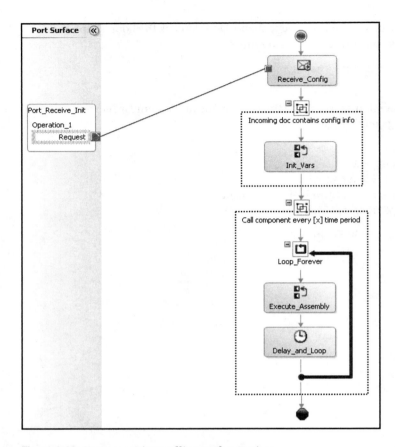

Figure 4-26. *Long-running polling orchestration*

4-12. Using the Transform Shape

Problem

You would like to transform an XML message, or multiple XML messages, into the format of another specified XML schema.

Solution

Using the Transform shape within the BizTalk Orchestration Designer allows you to transform XML messages into the format of another specified XML schema. As an example, assume an orchestration message (Customer schema) requires transformation (mapping) in preparation for a publication to another line-of-business application.

```
<Customer>
  <FirstName> </FirstName>
  <LastName> </LastName>
  <MiddleInit> </MiddleInit>
  <Age></Age>
```

```
  <Address>
  <AddrLine1> </AddrLine1>
  <AddrLine1> </AddrLine1>
  <AddrLine1> </AddrLine1>
  <Zip> </Zip>
  <State> </State>
  <Country></Country>
  </Address>
</Customer>
```

In this example, the outbound specification (`CustomerRecord`) has a different structure and form than that required by the line-of-business application.

```
<CustomerRecord >
  <Name> </Name>
  <MiddleInit> </MiddleInit>
  <Address> </Address>
  <Zip> </Zip>
  <State> </State>
  <Country> </Country>
  <DateTime> </DateTime>
</CustomerRecord>
```

To use the Transform shape within the Orchestration Designer, follow these steps:

1. Open the BizTalk project that contains the orchestration.

2. Ensure that two orchestration messages have been created. The `msgCustomers` message should reference the `Customer` schema, and the `msgCustomerRecords` message should reference the `CustomerRecord` schema.

3. Drag a Transform shape from the BizTalk Orchestrations section of the Toolbox. Place the shape under the Receive shape on the design surface. This automatically creates a Construct Message container and a Transform shape.

4. Click the exclamation mark on the Transform message shape (tool tip), within the Construct Message boundary.

5. Click the missing or invalid mapping configuration value in the drop-down list. The Transform Configuration dialog box will appear.

6. In the Enter Configuration Information Input section of the Transform Configuration dialog box, select the Existing Map radio button. (The New Map option allows you to configure the Construct shape by creating a new map.)

7. For the Fully Qualified Map Name Input option, select the map desired for the transformation. In this example, the `Transform_Sample.mapCustomer` map was selected.

8. Under the `Transform` node, select Source. Then click the `Source_Transform` input and select the `msgCustomers` orchestration message. This is the orchestration message assigned to the orchestration and is the same schema as that of the inbound map: `Transform_Sample.mapCustomer`.

9. Under the `Transform` node, select Destination. Then click the `Destination_Transform` input and select the `msgCustomerRecords` orchestration message. This is the orchestration message assigned to the orchestration and is the same schema as that of the outbound map: `Transform_Sample.mapCustomer`. Figure 4-27 shows the completed configuration.

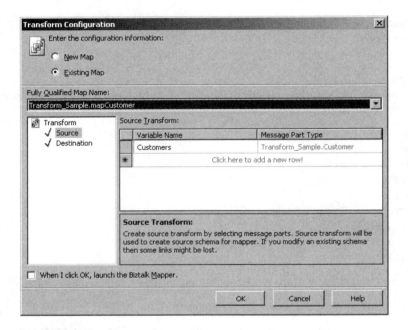

Figure 4-27. *Transform Configuration dialog box*

10. Click OK to complete the configuration of the Transform shape. Notice that the Construct Message shape is automatically configured with the `Messages Constructed` property of `CustomerRecords`. This indicates that the message constructed in the message transform is that of the destination schema specified in the transform map.

How It Works

The Transform shape allows you to map messages from one format to another within the BizTalk Orchestration Designer. This functionality assists in addressing common enterprise integration challenges, where destination processes and systems require a different format to that specified by the source process or system.

The Transform shape allows the assignment of an existing map or the creation of a new map within the Transform Configuration dialog box. Also, you can transform one or multiple source messages into one or multiple destination formats. To enable this, create a new map within the Transform shape configuration, by specifying multiple input messages and/or multiple destination messages. This will automatically create a map with the specified source and destination messages. This capability is useful when you need to partition message calls for the destination process or system. Figure 4-28 illustrates a BizTalk map with multiple messages.

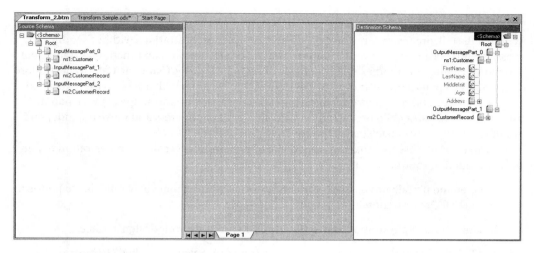

Figure 4-28. *Multiple message mapping*

■**Note** Native multiple message mapping can be done only inside an orchestration.

Message transformation may be required to perform deterministic data enrichment, required by the destination system. For example, this scenario is very common within the enterprise resource planning (ERP) application paradigm, where target integration processes (for example purchase orders, advance shipment notices, and invoices) require additional information to persist and update ERP process information based on the process and source context of a message.

A further consideration of using the Transform shape is that of implementing exception handling. By using the Transform shape in conjunction with a Scope shape, you can handle exceptions. Based on message transformation failure, orchestration logic can be implemented to take a course of action to handle the exception. This approach is different from that of implementing mapping within send or receive ports. Here, exceptions must be handled by the failure context of the port object.

Message transformation and message mapping are fundamental requirements for any enterprise integration platform, and BizTalk enables this capability via its mapping and orchestration tool set.

4-13. Using the Call Orchestration and Start Orchestration Shapes

Problem

Within a BizTalk orchestration, you would like to reuse common process logic across BizTalk processes.

Solution

Within a BizTalk orchestration, you can call or start other orchestrations without sending a message outside an orchestration's context. BizTalk orchestrations can function as traditional functions, calling one another synchronously or asynchronously. Using the Call Orchestration shape allows a parent orchestration to call a child orchestration with a set of parameters and receive an output back (synchronous). Using the Start Orchestration shape allows a parent orchestration to call a child orchestration with any set of parameters and move on, independent of receiving a result back (asynchronous).

As an example, assume that you would like to synchronously call an orchestration to perform a validation routine on a message.

1. Open the BizTalk project that contains the orchestration that you would like to perform the Call Orchestration functionality.

2. Drag a Call Orchestration shape from the Toolbox onto your design surface.

3. Click the exclamation mark on the shape (tool tip). Select No Called Orchestration - Click to Configure. The Call Orchestration Configuration dialog box appears.

4. In the Call Orchestration Configuration dialog box, select the orchestration you wish to call, as shown in Figure 4-29. In this dialog box, you can also select parameters that can be passed by an orchestration. Parameters are passed in the form of .NET variables. Only orchestration types that have `Activation` set to `False`—that is, only orchestrations that are invoked from another process—will be available for selection. In this instance, this is the calling orchestration rather than message instantiation.

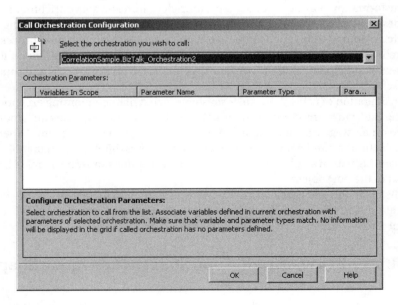

Figure 4-29. *Call Orchestration Configuration dialog box*

5. Click OK to complete the Call Orchestration shape configuration.

How It Works

Orchestration shapes in the BizTalk Orchestration Designer allow for the calling of other orchestrations synchronously or asynchronously. The choice of shape depends on the scenario and design requirements specified for the operating solution.

Calling an orchestration synchronously gives you the ability to nest functionality, similar to calling a method synchronously in any programming language. Calling an orchestration asynchronously allows an orchestration's functionality to be abstracted and performed independently without creating dependencies on the calling and invoking orchestration process.

In addition to calling an orchestration, you can optionally pass parameters to the calling orchestration. Parameters can be used to complement or aid in message processing without the need for custom code development to construct process-centric message context logic. To achieve this within a BizTalk orchestration, parameters are defined in the form of .NET BizTalk type variables. For example, messages, variables, and correlation sets are all BizTalk type variables eligible to passed with the calling orchestration.

4-14. Configuring Basic Correlations

Problem

You need to send a message out of an orchestration and receive a response back into the same orchestration instance.

Solution

You can use a correlation set to tell an orchestration to accept only messages that have the same information as a message sent by the orchestration. As an example, suppose you have a customer support website where customers can place support requests and expect a response to appear on the website within two days. When a customer places a request, the website sends a support request message containing a unique SupportID to BizTalk, which BizTalk forwards to a customer relationship management (CRM) system. Once support personnel monitoring the CRM system respond to the customer request, the response containing the same SupportID goes through BizTalk and posts to the customer support website for the customer to view.

Occasionally, the support personnel cannot respond within two days, either because the request is not clear or because it is an extraordinarily tough request. When support personnel cannot solve the customer's request in time, the business policy is to elevate the request to a special support team that will work one-on-one with the customer to help with the problem. Unfortunately, the CRM system does not have the functionality to escalate the support request after the standard time period. However, fortunately for your customers, BizTalk can implement the business process and coordinate these two messages easily using correlation sets.

The same orchestration instance that forwards the request to the CRM system must receive the correlating response. In this example, BizTalk will know to receive the response with the same SupportID as the message forwarded to the other system.

1. Create an orchestration that defines the basic flow of messages. Figure 4-30 illustrates a basic message flow where the orchestration receives a message, forwards the message on to another system, and waits for a response. If the orchestration does not receive a response within a specified amount of time, the orchestration sends the original message to another location for higher priority processing.

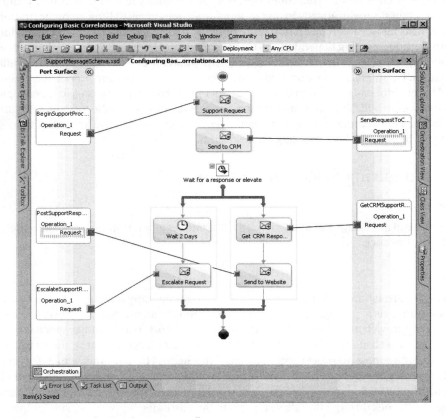

Figure 4-30. *Defining the message flow*

2. A correlation type defines the information that BizTalk uses to decide which orchestration instance gets the response. To create the correlation type, in the Orchestration View window, right-click Correlation Types and select New Correlation Type, as shown in Figure 4-31. The Correlation Properties dialog box appears.

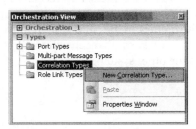

Figure 4-31. *Creating the correlation type*

3. In the Correlation Properties dialog box, select the promoted property that defines the correlation information and click the Add button. In this example, select the SupportID promoted property of the SupportMessage schema, as shown in Figure 4-32. Select OK to complete the creation of the new correlation type and rename it to SupportIDType.

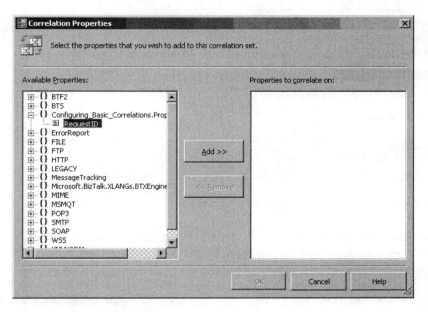

Figure 4-32. *Defining the members of the correlation type*

Note While a correlation set type can contain any promoted property, it cannot contain distinguished fields. See Recipe 1-3 for more information about promoted properties.

---

4. To create the correlation set, right-click Correlation Sets in the Orchestration View window and select New Correlation Set, as shown in Figure 4-33.

Figure 4-33. *Creating the correlation set*

5. In the Properties window, change the name of the new correlation set to SupportIDCorrelation and set the correlation type to the SupportIDType created in steps 2 and 3, as shown in Figure 4-34.

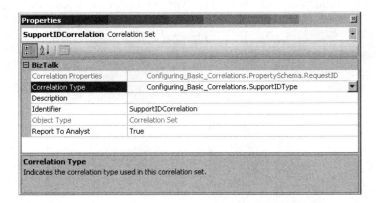

Figure 4-34. *Setting the correlation set properties*

6. Right-click the Send to CRM shape in the orchestration and select Properties. In the Properties window, set the Initializing Correlation Sets property to SupportIDCorrelation, as shown in Figure 4-35.

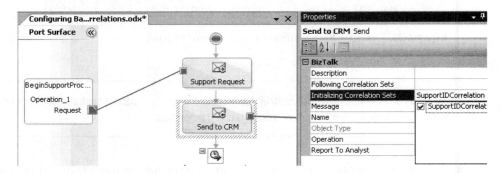

Figure 4-35. *Initializing the correlation set*

7. Right-click the Get CRM Response shape and select Properties. In the Properties window, set the Following Correlation Sets property to SupportIDCorrelation, as shown in Figure 4-36. This ensures that the orchestration will accept only messages with the same information at runtime, which is the specific support identifier in this example. While sending the outbound message, BizTalk creates an instance subscription with the properties of the correlation set to receive the correlated inbound message.

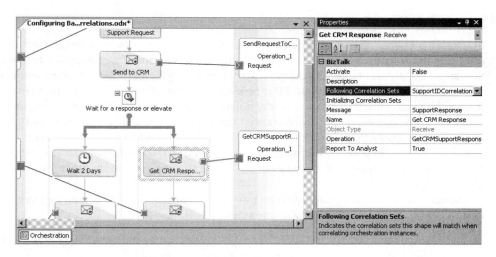

Figure 4-36. *Following the initialized correlation set*

How It Works

The orchestration in Figure 4-30 defines the basic flow of messages that BizTalk needs to coordinate. However, the time between when BizTalk sends the support message to the CRM system and receives a response could be as long as two days. You would expect that there could be any number of outstanding customer support requests during two days. Moreover, because there are many support requests sent to the CRM system, there would be many BizTalk orchestrations concurrently waiting for a response. Further, suppose that there is one request that has already taken over a day of research, when a new one arrives that will take only a few minutes to handle. BizTalk creates a new orchestration instance to forward each message to the CRM system, but how will BizTalk know which orchestration instance should receive the response message?

By using a correlation set, you can tell an orchestration to accept only messages that have the same information as a message sent by the orchestration. A *correlation set* is a container for holding information of a particular correlation type. A *correlation type* defines the correlation set, telling BizTalk the fields in a message that will create the correlation set. In this example, we have only one SupportID to keep track of, so we create only one correlation set. When BizTalk initially sends the support request to the CRM system, the orchestration instance initializes the correlation set containing the SupportID to keep track of the specific SupportID in the messages. The action receiving the response from the CRM system follows the same correlation set, meaning that the orchestration instance will accept only messages with the same SupportID as the message sent to the CRM system.

4-15. Maintaining Message Order

Problem

You are implementing an integration point where message order must be maintained. Messages must be delivered from your source system to your destination system in first-in/first-out (FIFO) sequence.

Solution

In scenarios where FIFO-ordered delivery is required, *sequential convoys* handle the *race condition* that occurs as BizTalk attempts to process subscriptions for messages received at the same time. Ordered message delivery is a common requirement that necessitates the use of sequential convoys. For example, FIFO processing of messages is usually required for financial transactions. It is easy to see why ordered delivery is required when looking at a simple example of a deposit and withdrawal from a bank account. If a customer has $0.00 in her account, makes a deposit of $10.00, and then makes a withdrawal of $5.00, it is important that these transactions are committed in the correct order. If the withdrawal transaction occurs first, the customer will likely be informed that she has insufficient funds, even though she has just made her deposit.

Sequential convoys are implemented by message correlation and ordered delivery flags in BizTalk Server, as outlined in the following steps.

1. Open the project that contains the schema. (We assume that an XSD schema used to define a financial transaction message is already created.)

2. Add a new orchestration to the project and give it a descriptive name. In our example, the orchestration is named SequentialConvoyOrchestration.

3. Create a new message, and specify the name and type. In our example, we create a message named FinancialTransactionMessage, which is defined by the FinancialTransactionSchema schema.

4. In the Orchestration View window, expand the Types node of the tree view so that the Correlation Types folder is visible.

5. Right-click the Correlation Types folder and select New Correlation Type, which creates a correlation type and launches the Correlation Properties dialog box.

6. In the Correlation Properties dialog box, select the properties that the convoy's correlation set will be based on, as shown in Figure 4-37. In our example, we select the BTS.ReceivePortName property, which indicates which receive port the message was received through.

7. Click the new correlation type and give it a descriptive name in the Properties window. In our example, the correlation type is named ReceivePortNameCorrelationType.

8. In the Orchestration View window, right-click the Correlation Set folder, select New Correlation Set, and specify a name and correlation type, as shown in Figure 4-38. In our example, we create a correlation set named ReceivePortNameCorrelationSet and select ReceivePortNameCorrelationType.

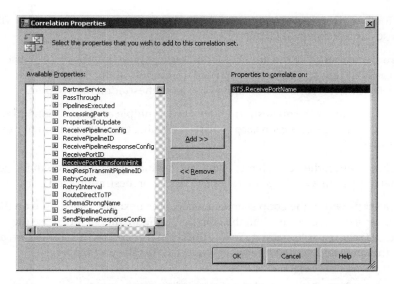

Figure 4-37. *Configuring a correlation type for a sequential convoy*

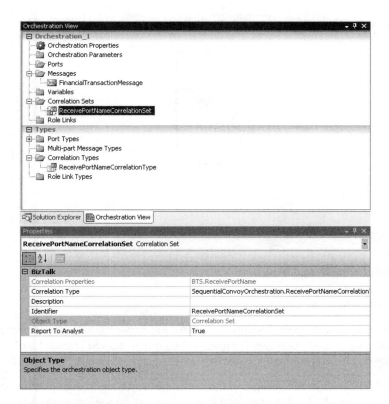

Figure 4-38. *Configuring a correlation set for a sequential convoy*

9. From the Toolbox, drag the following onto the design surface in top-down order. The final orchestration is shown in Figure 4-39.

- Receive shape to receive the initial order message. Configure this shape to use the FinancialTransactionMessage, activate the orchestration, initialize ReceivePortNameCorrelationSet, and to use an orchestration receive port.

- Loop shape to allow the orchestration to receive multiple messages. Configure this shape with the expression Loop == true (allowing the orchestration to run in perpetuity).

- Send shape within the Loop shape, to deliver the financial transaction message the destination system. Configure this shape to use an orchestration send port.

- Receive shape within the Loop shape, to receive the next message (based on the order messages were received) in the convoy. Configure this shape to use the FinancialTransactionMessage, to follow the ReceivePortNameCorrelationSet, and to use the same orchestration receive port as the first Receive shape.

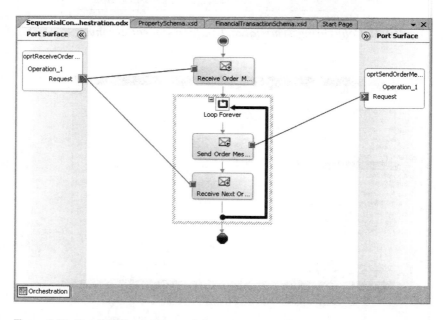

Figure 4-39. *Configuring a sequential convoy*

10. Build and deploy the BizTalk project.

11. Create a receive port and receive location to receive messages from the source system. In our solution, we receive messages from an MSMQ queue named TransactionIn. Configure the receive adapter to use Ordered Processing, as shown in Figure 4-40.

12. Create a send port to deliver messages to the destination system. In our solution, we send messages to an MSMQ queue named TransactionOut. In the Transport Advanced Options section of the Send Port Properties dialog box, select the Ordered Delivery option, as shown in Figure 4-41.

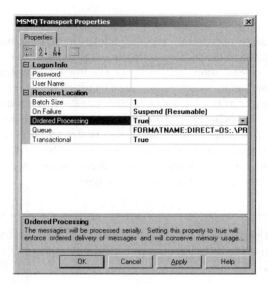

Figure 4-40. *Configuring an ordered delivery receive location*

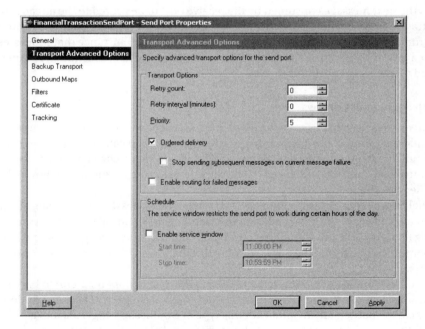

Figure 4-41. *Configuring an ordered delivery send port*

13. Bind the orchestration to the receive and send ports, configure the host for the orchestration, and start the orchestration.

How It Works

In this solution, we show how a convoy can be used to sequentially handle messages within an orchestration. The sequential convoy consists of the ReceivePortNameCorrelationSet and the ordered delivery flags specified on the receive location and send port. The first Receive shape initializes the correlation set, which is based on the receive port name by which the order was consumed. Initializing a correlation set instructs BizTalk Server to associate the correlation type data with the orchestration instance. This allows BizTalk to route all messages that have identical correlation type criteria (in our case, all messages consumed by the receive port bound to the orchestration) to the same instance. The Ordered Processing flag further instructs BizTalk Server to maintain order when determining which message should be delivered next to the orchestration. (See Recipe 4-14 for more information about correlation types.)

■**Note** The adapter used to receive messages into sequential convoy orchestrations must implement ordered delivery. Currently, the SQL, MSMQ, MSMQT, and MQ Series receive adapters support ordered delivery.

The Send shape in the orchestration delivers the financial transaction message to a destination system for further processing. The second Receive shape follows the correlation set, which allows the next message consumed by the receive port to be routed to the already running orchestration instance. Both the Send and second Receive shapes are contained within a loop, which runs in perpetuity. This results in a single orchestration instance that processes all messages for a given correlation set, in sequential order. This type of orchestration is sometimes referred to as a *singleton* orchestration.

Working with Sequential Convoys

The term *convoy set* is used to describe the correlation sets used to enforce convoy message handling. While our example used only a single correlation set, you can use multiple correlation sets to implement a sequential convoy. Regardless of how many correlation sets are used, sequential convoy sets must be initialized by the same Receive shape, and then followed by a subsequent Receive shape.

Sequential convoys can also accept untyped messages (messages defined as being of type XmlDocument). You can see how this is important by extending the financial transaction scenario, and assuming that a deposit and withdrawal are actually different message types (defined by different schemas). In this case, a message type of XmlDocument would be used on the convoy Receive shapes.

When troubleshooting issues with sequential convoys, it can often be useful to have a view into the subscriptions that are created in the MessageBox database. The Subscription Viewer utility can be particularly helpful with this type of troubleshooting. This tool is included with the BizTalk Server SDK, and is located in <Install Path>\SDK\Utilities\ BTSSubscriptionViewer.btq. The Subscription Viewer displays subscriptions for message types, including the destinations to which they are routed and any specific values on which they are based.

Fine-Tuning Sequential Convoys

While our example does implement a sequential convoy, you can fine-tune the solution to handle sequential processing in a more efficient and graceful manner. As it stands now, the SequentialConvoyOrchestration handles each message received from the source MSMQ queue in order. This essentially single-threads the integration point, significantly decreasing throughput. Single-threading does achieve FIFO processing, but it is a bit heavy-handed. In our example, *all* transactions do not have to be delivered in order—just those for a particular customer. By modifying the convoy set to be based on a customer ID field in the financial transaction schema (instead of the receive port name), you can allow transactions for different customers to be handled simultaneously. This change would take advantage of BizTalk Server's ability to process multiple messages simultaneously, increasing the performance of your solution.

■**Note** In this scenario, you must use a pipeline that promotes the customer ID property (such as the Xml-Receive pipeline) on the receive location bound to the sequential convoy orchestration. The PassThru receive pipeline cannot be used in this scenario. See Recipe 1-3 for more information about property promotion.

Changing the convoy set to include a customer ID field would also impact the number of orchestrations running in perpetuity. Each new customer ID would end up creating a new orchestration, which could result in hundreds, if not thousands, of constantly running instances. This situation is not particularly desirable from either a performance or management perspective. To address this issue, you can implement a timeout feature allowing the orchestration to terminate if subsequent messages are not received within a specified period of time. Take the following steps to implement this enhancement. The updated orchestration is shown in Figure 4-42.

1. Add a Listen shape in between the Send shape and second Receive shape.

2. Move the second Receive shape to the left-hand branch of the Listen shape.

3. Add a Delay shape to the right-hand branch of the Listen shape. Configure this shape to delay for the appropriate timeout duration. In our example, we set the timeout to be 10 seconds by using the following value for the Delay property:

   ```
   new System.TimeSpan(0,0,0,10)
   ```

4. Add an Expression shape directly below the Delay shape. Configure this shape to exit the convoy by using the following expression:

   ```
   Loop = false;
   ```

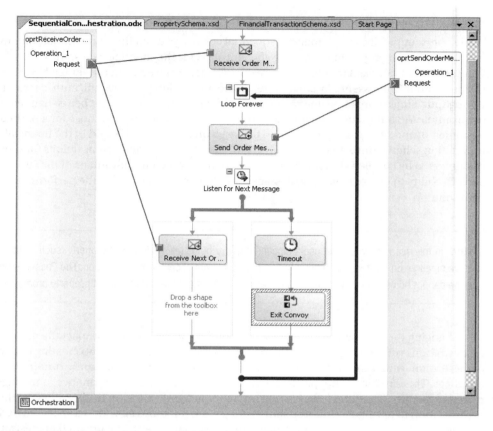

Figure 4-42. *Configuring a terminating sequential convoy*

Finally, you can enhance the solution to ensure that messages are successfully delivered to the destination system before processing subsequent messages. In the current solution, messages are sent out of the orchestration to the MessageBox database via the orchestration port. Once this happens, the orchestration continues; there is no indication that the message was actually delivered to its end destination. For example, if the destination MSMQ queue was momentarily offline, a message may be suspended while subsequent messages may be delivered successfully. Take the following steps to implement this enhancement. The updated orchestration is shown in Figure 4-43.

1. Change the orchestration send port's Delivery Notification property to Transmitted.

2. Add a Scope shape directly above the Send shape.

3. Move the Send shape inside the Scope shape.

4. Add an exception handler by right-clicking the Scope shape. Configure this shape to have an `Exception Object Type` property of `Microsoft.XLANGs.BaseTypes.DeliveryFailureException`. Enter a descriptive name for the `Exception Object Name` property.

5. Add an Expression shape inside the exception handler block added in the previous step. Configure this shape to appropriately handle delivery failure exceptions. In our solution, we simply write the event to the trace log via the following code:

```
System.Diagnostics.Trace.Write("Delivery Failure Exception Occurred - " +
deliveryFailureExc.Message);
```

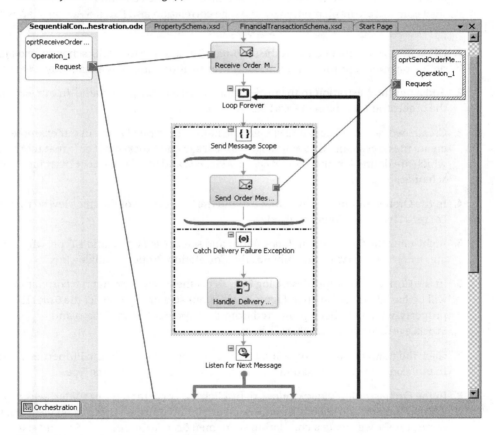

Figure 4-43. *Capturing delivery failure exceptions*

4-16. Configuring Parallel Convoys

Problem

You are implementing a data aggregation integration point, which requires data to be retrieved from multiple systems. Each source system publishes messages, and a message from each system must be received before further processing can take place.

Solution

A *parallel convoy* is a business process (orchestration) that receives multiple messages in parallel (at the same time) that relate to each other. Parallel convoys handle the *race condition* that occurs as BizTalk attempts to process subscriptions for messages received at the same time.

A common scenario requiring parallel convoys is where multiple messages for a specific event must be received before a business process can start. As an example, suppose your company's policy allows an order to be shipped only once payment has been approved and stock level has been verified. Payment approval comes from a financial system, and stock-level information comes from an inventory system. Once both systems publish their respective messages for a specific order, that order can be delivered to the customer.

Parallel convoys are implemented by message correlation and Parallel Action shapes in BizTalk Server, as shown in the following steps.

1. Open the project that contains the schemas. (We assume that XSD schemas used to define payment approval and stock-level verification messages are already created.)

2. Add a new orchestration to the project and give it a descriptive name. In our example, the orchestration is named ParallelConvoyOrchestration.

3. Create two new messages and specify the name and type of each. In our example, we create messages named PaymentApprovalMessage and StockLevelConfirmationMessage, which are defined by the PaymentApprovalSchema and StockLevelConfirmationSchema schemas, respectively.

4. In the Orchestration View window, expand the Types node of the tree view so that the Correlation Types folder is visible.

5. Right-click the Correlation Types folder and select New Correlation Type, which creates a correlation type and launches the Correlation Properties dialog box.

6. In the Correlation Properties dialog box, select the properties that the correlation will be based on, as shown in Figure 4-44. In our scenario, we select the OrderID property, which has been promoted from the PaymentApprovalSchema and StockLevelConfirmationSchema schemas.

7. Click the new correlation type and give it a descriptive name in the Properties window. In our example, the correlation type is named OrderIDCorrelationType.

8. In the Orchestration View window, right-click the Correlation Set folder, select New Correlation Set, and specify a name and correlation type, as shown in Figure 4-45. In our example, we create a correlation set named OrderIDCorrelationSet and select OrderIDCorrelationType.

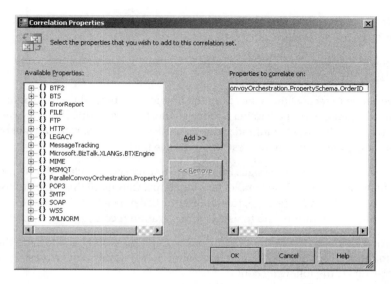

Figure 4-44. *Configuring a correlation type for a parallel convoy*

Figure 4-45. *Configuring a correlation set for a parallel convoy*

9. From the Toolbox, drag the following onto the design surface in top-down order. The final orchestration is shown in Figure 4-46.

- Parallel Actions shape to receive the response from the financial and inventory systems.

- Receive shape to receive messages from the financial system. Place this shape on the left-hand branch of the Parallel Actions shape. Configure this shape to use the `PaymentApprovalMessage`, to initialize the `OrderIDCorrelationSet`, to activate the orchestration, and to use an orchestration receive port.

- Receive shape to receive messages from the inventory system. Place this shape on the right-hand branch of the Parallel Actions shape. Configure this shape to use the `StockLevelConfirmationMessage`, to initialize the `OrderIDCorrelationSet`, to activate the orchestration, and to use an orchestration receive port.

- Expression shape to deliver the ship the order. Configure this shape to send the order to the appropriate recipient. In our solution, we simply write a message to the trace log via the following code:

```
System.Diagnostics.Trace.Write("Shipping Order with ID = " +
    PaymentApprovalMessage
    (ParallelConvoyOrchestration.PropertySchema.OrderID));
```

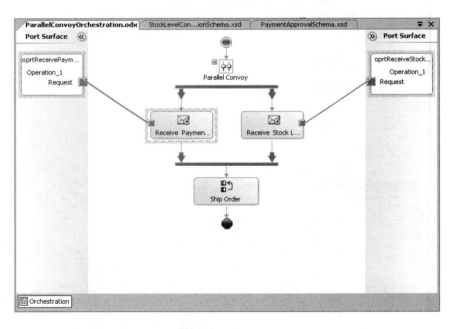

Figure 4-46. *Configuring a parallel convoy*

How It Works

In this solution, we show how a convoy can be used to concurrently handle messages within an orchestration. The parallel convoy, also referred to as a *concurrent convoy*, consists of the OrderIDCorrelationSet and the Parallel Actions shape. Each Receive shape in the Parallel Actions shape initializes the correlation set, which is based on the order ID. Initializing a correlation set instructs BizTalk Server to associate the correlation type data with the orchestration instance. This allows BizTalk to route all messages that have identical correlation type criteria (in our case, all messages with a specific order ID) to the same instance.

Each of the Receive shapes has its Activate property set to True and its Initializing Correlation configured to the same correlation set. The Receive shape that receives the first message will handle the activation of the orchestration instance and the initializing of the correlation set. The second Receive shape will not activate a new orchestration instance (even though its Activate property is set to True), and will actually follow the correlation set that the other Receive shape initialized.

Based on this example, messages for two order IDs would be handled in the following manner:

1. A payment approval message for order ID 1 is received, which instantiates orchestration instance 1.

2. A stock-level confirmation message for order ID 2 is received, which instantiates orchestration instance 2.

3. A payment approval message for order ID 2 is received, which is correlated and delivered to orchestration 2. The orchestration continues processing, ships order ID 2, and terminates successfully.

4. A stock-level confirmation message for order ID 1 is received, which is correlated and delivered to orchestration 1. The orchestration continues processing, ships order ID 1, and terminates successfully.

While our example used only a single correlation set, multiple correlation sets can be used to implement a parallel convoy. Parallel convoys are defined as having a convoy set that is initialized on multiple branches of a Parallel Actions shape within an orchestration. Regardless of how many correlation sets are used, if multiple Receive shapes initialize a convoy set in a Parallel Actions shape, the same correlation sets must be initialized on all of the Receive shapes.

4-17. Using XPath Queries on Messages

Problem

You need to get and/or set values in a message within an orchestration. There are a number of nodes that cannot be promoted because they are not unique, and you need to be able to access these values.

Solution

To access values in a message, you can use XPath. XPath queries are used to navigate the tree of a given XML document, and are typically used within orchestration Message Assignment and Expression shapes. BizTalk XPath queries require two parameters: the first parameter references the XML message, and the second is the query path.

As an example, assume that an orchestration message called msgDemo contains the XML shown in Listing 4-3.

Listing 4-3. *Sample XML Instance for XPath Query Example*

```
<ns0:NewHireList xmlns:ns0="http://SampleSolution.NewHireList">
  <DateTime>1999-04-05T18:00:00</DateTime>
  <ns1:Person xmlns:ns1="http://SampleSolution.Person">
    <ID>1</ID>
    <Name>S. Jonesy</Name>
    <Role>Embedded Programmer</Role>
    <Age>40</Age>
  </ns1:Person>
  <ns1:Person xmlns:ns1="http://SampleSolution.Person">
    <ID>2</ID>
    <Name>D. Hurley</Name>
    <Role>Artist</Role>
    <Age>45</Age>
  </ns1:Person>
</ns0:NewHireList>
```

The following steps demonstrate getting values, getting a node count, getting an entire XML node, and setting values.

1. To get the value of the <DateTime> element, use the following XPath query. The output of this query is 1999-04-05T18:00:00.

    ```
    xpath(msgDemo,"string(//*[local-name()='DateTime'])")
    ```

2. To get the value of the <Name> element that is in the same <Person> node as the <ID> which is equal to 2, use the following XPath query. The output of this query will be D. Hurley.

    ```
    xpath(msgDemo,"string(//*[local-name()='Name' and ../*
    [local-name()='ID'] = '2'])")
    ```

3. To get the count of <Person> nodes within the document, use the following XPath query. The output of this query is 2.

    ```
    xpath(msgDemo,"count(//*[local-name()='Person'])")
    ```

4. To get the entire XML node representation of the second <Person> node, use the following XPath query. Note that this requires formatting the query using the System.String.Format function. The result of this query will be a full XML node.

    ```
    strXPathQuery = System.String.Format("//*[local-name()='Person'][{0}]",2);
    xmlDoc = xpath(msgIncoming,strXPathQuery);
    ```

```
<ns1:Person xmlns:ns1="http://SampleSolution.Person">
 <ID>2</ID>
 <Name>D. Hurley</Name>
 <Role>Artist</Role>
 <Age>45</Age>
</ns1:Person>
```

5. To set the value of the `<DateTime>` element, use the following XPath query. Note that this must be done in a Message Assignment shape, since the value of the message is changing. The message used must first be constructed.

```
xpath(msgDemo, "//*[local-name()='DateTime']") = strDateTime;
```

How It Works

This recipe's solution demonstrated several of the many uses of XPath. One question that often arises is when to use XPath vs. when to use promoted properties. The ability to promote properties is limited. Elements that repeat within a schema cannot be promoted. Only unique values can be promoted. When you need to set the value of repeating nodes, XPath is the quickest and most versatile approach.

4-18. Using Nontransactional Orchestration Scopes

Problem

You need to define how your orchestration behaves under possible exception conditions.

Solution

Any orchestration can have Scope shapes in it. Place other orchestration shapes within the Scope shape to define the expected behavior of the orchestration. If BizTalk encounters an exception performing the steps inside a Scope shape, it will jump to separate actions defined in an exception handler. The solution demonstrates how to add exception handling to an orchestration.

1. Create a new orchestration. Drag a Scope shape from the Toolbox onto the orchestration design surface.

2. Right-click the name of the Scope shape and select Properties from the context menu.

3. Set the `Transaction Type` property to `None` and the `Name` property to `Controlled Exceptions Scope`.

4. Right-click the name of the new Scope shape and select New Exception Handler from the context menu, as shown in Figure 4-47.

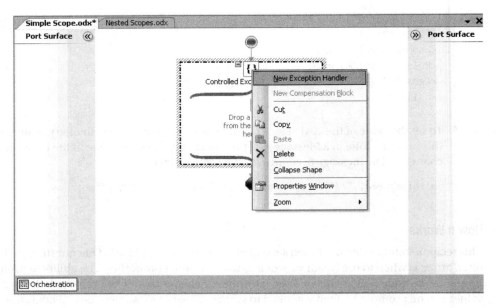

Figure 4-47. *Creating an exception handler*

5. Right-click the name of the exception handler created in the previous step and select Properties Window from the context menu.

6. Set the Exception Object Type property to General Exception and the Name property to Log Exception, as shown in Figure 4-48.

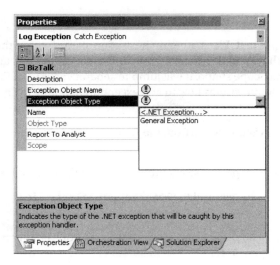

Figure 4-48. *Setting the Exception object type and name*

7. From the Toolbox, drag an Expression shape into the exception handler.

8. Double-click the Expression shape to open the Expression Editor, and add the following code to record the exception.

```
System.Diagnostics.EventLog.WriteEntry("A Simple BizTalk Source",
        "An exception was encountered in my sample orchestration.  ");
```

9. Build the orchestration logic inside the Scope shape. If BizTalk encounters an exception processing the orchestration logic, it will invoke the Expression shape.

How It Works

The BizTalk Orchestration Designer is a development tool. Just as when building a component with any other development tool, exception conditions can occur long after the component is constructed. The developer may misunderstand how the component should behave, or changes to the other systems BizTalk interacts with may cause exception conditions. Regardless of the cause, the developer always needs to plan for the unexpected.

■**Note** In addition to defining how an orchestration reacts to possible exception conditions, orchestration scopes can also define atomic or long-running transactions. See Recipes 4-19 and 4-20 for more information about using transactions in an orchestration.

This recipe demonstrates how to respond to exception conditions by invoking an Expression shape that writes an error message to the Windows application log. However, an exception handler can define more rigorous error-resolution procedures. The compensation block can simply log the exception, can invoke an exception-handling framework, or can invoke another BizTalk orchestration defining a series of resolution actions. In addition, if an orchestration defines the procedures for resolving exceptions, then the BizTalk Business Activity Monitor (BAM) can generate reports on exception-resolution processes.

Error Information

This solution's example uses the default General Exception object type, as shown earlier in Figure 4-48. This is useful when you want to log where and when errors occur, but do not need specific information about the actual errors encountered.

An exception handler can identify more specific error information when the exception handler's Object Type property is set to any class inheriting from System.Exception. When the Object Type is .NET Exception, as shown in Figure 4-49, the exception object can retrieve additional information such as an error message.

Modify the Expression shape as follows to include the error message in the application log entry.

```
System.Diagnostics.EventLog.WriteEntry("A Simple BizTalk Source",
        "An exception was encountered: " + ex.Message);
```

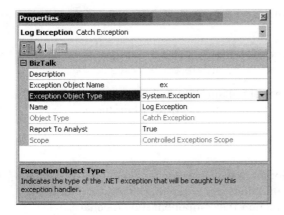

Figure 4-49. *Setting the exception handler type*

Multiple Exception Handlers

A single Scope shape can also specify multiple exception handlers to define different reactions to different exceptions encountered by the orchestration. When the Scope shape encounters an exception, it will check each exception handler from top to bottom. The Scope shape invokes the first exception handler matching the type of exception encountered, and stops looking for a match. Therefore, more specific exception handlers must appear above more general exception handlers, or the general exception handler will handle all errors and the Scope shape will never invoke the specific exception handlers. Define an additional exception handler with the following steps.

1. Define the first exception handler as presented in this recipe's solution.

2. Right-click the name of the Scope shape and select New Exception Handler.

3. Move the handler for the General Exception defined in the solution by selecting the name and dragging the mouse over the lower line defining the new exception handler. The General Exception handler should appear below the new one.

4. Right-click the name of the new exception handler and select Properties Window.

5. Change the Name property to Handle Arithmetic Exception.

6. For the Exception Object Type property, select <.NET Exception...>. In the Select Artifact Type dialog box that appears, select the Arithmetic Exception, as shown in Figure 4-50, and then click OK.

7. Change the Exception Object Name property to ex.

8. Add shapes to the new exception handler to handle arithmetic exceptions specifically, as shown in Figure 4-51.

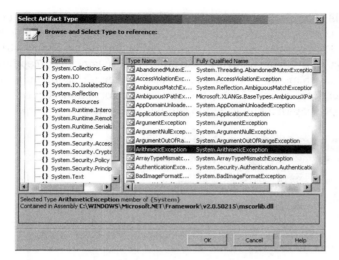

Figure 4-50. *Selecting specific exception types*

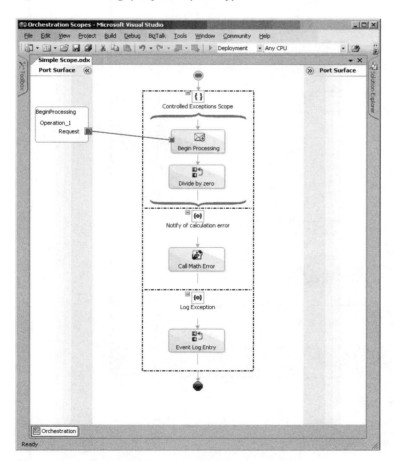

Figure 4-51. *Defining arithmetic exception-specific shapes*

While a Scope shape will invoke only the first exception handler matching the type of exception encountered, sometimes there are consistent actions the orchestration should take for different kinds of errors. For example, what if the orchestration depicted in Figure 4-51 should call the orchestration for resolving math errors in addition to logging the exception to the application log? The Throw shape can propagate an exception from the Scope shape that initially catches it to an outer Scope shape defining the consistent error actions. Figure 4-52 depicts an example of a Scope shape contained within another Scope shape.

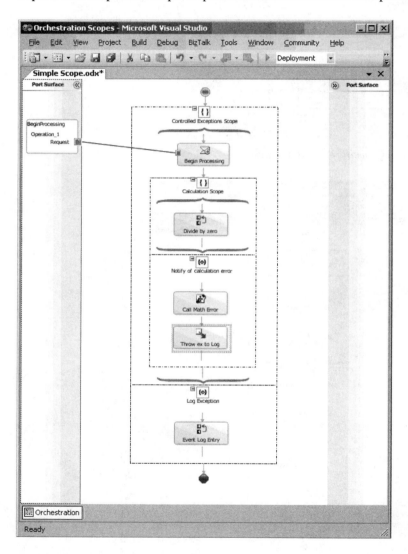

Figure 4-52. *Nested scopes*

4-19. Creating Atomic Scopes

Problem

You are building an orchestration process that contains actions that must complete together as a group or fail as a group.

Solution

BizTalk supports the notion of completing small units of work following the Atomicity, Consistency, Isolation, and Durability (ACID) transaction model. The Atomic Scope shape implements the ACID transaction model. Atomic scopes are the most flexible and restrictive of the transaction models in BizTalk. The use of an atomic scope within BizTalk ensures that a group of steps either succeeds or fails together. The following instructions outline the steps required to create and configure an atomic scope.

1. Open the project containing the orchestration that will contain the atomic scope transaction.

2. Verify the Transaction Type property of the orchestration is set to Long Running. This is required for orchestrations containing atomic scopes.

3. Select and drag the Scope shape from the BizTalk Orchestrations section of the Toolbox to the appropriate location within the orchestration.

■**Note** Atomic scopes may not contain nested Atomic Scope or Long Running Scope shapes.

---

4. Select the Scope shape and update the properties as follows. The shape properties should resemble Figure 4-53.

   • Change the Transaction Type to Atomic.

   • Change the Compensation from Default to Custom if your scope will contain a compensation handler.

   • Change the Isolation Level to the correct value.

   • Change the Name if desired.

   • Set the Report To Analyst property. Leave the property as True if you would like the shape to be visible to the Visual Business Analyst Tool.

   • Change the Retry value from True to False if you do not want the Scope shape to retry in the event of a failure. The Retry value must be set to True if you plan on throwing an exception to cause the atomic scope to retry. However, setting the value to true does not mean the atomic scope will retry by default.

- Change the `Synchronized` value from `False` to `True` if you are using the Atomic Scope shape within a Parallel Actions shape and manipulating the same set of data. (Refer to Recipe 4-10 for more information about the Parallel Actions shape.)

- Change the `Timeout` value if desired. Scope timeouts indicate the period of time to wait (in seconds) before the transaction fails. Atomic scopes that contain a timeout value will stop the transaction and be suspended if the timeout value is reached.

- Change the `Transaction Identifier` if desired.

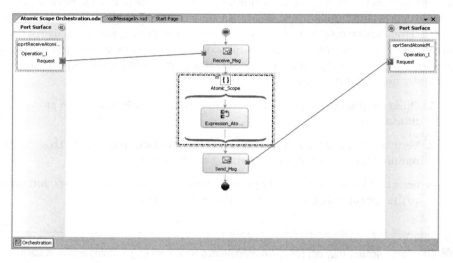

Figure 4-53. *Setting atomic scope properties*

5. Add the appropriate orchestration actions to the Atomic Scope shape. Your orchestration should look like Figure 4-54.

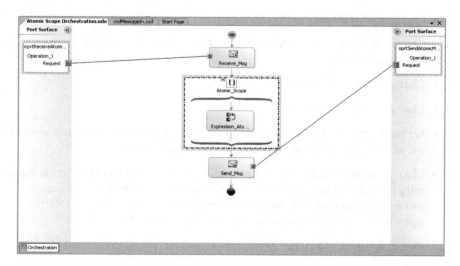

Figure 4-54. *Orchestration with an atomic scope*

How It Works

BizTalk supports the ACID model by providing the following features:

- *Atomicity*: Atomic Scope shapes guarantee all actions within the Scope shape are either performed completely or not performed at all.

- *Consistency*: System properties (messages and variables) are preserved through the transaction. In the situation where an atomic scope cannot be committed and the system properties are updated, then the system properties are rolled back to their previous state.

Note All variables, regardless of whether they are local to scope or global to the orchestration, will be rolled back to their previous state when an atomic scope fails.

- *Isolation*: Each atomic scope allows controlled visibility to other scopes' and transactions' data.

- *Durability*: Once an atomic scope has been committed, the only way the action can be undone is through the use of a BizTalk compensation handler.

Atomic Scope Considerations

Atomic scopes are extremely useful, but there is an associated cost with the use of any transactional model inside an orchestration. Consider the following when deciding whether to use an atomic scope:

- Atomic scopes cannot contain a send and a receive port that are referencing the same two-way request/response orchestration port. For example, if you are referencing an HTTP/SOAP port in your orchestration, you cannot have the Send and Receive shapes in a single Atomic Scope shape. Additionally, you cannot have Send and Receive shapes that implement the same correlation set within the same Atomic Scope shape. The rationale for this is that as soon as context has left the orchestration (a message is sent via a Send shape), the atomic scope action is complete and a response cannot be matched to the request.

- If an Atomic Scope shape contains a Send, Receive, or Start Orchestration shape, BizTalk will wait to perform those actions until the scope has been committed. BizTalk considers the boundary of the transaction to be the point that a message has been committed to the BizTalk MessageBox.

- A single atomic scope is not that expensive in the context to processing of an entire orchestration. However, the use of multiple atomic scopes can be expensive because BizTalk sets a checkpoint before and after an atomic scope is executed. Consider ways to combine multiple atomic scopes into fewer atomic scopes. The checkpoint takes place so that the orchestration can be resumed if it is suspended due to an exception in the atomic scope.

■**Note** Think of a checkpoint as BizTalk serializing its current processing state to persist and prepare for a rollback in the case of an exception in the atomic scope. The serialization and persistence of the current processing state reduces performance incrementally. The more atomic scopes in an orchestration, the more points of persistence that will be created and the greater the overall degradation in the performance of the orchestration.

- An object that is not serializable (does not implement the ISerializable interface or is not marked with a serializable attribute) must be in an atomic scope. For example, if you are using the XmlNodeList object, the variable must be declared local to the scope and referenced within the Atomic Scope shape. The XmlDocument data type is an exception to this rule.

- Using an Atomic Scope shape to perform multiple send operations does not guarantee that the send operations will be rolled back in the case one send fails. For example, if you have two Send shapes each sending a message to a SQL database, if there is a failure in one or both SQL databases, the Atomic Scope shape does not guarantee that the data will be backed out from either database call. BizTalk considers the boundary of a transaction to be the point that a message is committed to the MessageBox. True rollbacks are guaranteed only in true Microsoft Distributed Transaction Coordinator (MSDTC) transactions.

Atomic Scope Benefits

Even though atomic scopes are the more restrictive of the two transaction models, they offer significant benefits over the use of long-running scopes. Atomic scopes allow the specification of an Isolation Level property, as follows:

- Specifying Serializable means that concurrent transactions will not be able to make data modifications until the transaction is committed.

- Specifying Read Committed means that the existing transaction is prevented from accessing data modifications until the transaction is committed.

- Specifying Repeated Read means that read locks are required until the existing transaction is committed.

Atomic scopes also implement a retry capability that is enabled through the use of the Retry flag. An atomic scope will retry if the Scope shape's Retry property is set to True and at least one of the following exceptions occurs:

- Microsoft.XLANG.BaseTypes.RetryTransactionException is thrown or in the event that BizTalk cannot commit the transaction. Additionally, all variables will be reset to their state prior to entry of the scope.

- Microsoft.XLANG.BaseTypes.PersistenceException occurs due to BizTalk's inability to persist state.

■**Note** The Atomic Scope shape will retry 21 times before the orchestration is suspended with a two-second delay. The retry count is not user-configurable, but the two-second delay can be configured by overriding the `DelayFor` public property on `RetryTransactionException`.

Exception Handling

One challenge to using atomic scopes is the fact that you cannot have an exception handler on the Atomic Scope shape itself. Atomic scopes are defined to either succeed or fail, hence there is no direct need to have an exception handler. In the situation where an exception should be caught in an error handler, the items that cause an exception can be enclosed in a nontransactional scope (with an error handler) inside the atomic scope.

Consider the following scenario: you must pass a nonserializable object to a custom assembly that in turn makes a database call. You want to catch any communication exceptions and force the atomic scope to retry. One option for this scenario would be to implement an atomic scope to manipulate the nonserializable object and within that Atomic Scope shape, include a nontransactional Scope shape with an error handler that will throw a `Microsoft.XLANG.BaseTypes.RetryTransactionException`. This scenario would allow you use a nonserializable object and force a retry in the case of a communication problem. Figure 4-55 illustrates the use of a nested nontransactional scope with an error handler inside an Atomic Scope shape.

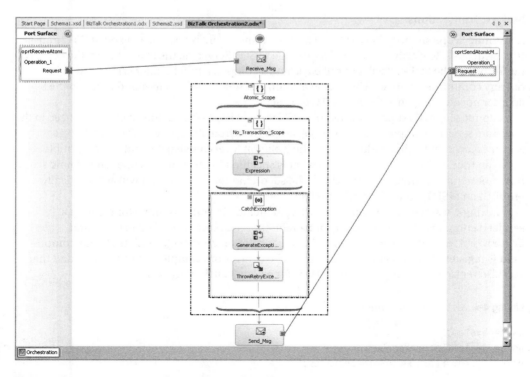

Figure 4-55. *Atomic scope with nested error handler*

Note When throwing a `RetryTransactionException` to perform a retry, validate that conditions have changed so that you do not continually throw a `RetryTransactionException` and create an infinite retry loop.

Compensation Handling

Atomic Scope shapes (as well as other Scope shapes) support the notion of compensation to facilitate undoing a logical piece of work regardless of the successful commit. Suppose that the atomic scope executes and commits successfully, but there is a business-error problem with the message data. The atomic scope, from a technical aspect, executed and committed correctly. However, due to the business validation failing, the transaction must be undone. Compensations allow definition of a process that details how the previously committed atomic transaction is to be rolled back.

The structure of a compensation handler is similar to that of an exception handler but functionally different. BizTalk will use the default compensation handler if no custom compensation handler is defined. The default BizTalk compensation handler calls the compensation blocks of any nested transactions, in reverse order of completion. Compensation handlers must be called explicitly, unlike error handlers, through the use of the Compensation shape. A common use for a compensation handler is to create a message that indicates business data needs to be backed out of a specific system or process.

MSDTC Transactions

An Atomic Scope shape behaves like an MSDTC transaction, but is not an explicit DTC transaction by default. To clarify, if you send a message to SQL Server via the SQL adapter, the actions performed in the SQL call will not roll back, and a compensation handler is required to back out any committed changes. The reason a compensation handler is required is due to the SQL adapter not enrolling in an explicit DTC transaction.

Atomic scopes do support the use of a DTC transaction as long as the objects referenced in the scope are serviced components (COM+ objects) derived from the `System.EnterpriseServices.ServicedComponents` class. Additionally, the isolation levels must agree and be compatible between transaction components and what is specified in the atomic scope. The atomic scope does not require a configuration value to be set on the shape itself, as it will automatically enroll in an MSDTC transaction if possible.

Listing 4-4 serves as an outline for what to include in your assembly for creating a serviced component. Your assembly must reference `System.EnterpriseServices` and `System.Runtime.InteropServices` (for the `Guid` attribute reference). Verify that your component is registered in the Global Assembly Cache (GAC) (for example, using `gacutil`) and that you also register the component in COM+ (for example, using `regsvcs`).

Listing 4-4. *Serviced Component*

```
using System;
using System.EnterpriseServices;
using System.Runtime.InteropServices;
```

```
namespace MSDTCTestLibrary
{
    /// <summary>
    /// Summary description for Class1.
    /// </summary>
    ///
    [Guid("9943FB26-F4F5-4e80-B746-160AB9A6359E")]
    [Transaction(TransactionOption.Required)]
    public class ClassMSDTCTest : ServicedComponent
    {
        public ClassMSDTCTest(){}

        public String Test()
        {
            try
            {
                // Commit the transaction
                ContextUtil.SetComplete();
                return "Test";
            }
            catch (Exception ex)
            {
                // Abort the transaction
                ContextUtil.SetAbort();
                return ex.ToString();
            }

        }

    }
}
```

4-20. Using Long-Running Transactions

Problem

You have separate tasks to accomplish in an orchestration that must all succeed or fail together. These tasks may take a long time to complete.

Solution

Long-running transactions can help ensure a single consistent outcome across multiple BizTalk tasks. As an example, suppose you have a website where customers can make purchases using credit. Creating a new customer involves two steps. First, the customer needs a login to access your website. Second, the customer also needs credit established so he can make purchases. Sometimes your website cannot create a login because the customer has chosen a login already assigned to another customer. Other times, BizTalk cannot establish credit for the customer. If one of these tasks succeeds and the other fails, the user may experience undesirable behavior on your website.

By defining actions to reverse each of the two tasks required in this example, BizTalk can automatically reverse the effects of one task in the event that the other fails. If BizTalk creates a login but cannot establish credit, then BizTalk will detect the failure and invoke the compensation logic to disable the login. If credit is established but BizTalk cannot create the login, BizTalk will invoke the compensation logic to suspend credit.

The following steps demonstrate how to set up a long-running transaction for this example.

1. Create a new BizTalk project and add an orchestration.

2. Right-click the orchestration design surface and select Properties Window.

3. Set the Transaction Type property to Long Running.

4. Place a Receive shape on the design surface with the Activate property set to True. Configure BizTalk to receive a NewCustomerMsg message.

5. Place a Parallel Actions shape under the Receive shape.

6. Place a Scope shape under the left branch of the Parallel Actions shape.

7. Select the icon in the upper-right corner of the Create Login shape, and select Long Running from the menu, as shown in Figure 4-56.

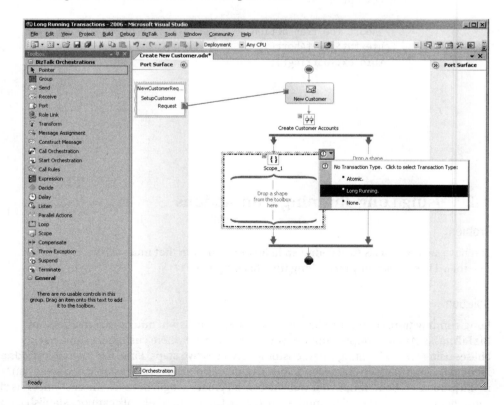

Figure 4-56. *Setting the scope transaction type*

8. Place a Send shape inside the Scope shape.

9. Set the Send shape's `Message` property to `NewCustomerMsg`.

10. Create a one-way send port named `CustomerActivation`.

11. Set the `CustomerActivation` send port's `Delivery Notification` property to `Transmitted`.

■**Note** Use delivery notification to determine if a delivery failure occurs. BizTalk will not complete the long-running transaction until the messages with delivery notification are successfully delivered, and will report an error if any of the messages are suspended.

---

12. Right-click the top portion of the Scope shape and select New Compensation Block from the context menu, as shown in Figure 4-57.

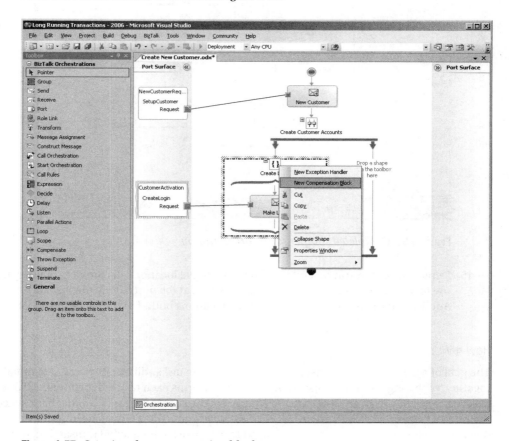

Figure 4-57. *Creating the compensation block*

13. Place a Send shape inside the compensation block, and attach it to a new port. This defines the actions to reverse the transaction if another transaction fails.

14. Repeat steps 6 to 13 to define the Create Credit Account scope. When completed, the orchestration should appear as depicted in Figure 4-58.

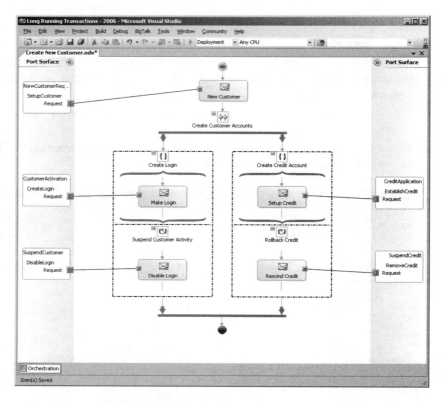

Figure 4-58. *Completed compensating orchestration*

15. Deploy the orchestration and bind the ports to file locations. To simulate delivery failure to the CustomerActivation and CreditApplication ports, deny the BizTalk Application Users group access to the file locations bound to the orchestration ports.

How It Works

The goal of a *transaction* is to ensure that many separate tasks will all either succeed or fail together. With long-running transactions, BizTalk performs each task independently. If one task fails, then BizTalk must roll back the changes of the successful tasks. Rolling back successful tasks because of another's failure is called *compensation*. A BizTalk orchestration can determine when successful transactions need to compensate for a failed transaction, but the BizTalk developer must define the specific compensation logic.

The solution's example consists of two tasks, each with custom compensation logic defined. If BizTalk cannot establish credit for the customer, then the Create Login transaction must compensate by taking actions to disable the login. Similarly, BizTalk compensates the Create Credit Account transaction by taking action to rescind credit. BizTalk will detect the error in the Create Credit Account transaction, and call the compensation logic of all the long-running transactions in the same scope that have completed successfully. If the Create Login transaction also fails, then both transactions arrived at the same result and BizTalk has nothing to compensate for. BizTalk will compensate only long-running transactions that complete successfully.

Long-running transactions are a great way to ensure a consistent outcome under circumstances such as the following:

- Tasks take longer than a split-second to complete.

- Results can be inconsistent for a short while before the compensating logic completes.

- BizTalk needs to send or receive messages with a transport that cannot participate in an atomic transaction, like an ASMX web service.

In addition to long-running transactions, BizTalk scopes can also support atomic transactions. An atomic transaction differs by locking all the resources involved until the transaction knows they can all succeed. If they cannot all succeed, then the transaction reverses all changes before releasing the resources. Because of this locking behavior, atomic transactions should be very quick. A long-running transaction executes each task separately, and follows up with compensating logic if one task encounters an error. This approach allows separate tasks to have different results for a short time while the compensating logic executes, but also allows greater processing flexibility.

4-21. Catching Exceptions Consistently

Problem

You want to be able to catch all exceptions in the same way, and be able to handle retries automatically with a configurable delay. You also want to be able to resubmit documents that have failed without losing context to what step in the orchestration flow was last executed.

Solution

The ExceptionHandlerPatternDemo project shows the use of the pattern, with a single Business Flow orchestration calling two different paths in a single Task Processing orchestration. Neither the Business Flow orchestration (SAMPLEMainBusinessFlow.odx) nor the Task Processing orchestration (SAMPLEExternalComponentCall.odx) are required in a true implementation. They are provided for demonstration purposes only. All of the files in the Common Schemas project and all of the files in the Exception Handler Buffer project are required, and *need no modifications (aside from possible namespace modifications) to be used in any other solution*.

The SAMPLEMainBusinessFlow orchestration demonstrates calling the other orchestrations with multiple input parameters (as demonstrated in the first Task Request grouping) and with an XML document that needs to be mapped (as demonstrated in the second Task Request grouping). Use the following steps to deploy and test the solution.

1. Open the ExceptionHandlerPatternDemo project.

2. Deploy the project using Visual Studio. All of the files necessary for a complete deployment are included in the solution (including the strong name key). For ease of deployment, place the base folder, ExceptionHandlerPatternDemo, on the C:\ drive root. If the C: drive is not available, several of the ports will need to be modified, as they reference physical paths for file send and receive locations.

3. Once the orchestrations and schemas are deployed, bound, and started, drop the SampleKickOff.xml file in the Input folder. This will kick off the flow. Monitor the progress in the Windows Event Viewer (all steps are logged to the Event Viewer).

How It Works

Based on a publish/subscribe architecture, the Exception Handler pattern can be used to buffer calls to components that may throw exceptions from the actual business flow of a process. The Exception Handler buffer allows for a common mechanism to catch, process, and retry exceptions (including notification to an administrator) that can be reused across multiple solutions. Figure 4-59 shows the high-level architecture of a request, and Figure 4-60 shows the high-level architecture of a response.

The orchestrations are built in such a way that the business workflow is separate from the actual calls to external tasks. The only orchestration that references anything besides ports that are directly bound to the MessageBox are the Task Processing orchestrations. So, too, these orchestrations are the only ones that will throw exceptions that need to be handled in a common way.

Any time an exception is thrown for any reason (such as a call to an external assembly throws an error, a web service is down, a database cannot be connected to, and so on), the Task Processing orchestration will catch the error, wrap the error information in a message, and return the message back to the Exception Handler orchestration. The Exception Handler orchestration will then decide whether to retry the call to the task (for system exceptions—for example, if a database cannot be connected to, the orchestration will delay for a specified period of time and then retry), or simply notify an administrator and wait for a response. The response back from an administrator could indicate that the call to the task should be retried, or that the entire process should be cancelled.

The Exception Handler pattern can be used in a variety of scenarios, with the following benefits:

- It offers configurable automatic retries of system exceptions.

- An administrator is notified (via any type of BTS adapter) for business rule exceptions and after a maximum number of automatic retries of system exceptions.

- It allows multiple unrelated orchestrations to publish to a single version of the Exception Handler orchestration.

- There are no uncaught or unhandled exceptions.

- No messages end up suspended in Health and Activity Tracking (HAT).

- It offers complete visibility into the life cycle of an orchestration.

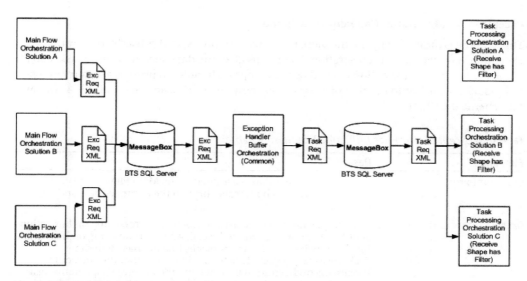

Figure 4-59. *High-level architecture (request)*

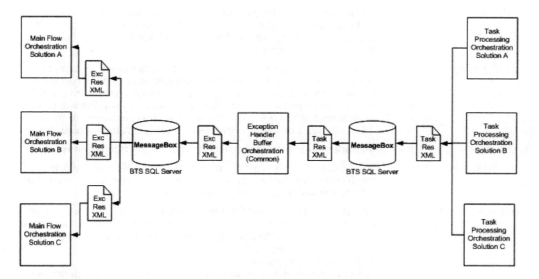

Figure 4-60. *High-level architecture (response)*

The orchestrations communicate with one another through the publish/subscribe model, meaning that the publishing orchestration drops a message on the BizTalk MessageBox to which the subscribing orchestration is subscribing. The following sections describe these schemas and how they are used.

Exception Handler Buffer Call Request Schema

This schema is published by the Business Flow orchestration(s) and subscribed to by the Exception Handler Buffer orchestration. It contains all of the data needed to call a task, and all of the configurable information needed by the exception handler to process and retry exceptions (such as maximum number of retries, delay between retries, and so on). Table 4-5 shows the schema definition.

Table 4-5. *Exception Handler Buffer Call Request Schema*

Element	Description
CorrelationID	A unique identifier that is assigned in the Main Flow orchestration and travels with each message through the entire request and full response.
OrchestrationFilter	The unique identifier specifying which Task Processing orchestration should instantiate based on the call. All Task Processing orchestration instances will subscribe to messages that are based on the TaskProcessingLogicCall schema. To ensure that the correct Task Processing orchestration is kicked off, the Receive shape in the Task Processing orchestration must be filtered on this field. Note that if there is only one instance of the Task Processing orchestration being used, there is no need to implement this filter.
TaskName	The name of the task that is to be executed in the Task Processing orchestration. The Task Processing orchestration can have multiple branches in a Decide shape. The branch that is executed is based on the value in this parameter.
MaxRetryCount	Maximum number of retries for a task that has thrown an exception. For example, if a call is being made to a database, and the connection to the database is unavailable, the Task Processing orchestration will return an exception. The Exception Handler orchestration will then retry (after a delay) the call to the task. Use this parameter to specify the maximum number of retries before notifying an administrator.
RetryDelay	Amount of time between retries. This parameter is in seconds.
InputParameter	If the call to the task is a call with one single simple type parameter (such as a string, integer, and so on), this parameter can be used. It is a distinguished field and can be easily accessed.
InputParameter (Node)	This is a repeating node allowing for multiple input parameters. Use this structure when multiple input parameters are needed. Values can be accessed using XPath queries in the Task Processing orchestration (see the demo for examples). Name: Name of the parameter. Type: The parameter type (integer, string, and so on). This parameter is not required. Value: The value of the parameter. The XPath query can find the Value based on the Name.
XMLParameter	This <Any> element can be populated with any type of XML document that may need to be passed to the Task Processing orchestration. There can be multiple XMLParameter values passed. See the demo for examples of how this parameter can be populated and read.

Exception Handler Buffer Call Response Schema

This schema is published by the Exception Handler orchestration and subscribed to by the Main Business Flow orchestration(s). It contains the output information needed by the Main Business Flow to determine what (if any) the result of the Task Processing call may have been. Table 4-6 shows the schema definition.

Table 4-6. *Exception Handler Call Buffer Response Schema*

Element	Description
CorrelationID	A unique identifier that is assigned in the Main Flow orchestration and travels with each message through the entire request and full response.
SuccessFlag	Boolean value indicating success or failure of call. If an administrator canceled the process, this value would be returned as false. If the call was made, regardless of the outcome, this value will be returned as true.
OutputParameter	If the response from the Task is a one single simple type parameter (such as a string, integer, and so on), this parameter can be used. It is a distinguished field and can be easily accessed.
OutputParameter (Node)	This is a repeating node allowing for multiple output parameters. Use this structure when multiple output parameters are needed. Values can be set and accessed using XPath queries in the Task Processing orchestration (see the demo for examples). Name: Name of the parameter. Type: The parameter type (integer, string, and so on). This parameter is not required. Value: The value of the parameter. The XPath query can find the Value based on the Name.
XMLParameter	This <Any> element can be populated with any type of XML document that may need to be passed back from the Task Processing orchestration. There can be multiple XMLParameter values passed. See the demo for examples of how this parameter can be populated and read.

Task Processing Logic Call Schema

This schema is published by the Exception Handler orchestration and is subscribed to by the Task Processing orchestration(s). All Task Processing orchestration instances subscribe to this schema type. Use a filter expression on the individual Task Processing orchestration initial Receive shape to indicate which instance to kick off (based on the OrchestrationFilter parameter). Table 4-7 shows the schema definition.

Table 4-7. *Task Processing Logic Call Schema*

Element	Description
CorrelationID	A unique identifier that is assigned in the Main Flow orchestration and travels with each message through the entire request and full response.
OrchestrationFilter	The unique identifier specifying which Task Processing orchestration should instantiate based on the call. All Task Processing orchestration instances will subscribe to messages that are based on the TaskProcessingLogicCall schema. To ensure that the correct Task Processing orchestration is kicked off, the Receive shape in the Task Processing orchestration must be filtered on this field. Note that if there is only one instance of the Task Processing orchestration being used, there is no need to implement this filter.
TaskName	The name of the Task that is to be executed in the Task Processing orchestration. The Task Processing orchestration can have multiple branches in a Decide shape. The branch that is executed is based on the value in this parameter.
InputParameter	If the call to the Task is a call with one simple type parameter (such as a string, integer, and so on), this parameter can be used. It is a distinguished field and can be easily accessed.
InputParameter (Node)	This is a repeating node allowing for multiple input parameters. Use this structure when multiple input parameters are needed. Values can be accessed using XPath queries in the Task Processing orchestration (see the demo for examples). Name: Name of the parameter. Type: The parameter type (integer, string, and so on). This parameter is not required. Value: The value of the parameter. The XPath query can find the Value based on the Name.
XMLParameter	This <Any> element can be populated with any type of XML document that may need to be passed to the Task Processing orchestration. There can be multiple XMLParameter values passed. See the demo for examples of how this parameter can be populated and read.

Task Processing Logic Response Schema

This schema is published by the Task Processing Logic orchestration(s) and subscribed to by the Exception Handler Buffer orchestration. It contains the output information needed by the Main Business Flow to determine what (if any) the result of the Task Processing call may have been and by the Exception Handler Buffer orchestration to determine what exceptions may be present and if the call needs to be retried (based on the presence of exceptions). Table 4-8 shows the schema definition.

Table 4-8. *Task Processing Logic Response Schema*

Element	Description
CorrelationID	A unique identifier that is assigned in the Main Flow orchestration and travels with each message through the entire request and full response.
SuccessFlag	Boolean value indicating success or failure of call. This is not a success/failure indicating the result of the call, but an actual indicator of whether the call was made or not. If an exception was thrown, or an administrator canceled the process, this value would be returned as false. If the call was made, regardless of the outcome, this value will be returned as true.
ErrorMessage	The text of the exception message (if an exception was thrown).
BaseException	The base exception type (if an exception was thrown).
StackTrace	The full stack trace thrown (if an exception was thrown).
OutputParameter	If the response from the Task is a single simple type parameter (such as a string, integer, and so on), this parameter can be used. It is a distinguished field and can be easily accessed.
OutputParameter (Node)	This is a repeating node allowing for multiple output parameters. Use this structure when multiple output parameters are needed. Values can be set and accessed using XPath queries in the Task Processing orchestration (see the demo for examples). Name: Name of the parameter. Type: The parameter type (integer, string, and so on). This parameter is not required. Value: The value of the parameter. The XPath query can find the Value based on the Name.
XMLParameter	This <Any> element can be populated with any type of XML document that may need to be passed back from the Task Processing orchestration. There can be multiple XMLParameter values passed. See the demo for examples of how this parameter can be populated and read.

Error To Administrator Schema

This schema is published by the Exception Handler orchestration and is published to an administrator. This may be as simple as writing to a file, or could be set up to write to a database or any other protocol desired. The Error To Administrator schema contains all of the information that an administrator would need to understand what error was thrown. Once the administrator is ready to resubmit the document to the process, the same schema type is resubmitted. Table 4-9 shows the schema definition.

Table 4-9. *Error To Administrator Schema*

Element	Description
CorrelationID	A unique identifier that is assigned in the Main Flow orchestration and travels with each message through the entire request and full response.
CancelFlag	Boolean value indicating that the administrator wants to cancel the entire process. There may be times when the exception being thrown may require some amount of rewrite. For whatever reason, an administrator may cancel the process by simply dropping the XML file back into the process with this flag set to true.

continued

Table 4-9. *Continued*

Element	Description
OriginalMessage	This node will contain the XML of the original message passed into the Exception Handler orchestration.
ErrorMessage	The text of the exception message (if an exception was thrown).
BaseException	The base exception type (if an exception was thrown).
StackTrace	The full stack trace thrown (if an exception was thrown).

4-22. Creating Role Links

Problem

You need to send a specific type of request based on a certain element within a document.

Solution

You can send specific request types based on certain document elements by using role links. Role links offer the flexibility of defining functions or roles for the inbound and outbound ports of your orchestration. Additionally, role links also offer the flexibility of abstracting the interactions between orchestration and external parties.

The following instructions outline the steps required to create and configure role links within a BizTalk orchestration and outside the context of Business Activity Services (BAS). Before implementing role links, you must create an orchestration and role links within the orchestration. Next, you must deploy the orchestration and create the parties that participate in the processes.

This solution uses two sample XML files to demonstrate how role links route messages based on message content. The first XML instance requires a manager party approval, and the second XML instance requires a HR party approval.

We've divided the solution for this recipe into several tasks, as described in the following sections.

Create the BizTalk Solution

First, you must create a BizTalk orchestration for this example.

1. Create a new BizTalk solution that will process new hire requests that require approvals. The message structure should match the sample outline in Listing 4-5.

   Listing 4-5. *Sample New Hire XML Instance*

```
<ns0:ApplicantApproval
    xmlns:ns0="http://Sample_Role_Link_Recipe.SampleNewHireRequest">
  <ApplicantID>1000</ApplicantID>
  <Approver>Manager</Approver>
  <Detail>
```

```
        <SSN>508-03-4433</SSN>
        <Name>Wally McFally</Name>
        <Position>Technician</Position>
      </Detail>
    </ns0:ApplicantApproval>
```

2. Create an orchestration to process the new hire requests. The orchestration requires the artifacts listed in Table 4-10. When complete, the orchestration should resemble Figure 4-61.

Table 4-10. *Role Links Recipe Artifacts*

Name	Type	Description
ReceiveNewHireRequest	Receive port	Receive port.
ReceiveRequest	Receive shape	Receive shape to receive message.
InitializeRoleLinks	Send shape	Expression shape to initialize role links for outbound message routing.
SendRequest	Expression shape	Send shape for outbound message.
msgNewHire	Message matching schema defined in step 1.	The name of the message is crucial as it must match the name referenced in the expression code that is entered to initialize role links. Make sure that the Approver element in the message is a distinguished property because the value in this field is used for routing.

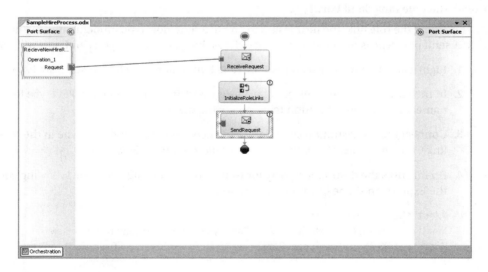

Figure 4-61. *New Hire orchestration*

Create the Orchestration Role Links

Next, you need to create and initialize the role links send port for message approval. The Role Link shape will contain a single Approval consumer role.

1. Select the Role Link shape form the BizTalk Orchestrations section of the Toolbox and drag the shape to the orchestration.

2. The Role Link Wizard will launch. Follow the Role Link Wizard and specify the following:

    - For the role link name, specify NewHireApproval.

    - For the role link type, specify NewHireApprovalRoleLinkType.

    - For the role link usage, specify that you are creating a Consumer role, as this orchestration will be providing messages.

3. Click the Finish button to complete the wizard.

4. Once the wizard has completed, remove the Provider role from the newly created role link, as the Provider role will not be used in this example.

■**Note** When following the Role Link Wizard, select either the Provider role or Consumer role for your application. The Role Link Wizard will create both roles, but you are free to remove the role that does not apply to your given situation.

Create the Role Link Send Port Type

After creating the role link, the next task is to create a send port type implemented by the role link. A send port type is required because it defines the type of message a send port will send.

1. Right-click the Provider section of the Role Link shape and choose Add Port Type.

2. In the Port Type Wizard, select Create a New Port Type and enter SendPortType for the name. Click the Finish button to complete the wizard.

3. Connect the orchestration send port to the newly created send port type in the role link Consumer role. The orchestration should resemble Figure 4-62.

4. BizTalk uses the destination party for routing of the message. Add the following code to the Expression shape in your orchestration.

```
//set the approver name
NewHireApproval(Microsoft.XLANGs.BaseTypes.DestinationParty) = new
Microsoft.XLANGs.BaseTypes.Party(msgNewHire.Approver, "OrganizationName");
```

5. Build and deploy the solution after completing the orchestration. When you deploy the solution, a new Consumer role is created in the `Roles` folder located under the BizTalk Explorer.

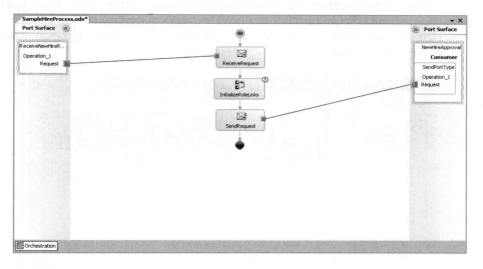

Figure 4-62. *New Hire orchestration with role links*

■**Note** The Expression shape code performs the party resolution. The line of code uses the `Approver` distinguished field to determine to which party to route the message. When you create a party, a party alias is also created to use for party resolution. In the Expression shape, we use the default alias, `OrganizationName`, which is created with each party. However, multiple aliases can be created for a party and then referenced in an Expression shape. For example, an alias of `PhoneNumber` could be created during the party creation and then referenced in the Expression shape.

Create Parties and Physical Send Ports

The final steps involve creating the BizTalk parties and physical send ports for the solution. Within the BizTalk Explorer, create the physical send ports and parties that will receive the approval messages.

1. Create a file send port named `HRPartySendPort`. This is the send port for messages that are routed to the HR department.

2. Create another file send port named `ManagerPartySendPort`. This is the send port for messages that are routed to the Manager department.

3. Create a party named ManagerParty. Make sure that the ManagerParty refers to the ManagerPartySendPort. Use the standard OrganizationName alias that is created when the party is created.

4. Create a party named HRParty. Make sure that the HRParty refers to the HRPartySendPort. Use the standard OrganizationName alias that is created when the party is created. Figure 4-63 shows the Party Properties - Configurations - Aliases dialog box and demonstrates the use of an alias.

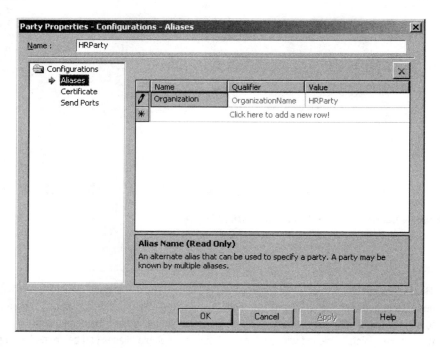

Figure 4-63. *Configuring party properties*

■**Note** The Approver name value in the message must match the name of the party you created. If a message is sent referencing an invalid party, BizTalk will suspend the message when trying to route the message to the party specified.

---

5. Enlist the two parties within the Consumer role that was created when the orchestration was deployed. The completed BizTalk Explorer view will resemble Figure 4-64.

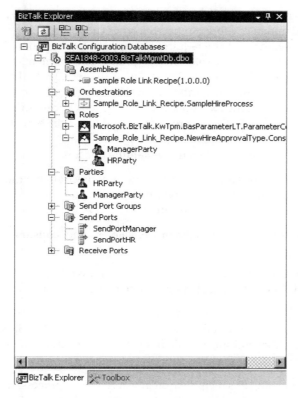

Figure 4-64. *BizTalk Explorer view with role links*

Test the Role Links

After completing the preceding tasks, you will be able to enlist and start your solution to test the implemented role links. When you submit a message with Manager as the value for the Approver element, the message will be routed to the send port associated with the Manager party. When you submit a message with HR as the value for the Approver element, the message will be routed to the send port associated with the HR party.

How It Works

Role links are extremely useful for loosely coupling your physical solution from the trading partner or disparate system. Processes that implement role links benefit from the abstraction by being able to stand independent of the implementation of the trading partner or subscribing system.

Imagine having a business process that is the same for multiple trading partners or systems. Some of the consumers of the process need the information in a flat file format or must receive the information using a proprietary communication protocol. You could implement this scenario through the use of dynamic ports or a send port group, however the maintenance of subscribers becomes a challenge. Updating a dynamic send port requires updating the process that provides the configuration information. Implementing role links allows the subscribers to be independent and updated without impacting other subscribers.

Implementing role links is straightforward and requires few steps in configuration. The first set of configuration steps is performed in the solution design-time environment. The final set of steps is performed after the process has been deployed. You must identify whether you are consuming or providing a service, identify the parties that will be interacting with the service, and specify the role under which the parties will operate. The Role Link Wizard in Visual Studio will create two default roles automatically. You are not required to use the two roles, and you can create additional roles after the wizard has executed.

The following are the required components when implementing role links:

Parties: The specific entities interacting with your organization's orchestration either providing or consuming information from that orchestration. Typically, each party represents a single organization that interacts with your organization.

Roles: Logical entities that define a specific business process. Roles either consume or provide services.

Role links: Describe the relationship or connection (link) between two roles. The Role Link shape within Visual Studio will launch the Role Link Wizard to assist in creating roles within your orchestration.

Role link types: Describe how your orchestration participates in the service. Role link types are similar to port types in that you specify whether you are consuming a message or publishing a message.

In the sample solution accompanying this recipe, we created a New Hire process that contains a single Approver role. We required only a single role and removed one role from the role link after the wizard was complete. For the role created in our role link, we specified a send port type. Each role must implement a port type for communication to outside entities. The final step was to programmatically determine party resolution. For illustration purposes, an Expression shape implemented party resolution via code. BizTalk must always know which party will be receiving the message, and the party resolution can either be performed in the orchestration or within a pipeline.

4-23. Calling Web Services

Problem

You want to call a web service from within your business process, using the standard SOAP adapter.

Solution

When calling a web service, the first item that is needed is the Web Services Description Language (WSDL). The WSDL contains the interfaces indicating how a web service can be called. BizTalk imports this WSDL and turns it into a schema that can be read in the same way as a standard XSD, with each web method defining its own schema. This solution will walk through the steps required to reference a WSDL, create a message to post to a web service (via a web method), and get the web service result message.

1. Open a BizTalk project in Visual Studio.

2. In the Solution Explorer, right-click the References node under the project header and select Add Web Reference.

3. In the Add Web Reference dialog box, you can manually enter the URL of the WSDL into the URL box at the top of the window. This can be a standard web URL (http://) or a file path to a WSDL file (useful for developing in a disconnected environment). Alternatively, use any of the other Browse methods to locate the web service.

4. After entering a valid URL path, all available web services will be displayed on the right side of the dialog box. Select the desired web service from this list. Make sure that the web reference name shown in the text box is appropriate (usually you will want to rename this to something more descriptive than the default; the name entered here will be how the web service is referred to in the rest of the project).

5. Click the Add Reference button, and then click OK. The newly referenced web service should now appear under the Web References folder in the Solution Explorer.

6. In an orchestration, right-click the Port Surface and select New Configured Port. This will start the Port Configuration Wizard. Use the following settings to configure the new port.

   - Name the port appropriately.

   - For Port Type, select Existing Port Type. In the window that appears, highlight the web port that is a post (as opposed to a response back), and then click Next.

   - The final screen should be automatically configured indicating that BizTalk will always be set to sending a request and receiving a response, with the port binding set to Specify Now. There is no need to make any changes. Click Next, and then click Finish.

■**Note** Web service calls can be request-response (two-way) or simply request (one-way). Some of the parameters in the configuration will be slightly different in the case of a one-way web service.

---

7. In the orchestration, add a new Send shape. This shape will require a message to be associated with it. You will want to create a message that has the same type as the outgoing port you configured in step 6, as follows:

   a. In the Orchestration View window, right-click the Messages folder and select New Message.

   b. Give this message an appropriate name, such as msgRequest.

   c. In the Properties window of the message, click the Message Type drop-down list, expand Web Message Types, and select the message type that corresponds to the port type you indicated in step 6.

   d. Set the Send shape Message Type property to this message.

8. Connect the Send shape to the outgoing method on the port created in step 6.

9. Drop a Receive shape on the orchestration, immediately after the Send shape created in step 7. You will need to create a message that has the same type as the response back from the web service call, as follows:

   a. In the Orchestration View window, right-click the Messages folder and select New Message.

   b. Give this message an appropriate name, such as msgResponse.

   c. In the Properties window of the message, click the Message Type drop-down list, expand Web Message Types, and select the message type that corresponds to the response of the web service web method indicated in step 6.

   d. Set the Receive shape Message Type property to this message.

10. Create an instance of the message that you are sending to the web service (msgRequest). This can be done through a map or a Message Assignment shape. The following steps will show how to do this through a map.

    a. Drop a Transform shape in the orchestration immediately before the Send shape created in step 6. This will automatically create a Construct Message shape.

    b. In the Properties window of the Construct Message shape, click the Messages Constructed property and select the message created in step 6 (msgRequest).

    c. Double-click the Transform shape. In the Transform Configuration dialog box, the target document should be msgRequest, and the source document can be any document (you will need to create a message, not included in these steps, of any given schema type and set it to the source).

    d. After setting the source and target schemas, click OK. The map should open, and you can map fields as needed.

How It Works

The complexity around calling and mapping to web services is greatly reduced by using a BizTalk orchestration, the standard SOAP adapter, and the steps described in this solution. However, there may be times when these steps do not provide the result needed. One example would be the need for Web Services Enhancements (WSE) 2.0, which requires certain authentication properties to be passed at the SOAP Header level, a level not explicitly available on a standard SOAP adapter. When WS-Security is used to secure a web service, invoke it with the WSE 2.0 BizTalk adapter. Additionally, the web service could be called from an external .NET component, removing the complexity of calling the web service from BizTalk altogether.

Calling a web service from an external assembly lets developers use the full functionality of .NET to make the call. While complex web services with arrays or strongly typed data sets can be called from an orchestration (much more easily with BizTalk 2006 than with BizTalk 2004), moving the call to an external component may be easier.

There are important benefits to calling a web service with the BizTalk SOAP adapter and following the steps described in this solution. The ability to turn the WSDL into a schema, the ability to have retries automatically occur, and the simplicity of creating the message through the BizTalk Mapper are all excellent reasons to invoke the web service from within an orchestration.

4-24. Exposing an Orchestration As a Web Service

Problem

You would like to expose an orchestration process as a web service to be called from an outside application.

Solution

Using BizTalk, an orchestration can be exposed as a web service via the BizTalk Web Services Publishing Wizard. Using this tool, the effort to expose an orchestration as a web service is considerably simplified. To expose an orchestration as a web service, take the following steps:

1. Open the BizTalk Web Services Publishing Wizard by selecting Start ➤ Programs ➤ BizTalk 2006 ➤ BizTalk Web Services Publishing Wizard.

2. On the Welcome page, click the Next button.

3. On the Create Web Service page, click the "Publish orchestration as a web service" radio button.

4. On the BizTalk Assembly page, click the Browse button and navigate to your assembly DLL containing the orchestration that you wish to expose as a web service. The wizard will now examine the assembly and return all orchestrations and orchestration ports deployed to the BizTalk configuration database. Only orchestration receive ports defined as public - No Limit will have permissions to be exposed as web service.

5. On the Orchestrations and Ports page, select the orchestrations and receive ports you desire to export and expose as a web service, as shown in Figure 4-65.

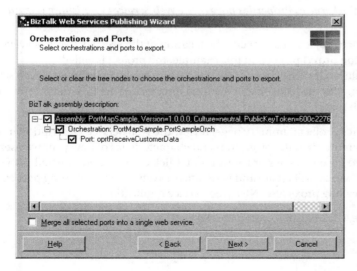

Figure 4-65. *Orchestrations and Ports page of the Web Services Publishing Wizard*

■**Note** If there are multiple receive orchestration ports, the Web Services Publishing Wizard gives you the ability to merge all ports into a single web service. To enable this, at the bottom of the dialog box, check the "Merge all selected ports into a single Web Service" option.

---

6. On the Web Services Properties page, enter the namespace of the web service, as shown in Figure 4-66. In this example, the namespace is called OrchestrationWebServiceSample. You can also configure other common properties of a standard web service, such as the specification of additional SOAP Headers and other Web Services Interoperability (WSI) properties.

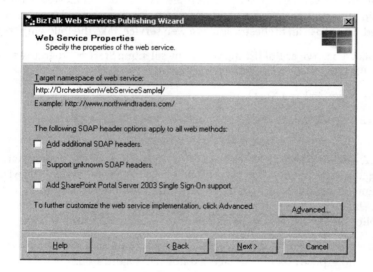

Figure 4-66. *The Web Services Properties page of the Web Services Publishing Wizard*

7. On the Web Service Project page, specify the location of the ASP .NET Web Service (calling application proxy) project. In this example, the project is called OrchestrationWebServiceProxySample. This step will automatically create a web service web application under the local host as a virtual directory of the Internet Information Services (IIS) web server.

8. On the Web Service Project Summary page, review the Web Service Description input scroll box. This summarizes the properties and characteristics of how your web service will be configured based on your previous input. Click Create when satisfied with your web service. The wizard will create and generate the web service exporting port configuration and the calling proxy ASP .NET Web Service application.

9. On the final page, click Finish to complete the web service configuration.

How It Works

Exposing orchestrations as web services allows you to reuse orchestration processes by creating BizTalk configurations to support the passing of a web service call to a BizTalk orchestration. This way, you can take advantage of core BizTalk capabilities such as error handling, document tracking, and integration into downstream BizTalk via the publish/subscribe architecture. In addition, you can extend outside your BizTalk environment, to enable a service-oriented approach, composite application paradigms, and so on.

The Web Services Publishing Wizard interrogates the BizTalk orchestration and receive ports and creates a web service application to support the calling of the target BizTalk orchestration. This is achieved by creating a web service (ASMX) that calls a C# .NET code behind that implements the mechanism of publishing the message instance to the BizTalk MessageBox.

Just as BizTalk orchestrations can be exposed as web services, so too can XSD schemas. XSD schema web services are also generated using the Web Services Publishing Wizard, where one or more XSD schemas are selected and corresponding web services are generated. The web service handles sending the message directly to the BizTalk MessageBox, offering a way to implement publish/subscribe without the need to create a BizTalk orchestration.

Within a web service implementation, security is a paramount consideration. You should consider security at the transport, SOAP, receive adapter, and receive port. It is worth noting that the Web Service Publishing Wizard will not automatically configure Secure Socket Layer (SSL) security for the web service application and Web Services Security (WS-Security). You can address this security concern by configuring IIS and by using standard Windows Server infrastructure security configuration and deployment tasks.

CHAPTER 5

Business Rules Framework

Business processes are changing at an unprecedented speed, and the IT systems that power business processes are being asked to keep up. In today's environment, in order to maintain a market advantage, organizations must react quickly to new markets, shifting consumer demand, shifting cost structures, and shifting business differentiators. The IT changes required to support dynamic business policies are taxing IT departments in terms of cycle time and hard costs.

At the root of this taxation are the complexities involved in designing and deploying traditional technical solutions. Current software development life cycle (SDLC) methodologies are time-consuming and expensive, and they often fail to deliver the set of features required by businesses within their time frames and budget targets. Although technologies such as .NET and BizTalk have shortened the cycle time to develop, test, and deploy solutions, often these technologies still don't meet the demanding cycle time requirements demanded by an agile business. For instance, consider a bank's business policy for granting credit to a customer. If you implement this logic within a BizTalk orchestration, the steps required to change the logic, compile the program, and redeploy are too numerous to enumerate here. In addition, this change requires that the system be taken offline while you enact the changes. Also, if the bank has a strong development methodology, it may require additional time to follow the process and obtain the necessary approvals. All this adds up to a sluggish, expensive process for changing the business policy.

The business rules framework is BizTalk's answer to reducing the business agility problem faced by traditional technologies. The business rules framework is a rules execution engine that allows you to create business policies that you can develop, deploy, and dynamically execute quickly without bringing your BizTalk process down. The framework comprises policies, facts, vocabularies, and rules. In conjunction, these artifacts combine to create a powerful tool for quickly changing business rules in near real time.

5-1. Creating a Business Policy

Problem

You want to understand the process for creating business rule policies. These policies are core components to all business rule development.

Solution

The business rules framework consists of policies, rules, vocabularies, and facts. A *business policy* is the container in which business rules are defined, versioned, tested, deployed, and executed. From within the business policy editing window, the first step before creating rules is to create a policy. The policy then may contain one or more rules for deployment. To create a policy, take the following steps:

1. Open the Business Rule Composer by selecting Start ➤ Programs ➤ Microsoft BizTalk Server 2006 ➤ Business Rule Composer.

2. Within the Policy Explorer, right-click the Policies node, and click Add New Policy.

3. Give the policy a name.

4. By default, version 1.0 of the policy is created. You may change the version number if you want by selecting the version, navigating to the Properties window, and setting the Version property.

5. Add an optional description for the policy.

6. Right-click the version, and choose Save.

How It Works

Creating a business rules policy is a relatively simplistic exercise but is the foundation to the business rules framework. Once you have created the policy, you can add rules and facts to the policy for testing and deployment. When calling the policy from BizTalk, the latest version will be selected for execution, unless you specify a specific version. The rules engine detects and deploys new versions of a policy, allowing changes to be made to the business policy in a live, deployed process. This creates a powerful environment to apply a dynamic business policy to deployed solutions with minimal work. The recipes in this chapter will guide you through adding rules, facts, and vocabularies to your business rules policy.

5-2. Creating and Testing Rules

Problem

You need to create and test a simple business rule that a business process can use. The business process needs to validate a document and receive the result.

Solution

You need to perform a number of basic steps to create a rule. These include the following:

1. Define the rule logic.

2. Define the input schema and XML instance.

3. Define the output schema and XML instance.

4. Define the facts that the rule uses, such as constants, functions, and predicates (vocabularies).

The first step to creating a rule is determining the logic of the rule. This example will use the logic in Listing 5-1 to construct the rule.

Listing 5-1. *Rule Logic*

```
If Age < Minimum Age Then Deny Application
If Age > or = Minimum Age Then Accept Application
```

We will show how to execute the rule in Listing 5-1 against an XML document containing the data that will be validated. For this example, we will use the NewHire schema (Figure 5-1) with the schema and XML instance (Listing 5-2).

Figure 5-1. *NewHire schema*

Listing 5-2. *NewHire XML Instance*

```
<ns0:NewHireList xmlns:ns0="http://SampleSolution.NewHireList">
  <DateTime>1999-04-05T18:00:00</DateTime>
  <ns1:Person xmlns:ns1="http://SampleSolution.Person">
    <ID>1</ID>
    <Name>Mary</Name>
    <Role>Dog Walker</Role>
    <Age>17</Age>
  </ns1:Person>
  <ns1:Person xmlns:ns1="http://SampleSolution.Person">
    <ID>2</ID>
    <Name>Windy</Name>
    <Role>Baby Changer</Role>
    <Age>35</Age>
  </ns1:Person>
</ns0:NewHireList>
```

■**Note** The schema must define the `<Age>` element as an integer for the comparison to work in the business rule, which you will create in this solution. The rules engine will not implicitly convert a String to an Int.

The next step in this solution is to output a document. The document that is sent to the rules engine will be modified and returned to the calling entity. If the applicant's age is not a valid age, the document will be modified to display the text "INVALID APPLICANT" in the `<Role>` element. (This element must exist in order for it to be set.)

The following steps describe how to create the vocabulary using the Business Rule Composer:

1. Open the Business Rule Composer from the Start menu. If the Open Rule Store dialog box appears, select the appropriate SQL Server instance and authentication to log on (this should be the instance against which you want to develop).

2. Add a new vocabulary, which will contain the definition for the Minimum Age constant and the Age node in the input XML document. In the Facts Explorer, right-click the Constants folder (or create a folder of your own—it could be named according to the rule, such as AgeValidation), and select Add New Version. Name it appropriately (the version number).

3. To add the Minimum Age constant, right-click the Version subfolder created in the previous step, and select Add New Definition. The Vocabulary Definition Wizard appears. Once the wizard is open, do the following:

   a. Add a new constant by selecting the Constant Value option. Enter **MinimumAge** for the Definition Name field. Give a description of the minimum age of the applicant. Click Next.

   b. On the final page of the wizard, set Type to System.Int32, and set Value to 18. Set Display Name to an appropriate value. Click Finish.

4. To add the reference to the Age node in the NewHire XML document, right-click the subfolder of the version that was created in step 2, and select Add New Definition. The wizard appears, and you should then perform the following steps (shown in Figure 5-2):

   a. Select the XML Document Element or Attribute option, and click Next.

   b. Enter **ApplicantAge** for the Definition Name field. Give a description of the actual age of the applicant.

   c. Click the Browse button, and find the NewHire XSD schema (based on Figure 5-1). Once you have selected the schema, a new dialog box appears where you can select the Age node. Select this node, and click OK.

   d. Modify the Document type namespace. This namespace must match the namespace of the schema that references it—ensure that it has been set correctly to SampleSolution.NewHireList.

   e. In the Select Operation section, select the Perform "Get" Operation radio button.

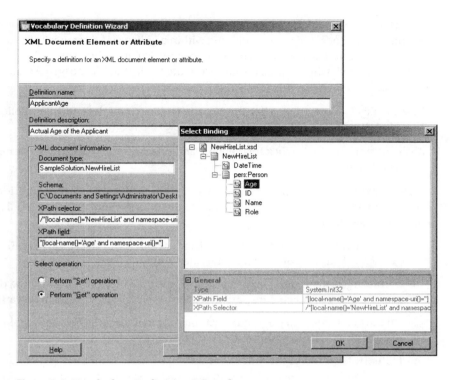

Figure 5-2. *Vocabulary Definition Wizard*

5. Add a reference to the Role node in the NewHire XML document. Following the same procedure as defined in step 4, use these substeps:

   a. Select the XML Document Element or Attribute option, and click Next.

   b. Enter **ApplicantRole** for the Definition Name field. Give a description of the role of the applicant, which will be set to INVALID APPLICANT.

   c. Click the Browse button, and find the NewHire XSD schema. Once you have selected the schema, a new dialog box appears where you can select the Role node. Select this node, and click OK.

   d. Modify the Document type namespace. This namespace must match the namespace of the schema that references it—ensure that it has been set to SampleSolution.NewHireList.

   e. In the Select Operation section, select the Perform "Set" Operation radio button.

6. Now publish the vocabulary by right-clicking the newly created Vocabulary folder created in step a and selecting Publish. This allows the vocabulary to be used by a policy, which is where you define an actual business rule.

The steps up to this point have been putting into place the components needed to create a business rule. A rule (or set of rules) is defined within a policy and references preexisting functions, predicates, and any custom-defined constants (such as what you defined in the previous steps). The following steps show how to create the actual business rule and policy and use the vocabulary created previously:

1. In the Policy Explorer, right-click the `Policies` folder, and select Add New Policy. Enter **SamplePolicy** for the policy name.

2. A version appears. Right-click this version, and select Add New Rule. Enter **SampleRule** for the rule name.

3. Select the rule you created in the previous step. You will see an empty condition in the right pane. Take the following steps to create the rule. (See Figure 5-3 for a full picture of the completed steps.)

   a. In the Facts Explorer, expand the `Predicates` folder, and select the `Less Than` predicate. Drag and drop this on the rule condition.

   b. On the `argument1` entry in the `IF` section of the Rule Composition window, drag and drop the custom vocabulary parameter `ApplicantAge` you created in an earlier step.

   c. On the `argument2` entry in the `IF` section, drag and drop the custom vocabulary parameter `MinimumAge` you created earlier.

   d. In the `THEN` section of the Rule Composition window, drop the `ApplicantRole` parameter (created earlier). Next to this you will see an `empty string` blank. Click this, and type **INVALID APPLICANT**.

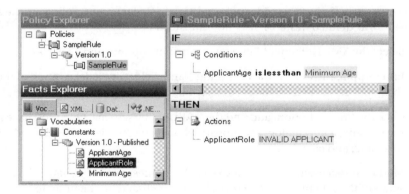

Figure 5-3. *Creating the rule*

The rule is complete at this point. Save the rule (right-click, and select Save). You can now test the rule (and policy). Use these steps to validate and test the rule:

1. Right-click the `Version` folder of the rule you just created, and select Test Policy.

2. In the Select Facts dialog box that appears, click the schema name. The option Add an Instance of the NewHireList XML will be available. You saw an example of this earlier in this recipe (refer to Listing 5-2). Click Add Instance, and browse to an instance of this XML document.

3. Once you have declared an instance, click the Test button. This causes the XML instance to be passed to the rule. A full trace appears in an Output window where you can verify whether the rule executed as expected (the value of the XML node should change).

4. Right-click the policy, and select Publish.

5. Right-click the policy, and select Deploy.

You can now call the rule and policy from an orchestration. To call the rule and policy from an orchestration, perform the following steps:

1. In an orchestration, create a message of the type that is to be passed into the rule and a message of the type that is expected back (in this case, the messages will both be the same NewHireList XSD type).

2. Drop a Call Rules shape in an Atomic Scope (or in an orchestration that has a transaction type of Atomic).

3. Right-click the Call Rules shape, and select the policy you created. You will see one input parameter, which will be the message created in step 1.

Note The document type must match the namespace of the schema that will call it for the rule to be callable from an orchestration.

The XML instance shown in Listing 5-3 represents the generated output from testing the business rule created in this solution.

Listing 5-3. *Output XML Instance*

```
<ns0:NewHireList xmlns:ns0="http://SampleSolution.NewHireList">
  <DateTime>1999-04-05T18:00:00</DateTime>
  <ns1:Person xmlns:ns1="http://SampleSolution.Person">
    <ID>1</ID>
    <Name>Mary</Name>
    <Role>INVALID APPLICANT</Role>
    <Age>17</Age>
  </ns1:Person>
  <ns1:Person xmlns:ns1="http://SampleSolution.Person">
    <ID>2</ID>
    <Name>Windy</Name>
    <Role>Baby Changer</Role>
    <Age>35</Age>
  </ns1:Person>
</ns0:NewHireList>
```

How It Works

There are additional uses of the rules engine, including the ability to store parameters that can be accessed from orchestrations. Similar in nature to a configuration file that stores parameters that may need to change (such as connection strings, etc.) once a solution is in production, these constants allow for runtime modifications. Benefits to using the rules engine to store configurable parameters include ease of access, simple user interface, and enhanced read/write permissions (compared with a text file containing configurable parameters).

To add parameters that can be accessed from an orchestration, there are two basic steps: create the parameters, and access the constants through the rules engine API.

The first step is to create the parameters in a vocabulary in the rules engine and save them. You don't need to publish them unless versioning would be helpful. If they are not published, it is easier to modify them at runtime, because all that is required is to right-click the value that needs to be changed and select Modify. Once you have saved the vocabulary, running instances of orchestrations that reference these parameters will pick up the new values.

The second step is to add .NET code to a BizTalk Helper class to access the vocabulary through the rules engine API. The code shown in Listing 5-4 can be placed into a .NET assembly and should be referenced by a BizTalk project. The method can then be called from an Expression shape within an orchestration. This code also allows for a specific version to be called, if desired.

Listing 5-4. *Accessing Constants Through the Rules Engine API*

```
public bool blnGetVocabularyConstantValue(string strVocabularyName,
                                          string strConstantName,
                                          string strVersion,
                                          ref string strConstantValue,
                                          ref string strConstantType) {

    RuleStore rlsRuleStore;
    VocabularyInfoCollection vicVocabInfo;
    Vocabulary vocVocab;
    RuleSetDeploymentDriver rsdDriver = new RuleSetDeploymentDriver();
    Hashtable hshTable;
    LiteralDefinition litDef;
    Boolean blnConstantFound = false;

    rlsRuleStore = rsdDriver.GetRuleStore();

    if((strVersion == null) || (strVersion == "")) {
     vicVocabInfo = rlsRuleStore.GetVocabularies(strVocabularyName,
                                RuleStore.Filter.Latest);
    }
    else {
     vicVocabInfo = rlsRuleStore.GetVocabularies(strVocabularyName,
                                RuleStore.Filter.All);
    }
```

```
// check to see that the vocabulary searched on has returned data
if(vicVocabInfo.Count > 0) {
 for(int x=0;x<vicVocabInfo.Count;x++) {

 vocVocab = rlsRuleStore.GetVocabulary(vicVocabInfo[x]);

 // Check to see that the version equals the version being searched for
 // or that the version passed in was a wildcard (Null)
 if((strVersion == null) || (strVersion == "") ||
 ((vocVocab.CurrentVersion.MajorRevision + "." +
   vocVocab.CurrentVersion.MinorRevision) == strVersion)) {

  // Initialize the hashtable to the number of definitions on the vocabulary
  hshTable = new Hashtable(vocVocab.Definitions.Count);
  hshTable = (Hashtable)vocVocab.Definitions.SyncRoot;

  // check that the constant being searched for exists in the vocabulary
  if(hshTable.ContainsKey(strConstantName)) {
   litDef = (LiteralDefinition)hshTable[strConstantName];

   strConstantType = litDef.Value.GetType().ToString();
   strConstantValue = litDef.Value.ToString();

   blnConstantFound = true;

   // exit loop
   break;
   }
  }
 }
}
 return blnConstantFound;
}
```

You can use the code in Listing 5-5 to invoke the previous class from an orchestration Expression shape. This allows for an alternate method of access to the rules engine without needing the standard call using the Call Rules shape and is useful when getting the value of a constant or other scalar value.

Listing 5-5. *Calling the Object from the Orchestration Expression Shape*

```
// the following string is the name of the vocabulary
strVocabularyName = "Project.BizTalk.Constants";
objVocab.GetVocabularyConstantValue(strVocabularyName, "ConstantName", "",
                                    "10", ref strValue,ref strType);
```

5-3. Creating Facts

Problem

You need to understand how to use the Facts Explorer to create a vocabulary that will be used within a business rule fact. You want to be able to store constants, predicates, and so on, that can be changed easily without redeploying code.

Solution

This solution will demonstrate how to create a vocabulary using a node in an imported XML schema. *Facts* are those items that are used to create rules. The Facts Explorer has four tabs, as follows:

- *Vocabularies*: These consist of all defined values that you can use when creating a rule, including constants, predicates, XML nodes, and so on.

- *XML Schemas*: You can use all schemas imported onto this tab when creating vocabularies or predicates (actions). You can drag and drop nodes on the XML Schemas tab in the Vocabulary window.

- *Databases*: You can add references to databases that will be used for creating facts on this tab. You can drag and drop tables onto the Vocabulary window.

- *.NET Assemblies*: Assemblies, like databases and XML schemas, can be references in the Facts Explorer and used to create vocabularies.

Use the following steps to import an XML schema and create a new vocabulary:

1. In the BizTalk Business Rule Composer, click the XML Schemas tab in the Facts Explorer.

2. Right-click the Schemas folder, and select Browse. Locate a schema to import, and click Open. This imports the full schema into the window, as shown in Figure 5-4.

Figure 5-4. *XML Schemas tab*

3. Create a new vocabulary by clicking the Vocabulary tab. Right-click the Vocabularies folder, and select Add New Vocabulary. Give the vocabulary a name.

4. Now drag a node from the XML schema that was imported, and drop it on the vocabulary you created in the previous step. By holding down the mouse button as you drag the node, you can navigate between tabs.

5. The Vocabulary Definition Wizard immediately opens, with the XML Document or Attribute option automatically selected. Navigate through the wizard to finish creating the vocabulary. The fields will already be filled in for you.

How It Works

You can add the Database and .NET Assembly facts to the Vocabulary tab in a similar manner as described in this solution. Additionally, you can drop all facts in the condition or action (IF...THEN) of a rule. Once you have added a fact to a rule, right-clicking the condition or action allows you to browse to the original fact, as shown in Figure 5-5. Complex rules will have many facts referenced in them, and this allows you to keep track of all the disparate definitions.

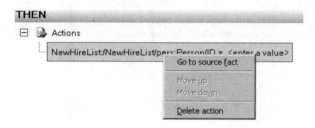

Figure 5-5. *Action with fact*

5-4. Setting Rule Priorities

Problem

You need to control the order in which the BizTalk rules engine executes rules. The order BizTalk executes rules in determines which rules take precedence, with the results of the last rule executing and potentially overwriting the results of the previous rules.

Solution

In many real-world scenarios, multiple business rules must execute in a predetermined order. In these situations, the second rule may overwrite the result of the first rule. Control the order in which the BizTalk rules engine executes rules by assigning a priority to each rule.

This recipe defines two business rules for determining which shipper should deliver a package to a customer. A customer can specify a preferred shipper to deliver their items. However, sometimes customers receive promotional discounted shipping rates, and a customer can specify they would like to take advantage of these special shipping rates. The promotional shipping rate rule must execute after and override the results of the preferred shipper rule.

> **■Note** This example assumes that the business rules already exist. For more information about creating business rules, please see the earlier recipes in this chapter.

The following steps demonstrate how to set the priority of a business rule:

1. From the Start menu, select All Programs ➤ Microsoft BizTalk Server 2006 ➤ Business Rule Composer.

2. Navigate to the policy containing the shipping business rules.

3. Select the Use Preferred Shipper rule in the Policy Explorer, and change the `Priority` property to the value 1, as shown in Figure 5-6.

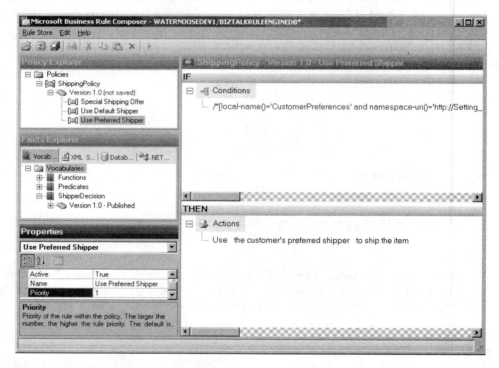

Figure 5-6. *Setting the Use Preferred Shipper rule's priority*

> **■Note** The BizTalk rules engine executes higher-priority rules first. Since the promotional shipping rate rule should override the preferred shipper rule, it must execute after the preferred shipper rule and must have a lower priority.

4. Select the Special Shipping Offer rule in the Policy Explorer, and verify that the Priority value is set to the value 0.

How It Works

The BizTalk rules engine executes high-priority rules first. Consequently, lower-priority rules execute after higher-priority ones and potentially can override the results of higher-priority rules. The BizTalk rules engine may execute rules with the same priority in any order. Remember that the priority of rules will affect the order BizTalk executes them in and has no direct effect on the importance of the rule's actions.

5-5. Creating Custom Fact Retrievers

Problem

You need to define business rules using facts that an orchestration cannot provide. The facts may not be available in the orchestration, or you may need to reuse a fact across many instances of the orchestration.

Solution

A business rule performs actions when conditions defined in the Business Rule Composer are true. For example, an action may modify a value in a message. The BizTalk developer creates a condition from facts, which are pieces of information the rules engine can examine. Most often, the rules engine will examine facts from the messages BizTalk directly processes. The orchestration invoking the rules engine directly provides these facts. However, sometimes a rule needs to be based on facts that are not available in the orchestration. The rules engine can retrieve these external facts with a custom fact retriever.

In this example, a business rule will schedule a customer's service request only if the customer's address is in the Northwind database. The customer's address may be different each time the orchestration invokes the rules engine. The customer's address is called a *short-term* fact because the orchestration provides the fact every time it invokes the rules engine. However, instead of opening a new connection to the database each time the orchestration invokes the rules engine, this example reuses the same connection to the Northwind database over and over again. Reusing the database connection makes it a *long-term* fact. The BizTalk developer must provide long-term facts to the rules engine with the IFactRetriever interface. The custom fact retriever created in this recipe provides the connection to the Northwind database to the rules engine.

Use the following steps to create the custom fact retriever:

1. Open Visual Studio .NET, and create a new class library project.

2. Add a reference to the Microsoft.RuleEngine.dll assembly. This assembly is located in the root of the BizTalk installation directory. The default location of this folder is C:\Program Files\Microsoft BizTalk Server 2006\.

3. Implement the Microsoft.RuleEngine.IFactRetriever interface. This interface defines one method called UpdateFacts.

4. Within the UpdateFacts method, add code to check whether the factsHandleIn parameter is null. If the factsHandleIn parameter is null, create and return an instance of the Microsoft.RuleEngine.DataConnection class. If the factsHandleIn parameter is not null, then simply return it from the method. When completed, the code should appear as in Listing 5-6.

Listing 5-6. *Completed Custom Fact Retriever*

```
using System.Data.SqlClient;
using Microsoft.RuleEngine;

namespace CustomFactRetriever
{
    public class AssertDBConnection : IFactRetriever
    {
        public object UpdateFacts(RuleSetInfo ruleSetInfo,
                                  RuleEngine engine, object factsHandleIn)
        {
            object factsHandleOut;
            if (factsHandleIn == null)
            {
                SqlConnection SQLConn = new SqlConnection("
                                            Initial Catalog=Northwind;
                                            Data Source=(local);
                                            Integrated Security=SSPI;");
                DataConnection RulesConn = new DataConnection("Northwind",
                                            "Customers", SQLConn);
                engine.Assert(RulesConn);
                factsHandleOut = RulesConn;
            }
            else
                factsHandleOut = factsHandleIn;

            return factsHandleOut;
        }
    }
}
```

5. Compile the class library assembly, and deploy it to the Global Assembly Cache (GAC). After creating the custom fact retriever, define a vocabulary and business rules. This example will schedule a service appointment only if the customer's address is in the database.

6. Open the Business Rule Composer, and create a new policy with one rule. Define a vocabulary for accessing facts defined by an XML message. An orchestration must provide the message when the policy executes. This example gets the address a customer requested service at and decides whether to approve the service request.

7. Right-click the new vocabulary, and select Add New Definition. Select the option to create a new database table or column definition in the vocabulary, and click Next, as shown in Figure 5-7.

8. Give the definition an appropriate name, and leave the Binding Type set to Data Connection.

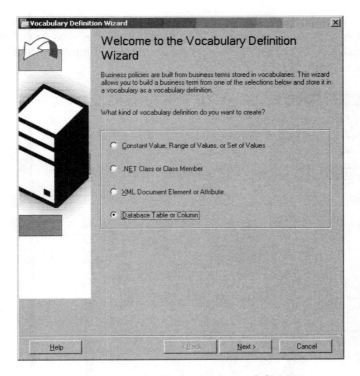

Figure 5-7. *Creating a new database column definition*

9. Within the Database Information section of the window, click the Browse button. After selecting a SQL Server instance with a Northwind database, browse to the Customer table. Select the Address column of the Customer table, as shown in Figure 5-8, and click OK.

Figure 5-8. *Setting the location of the customer's registered address*

10. Within the Select Operation section of the window, select the Perform "Get" Operation radio button. Set an appropriate display name for display in the Business Rules Composer. When complete, the Database Table or Database Table Column Definition window appears, as shown in Figure 5-9.

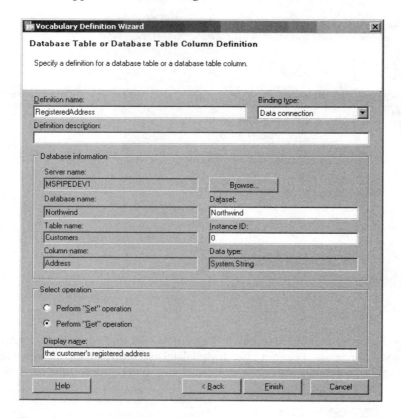

Figure 5-9. *Completing the definition*

11. Click the Finish button to complete the vocabulary definition.

12. After creating the vocabulary definition, specify the custom fact retriever to provide the connection to the database when the rule executes. Then, select the policy version in the Policy Explorer section of the Business Rule Composer. The properties should appear in the lower-left region of the Business Rule Composer.

13. Select the Fact Retriever property of the policy version, and click the ellipsis that appears.

14. In the Select Configuration component, click the Browse button. In the list of assemblies that appears, select the custom fact retriever created previously in this example.

■Note If you cannot locate the custom fact retriever, verify that it is deployed to the GAC.

---

15. Select the class implementing UpdateFacts to complete configuring the custom fact retriever, as shown in Figure 5-10.

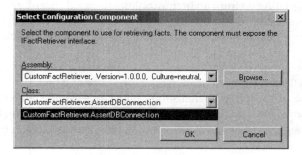

Figure 5-10. *Configuring the custom fact checker*

16. After creating the custom fact retriever to retrieve the DataConnection and configuring the policy to use the custom fact retriever, it is time to define the rules. So, define the business rule to compare the requested service address with the customer addresses already in the Northwind database. If there is a match, then the service request will be scheduled. When completed, the rule should appear, as shown in Figure 5-11.

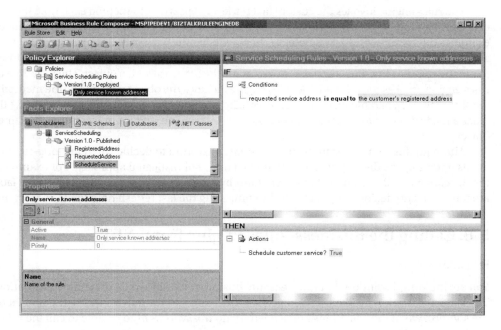

Figure 5-11. *Completed service address verification rule*

17. Deploy the rules and invoke them from an orchestration, specifying the XML messages that the policy expects. The rules engine will invoke the UpdateFacts method of the custom fact retriever. The method will add a DataConnection fact to the Northwind database to the rules engine facts.

How It Works

The rules engine examines facts provided either directly from an orchestration or from a custom fact retriever. The facts provided directly from an orchestration are called *short-term* facts, and the orchestration supplies them each time BizTalk invokes the rules engine. The facts provided from a custom fact retriever are called *long-term* facts, and they can be reused each time BizTalk invokes the rules engine.

A BizTalk orchestration can also treat the DataConnection in this example as a short-term fact. Accomplish this by creating a DataConnection in an Expression shape and including it as a parameter to the Call Rules shape. However, each orchestration instance would create its own DataConnection. You can improve the scalability and performance of the application by treating the DataConnection as a long-term fact and sharing it each time BizTalk invokes the rules engine.

In general, treating a fact as long-term is preferable under the following conditions:

- The fact value can be shared each time BizTalk invokes the rules engine.

- Retrieving the fact incurs a significant performance penalty.

- Caching the fact value will still allow the rules to execute correctly.

- The fact is not directly available in the orchestration that invokes the rules.

The rules engine invokes the custom fact retriever's UpdateFacts method each time the policy executes. This method decides when to update the facts. In this example, the UpdateFacts method examines the factsHandleIn parameter to check whether the DataConnection was already created. If the factsHandleIn parameter is null, then the method creates the DataConnection, inserts it into the rules engine, and completes by returning the DataConnection object. The next time the rules engine invokes the method, the rules engine includes the object returned by the method in the factsHandleIn parameter. If the factsHandleIn parameter is not null, the method knows that it has already inserted the DataConnection into the rules engine, and it simply returns the same object.

Although this solution example uses a simple algorithm to decide when the long-term fact needs updating, the developer can implement a more sophisticated approach. For example, the developer could refresh the facts every hour by returning a DateTime object when the facts are refreshed and decide to update facts by comparing the last refresh time to the current time.

5-6. Calling the Business Rules Engine from .NET

Problem

You are building a solution that must execute business rules based on dynamic information. These business rules are likely to change over time, and you want to minimize the impact on the solution when modifications are needed. To do this, you want to be able to call the rules engine from a .NET assembly.

■**Note** The problem within this recipe is the same as in Recipe 5-7. The solutions in the two recipes differ in how the business rules are executed.

Solution

This solution describes the steps necessary to call the business rules engine from a C# assembly. The steps detail how to build a .NET Windows application to process job applications and dynamically determine whether applicants meet a minimum age requirement. If the applicant is younger than 18, then they cannot be considered for employment. The minimum age is likely to change over time and needs to be easily configurable. The business rules engine that comes with BizTalk Server captures the business rule determining the minimum working age. Other recipes within this chapter detail the steps for creating rules.

■**Note** This recipe is based on the policy and vocabulary defined in Recipe 5-2.

This solution assumes that a rule exists in the business rules engine to determine whether an applicant meets the minimum age requirements. To call this rule from a .NET application, follow these steps:

1. Open the project containing the .NET application.

2. Add a project reference to the `<Install Folder>\Microsoft BizTalk Server 2006\ Microsoft.RuleEngine.dll` assembly, which contains the classes required to call the business rules engine.

3. Create the necessary policy and fact objects, and execute the business rule policy, as shown in Listing 5-7.

Listing 5-7. *Calling a Business Rule from .NET*

```
public void callSamplePolicy(ref System.Xml.XmlDocument newHireListDoc)
{
    // create the SamplePolicy policy object
    // specify policy name and version
    Microsoft.RuleEngine.Policy policy =
            new Microsoft.RuleEngine.Policy("SamplePolicy", 1, 0);

    // create the facts object array to hold the input parameters for the policy
    object[] facts = new object[1];

    // create the input parameter for the SamplePolicy policy
    // based on a typed BizTalk schema (fully qualified .NET type)
    Microsoft.RuleEngine.TypedXmlDocument typedXmlDoc =
      new Microsoft.RuleEngine.TypedXmlDocument("SampleSolution.NewHireList",
                                                    newHireListDoc);

    // add the input parameter to the facts object array
    facts[0] = typedXmlDoc;
```

```
    // execute the policy against the facts
    policy.Execute(facts);
    policy.Dispose();

    // set the parameter object
    newHireListDoc.LoadXml(typedXmlDoc.Document.OuterXml);
}
```

How It Works

Although the business rules engine comes as part of BizTalk Server, this solution shows that
.NET assemblies outside the BizTalk environment can call into it. This allows external applications to use the same rule framework that the integration hub does, enabling companies to
consolidate their business rules functionality onto one platform.

■**Note** You can extend this solution by using a web service method to access the business rules engine,
allowing code on any platform to call into a common rule framework.

For a .NET project to call into the business rules engine, it must reference the Microsoft.
RuleEngine.dll assembly. This assembly contains the classes used to access the rules framework, including those to execute policies. In this solution, you first create an instance of the
policy object, with the appropriate name and version. The name must exactly match the name
of the policy you want to execute, as shown in Figure 5-12. This solution specifies SamplePolicy
as the policy name, which maps to the highlighted name in Figure 5-12.

Following the policy name, you specify the major and minor versions of the policy you
want to execute. You specify 1.0, which is the only version of the policy currently deployed.
Alternatively, you could specify the name only when creating the policy object (no version
parameters supplied to the policy's constructor method), which executes the most recently
deployed version of the policy.

Next, you create a collection (array) of fact objects. This array holds all the objects necessary to execute the policy. These objects map to the different types of facts that the Business
Rule Composer can create, including XML documents, .NET classes or class members, and
database connections. The SamplePolicy policy uses only a single XML document fact, which
you create next.

You use the Microsoft.RuleEngine.TypedXmlDocument class to create an XML document fact,
specifying the document type (the fully qualified .NET type name) and XML document instance.
Add this TypedXmlDocument to the fact collection.

Finally, you execute the policy against the facts collection. As shown in Recipe 5-7, the
facts collection is passed as a *reference* parameter, meaning any changes to the facts will be
committed to the original instances. In this solution, the XML document fact will have the
appropriate minimum age requirement logic applied.

It is also possible to execute a policy directly from an Expression shape within an orchestration. Listing 5-8 illustrates how you would execute the same policy as described in the
"Solution" section of this recipe but from an Expression shape.

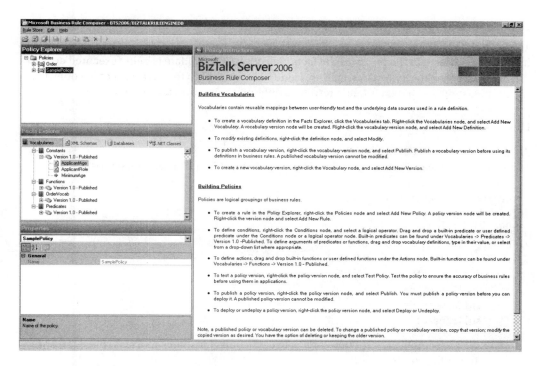

Figure 5-12. *Specifying a policy name*

Listing 5-8. *Calling Policy from Expression Shape*

```
// create the SamplePolicy policy object
// policy variable has type of Microsoft.RuleEngine.Policy
policy = new Microsoft.RuleEngine.Policy("SamplePolicy", 1, 0);

// create the input parameter for the OrderShipping policy
// typedXmlDoc variable has type of Microsoft.RuleEngine.TypedXmlDocument
// NewHireListMessage has type of SampleSolution.NewHireList
typedXmlDoc =
  new Microsoft.RuleEngine.TypedXmlDocument("SampleSolution.NewHireList",
                                                NewHireListMessage);

// execute the policy against the facts
policy.Execute(typedXmlDoc);
policy.Dispose();
```

Although the policy executed in this recipe requires only a single XML document fact, facts can also be .NET classes or class members and data connections. By default, BizTalk Server requires you to provide an object instance for each fact used in a policy.

Data Connection Facts

To pass a data connection fact to a policy, initialize a `Microsoft.RuleEngine.DataConnection` instance and pass it to the policy in the facts collection. If an update is being executed against the underlying database, you must also provide a transaction to the `DataConnection` object, as shown in Listing 5-9. If data is being retrieved only, no transaction is required.

Listing 5-9. *Providing a Transaction*

```
// create SQL connection object
sqlConnection = new System.Data.SqlClient.SqlConnection("ConnectionString");

// create SQL transaction object
sqlTransaction = sqlConnection.BeginTransaction();

// create Data Connection object
dataConnection = new Microsoft.RuleEngine.DataConnection(
        "SqlDataSetName",
        "SqlTableName",
        sqlConnection,
        sqlTransaction);
```

The .NET assembly can add this `DataConnection` object instance to a fact collection and pass it to the policy for execution.

5-7. Calling the Business Rules Engine from an Orchestration

Problem

You are building a workflow that must execute business rules based on dynamic information. These business rules are likely to change over time, and you want to minimize the impact on the solution when modifications are needed.

■**Note** The problem within this recipe is the same as in Recipe 5-6. The solutions in the two recipes differ in how the business rules are executed.

Solution

This solution will demonstrate how to call the business rules engine from an orchestration, without using a .NET assembly. The basic problem is similar to the previous recipe (Recipe 5-6). The key points of the problem are as follows:

- Job applications must be processed, and it must be determined whether they meet the minimum age requirement.

- If the applicant is younger than 18, then they cannot be considered for employment.

- The minimum age is likely to change over time and needs to be easily configurable.

Note This recipe is based on the policy and vocabulary defined in Recipe 5-2.

This solution assumes that a rule exists in the business rules engine to determine whether an applicant meets the minimum age requirements. To call this rule from an orchestration, follow these steps:

1. Open the project containing the orchestration.

2. In the orchestration's Properties window, configure it to act as a long-running transaction.

3. Create a new message, and specify the name and type. In this scenario, create a message named `NewHireListMessage` defined by the `NewHireList` schema.

4. From the Toolbox, drag the following onto the design surface in top-down order:

    a. Receive shape to receive the initial order message—configure this shape to use the `NewHireListMessage` message, to activate the orchestration instance, and to use an orchestration receive port.

    b. Send the shape to deliver the `NewHireListMessage` message to an external system—configure this shape to use an orchestration send port.

5. From the Toolbox, drag a Scope shape onto the design surface, in between the Receive and Send shapes configured in the previous step—configure this shape to act as an Atomic transaction, as shown in Figure 5-13.

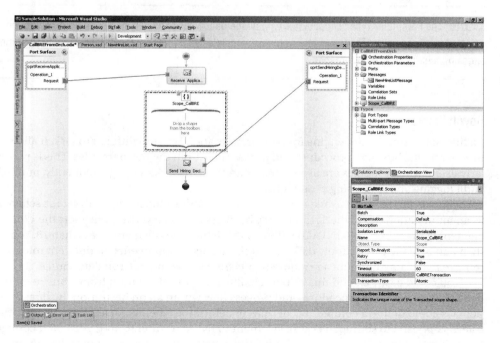

Figure 5-13. *Configuring the Scope shape*

6. From the Toolbox, drag a Call Rules shape onto the design surface, inside the Scope shape configured in the previous step. Configure this shape by double-clicking it, which launches the CallRules Policy Configuration dialog box, as shown in Figure 5-14. Select the appropriate business policy to call and the parameters to pass into the policy (SamplePolicy and NewHireListMessage in this scenario).

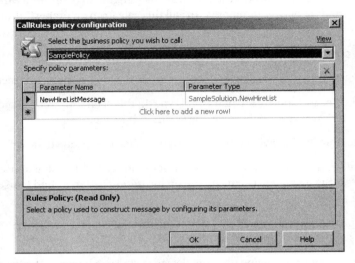

Figure 5-14. *Configuring the Call Rules shape*

■**Note** The Parameter Type list populates with all the data types expected as input parameters to the selected business policy. The Parameter Name list populates with all the orchestration variables and messages matching the parameter types.

How It Works

Calling the business rules engine from an orchestration is a straightforward task. It allows you to separate the business procedure and process flow from the business rules. This is particularly useful when the rules are used across many process flows, change frequently, or need audit logging and versioning capabilities.

This recipe's solution uses a message instance conforming to the NewHireList schema as an input parameter to the SamplePolicy business rule policy. This policy sets the <Role> element of the message to INVALID APPLICANT if the <Age> element is less than 18. You could then enhance the rule to apply different minimum age requirements for different roles or to retrieve real-time minimum age requirements from a government-run data source.

You could easily extend this solution to illustrate how the output from a business rule can facilitate business procedures and process flow within an orchestration. Business rule policies could define a complex set of rules to determine whether an applicant is valid for a role. As opposed to setting the <Role> element to INVALID APPLICANT, you could configure the policy to return a Boolean value indicating whether the applicant meets the minimum age requirements. The orchestration could then use this Boolean value in a Decide shape, allowing separate process flows to determine whether an applicant is valid for a role based on previous work experience, personal references, and salary requirements.

For an orchestration to successfully call a policy, you must make a few settings:

- The Call Rules shape must be within an Atomic Scope shape (this necessitates that the orchestration's Transaction property is set to Long Running).

- The Policy must be published and deployed within the business rules engine.

■**Note** The Call Rules shape will always access the most recently deployed version of a policy.

- An initialized instance of all variables referenced in the policy must be in the same scope as the Call Rules shape.

Although this solution uses only an XML message instance as input to the rules policy, policies can accept other types of input parameters as well. The Vocabulary Definition Wizard allows a .NET class/class member or a data table/column to be used as business terms. As previously stated, an initialized instance of all variables referenced in a policy must be in scope at the Call Rules shape in the orchestration. This means that if a .NET class and a data table/column are used in a policy, there must be an initialized instance of the .NET class and rules engine Microsoft.RuleEngine.DataConnection object available in the orchestration to pass into the policy as input parameters.

■**Note** If there is no instance matching an input used in a policy's rules, that input parameter will not appear in the Call Rules Policy Configuration dialog box's Parameter list. This will prevent the policy from being successfully called from the orchestration.

The policy used in this scenario references vocabulary definitions based on two XML elements in the NewHireList schema: <Age> and <Role>. Take care when creating these vocabulary definitions, or the rule policy won't be able to appropriately handle the orchestration message. Specifically, set the Document Type property of the business term to be the fully qualified type name—SampleSolution.NewHireList in this case. If the fully qualified .NET type name is not used to define the BizTalk schema, BizTalk Server will not have enough information to uniquely identify the data field.

Note In BizTalk Server 2004, the default value supplied for the Document Type property is the schema file name with no extension. If this value is not changed to use the fully qualified .NET type name, orchestrations will not be able to call the policy rules using the definition. You can find the fully qualified .NET type name by selecting a schema in the Visual Studio Solution Explorer and viewing the Fully Qualified Name property.

Figure 5-15 illustrates how to set the Document Type property for the <Age> element within the Business Rule Composer.

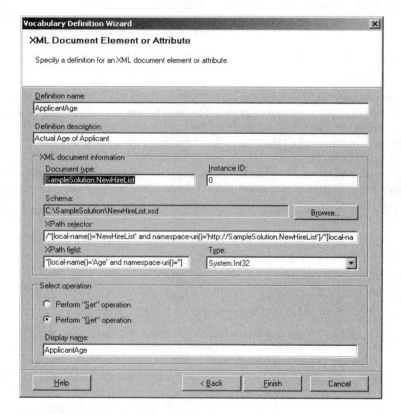

Figure 5-15. *Configuring the vocabulary definition*

A finer point regarding the Call Rules shape is that it treats input parameters as *reference* parameters, which means rules may modify the objects passed and return them to the orchestration. The solution in this chapter passes a new hire list message into the SamplePolicy policy. The policy modifies the message by applying the appropriate minimum age requirements logic and passes back the message. Given that messages are immutable (once they are created, they cannot be modified) in BizTalk, how does this work? The answer is that, behind the scenes, the policy creates a modified copy of the original message. Although this saves the developer's time when creating their orchestration, it also has an important side effect: all promoted properties on the original message are removed from the message context. If properties on the message need to be maintained, make a copy of the message, allowing the message context to be reset after the business rules engine is called.

5-8. Deploying and Undeploying Policies

Problem

You want to know the components that make up a rules engine policy and perform the steps necessary to deploy and undeploy a policy to make the rule sets available to business processes.

Solution

Deploying a policy requires that several components be in place prior to the deployment. The deployment is quite straightforward, and you can deploy in several ways. This solution describes the prerequisites to the policy deployment and walks through the deployment steps using the Business Rule Composer. See the "How It Works" section for information about using the Rules Engine Deployment Wizard.

A policy consists of one or more rules. A rule comprises a set of facts. In this solution, we describe the process to deploy and undeploy all the components that make up a policy. Your first task is to define any facts that may need to be used in any rules that are part of the policy:

1. Define all the custom facts. Using the Business Rule Composer, open the Facts Explorer. Define any vocabulary, schemas, databases, or .NET assemblies that may be needed for any rule.

2. Once completed, save and publish any vocabularies that may have been defined. Right-click the vocabulary version, which will be used by a rule, and click Save. Right-click the version again, and select Publish. Once you have published a vocabulary version, you cannot modify it directly. Instead, it must be versioned—you can do this by copying the most recent version and then pasting a new version. The new version can be modified.

3. Your next task is to create a new policy and add all the rules that are part of the policy. In the Policy Explorer, create a new policy, and add one or more rules. As you create each rule, reference the appropriate version of the vocabularies, which have been published.

4. Save, publish, and test the policy by right-clicking the policy version and selecting the appropriate menu item.

5. The final task is to actually deploy the policy. Once the policy has been deployed, it cannot be deleted unless it is first undeployed. In the same manner as the vocabularies, it cannot be modified unless a new version is first created. Deploy the policy as follows: right-click the policy version that is to be deployed, and select Deploy, as shown in Figure 5-16. (You can undeploy policies by selecting Undeploy.)

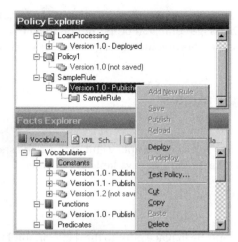

Figure 5-16. *Deploying via the Business Rule Composer*

How It Works

You have two basic approaches for deploying and undeploying policies. The first is to use the Business Rule Composer. Using the Business Rule Composer, you can define facts and policies that can be modified, published, and deployed. The second is to use the Rules Engine Deployment Wizard, as shown in Figure 5-17. The wizard allows policy files to be exported and imported onto machines where they may not have been created. Use the following basic steps to deploy a policy in a distributed environment:

1. Export the policy file. Open the BizTalk Rules Engine Deployment Wizard on the machine where the policy was created. Select Export Policy/Vocabulary File from Database. Walk through the options, selecting the policy you want to deploy on a target machine. This process will create an XML file (or multiple files if exporting multiple vocabularies and policies) that can be copied to another machine.

2. Copy the XML file(s) created in the first step to the target machine. Open the wizard on the target machine, and select the Import and Publish Policy/Vocabulary File to Database option. Walk through the options to publish the data to the target machine's rules engine (the vocabularies must first be deployed, and all referenced .NET assemblies must be placed in the GAC).

3. Run the wizard again on the target machine. This time, select the Deploy Policy option. All policies and vocabularies that have not been deployed will be available in the drop-down list. Select the object(s) you want to deploy, and walk through the rest of the wizard. The vocabularies and policies can now be referenced on the target machine by orchestrations or other components.

4. To undeploy, follow step 3, selecting Undeploy rather than Deploy from the first option list. Only those vocabularies and policies that have been deployed successfully will be available for undeployment.

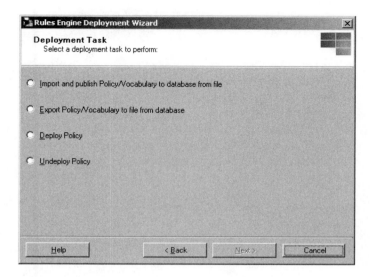

Figure 5-17. *Using the Rules Engine Deployment Wizard*

CHAPTER 6

■ ■ ■

Adapters

The BizTalk engine uses adapters to communicate with outside systems, and adapters start and end any process within BizTalk. Adapters come in three basic flavors: protocol adapters, database adapters, and ERP adapters.

Hundreds of adapters are available from third-party vendors that enable the BizTalk engine to communicate with just about any system. In addition, if an adapter is not available, the BizTalk adapter framework facilitates custom adapter development in .NET. Commonly used adapters include the following:

- *Protocol adapters*: HTTP, File, and SOAP

- *Database adapters*: SQL, DB2, and Oracle

- *ERP adapters*: SAP, PeopleSoft, and Siebel

An entire book would be necessary to cover all the adapters available and their proper use. ERP adapters in particular require an in-depth discussion of the ERP system in question before you are able to use the adapter for that system. This chapter will therefore focus on a few of the more basic protocol and database adapters that are included with BizTalk out of the box.

6-1. Configuring File Sends

Problem

You need to send a message from BizTalk with the File adapter.

Solution

The BizTalk platform offers numerous options to facilitate sending files. Within the BizTalk File adapter, various send options are natively available for the user to configure. The following steps demonstrate how to configure a send port:

   1. Open the BizTalk Explorer, and create a send port that uses the File adapter.

■**Note** In alignment with standard BizTalk functionality, only static ports are defined to use a named File adapter.

---

2. In the send port properties, under the General options, click the ellipses for the Address (URI) property. The FILE Transport Properties dialog box appears.

3. Click the Destination Folder input box. Enter the value of the folder where you would like BizTalk Server to write the file. In this example, we are using the folder C:\Book.

4. Click the Copy Mode drop-down list, and ensure that the default value, Create New, is selected, as shown in Figure 6-1.

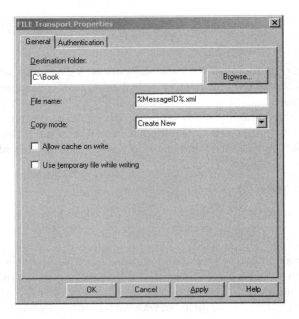

Figure 6-1. *Configuring file sends in the FILE Transport Properties dialog box*

■**Note** The Copy Mode drop-down list offers the Create New, Append, and Overwrite options. In this recipe, we will use Create New.

---

5. Click the Authentication tab, ensure that the Use These Credentials When Host Does Not Have Access to Network Share check box is unchecked.

■**Note** BizTalk gives you the ability to specify a different user account if the security permissions are different from the running host user account.

---

6. Click OK.

How It Works

In this recipe, we demonstrated how to use the File adapter and explored the native configuration options. You can configure the File adapter either within the BizTalk Explorer (under a send port) or through code programmatically. The File adapter send configuration options encompass naming a file, using copy mode, implementing caching, and implementing security.

When naming files on the General tab of the FILE Transport Properties dialog box, you can configure a file send in conjunction with numerous macros to assist in making a file name more meaningful. For example, as shown in Figure 6-1, the File Name value is %MessageID%.xml. The macro, %MessageID%, will be substituted with the Globally Unique Identifier (GUID) of the message in BizTalk Server at runtime when the file is named. This GUID comes directly from the message context property, BTS.MessageID. (Please see the BizTalk documentation for a complete list of all of the macros available when naming files.) It is important to note you can use only these macros. Currently, the product does not support creating custom or "user-defined" macros, and it doesn't support using any other BizTalk context properties other than what is available via the macros. Using these file-naming macros has been described as somewhat problematic within the BizTalk user group community. It is worth noting that a macro will fail if the following is true:

- A corresponding system property is not set, for example, the exclusion of SourceParty or SourcePartyID.

- The file send macro is misspelled (including case-sensitive considerations).

- The value of the macro result causes an invalid file name, for example, the usage of the following characters:

  / \ ! . , * " |

A further consideration when using the File send adapter is to ensure the security/access permissions are set appropriately. This encompasses standard Active Directory security considerations for related share and folder permissions, as well as security considerations related to non-Windows environments. By default, the File adapter write activity uses the user account of the running BizTalk host. It is always a good idea to unit test a security scenario first to ensure a file can be written to the desired destination before introducing the File send adapter. This way, you can isolate permission issues, saving possible issue detection and resolution time.

6-2. Configuring File Receives

Problem

You need to receive a message in BizTalk using the File adapter.

Solution

Within the BizTalk File adapter, numerous options are available to facilitate receiving files. You can configure all these options natively within the adapter. The following steps outline configuring the File receive adapter:

1. Open the BizTalk Explorer, and create a receive port and a corresponding file receive location.

2. Within the receive location, click the ellipsis for the Address (URI) property. The FILE Transport Properties dialog box appears.

3. Click the Receive Folder input box. Enter the value of the file folder you want BizTalk Server to pull for files. In this example, we are using the folder C:\Book\Receive, as shown in Figure 6-2.

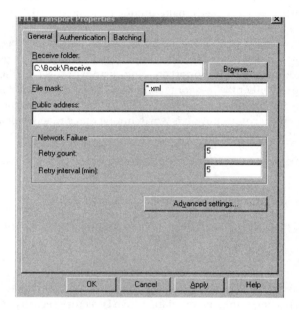

Figure 6-2. *Configuring file receives in the FILE Transport Properties dialog box*

4. Click the File Mask input area. Enter the value ***.***.

■**Note** The File Mask property allows the File adapter to consume files that match a specific file mask. In the instance of *.*, all files will be consumed by the wildcard mask. However, it is worth noting that you cannot set up two receive locations with the same mask, monitoring the same location.

---

5. Click the Public Address input box. Enter the address in the format of file://<Receive folder>/<File Mask>.

6. Under the Network Failure options, ensure the default options are 5 and 5 for Retry Count and Retry Interval.

7. Click the Authentication tab; ensure that the Use These Credentials When Host Does Not Have Access to Network Share check box is unchecked.

■**Note** BizTalk gives you the ability to specify a different user account, if the security permissions are different from the running host user account.

---

8. Click OK.

How It Works

In this recipe, we demonstrated how to use the File receive adapter and explored the native configuration options. You can configure the File adapter either using the BizTalk Explorer (within a receive location), programming code, or using the BizTalk Administration Console. The File adapter receive configuration options encompass receive location parameters, network failure options, and authentication.

In addition to the basic configuration options, you can configure other advanced options to assist in the process of receiving files. The General tab contains some advanced configuration options, as shown in Table 6-1.

Table 6-1. *Advanced Settings for File Transport*

Option	Description
Rename Files While Reading	Ensures that a file is renamed while BizTalk is reading the file during the receive process. This might assist in ensuring that an incoming file is not overwritten if the source address has the ability to write files with identical names.
Receive Location Polling	Gives the ability to set the polling interval for BizTalk to check for new files on a given receive location.
Removing of Files	Specifies timing values that control when BizTalk deletes the source files after a file has been read and submitted to the BizTalk MessageBox. This might be useful when trying to avoid overwrites in a scenario where multiple files are written to the same file source.

The File receive adapter also allows for the configuration of file batching. Batching allows destination files to be submitted in a collective batch, allowing for the configuration of file consumption and file exception options on the entire batch. Within BizTalk's batch processing model, files that are processed successfully to the MessageBox are deleted from the source, files that are processed to the MessageBox with exception are suspended, and messages that fail to write to the MessageBox cause the entire batch to be rolled back. For example, a security permission issue might prevent the file from being open and consumed. This premise ensures that all files are preserved on the source file location. That is, the physical file deletion process does not occur until the entire batch has been processed.

6-3. Configuring SMTP Send Ports

Problem

You need to send a message from BizTalk with the Simple Mail Transport Protocol (SMTP).

Solution

This example configures a BizTalk send port using the SMTP adapter to send a message to a single email recipient. If BizTalk needs to send each message to a different email address, use a dynamic port from an orchestration. For more information about configuring dynamic ports, please see Recipe 4-6. The following steps outline how to configure the SMTP adapter:

1. From the Start menu, select All Programs ➤ Microsoft BizTalk Server 2006 ➤ BizTalk Server Administration.

2. Expand the BizTalk Server group, select the default BizTalk Application 1, and select the Send Ports folder.

3. Right-click the Send Ports folder, and select New ➤ Static One-Way Send Port to open the Send Port Properties dialog box. Enter **Sample SMTP Send Port** in the Name box.

4. Within the Transport section of the General tab, select SMTP from the Type drop-down list, as shown in Figure 6-3.

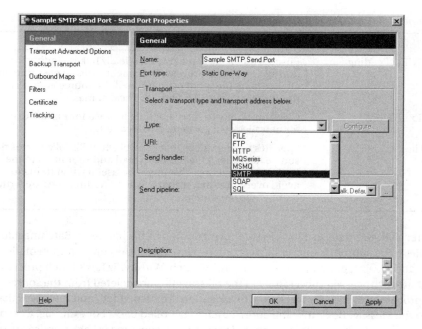

Figure 6-3. *Specifying the SMTP transport type*

5. Click the Configure button to open the SMTP Transport Properties dialog box.

6. On the General tab, enter the message recipient's email address and the email message subject, as shown in Figure 6-4. Additionally, request delivery and read receipts to get a notification email when the message recipient receives or marks the message as read.

Figure 6-4. *Configuring the general options for the SMTP adapter*

7. The settings on the Compose tab provide three options for specifying the message body. First, the message body may directly contain the sent message. Second, you can set the message to a fixed value, as shown in Figure 6-5. Third, BizTalk can retrieve the message from a file location. Set these options as necessary.

Figure 6-5. *Configuring the Compose tab*

8. The Attachments tab allows you to configure the different ways BizTalk can include attachments. BizTalk can include the message being sent with the SMTP adapter as an attachment or include an external file as an attachment, as shown in Figure 6-6. Set these options as necessary.

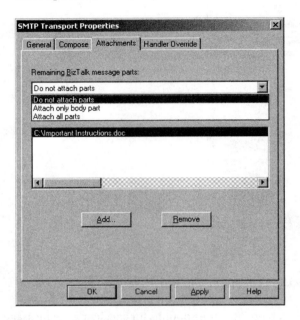

Figure 6-6. *Setting the SMTP attachment*

9. The Handler Override tab contains SMTP configuration settings such as the SMTP server name, the From address used when sending email messages, and authentication settings. Instead of setting these configuration values for each send port using the SMTP transport, all SMTP send ports can share configuration values for the SMTP handler. Only change these values from the default settings if you need to override the default SMTP handler configuration.

In addition to configuring a send port to use the SMTP adapter, you can configure settings on the adapter to be used by all send ports via the adapter. Configure the SMTP handler with properties that any SMTP send port can reuse with the following steps:

1. Connect to the BizTalk group in the BizTalk Administration Console, expand the Platform Settings folder, and expand the Adapters folder. Select the SMTP adapter.

2. Right-click the host appearing in the right pane of the BizTalk Administration Console, and select Properties.

3. Click the Properties button in the SMTP Transport Properties dialog box.

4. Set the default configuration values for the SMTP adapter. Figure 6-7 shows a sample configuration.

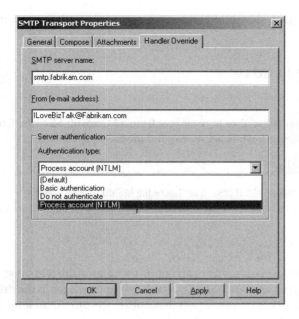

Figure 6-7. *SMTP handler configuration*

You have three handler configuration options for authenticating with the SMTP server, as shown in Table 6-2. SMTP send ports have a fourth default authentication option, which specifies to use the handler configuration setting.

Table 6-2. *SMTP Handler Authentication Options*

Authentication Option	Description
Basic Authentication	Specifies specific credentials to authenticate with the SMTP server. BizTalk may pass these credentials over the network in clear text.
Do Not Authenticate	BizTalk provides no authentication credentials when sending an email message via SMTP.
Process Account (NTLM)	The adapter uses the host instance identity to authenticate with the SMTP server.

How It Works

BizTalk can only send email messages with the SMTP adapter. To receive a message via email, you must use the POP3 adapter available in BizTalk 2006. BizTalk 2004 does not include the POP3 adapter.

The security settings of some SMTP servers disallow impersonation. Under these circumstances, the From address in an email must match the account credentials provided to the SMTP server. The SMTP server must have an email account created specifically for the credentials provided by BizTalk. For example, when specifying process account (NTLM) authentication, the identity of the BizTalk host instance must also have a valid email address. If the

From address does not match the email address of the host instance identity, the email will not be sent.

6-4. Configuring MSMQ Sends

Problem

You are integrating with a system that subscribes to messages from a Microsoft Message Queue (MSMQ) queue, and you must configure BizTalk Server to send messages to MSMQ.

▪Note See Recipe 6-5 for further information about how to configure the MSMQ receive adapter.

Solution

You are building a solution that processes orders from an online commerce site and must deliver those messages to an ERP system via an MSMQ queue. To send messages to the destination queue, you must create a BizTalk Server send port that utilizes the MSMQ adapter. To configure the send port, follow these steps:

1. From the Start menu, select All Programs ➤ Microsoft BizTalk Server 2006 ➤ BizTalk Server Administration.

2. Expand the BizTalk Server group, select the default BizTalk Application 1, and select the Send Ports folder.

3. Right-click the Send Ports folder, and select New ➤ Static One-Way Send Port to open the Send Port Properties dialog box.

4. Select Static One-Way Way Port in the drop-down list, and click OK.

5. Give your send port a descriptive name, select the XMLTransmit pipeline, ensure the correct subscriptions are implemented (on the Filters tab), and select MSMQ as the transport type.

6. Click the Configure button to the right of the Transport Type field. This launches the MSMQ Transport Properties dialog box.

7. Set the Destination Queue property to the queue name that the ERP system accepts messages from, as shown in Figure 6-8. In this scenario, we are using a queue named ERPCommerceOrder.

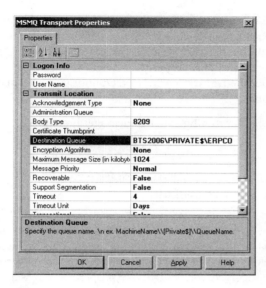

Figure 6-8. *Configuring an MSMQ send port*

8. Leave all other properties with their default values, and click OK.

9. Click OK in the Send Port Properties dialog box to save the send port.

■**Note** You can also create send ports in the BizTalk Editor view in Visual Studio.

---

10. Right-click the send port created in the previous step, and select Start.

How It Works

The BizTalk Server MSMQ adapter allows easy access to messages in MSMQ queues (MSMQ versions 2.0 and 3.0). The adapter relies on the local MSMQ service, which must be installed on the same computer hosting the adapter.

MSMQ Send Options

Although this example illustrates the simplest scenario for sending MSMQ messages to a specified queue, you can make a number of configurations against the MSMQ adapter:

Destination Queue: Specifies the queue to which to send messages. See the following section for further information about how to format queue names.

Ordered Delivery: Specifies whether the message order is persisted when delivering messages to the destination queue. This property enables a solution to implement ordered message delivery, although you must also ensure that all the previous processing (including the receipt of the message from the source queue) is handled serially if the order is to be maintained. See Recipe 4-15 for further information about implementing ordered delivery in BizTalk orchestrations.

You can additionally specify whether the send port should be stopped if errors are encountered when delivering a message to the destination queue. This setting helps enforce a strict ordered delivery requirement, although it has the side effect of completely disabling an interface if a single error occurs. This property is available only via the BizTalk Administration Console, under the Transport Advanced Options grouping of an MSMQ Send Port Properties dialog box.

`Failed Message Routing`: Specifies whether routing of failed messages is enabled.

■Note You can make this setting only via the BizTalk Administration Console, under the Transport Advanced Options grouping of an MSMQ Send Port Properties dialog box.

`Encryption Algorithm`: Specifies the algorithm used to encrypt messages as they are written to the destination queue. The available values are RC2, RC4, and None. This property results in the `Message.UseEncryption` and `Message.EncryptionAlgorithm` properties being set.

`Body Type`: Specifies the body type of MSMQ messages written to the destination queue.

`Maximum Message Size (in kilobytes)`: Specifies the maximum size of the message batch to be delivered to the destination queue. The MSMQ adapter will fill the batch with messages from the MessageBox until this setting is reached.

`Message Priority`: Specifies the priority for delivering messages. This setting is relative to the other send ports within your BizTalk environment. To nullify the functionality of this property, set the priority on all the send ports in your environment to the same value.

`Recoverable`: Specifies whether messages will be recoverable if errors are encountered during the delivery to the destination queue. When this value is set to `True`, messages are persisted to disk in between being pulled from the MessageBox and delivered to the destination queue. If errors occur during delivery, messages can be recovered from the disk.

`Support Segmentation`: Specifies whether the adapter allows large messages (larger than 4MB) to be segmented. This property should be set to `True` if you have implemented the large message extension—if the adapter attempts to deliver a message larger than 4MB and this property is set to `False`, an error is thrown and the message is not delivered.

`Timeout`: Specifies the timeout value for which messages must be delivered (combined with the `Timeout Unit` property). This value applies only when the `Transaction` property is set to `True`. The MSMQ adapter treats messages not delivered within the specified timeout period as error scenarios.

`Timeout Unit`: Specifies the timeout unit for which messages must be delivered (combined with the `Timeout` property). The available values for this property are `Days`, `Hours`, `Minutes`, and `Seconds`.

Use Journal Queue: Specifies whether messages will be copied to the journal queue.

■Note The journal queue is a system queue that is automatically created when MSMQ is installed and is meant to contain copies of messages that are sent or received.

Use Dead Letter Queue: Specifies whether error messages will be sent to the dead letter queue.

■Note The dead letter queue is a system queue that is automatically created when MSMQ is installed and is meant to contain undelivered messages.

User Name: Specifies the user for accessing a remote queue. This property applies only when accessing remote queues. The MSMQ adapter's host account is used to access all local queues.

Password: Specifies the password for accessing a remote queue. This property applies only when accessing remote queues.

Acknowledgement Type: Specifies the type of acknowledgment to send upon the successful delivery of a message batch to the destination queue. The available acknowledgment types are defined in the System.Messaging.AcknowledgeTypes enumeration. You can select multiple acknowledgment types for this property.

Administration Queue: Specifies the administration queue where acknowledgment messages are sent upon the successful delivery of messages to the destination queue.

Use Authentication: Specifies that a certificate thumbprint will be used when delivering messages to the destination queue.

Certificate Thumbprint: Specifies the certificate thumbprint used to attach to the message batch. You can use this certificate thumbprint to authenticate your BizTalk environment as the sender of the messages, helping increase the overall security of your integration solution. The certificate is stored in the System.Messaging.Message.SenderCertificate property.

■Note You can find certificate thumbprints by viewing a certificate's details in the Certificate MMC snap-in.

Transactional: Specifies whether the send port will deliver messages transactionally. This property must be set to True if the destination queue is transactional and False if the destination queue is not transactional.

If the Transactional property is set to True, the MSMQ adapter transactionally retrieves the appropriate amount of messages (as defined by the Maximum Message Size property) into a batch from the MessageBox and attempts to deliver the batch to the queue within the transaction. If any errors are encountered when delivering the batch (including a timeout, as defined by the Timeout and Timeout Unit properties), the MSMQ adapter attempts to redeliver the messages. If any errors are encountered when redelivering the batch, MSMQ suspends the messages, leaving them in a recoverable state in the Message-Box. Setting this property to True automatically implements the behavior defined by the Recoverable property. Messages within a batch are handled individually—those messages that do not encounter errors are delivered to the destination queue, even if other messages in the batch have errors.

If the Transactional property is set to False, the MSMQ adapter retrieves the appropriate number of messages (as defined by the Maximum Message Size property) into a batch from the MessageBox and attempts to deliver the batch to the queue. If any errors are encountered when delivering the batch (including a timeout, as defined by the Timeout and Timeout Unit properties), the MSMQ adapter attempts to suspend the messages. If any errors are encountered when suspending the batch, the messages are lost.

■**Note** As a batch is delivered to the destination queue, errors can occur as messages. They pass through the send pipeline configured on the send port, pass through the map configured on the receive port, or are written to the destination queue.

MSMQ Queue Name Formats

To successfully send documents to an MSMQ queue, you must appropriately format the name of the queue via the Destination Queue property. The appropriate name depends on the type and location of the queue. The following list defines the way the Queue property should be entered for the commonly implemented queues:

Public queue: ComputerName\QueueName

Private queue: ComputerName\Private$\QueueName

Direct access to a queue via TCP: DIRECT=TCP:IPAddressOfComputer\QueueName

Direct access to a queue via HTTP: DIRECT=http://ComputerName/MSMQVirtualDirectory/QueueName, where MSMQVirtualDirectory is the Internet Information Services (IIS) virtual directory name of the MSMQ service

Direct access to a queue via HTTPS: DIRECT=https://ComputerName/MSMQVirtualDirectory/QueueName, where MSMQVirtualDirectory is the IIS virtual directory name of the MSMQ service

Journal queue: ComputerName\QueueName\Journal$

Dead letter queue: ComputerName\Deadletter$

Transaction dead letter queue: ComputerName\XactDeadletter$

By default, the MSMQ adapter prepends `FORMATNAME:DIRECT=OS:` to the `Queue` property, assuming the queue is referenced directly via the host computer's name.

6-5. Configuring MSMQ Receives

Problem

You are integrating with a system that publishes messages to an MSMQ queue, and you must configure BizTalk Server to receive messages from MSMQ.

■**Note** See Recipe 6-4 for further information about how to configure the MSMQ send adapter.

Solution

You are building a solution that processes orders from an online commerce site that outputs order messages to an MSMQ queue. To receive messages from the queue, you must create a BizTalk Server receive location that utilizes the MSMQ adapter. To configure the receive location, follow these steps:

1. From the Start menu, select All Programs ➤ Microsoft BizTalk Server 2006 ➤ BizTalk Server Administration.

2. Expand the BizTalk Server group, select the default BizTalk Application 1, and select the `Receive Ports` folder.

3. Right-click the `Receive Ports` folder, and select New ➤ One-Way Receive Port to open the Receive Port Properties dialog box.

4. Give your new receive port a descriptive name, and click OK.

5. Right-click the receive port created in the previous step, and select New ➤ Receive Location. The Receive Location Properties dialog box appears.

6. Give your receive location a descriptive name, select the XMLReceive pipeline, and select MSMQ as the transport type.

7. Click the Configure button to the right of the Transport Type field. This launches the MSMQ Transport Properties dialog box.

8. Set the `Queue` property to the queue name that the online commerce site outputs messages to, as shown in Figure 6-9. In this scenario, we are using a queue named `CommerceOrder`.

9. Leave all the other properties with their default values, and click OK.

10. Click OK in the Receive Location Properties dialog box to save the receive location.

■**Note** You can also create receive ports and receive locations in the BizTalk Editor view in Visual Studio.

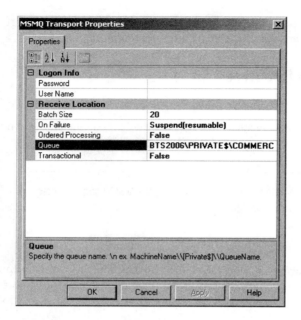

Figure 6-9. *Configuring an MSMQ receive location*

   11. Select the Receive Locations folder in the BizTalk Administration Console, right-click the receive location created earlier, and select Enable.

How It Works

The BizTalk Server MSMQ adapter allows easy access to messages in MSMQ queues (MSMQ versions 2.0 and 3.0). The adapter relies on the local MSMQ service, which must be installed on the same computer hosting the adapter.

MSMQ Receive Options

Although this example illustrates the simplest scenario for receiving MSMQ messages from a specified queue, you can make a number of configurations against the MSMQ adapter:

   Queue: Specifies the queue from which to receive messages. Each queue must be polled by only one receive location per BizTalk environment. See the following section for further information about how to format queue names.

   Ordered Processing: Specifies whether the message order is persisted in the MessageBox. If this property is set to True, only one message is received in each batch (one message retrieved each time the receive location polls the queue). This property enables a solution to implement ordered message delivery, although you must also ensure that any subsequent processing (including the delivery of the message to a destination system) is handled serially if order is to be maintained. A True value for this property overrides the Batch property, essentially setting its value to 1. See Recipe 4-15 for further information about implementing ordered delivery in BizTalk orchestrations.

On Failure: Specifies the action the adapter should take on the receive location if an error occurs. These are the available values:

- Stop: The receive location will be stopped.

- Suspend (nonresumable): The receive location will remain enabled, with error messages being suspended in a nonresumable state.

- Suspend (resumable): The receive location will remain enabled, with error messages being suspended in a resumable state.

Batch Size: Specifies the number of MSMQ messages to be handled in a single batch. The default value of 0 indicates an unlimited number of messages in a batch. The MSMQ adapter retrieves messages from a queue and submits them to the MessageBox in batches of one to many messages.

User Name: Specifies the user for accessing a remote queue. This property applies only when accessing remote queues. The MSMQ adapter's host account is used to access all local queues.

Password: Specifies the password for accessing a remote queue. This property applies only when accessing remote queues.

Transactional: Specifies whether the receive location will retrieve messages transactionally. This property must be set to True if the source queue is transactional and False if the source queue is not transactional.

■**Note** The MSMQ adapter does not support transactionally receiving messages from a remote queue. If the queue is remote, message batches will be retrieved nontransactionally, regardless of the configuration of this property.

If the Transactional property is set to True, the MSMQ adapter transactionally retrieves the appropriate number of messages into a batch and attempts to submit the batch to the MessageBox within the transaction. If any errors are encountered when submitting the messages, the MSMQ adapter attempts to suspend the messages that have errors. If any errors are encountered when suspending the error messages, the MSMQ adapter rolls back the receive transaction (which leaves the messages in their original location—in the MSMQ queue). Messages within a batch are handled individually; those messages that do not encounter errors are submitted to the MessageBox, even if other messages in the batch have errors.

If the Transactional property is set to False, the MSMQ adapter retrieves the appropriate number of messages in a batch and attempts to submit the batch to the MessageBox. If any errors are encountered when submitting the batch, the MSMQ adapter attempts to suspend the messages. If any errors are encountered when suspending the batch, the messages are lost.

■**Note** As a batch is submitted to the MessageBox, errors can occur as messages. They pass through the receive pipeline configured on the receive location, pass through the map configured on the receive port, or are written to the MessageBox database.

You should consider the performance impact when using the MSMQ adapter. It is important to understand the volume and size characteristics of the messages you expect to receive via MSMQ, because they can significantly impact your BizTalk Server resources. You should pay particular attention to the following:

Threading: BizTalk Server attempts to allocate threads to each MSMQ receive location as it polls its queue. Depending on how many messages are in the source queue, multiple threads may be allocated to each receive location. By default, the number of active threads allocated to the MSMQ adapter cannot exceed 25. If you have more than 25 messages being retrieved at any one time, it is possible to have latency.

To allow BizTalk to allocate additional threads to the MSMQ adapter, increase the value of the HKEY_LOCAL_MACHINE\SYSTEM\CurrentControlSet\Services\BTSSvcguid registry setting. The flip side to allocating additional threads to the MSMQ adapter is that the adapter can use additional system resources, such as memory. This could result in an overall degradation in system performance.

Memory allocation: As message batches are retrieved by MSMQ receive locations, they are stored in memory until they are written to the MessageBox. The larger these batches are, the more memory is allocated. To throttle the amount of memory used by the Message-Box adapter, you can use the Batch and Serial Processing properties. You can limit the number of messages in any given batch by setting the Batch property to a low value. You can also set the Serial Processing property to True, which limits the MSMQ receive location to retrieving a single message in each batch.

Memory allocation is particularly important if you have implemented the large message extension for message queuing, which allows messages larger than 4MB in size to be handled by the MSMQ adapter. See the SDK example devoted to this topic for further information.

It is important to understand the relationship of these configurations and the impact they have on system resources. The ideal configuration of threading, serial processing, and batch processing is specific to each BizTalk environment. Optimization should be part of the performance-testing phase for all solutions you deploy to your BizTalk Server environment.

MSMQ Queue Name Formats

To successfully read messages from an MSMQ queue, you must appropriately format the name of the queue via the Queue property. The appropriate name depends on the type and location of the queue. The following list defines the way the Queue property should be entered for the commonly implemented queues:

Public queue: `ComputerName\QueueName`

Private queue: `ComputerName\Private$\QueueName`

Direct access to a queue via TCP: `DIRECT=TCP:IPAddressOfComputer\QueueName`

By default, the MSMQ adapter prepends `FORMATNAME:DIRECT=OS:` to the `Queue` property, assuming the queue is referenced directly via the host computer's name.

6-6. Sending Updategrams with the SQL Adapter

Problem

You need to create an orchestration that inserts a record into a table in your SQL database. Specifically, you need to create an orchestration that inserts a new customer record in your ERP system based on an inbound customer creation message from your CRM system.

Solution

The solution reviewed as part of this recipe outlines how to use the SQL adapter within the context of an orchestration. The following instructions outline the tasks required to create and configure the physical SQL send port as well as the orchestration that implements the SQL adapter.

The solution has sample XML files to demonstrate how the SQL adapter inserts message content into a SQL table. The solution also includes a sample SQL table structure.

Task 1: Create Supporting Artifacts

Your first task is to create supporting artifacts. These include a database table and a BizTalk solution. Here are the steps to follow:

1. Create a new SQL database and table for which to insert the record. Compile the table definition listed in Listing 6-1.

   Listing 6-1. *Listing Customer Table Definition*

   ```
   CREATE TABLE [dbo].[Customer] (
       [CustomerID][int] IDENTITY (1,1) NOT NULL,
       [CustomerName][nvarchar](30) COLLATE SQL_Latin1_General_CP1_CI_AS NOT
   NULL,
       [Address][nvarchar](60) COLLATE SQL_Latin1_General_CP1_CI_AS NOT NULL,
       [City][nvarchar](30) COLLATE SQL_Latin1_General_CP1_CI_AS NOT NULL,
       [Region][nvarchar](30) COLLATE SQL_Latin1_General_CP1_CI_AS NOT NULL,
       [PostalCode][nvarchar](10) COLLATE SQL_Latin1_General_CP1_CI_AS NOT NULL,
   ) ON [PRIMARY]
   ```

2. Create a new BizTalk solution that will insert customers into the Customer table in your SQL database. Next, create a sample message that matches the structure detailed in Listing 6-2. The schema for this message will be created as part of the solution as defined in the "Task 2: Create BizTalk Solution Artifacts" section of this recipe.

Listing 6-2. *Sample Customer Message*

```
<nsO:Customer_Request xmlns:nsO="http://SQLAdapterUpdategram">
  <nsO:sync>
    <nsO:after>
      <nsO:Customer CustomerName="Alice" Address="King" City="Seattle"
Region="WA" PostalCode="98005" />
    </nsO:after>
  </nsO:sync>
</nsO:Customer_Request>
```

Task 2: Create BizTalk Solution Artifacts

You will be using the Add Generated Items Wizard to generate the BizTalk artifacts for this recipe. The wizard will prompt you to specify your BizTalk environment (such as specifying the BizTalk MessageBox database, setting the connection string to the database you will be accessing, and identifying the type of SQL port you are creating, such as send or receive). The following steps describe this task in detail:

1. Choose Add Generated Items from the Solution Explorer tool menu. Verify that Add Adapter Metadata is selected. Figure 6-10 displays the Add Generated Items Wizard.

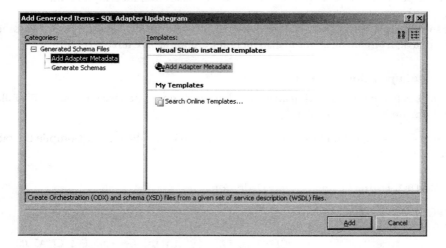

Figure 6-10. *Using the Add Generated Items Wizard*

2. On the Add Adapter page, select the SQL adapter, and verify the settings to your BizTalk MessageBox database.

Note You can leave the Port field empty unless you are specifying an already created SQL send or receive port. This sample will create a send port that you will specify later through the BizTalk Explorer.

---

3. Follow the wizard, and set the connection string for the database to which you are connecting. Next, in the SQL Transport Schema Generation Wizard, specify the target namespace as `http://SQLAdapterUpdategram`, the request document root element name as `Customer_Request`, and the response document root element name as `Customer_Response`. The wizard should look like Figure 6-11.

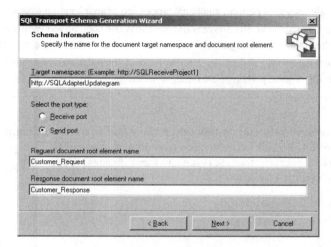

Figure 6-11. *Using the SQL Transport Schema Generation Wizard*

4. On the Statement Type page of the wizard, select Updategram as the type of statement. On the Statement Information page of the wizard, select Insert as the type of the update-gram to create. Additionally, on the same page, select the Customer table as the table name. In the Columns to Update list, multiselect the following columns: CustomerName, Address, City, Region and PostalCode. CustomerID is not required because SQL Server automatically generates the ID because of the column being an Identity column. The wizard should resemble Figure 6-12.

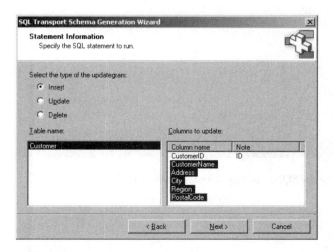

Figure 6-12. *Using the SQL Transport Generation Wizard—the Statement Information page*

5. Click Finish, completing the wizard. When you complete the wizard, notice that BizTalk creates two artifacts for you: the BizTalk orchestration and InsertCustomerService.xsd.

■**Note** The BizTalk orchestration allows you to perform additional processing of an inbound message before sending the message to the SQL database. The InsertCustomerService schema represents a multipart message within your orchestration. The first part of the message represents the request you will be sending to the SQL database, and the second part represents the response the database will return to you. In this recipe, we will use only the request portion of the multipart message.

---

6. Configure the BizTalk orchestration for an inbound receive and an outbound send. Additionally, configure your BizTalk orchestration to send a message of type SQL_Adapter_Updategram.InsertCustomerService.Customer_Request. Your orchestration should resemble Figure 6-13.

7. Build and deploy your BizTalk solution.

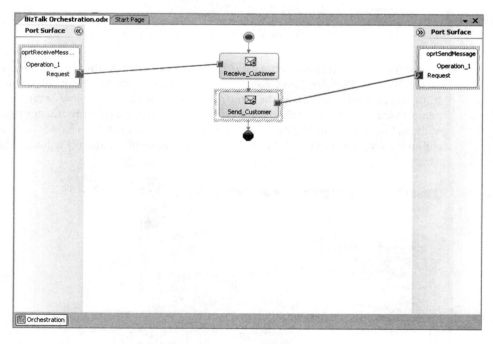

Figure 6-13. *Configuring the SQL updategram orchestration*

Task 3: Create Physical BizTalk Ports

To test this solution, you will need to create a physical file receive port to consume the inbound XML file and a SQL send port to send the message to the SQL database. A simple file receive port will consume the inbound XML document and activate the SQL updategram orchestration just created. Please see Recipe 6-2 for creating a file receive port. The following steps outline creating the SQL send port:

1. From the Start menu, select All Programs ➤ Microsoft BizTalk Server 2006 ➤ BizTalk Server Administration.

2. From the BizTalk Explorer, right-click the Send Ports folder, and select New ➤ Static One-Way Send Port to open the Send Port Properties dialog box. Enter **Sample SQL Updategram Send Port** for the new send port's name. Within the Transport section of the General tab, select SQL from the Type drop-down list.

3. In the SQL Transport Properties dialog box, configure the connection string to the appropriate database by clicking the ellipses next to the Connection String field. Additionally, configure the document target namespace as http://SQLAdapterUpdategram.

4. Set Send Pipeline to the Microsoft.BizTalk.DefaultPipelines.XMLTransmit pipeline.

5. Bind the deployed orchestration to the newly created send and receive ports.

Task 4: Test the Solution

Follow these steps to test the solution:

1. Place the customer test file in the file folder being monitored by BizTalk Server by the file receive port just created. BizTalk Server will consume the file, launch the orchestration, and send the updategram to SQL Server via the SQL send port configured.

2. Verify that the record inserted successfully into the Customer table.

How It Works

SQL updategrams are extremely useful when you need a lightweight implementation to insert, update, or delete data from a SQL table. This recipe demonstrates how to use the Add Generated Items Wizard as well as how to insert records into a SQL table. This recipe did not address the need to process exceptions that may occur when inserting records into a SQL table.

The focus of this recipe was to demonstrate how to insert a record into a single table; however, updategrams can also affect data in multiple tables. The Add Generated Items Wizard creates only a single schema for a single table. However, if you want to modify multiple tables in the same call, you can run the wizard multiple times and then copy the generated schemas into a single schema, or you can manually adjust the autogenerated schema and add the nodes. Consider if you have a Customer table and an Order table. For each customer you insert into the Customer table, you would also like to insert their corresponding orders to the Order table. If you knew the structure of the Order table, you could add the structure to the autogenerated schema, and BizTalk will know to insert the records into a table with the name of the node you specified. Figure 6-14 displays the structure of the modified schema to also insert records into the Order table. A better approach to modifying the autogenerate schema would be to consider using a SQL stored procedure to manage the insertion of data into multiple tables.

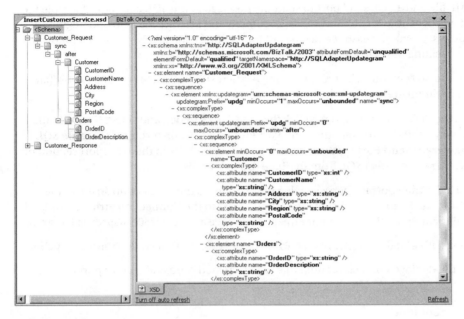

Figure 6-14. *Multiple table insert schema*

SQL updategrams allow you to update records at a table level, which is convenient. However, not all databases may allow access at a table level; they may require you to use other means to manipulate data in the specific table. Additionally, using an updategram "locks" you into using a deployed table structure, which presents a challenge from a maintenance perspective. When determining the best way to manipulate data in a SQL table, consider the following questions:

- Will the account with which you are accessing the SQL database have permissions at a table level?

- What is the likelihood of the table structure changing, and how does that affect the solution you are building?

- Is there logic at a database level that must be performed before the message from your orchestration can be processed?

- Do you need to affect data in many tables? Even though it is technically possible to insert data into multiple tables via an update datagram, inserting data into multiple tables can be better managed using a SQL stored procedure.

If any of the previous questions is true, then you should consider an alternative to using an updategram. Recipe 6-7 discusses using SQL stored procedures as an alternative.

6-7. Calling Stored Procedures Using the SQL Adapter

Problem

You need to create an orchestration that inserts a record into a table in your SQL database via a stored procedure. Specifically, you need to create an orchestration that inserts a new customer record based on an inbound message.

Solution

The solution reviewed as part of this recipe outlines how to use the SQL adapter within the context of an orchestration. The following instructions outline the tasks required to create and configure the physical SQL send port as well as the orchestration that implements the SQL adapter.

The solution has sample XML files to demonstrate how the SQL adapter inserts message content into a SQL table via a stored procedure. The solution also includes a sample SQL table structure.

Task 1: Create Supporting Artifacts

The steps outlined for this task create the supporting solution artifacts. You will create the table, stored procedure, and inbound message structure for the message consumed by BizTalk. Here are the steps to follow:

1. Create a new SQL database and table for which to insert the record. Compile the table definition listed in Listing 6-3.

   Listing 6-3. *Example Customer Table Definition*

```
CREATE TABLE [dbo].[Customer] (
    [CustomerID][int] IDENTITY (1,1) NOT NULL,
    [CustomerName][nvarchar](30) COLLATE SQL_Latin1_General_CP1_CI_AS NOT NULL,
    [Address][nvarchar](60) COLLATE SQL_Latin1_General_CP1_CI_AS NOT NULL,
    [City][nvarchar](30) COLLATE SQL_Latin1_General_CP1_CI_AS NOT NULL,
    [Region][nvarchar](30) COLLATE SQL_Latin1_General_CP1_CI_AS NOT NULL,
    [PostalCode][nvarchar](10) COLLATE SQL_Latin1_General_CP1_CI_AS NOT NULL,
) ON [PRIMARY]
```

2. If you do not have a stored procedure to insert individual customer records, then compile the stored procedure listed in Listing 6-4.

Listing 6-4. *Example Insert Customer Stored Procedure*

```
if exists  (select * from sysobjects where name = 'BizTalkToCustomerInsert'
and type = 'P')
    drop proc BizTalkToCustomerInsert
go
CREATE procedure BizTalkToCustomerInsert
                    @CustomerName nvarchar(60)
                    , @Address nvarchar(120)
                    , @City nvarchar(60)
                    , @Region nvarchar(60)
                    , @PostalCode nvarchar(60)
AS
/*
**
** Object: BizTalkToCustomerInsert
**
** Description: Inserts records into the Customer table for the SQL adapter
** stored procedure recipe
**
**
*/
BEGIN
    Declare @intReturnCode int
    select    @intReturnCode = 0

    /*Insert records that will be returned to caller*/
    Insert Customer (CustomerName, Address, City, Region, PostalCode)
    Values (@CustomerName, @Address, @City, @Region, @PostalCode)

    /* Set the outbound return code */
    select    @intReturnCode = @@error

    /* return the return code */
    return @intReturnCode
END

go
grant execute on dbo.BizTalkToCustomerInsert to public
go
```

3. Create a new BizTalk solution that will insert customers into the Customer table in your SQL database. Next, create a sample message that matches the structure detailed in Listing 6-5. The schema for this message will be created as part of the solution as defined in the "Task 2: Create BizTalk Solution Artifacts" section of this recipe.

Listing 6-5. *Example Customer Input Message*

```
<ns0:Customer xmlns:ns0="http://SQLAdapterStoredProcedure.schCustomer">
        <CustomerName>Sherrie Long</CustomerName>
        <Address>5015 48th Ave SW</Address>
        <City>Woodland Park</City>
        <Region>WA</Region>
        <PostalCode>98005</PostalCode>
</ns0:Customer>
```

Task 2: Create BizTalk Solution Artifacts

Next, you will be using the Add Generated Items Wizard to generate the BizTalk artifacts for this recipe. The wizard will prompt you to specify your BizTalk environment (such as specifying the BizTalk MessageBox database, setting the connection string to the database that you will be accessing, and identifying the type of SQL port you are creating such as send or receive). Follow these steps:

1. Choose Add Generated Items from the Solution Explorer's tool menu. Verify that Add Adapter Metadata is selected. Figure 6-15 displays the Add Generated Items Wizard.

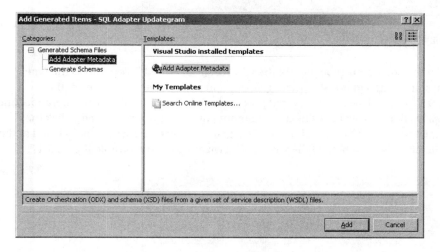

Figure 6-15. *Using the Add Generated Items Wizard*

2. On the Add Adapter Wizard page, select the SQL adapter, and verify the settings to your BizTalk MessageBox database.

■Note You can leave the Port field empty unless you are specifying an already created SQL send or receive port. This sample will create a send port that you will specify later through the BizTalk Explorer.

---

3. Follow the wizard, and set the connection string for the database to which you are connecting. Next, in the SQL Transport Schema Generation Wizard, specify the target namespace as `http://SQLAdapterStoredProcedure`, the request document root element name as `Customer_Request`, and the response document root element name as `Customer_Response`. The wizard should look like Figure 6-16.

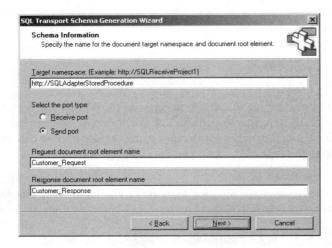

Figure 6-16. *Using the SQL Transport Schema Generation Wizard*

4. On the Statement Type page of the wizard, select Stored Procedure as the type of statement. On the Statement Information page of the wizard, select the `BizTalkToCustomerInsert` stored procedure from the drop-down enumeration, and leave all the check boxes next to the input parameters empty. Finally, click the Generate button because it results in a generated execute script that is listed in the Generated Script field of the wizard. The wizard should resemble Figure 6-17.

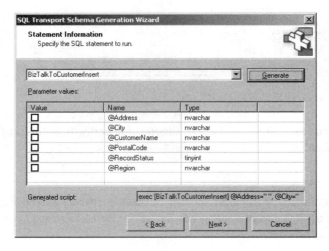

Figure 6-17. *Using the SQL Transport Generation Wizard—the Statement Information page*

■Note Because the stored procedure contains input parameters, they are displayed in the datagrid of the wizard. If there are default values that should be specified, then you can enter those parameters next to the name of the input parameter. If the check box is selected, then a null value will be submitted as the value for the input parameter.

5. Click Finish, completing the wizard. When you complete the wizard, notice that BizTalk creates two artifacts for you: the BizTalk orchestration and SQLService.xsd.

■Note The BizTalk orchestration allows you to perform additional processing of the inbound message, and the SQLService schema contains the physical representation of the data returned from the stored procedure.

6. Create a BizTalk map that maps the inbound Customer message to the outbound Customer_Request message that is being sent to the stored procedure. The map should resemble Figure 6-18.

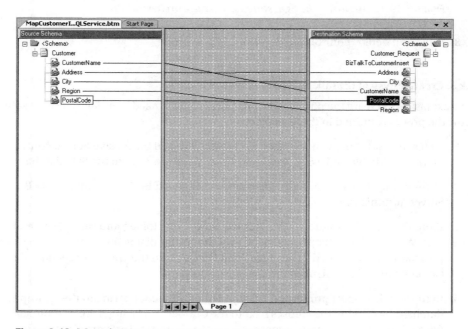

Figure 6-18. *Mapping* Customer *to* Customer_Request

7. Configure the BizTalk orchestration for an inbound receive and an outbound send. Additionally, configure your BizTalk orchestration to send a message of type SQL_Adapter_Stored_Procedure.SQLService.Customer_Request. Your orchestration should resemble Figure 6-19.

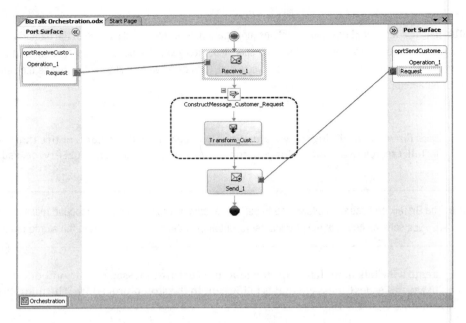

Figure 6-19. *Configuring the SQL stored procedure orchestration*

8. Build and deploy your BizTalk solution.

Task 3: Create Physical BizTalk Ports

Your next task is to create the physical BizTalk ports you will need in order to test the solution. Follow the process outlined in these steps:

1. To test this solution, you will need to create a physical file receive port to consume the inbound XML file and a SQL send port to send the message to the SQL database.

2. From the Start menu, select All Programs ➤ Microsoft BizTalk Server 2006 ➤ BizTalk Server Administration.

3. From the BizTalk Explorer, right-click the Send Ports folder, and select New ➤ Static One-Way Send Port to open the Send Port Properties dialog box. Name the new send port **Sample SQL Stored Procedure Send Port**. Within the Transport section of the General tab, select SQL from the Type drop-drop list.

4. In the SQL Transport properties, configure the connection string to the appropriate database by clicking the ellipses next to the Connection String field. Additionally, configure the document target namespace as http://SQLAdapterStoredProcedure.

5. Set Send Pipeline to the Microsoft.BizTalk.DefaultPipelines.XMLTransmit pipeline.

6. Bind the deployed orchestration to the newly created send and receive ports.

Task 4: Test the Solution

Your last task is to test your solution to be sure it works correctly. The procedure for testing is simple: place your sample customer test file in the folder being monitored by the file receive port, and verify that the record inserted successfully into the Customer table.

How It Works

Utilizing the SQL adapter to call stored procedures is a great way to insert data into a database or call a procedure to return data from a database. The benefits of using the SQL adapter over creating a component to make database calls include being able to use any BizTalk adapter (including guaranteed reliable message delivery, retry capabilities, and the ability to specify alternative mechanisms for message delivery). Additionally, a stored procedure is capable of taking an entire XML message or individual data elements as input parameters.

This recipe demonstrates how to use the SQL adapter and stored procedure to insert customer records in a SQL table. The stored procedure required input parameters but could have taken the entire contents of the XML message and parsed the contents of message.

6-8. Receiving with the SQL Adapter

Problem

You need to create an orchestration that retrieves messages from a SQL table via a SQL stored procedure. Specifically, you need to create an orchestration that will receive individual customer records from your SQL database via a SQL stored procedure.

Solution

The solution reviewed as part of this recipe outlines how to use the SQL receive adapter within the context of an orchestration. The solution has a sample table and stored procedure to demonstrate how the SQL receive adapter routes messages based on message content. The following instructions outline the tasks required to create and configure the physical SQL receive port as well as the orchestration that implements the SQL receive adapter.

Task 1: Create Supporting Artifacts

Perform the following steps to create the SQL support artifacts that are used by this recipe:

1. Create a new SQL database and table for which to insert the record. Compile the following table definition, and insert the statements listed in Listing 6-6.

■Note The table definition is different from the previous recipe. Make sure to use the table definition in Listing 6-6 or modify the previously created table definition.

Listing 6-6. *Example Customer Table Definition*

```
CREATE TABLE [dbo].[Customer] (
    [CustomerID][int] IDENTITY (1,1) NOT NULL,
    [CustomerName][nvarchar](30) COLLATE SQL_Latin1_General_CP1_CI_AS NOT NULL,
    [Address][nvarchar](60) COLLATE SQL_Latin1_General_CP1_CI_AS NOT NULL,
    [City][nvarchar](30) COLLATE SQL_Latin1_General_CP1_CI_AS NOT NULL,
    [Region][nvarchar](30) COLLATE SQL_Latin1_General_CP1_CI_AS NOT NULL,
    [PostalCode][nvarchar](10) COLLATE SQL_Latin1_General_CP1_CI_AS NOT NULL,
    [RecordStatus][tinyint] NOT NULL
) ON [PRIMARY]

Insert Customer (CustomerName, Address, City, Region, PostalCode, RecordStatus)
Values ('Shauna Marie', '9515 S Wally St', 'Bellevue', 'WA', '98004', 1)
Insert Customer (CustomerName, Address, City, Region, PostalCode, RecordStatus)
Values ('Pat Dean', '10034th 49th Ave NE', 'Redmond', 'WA', '95550', 1)
Insert Customer (CustomerName, Address, City, Region, PostalCode, RecordStatus)
Values ('Sherrie Long', '5015 48th Ave SW', 'Woodland Park', 'CO', '80863', 1)
```

    2. If you do not have a stored procedure to retrieve individual customer records, then compile the stored procedure listed in Listing 6-7.

■**Note** Notice that the select statement in Listing 6-7 contains a FOR XML AUTO, XMLDATA, ELEMENTS clause. The SQL adapter requires select statements returning records to return them in XML format. Additionally, the XMLDATA clause is required only when running the wizard to generate the schema for the result set from the stored procedure. When you test the solution, make sure to remove the XMLDATA clause from your stored procedure.

Listing 6-7. *Example Retrieve Customer Record Stored Procedure*

```
if exists(select * from sysobjects where name = 'CustomerToBizTalk' and type = 'P')
    drop proc CustomerToBizTalk
go
CREATE procedure CustomerToBizTalk
AS
/*
**
** Object: CustomerToBizTalk
**
** Description: Retrieves records from the Customer table for the SQL receive
**              adapter recipe
**
**
*/
```

```
BEGIN
    /*Populate temp table with records that will be returned to caller*/
    Select top 1 CustomerID
        , CustomerName
        , Address
        , City
        , Region
        , PostalCode
        , RecordStatus
    Into    #TempCustomer
    From    Customer
    Where    RecordStatus = 1

    /*Update Status of retrieved record from the Customer table*/
    Update    Customer
    Set        RecordStatus = 0
    Where    CustomerID = (select CustomerID from #TempCustomer)

    /*Return records to caller*/
    Select CustomerID
        , CustomerName
        , Address
        , City
        , Region
        , PostalCode
        , RecordStatus
    from    #TempCustomer as Customer FOR XML AUTO, XMLData, Elements

    /*Clean up temp table*/
    drop table #TempCustomer
END

go
grant execute on dbo.CustomerToBizTalk to public
go
```

Task 2: Create BizTalk Solution Artifacts

Next, use the Add Generated Items Wizard to generate the BizTalk artifacts for this recipe. The wizard will prompt you to specify your BizTalk environment (including specifying the BizTalk MessageBox database, setting the connection string to the database you will be accessing, and identifying the type of SQL port you are creating such as send or receive). This recipe assumes you have created an empty BizTalk solution. Here are the steps to follow:

1. Choose Add Generated Items from the Solution Explorer's tool menu. Select the Add Adapter Metadata template. Figure 6-20 displays the Add Generated Items Wizard and the selected template.

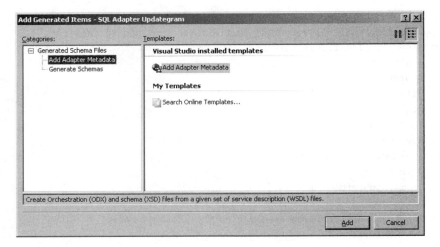

Figure 6-20. *Using the Add Generated Items Wizard*

2. On the Add Adapter Wizard page, select the SQL adapter, and verify the settings to your BizTalk MessageBox database.

■Note You can leave the Port field empty unless you are specifying an already created SQL send or receive port.

3. Follow the wizard, and set the connection string for the database to which you are connecting. Next, in the SQL Transport Schema Generation Wizard, specify the target namespace as http://SQLReceiveAdapter and the document root element name as Customer_Response. The wizard should resemble Figure 6-21.

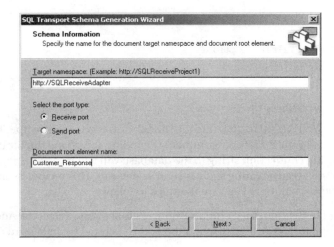

Figure 6-21. *Using the SQL Transport Schema Generation Wizard*

4. On the Statement Type page of the wizard, select Stored Procedure as the type of statement. On the Statement Information page of the wizard, select the `CustomerToBizTalk`
   stored procedure from the drop-down enumeration, and click the Generate button.
   The Generate button results in a generated execute script that is listed in the Generated Script field of the wizard. Figure 6-22 displays the completed wizard.

■**Note** If the stored procedure contained any input parameters, then those parameters would display in the
datagrid of the wizard. The wizard also depends on the select statement in the stored procedure to contain
the XMLDATA clause in the FOR XML statement. The XMLDATA clause returns the schema layout for the structure returned by the select statement.

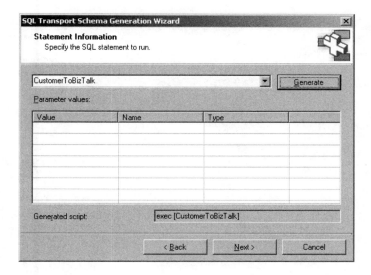

Figure 6-22. *Completed wizard*

5. Click Finish, completing the wizard. When you complete the wizard, notice that
   BizTalk creates two artifacts for you: the BizTalk orchestration and `SQLService.xsd`.

■**Note** The BizTalk orchestration allows you to perform additional processing of the inbound message, and
the SQLService schema contains the physical representation of the data returned from the stored procedure.

6. Create a BizTalk orchestration, configuring it based on the artifacts listed in Table 6-3.
   Configure the BizTalk orchestration for an inbound receive and an outbound send.

Table 6-3. *SQL Receive Orchestration*

ID	Name	Discussion
1	Receive Customer	Receive shape
2	oprtReceiveCustomerSQL	Receive port
3	oprtReceiveCustomerSQLType	Receive port type
4	msgSQLCustomer	Orchestration message pointed to the schema generated from the Add Generated Items Wizard
5	Send Customer	Send shape
6	oprtSendCustomer	Send port
7	oprtSendCustomerType	Send port type

Your orchestration should resemble Figure 6-23.

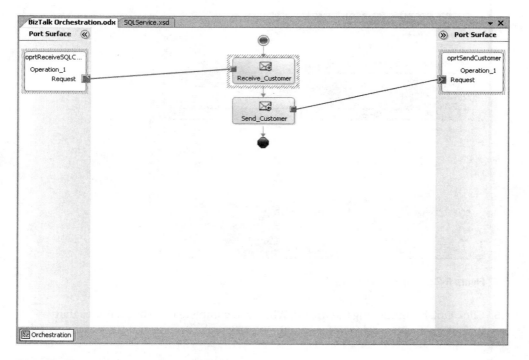

Figure 6-23. *Viewing the complete orchestration*

Once your orchestration is complete, build and deploy your solution.

Task 3: Create Physical BizTalk Ports

Execute the following steps to create the SQL receive port that will call the stored procedure and route the message received to the deployed BizTalk solution:

1. To test this solution, you will need to create a physical SQL receive port to consume the inbound XML file and a physical file send port to send the message to a file share for examination.

2. From the Start menu, select All Programs ➤ Microsoft BizTalk Server 2006 ➤ BizTalk Server Administration.

3. From the BizTalk Explorer, right-click the Receive Ports folder, and select Add Receive Port ➤ One-Way Port to open the One-Way Receive Port Properties dialog box. Name the new receive port **Sample SQL Receive Port**. Leave the rest of the settings with default values.

4. From the BizTalk Explorer, right-click the Receive Locations folder under the newly created port called Sample SQL Receive Port, and choose Add Receive Location. In the Receive Location Properties dialog box, configure the transport type, address, receive handler, and receive pipeline. Configure the dialog box settings specified in Table 6-4.

Table 6-4. *SQL Receive Location Configuration Settings*

Configuration Parameter	Value
Transport Type	SQL.
Address (URI)	Location of your SQL server. See step 5 for more information.
Receive Handler	BizTalk host instance (for example, BizTalkServerApplication).
Receive Pipeline	Microsoft.BizTalk.DefaultPipelines.XMLReceive.

5. When configuring the Address (URI) property in the Receive Port dialog box, leave the Receive Configuration settings to the default values:

   a. Set Document Root Element Name to Customer_Response.

   b. Set Document Target Namespace to http://SQLReceiveAdapter.

   c. On the SQL Command page, navigate to the deployed BizTalk project and schema to set the SQL command properly. The completed SQL Transport Properties dialog box should resemble Figure 6-24.

■**Note** BizTalk uses the root element name and the namespace to route the inbound XML file. If the root element name and the namespace do not match the root element name and namespace of the SQLService.xsd file you created in the BizTalk solution, you will receive document routing errors and suspended messages when BizTalk tries to route the message from the SQL receive adapter.

---

6. Bind the deployed orchestration to the newly created send and receive ports.

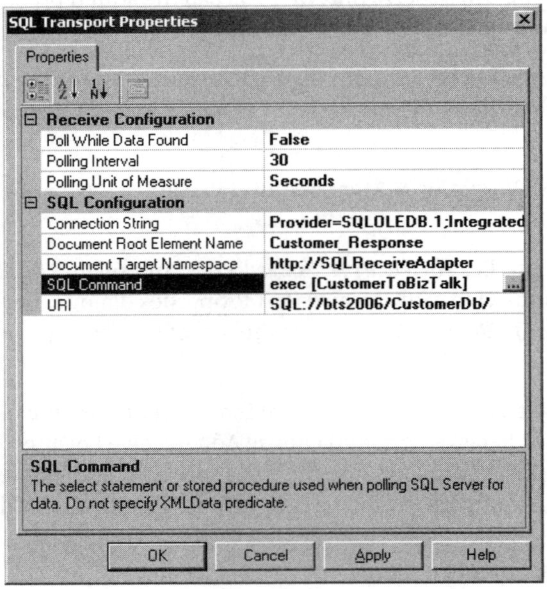

Figure 6-24. *Viewing the completed SQL Transport Properties dialog box*

Task 4: Test the Solution

Your final task is to test your solution. Here are the steps to follow:

1. Modify and recompile the CustomerToBizTalk stored procedure. Remove the XMLDATA clause in the FOR XML AUTO statement, and recompile it. The resulting stored procedure should resemble Listing 6-8.

Listing 6-8. *Revised Select Statement*

```
/*Return records to caller*/
    Select CustomerID
        , CustomerName
        , Address
        , City
        , Region
        , PostalCode
        , RecordStatus
    from     #TempCustomer as Customer FOR XML AUTO, Elements
```

2. Start your orchestration and SQL receive port, and validate that a single XML file is created for each customer in your Customer table with the RecordStatus of 1. Also verify that the records in the Customer table have had their status set to 0 indicating that BizTalk has consumed the record. The resulting XML file should resemble Listing 6-9.

Listing 6-9. *Customer Sample XML*

```xml
<?xml version="1.0" encoding="utf-16" ?>
<Customer_Response xmlns="http://SQLReceiveAdapter">
  <Customer>
      <CustomerID>1</CustomerID>
      <CustomerName>Shauna Marie</CustomerName>
      <Address>9515 S Wally St</Address>
      <City>Bellevue</City>
      <Region>WA</Region>
      <PostalCode>98004</PostalCode>
      <RecordStatus>1</RecordStatus>
  </Customer>
</Customer_Response>
```

How It Works

Retrieving records via the SQL receive adapter is extremely useful and powerful when coupled with the use of stored procedures. Implementing the SQL receive adapter requires configuring and managing how records are retrieved from SQL. This recipe outlined how to use a stored procedure that selects records in a temporary table, updates the status of the individual record in the SQL table, and then returns the records to the SQL adapter. Additionally, this sample demonstrated how to use the FOR XML AUTO clause within a stored procedure.

Stored Procedure Configuration

The SQL receive adapter operates on the "polling" principle of retrieving records. The adapter will call the stored procedure on a configurable interval to retrieve records. However, the adapter does not maintain the state of which records it has consumed. Therefore, any stored procedure that the SQL receive adapter executes must maintain a level of state identifying the processed records. If you examine the stored procedure listed previously, you will notice that there is a RecordStatus column that is updated to 0 when the records are polled. You have many options for determining unprocessed records. For example, you can use the status flag, physically remove the record from the database, use the date range, and so on. If the stored procedure does not maintain state, then BizTalk will continue consuming the same data.

In addition to maintaining state within the stored procedure, if you are returning a result via a select statement, then you must specify the FOR XML AUTO, XMLDATA clause for generating the SQLService.xsd schema. As explained, the XML AUTO clause instructs SQL Server to return the result set as XML, and the XMLDATA clause instructs SQL Server to return the schema layout for the returned result set. The SQL service adapter officially supports using the FOR XML AUTO clause.

You can also use the FOR XML Explicit clause, but it is not officially supported and should be used with care. Using FOR XML Explicit eliminates using the Add Generated Items Wizard to automatically generate the SQLService schema. However, you can create the SQLService schema manually. One benefit to using FOR XML Explicit over FOR XML AUTO is the greater level of control in the resulting XML structure that is returned to BizTalk. If you have a complicated XML message structure that is comprised of data from multiple tables, you can format the result set in the correct XML structure via the FOR XML Explicit clause. The select statement in Listing 6-10 demonstrates how to use the FOR XML Explicit clause.

Listing 6-10. *Return Result Set Using the FOR XML Explicit Clause*

```
select     1    as Tag, NULL     as Parent
    , NULL     as [Customer!1!element]
    , CustomerID as [Customer!1!CustomerID!element]
    , CustomerName     as [Customer!1!CustomerName!element]
    , Address as [Customer!1!Address!element]
    , City as [Customer!1!City!element]
    , Region as [Customer!1!Region!element]
    , PostalCode as [Customer!1!PostalCode!element]
    , RecordStatus as [Customer!1!RecordStatus!element]
from    Customer
FOR XML EXPLICIT
```

Adapter Configuration

The SQL receive adapter contains many items for configuration. Table 6-5 lists the items worth noting. The SQL adapter receive location differs from other BizTalk receive locations in that each SQL receive location identifies a specific message type that is received from a database. If you expect to receive multiple types of messages, then you must construct a SQL receive port for each unique message type. The SQL adapter is configured for each unique message type through the Document Root Element Name node and the Document Target Namespace node. Additionally, each SQL receive location is configured to execute a specific SQL stored procedure or command.

Table 6-5. *SQL Receive Adapter Configuration*

ID	Configuration Parameter	Description
1	Poll While Data Found	Indicates whether to continue polling for new records in additional batches or whether to submit a single query result for the entire polling window.
2	Polling Interval	Identifies how often to poll for records.
3	Polling Unit of Measure	Identifies the unit of measure for polling.
4	Connection String	Identifies the connection string for the database containing data to be polled.
5	Document Root Element Name	Identifies the Root node that BizTalk will assign the inbound message.
6	Document Target Namespace	Identifies the namespace that BizTalk will assign the inbound message.
7	SQL Command	Identifies the SQL command the SQL adapter will execute.
8	URI	Identifies a unique identifier for the receive location. This value is autogenerated.

In addition to the configuration items identified previously, you must verify that MSDTC is configured correctly on the target system that is hosting the SQL database because BizTalk enrolls every call from the SQL adapter into an MSDTC-styled transaction.

6-9. Configuring HTTP Sends

Problem

You want to programmatically configure an HTTP send port from an orchestration using a Message Assignment shape.

Solution

This solution will describe how to post a document using a send port configured with authentication to post via a secure HTTPS site. The following solution assumes you have a BizTalk 2006 project open in Visual Studio 2005 with a BizTalk orchestration and a schema that can be used to create an orchestration message.

Here are the steps to follow:

1. Create a new orchestration message by right-clicking the Messages folder in the Orchestration View window and selecting New Message. Enter **msgSend** for the message name, and give it a message type (this should be the schema of the document that will be sent via HTTP).

2. Setting HTTP properties requires constructing the message that will be sent. Drop a Message Assignment shape in the orchestration. This will create a Construct Message shape that should be configured such that the Message Constructed property is set to the message created in step 1. See Figure 6-25.

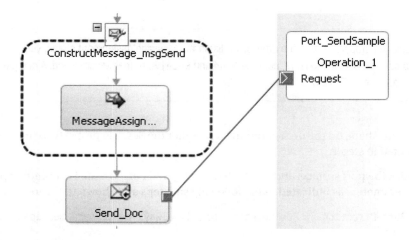

Figure 6-25. *Assigning messages in orchestration*

3. Double-click the Message Assignment shape, and enter the property settings as shown in Listing 6-11. Figure 6-26 shows the properties available in the Message Assignment Editor. Click OK when complete.

Listing 6-11. *Message Assignment Code*

```
// Set HTTP send port properties; the username and password can be
// configurable by using the config file or BizTalk rules engine
// rather than hard-coded values
msgSend(HTTP.AuthenticationScheme) = "Basic";
msgSend(HTTP.Username) = "User"; // can be loaded from config file, also
msgSend(HTTP.Password) = "Password"; // can be loaded from config file
// configure additional parameters as appropriate
```

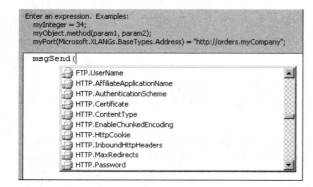

Figure 6-26. *Viewing the HTTP parameters in the Message Assignment Editor*

■Note When selecting properties from the drop-down list in the Message Assignment shape, you'll see all the properties you can set. Specific to HTTP, both the Send and Receive properties are listed. A complete list of Send properties appears in Table 6-6.

---

4. Drop a Send shape on the orchestration surface. Set the Message property to the message created in step 1.

5. Right-click the port surface, and select New Configured Port. On the Port Binding page, set the parameters as indicated in the following substeps and shown in Figure 6-27:

   a. Set Port Direction of Communication to I'll always be sending messages on this port.

   b. Set Port Binding to Specify now.

   c. Set Transport to HTTP.

   d. Set URI to the URL being posted to (https://Sample).

   e. Set the pipeline to the default XMLTransmit pipeline.

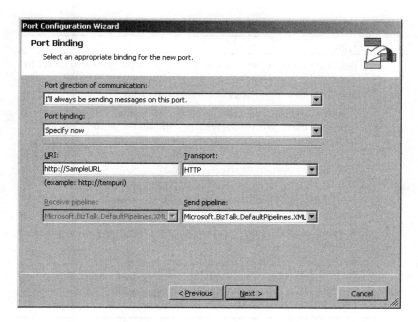

Figure 6-27. *Using the Port Configuration Wizard*

Table 6-6 describes the details of each of the port properties you can set for the HTTP port via code in an Expression shape of an orchestration. These are the same parameters you set when configuring an HTTP send port in the BizTalk Explorer.

Table 6-6. *HTTP Port Parameters*

Property	Type
AffiliateApplicationName	When using SSO, you can specify an affiliate application. You enter the name of the application as a string. When using this property, the UseSSO property must be set to True.
AuthenticationScheme	You can set four types of authentication: Anonymous, Basic, Digest, and Kerberos. When using Basic and Digest, you should set the Password and Username properties.
Certificate	If you are using a certificate (for HTTPS), you should enter the thumbprint of the certificate as a string here. Thumbprints are typically found in the properties of the certificate and are 40-digit hex values.
ContentType	The default value is Text/XML. This is a string.
EnableChunkedEncoding	Boolean value that indicates whether to send the document in chunked packets of information.
MaxRedirects	The HTTP adapter can be set to allow for 0 to 10 redirects.
Password	Password used when posting to a secure site. AuthenticationScheme should be set to Basic or Digest.
ProxyName	If a proxy server is used, enter the name of the server as a string.

continued

Table 6-6. *Continued*

Property	Type
ProxyPassword	Password for proxy server. The UseProxy property should be set to True, and UseHandlerProxySettings should be set to False.
ProxyPort	Port for proxy server. An example would be 80.
ProxyUsername	Username for proxy server. The UseProxy property should be set to True, and UseHandlerProxySettings should be set to False.
RequestTimeout	By default, the timeout will be managed based on the size of the document. This can be overridden with a specific timeout value entered as a numeric entry (in seconds).
UseHandlerProxySettings	If set to True, other proxy properties that may be set are overridden, and the send port will use the proxy handler configuration.
UseProxy	Boolean value. Use other proxy properties in conjunction with this value.
Username	Username used when posting to a secure site. AuthenticationScheme should be set to Basic or Digest.
UseSSO	A Boolean value indicating whether to use the SSO server. Use the AffiliateApplicationName property in conjunction with this.

How It Works

When sending documents via a send port, exceptions can occur—perhaps the HTTP server is unavailable or the URL is incorrect. In such cases, it is often useful to be able to catch the exception immediately in the orchestration, especially when specific error handling routines need to occur.

By default, send ports are set up to automatically retry in case of failure. This means an orchestration will call the send port and then continue processing asynchronously while the adapter manages the transmission of the document. If an exception is thrown, it is handled by the adapter and is never bubbled up to the orchestration. With the adapter operating asynchronously from the orchestration, exceptions that are thrown can result in lost messages and unexpected error messages.

To force the adapter to execute synchronously with the orchestration moving on to the next steps only when a message has been posted successfully by the adapter, you should set the Delivery Notification property on the send port to Transmitted, as shown in Figure 6-28.

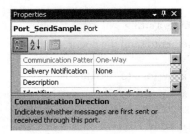

Figure 6-28. *Setting the* Delivery Notification *property*

6-10. Configuring HTTP Receives

Problem

You want to configure an HTTP receive location to allow posts from a client machine to BizTalk Server. Additionally, you want to understand how to configure IIS 6.0 and create a virtual directory to allow the receive location to operate correctly.

Solution

This solution will describe how to configure an HTTP receive location to allow documents to be posted to BizTalk. The first task is to configure IIS to allow for the redirection of documents to BizTalk. The second task is to create a virtual directory to handle specific requests, and the third step is to configure the HTTP receive. The majority of servers will have IIS 6.0 installed, and this solution describes the steps necessary for that version (IIS 5.0 has different configuration steps—refer to the BizTalk documentation for details). After IIS has been configured, you will work through the steps needed to create a virtual directory and configure an HTTP receive port.

To configure IIS 6.0, follow these steps:

1. Open Internet Information Services Manager by selecting Control Panel ➤ Administrative Tools.

2. Right-click Web Service Extensions, and select Add New Web Service Extension. Set the following properties in the dialog box that opens:

   a. Give an appropriate name to the extension (`SampleHTTPReceive`).

   b. Next to the Required Files box, click the Add button, and browse to `BTSHTTPReceive.dll` located in `\Program Files\Microsoft BizTalk Server 2006\HttpReceive`.

■Note If an error occurs indicating that the file is already required by another process, you don't need to continue, because the HTTP receive adapter has already been created and configured appropriately. Cancel out, and move to step 3.

---

   c. Check the Set Extension Status to Allowed check box.

   d. Click OK.

3. Right-click the `Application Pools` folder, and select New ➤ Application Pool. Give an appropriate name to this Application Pool (`CustomHTTPReceive`). Leave the default properties set, and click OK.

4. Right-click the application pool created in step 3, and select Properties. Set the following properties on the Identity tab in the dialog box that opens (all properties on other tabs should be left at their default values):

    a. Click the Configurable radio button.

    b. The Username property should be set to a user who has permissions to read and write to the BizTalk management database. Typically, during BizTalk installation, a Service account will be created that will be used to run the BizTalk services. You can use this account here.

    c. Type the password for the account entered in the previous step.

Once IIS is configured, the next order of business is to create a virtual directory. Each solution that requires an HTTP receive to be set up will require a separate virtual directory. BizTalk listens to this URL and, through the use of BTSHTTPReceive.dll and the HTTP receive adapter, passes the information to the BizTalk MessageBox.

The following steps demonstrate how to create a virtual directory. This directory is where clients will post HTTP requests to BizTalk.

1. In Internet Information Services Manager, expand the Web Site folder, right-click the Default Web Site folder, and select New ➤ Virtual Directory.

2. Click through the wizard, setting the following properties:

    a. The name of the virtual directory should be what you want exposed to clients. For example, SampleHTTPReceive would be exposed to the client as http://[server]/SampleHTTPReceive.

    b. Set the website content directory path to the location of the BTSHTTPReceive.dll file, located in \Program Files\Microsoft BizTalk Server 2006\HttpReceive.

    c. On the Access Permissions page, check the boxes next to Read and Execute. Leave all other permissions unchecked.

    d. Exit the wizard by clicking Finish.

3. Once you have created the virtual directory, right-click it and select Properties. Set the following two properties:

    a. Ensure that the Execute Permission property is set to Scripts and Executables.

    b. Set the Application Pool property to the application pool created earlier in this solution.

    c. Click OK.

Figure 6-29 shows the IIS configuration.

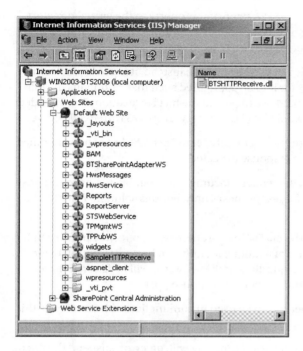

Figure 6-29. *Using the Internet Information Services (IIS) Manager*

At this point, IIS and the virtual directory are set up to route requests to BizTalk Server. The next steps are to create a receive port and configure a receive location for HTTP. These will be specific to each solution, so you will need to set up separate instances for different BizTalk solutions.

1. Using BizTalk Explorer, right-click the `Receive Ports` folder, and select Add Receive Port. In the dialog box that appears, select Request-Response Port and click OK. Give the receive port a name, and click OK to create the port.

2. Under the receive port you created, right-click the `Receive Location` folder and select Add Receive Location.

3. In the Receive Location Properties dialog box that opens, use the following settings:

   a. Set `Transport Type` to `HTTP`. This will automatically set the receive handler to `BizTalkServerIsolatedHost`.

   b. Set `Receive Pipeline` to `Microsoft.BizTalk.DefaultPipelines.XMLReceive`.

   c. Set `Send Pipeline` to `Microsoft.BizTalk.DefaultPipelines.XMLTransmit`.

4. Click the Address (URI) ellipsis button, and use the following settings:

a. Set the Virtual Directory plus ISAPI extension property to the virtual directory created during the IIS configuration earlier in this solution. The entry should follow this format: /SampleHTTPReceive/BTSHTTPReceive.dll.

b. The Public address property is not used by BizTalk; instead, it is used for reference purposes only. The intention is for it to be configured such that it contains the full external address that clients would use to post to the receive location. The intended format for this reference field would be http://[servername]/SampleHTTPReceive.

c. The Return Content-Type property is generally set to Text/XML but can be modified depending on the format of the response expected.

d. The Loopback flag is set when the request document is intended to be the response back. Generally, this flag is set for test purposes only. For this solution, it should be False.

e. The Return Correlation Handle on Success property is for one-way ports only. It is intended to allow the creation of a unique identifier to be able to correlate the request to the document sent. Regardless of the setting, it will be ignored in this solution, because you are creating a request-response port.

f. The Use Single Sign On property is to be used in conjunction with SSO. Leave this property unchecked.

g. If checked, the Suspend Failed Requests property will, on error, suspend the document in the BizTalk MessageBox and will send an accepted notification to the client that posted the request (meaning the client will have successfully posted the document, but the document will be in a suspended state and will require administrative attention). If unchecked, any errors receiving the document will result in an immediate response back to the client indicating failure. For this solution, keep this property unchecked.

Figure 6-30 shows the final configuration.

Figure 6-30. *Viewing the final HTTP transport properties*

How It Works

You can set several configurations at the HTTP receive adapter level that will affect the way the adapter functions. You can set certain properties in the Registry that will provide for more control and optimization over large implementations that use the HTTP adapter. In many cases, however, the server and solution infrastructure may require that this default be reduced or increased. You can set this property using the following steps:

1. In the Registry Editor, locate the following path: `HKEY_LOCAL_MACHINE\SYSTEM\ CurrentControlSet\Services\BTSSvc.3.0`.

2. Right-click this path, and select New ➤ Key. Enter **HttpReceive** for the key's name.

3. Right-click the `HTTPReceive` key, and select New ➤ DWORD. Name the key `RequestQueueSize`. Give this a decimal value from 10 to 2048.

You can take the previous steps for the keys listed in Table 6-7.

Table 6-7. *HTTP Receive Adapter Registry Entries*

Property	Description
DisableChunkEncoding	DWORD whose default is 0. Any nonzero number turns off this setting. Indicates whether communications back to the client will be sent using chunked encoding.
HTTPReceiveThreadsPerCPU	DWORD whose default is 2. Can be set to any value from 1 to 10. Indicates the number of threads per CPU that are allocated to the HTTP receive adapter.
RequestQueueSize	DWORD whose default value is 256. Can be set anywhere from 10 to 2048. The value indicates the total number of concurrent requests that BizTalk will process simultaneously.

6-11. Configuring SOAP Sends and Receives

Problem

You want to understand how to configure a static solicit-response SOAP send port using BizTalk Explorer to allow client machines posting to orchestrations that have been deployed as web services.

Solution

SOAP ports are generally two-way (solicit-response) ports, because consuming web services generally result in a response to the calling party. The following steps guide you through the process of configuring a two-way SOAP port:

1. In BizTalk Explorer, right-click the Send Ports folder, and select Add Send Port. In the dialog box that opens, select Static Solicit-Response Port.

2. On the Property Pages dialog box that opens, select a transport type of SOAP.

3. Click the ellipsis for the Address (URI) property entry box. The Transport Properties dialog box will open with the General tab active, as shown in Figure 6-31.

4. Configure the General tab according to the requirements of the web service, with the following guidelines.

    a. The value of the Web Service URL property should be entered in the format http://webservice.asmx.

    b. The four authentication types are Anonymous, Basic, Digest, and NTLM. The value selected for this property will depend on the requirements of the web service being consumed. Often it will take some experimentation to determine the proper authentication settings, especially when additional security measures, such as certificates, are required.

    c. If a web service requires an SSL certificate, enter a reference to it in the Certificate Thumbprint property. You can access the thumbprint through the certificate properties and copy and paste it into this property.

Figure 6-31. *Configuring the General tab*

5. Configure the proxy settings on the Proxy tab according to any proxies that may be necessary to call the web service.

6. Configure the Web Service tab using the following guidelines:

   a. Generally, all calls to web services should be handled through the orchestration web port; this provides the robust capabilities for posting over the supported protocols inherent to SOAP.

   b. Occasionally, it may be necessary to specify a proxy class for a call to a web service. In such cases a proxy class must be created. You can create a class using the command-line utility WSDL.exe. This tool will create an assembly that can be referenced using the Assembly Name property. Once referenced, the type and methods available on the original web service will be made available in the two remaining property fields.

7. Click OK to save the settings entered in the Transport Properties dialog box, and configure the remaining properties on the SOAP send adapter:

   a. Set the Send and Receive Pipelines settings according to the needs of the solution (generally XMLTransmit and XMLReceive).

   b. If a certificate is required for outbound encryption, set the Certificate Name property to the appropriate certificate. Only those certificates that have been installed on the machine will be available in the drop-down list.

   c. Set any inbound or outbound maps, and configure any filters that may be necessary.

8. Click OK to complete the configuration of the SOAP port.

How It Works

When calling a web service from an orchestration, it is often useful to be able to specify a dynamic URL. For instance, in a development environment, the URL being posted to will be a test URL, and the URL will need to change once the orchestration has been deployed to a production setting. You have several approaches to solving the need for supporting a dynamic URL, one of which is to set the address programmatically in an orchestration Expression shape.

■Note   For detailed steps on consuming a web service, see Recipe 4-24 in this book.

The following steps describe how to configure a SOAP port where the URL is assigned dynamically at runtime within the orchestration:

1. Create a web reference to a WSDL. Right-click the `Project Root` folder in Visual Studio, and select Add Web Reference. Browse to the appropriate WSDL, and add a reference. The web methods on this WSDL will define the interface on the send port.

2. Right-click the orchestration port surface, and select New Configured Port. Click through the wizard, and set the port type to be used for this port to Use an Existing Port Type. Select the web method that will be posted to, as shown in Figure 6-32.

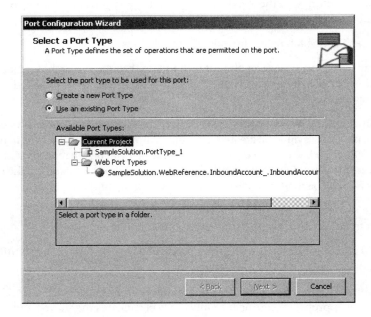

Figure 6-32. *Setting the web port type*

3. On the Port Binding page of the wizard, set the properties as shown here:

    a. Set Port Direction of Communication to always sending.

    b. Set Port Binding to Dynamic.

    c. The Send Pipeline property is generally set to Microsoft.BizTalk. DefaultPipelines.XMLTransmit.

4. Click Finish to complete the wizard.

At this point, you can create an Expression shape in the orchestration. Because the goal is to have a dynamic URL, the URL can be stored in a configuration file. Assuming that the BTSNTSvc.exe.config file is used to store a custom property, you can take the following steps:

1. In the BTNTSvc.exe.config file, add a new key, as follows (add this to the <appSettings> node):

```
[<appSettings>]
 <add key="WSURL" value="http://sample.asmx"/>
[</appSettings>]
```

2. Drop an Expression shape on the orchestration. You can enter the following code in the orchestration to read the configuration file and to set the address on the web port created in the previous steps:

```
strURL = System.Configuration.ConfigurationSettings.AppSettings.Get("WSURL");
Port_1(Microsoft.XLANGs.BaseTypes.Address) = strURL;
```

CHAPTER 7

■ ■ ■

Deployment

At the core of every BizTalk project is the necessity to deploy an integration project to the BizTalk execution environment. Given the complexity of the product, and the rich features it provides, this task has often been difficult and time-consuming. Every experienced BizTalk developer understands the time requirements to deploy, enlist, and start BizTalk artifacts, keeping in mind dependencies and ordering the steps accordingly. BizTalk 2006 makes great inroads into simplification of this process, so that less time is spent deploying solutions, and more time is available to develop new return-on-investment-producing solutions.

This chapter provides recipes for exporting and importing applications. It also covers how to start an application and begin processing within the BizTalk execution environment.

7-1. Exporting Applications

Problem

You have completed the build phase of a BizTalk project and need to migrate your work from the development environment to the test environment.

Solution

You must export the BizTalk application you have been building for use in the new environment. The BizTalk Administration Console provides the capability to export and import artifacts. Combined with the use of BizTalk applications, this allows for a simplified method of packaging your solutions and deploying them to new environments. The following steps outline the process for exporting a BizTalk application.

1. To open the BizTalk Administration Console, select Start ➤ All Programs ➤ BizTalk Server 2006 ➤ BizTalk Server Administration.

2. In the left pane, navigate through BizTalk Server 2006 Administration to your BizTalk group, and expand the `Applications` folder.

3. Right-click the application you wish to export and select Export ➤ MSI File, as shown in Figure 7-1. This launches the Export MSI File Wizard.

4. Click Next on the Welcome page of the wizard.

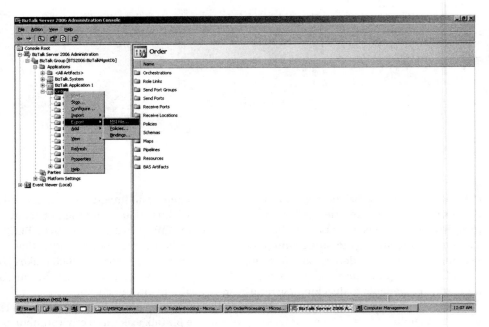

Figure 7-1. *Choosing to export an application*

5. On the Select Resources page, verify that the resources you need to include in the exported MSI package are selected. In the example shown in Figure 7-2, the resources consist of two BizTalk assemblies and their bindings, along with a web directory. Click Next to proceed.

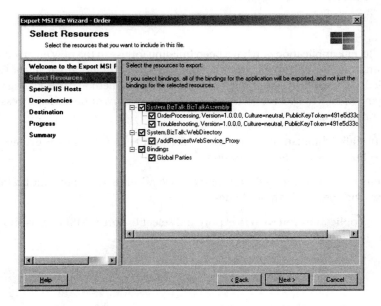

Figure 7-2. *The Select Resources page of the Export MSI Wizard*

Note Including bindings within your MSI package will automatically overwrite any existing bindings in the target application upon import. Exclude the bindings during the export process if you do not want to overwrite the bindings in your target application.

6. On the Specify IIS Hosts page, select the virtual directories you need to include in the exported MSI package. In the example shown in Figure 7-3, the web directory exists on the local machine. Click Next.

Note You must specify IIS hosts for all web directory resources that have not already been added to the BizTalk Management database. In our example, the Order application has a SOAP receive location, which is configured to receive messages from the /addRequestWebService_Proxy/ addRequestWebService_addRequestSPMLWebService_addRequest.asmx web service. Since the receive locations do not include the host, it must be specified during the export process.

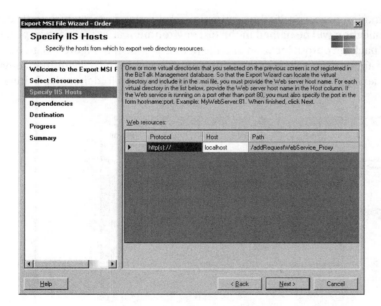

Figure 7-3. *The Specify IIS Hosts page of the Export MSI Wizard*

7. On the Dependencies page, review the BizTalk applications your exported MSI package depends on, as shown in Figure 7-4. Prior to importing your application into the test environment, you must ensure that all applications listed on this page are present in the test environment. In our example, the application depends on the BizTalk. System application. Click Next to proceed.

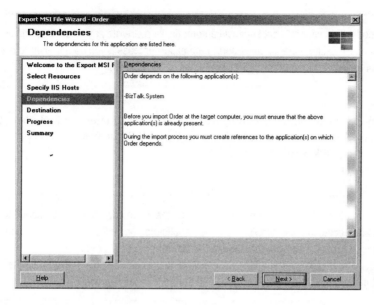

Figure 7-4. *The Dependencies page of the Export MSI Wizard*

8. On the Destination page, specify the destination application name (which indicates what the application will be named in the test environment after you have imported it) and the MSI package output location and file name, as shown in Figure 7-5. In our example, the application will be named the same as it was in the development environment (Order) and the MSI package will be written out to a folder on the C drive.

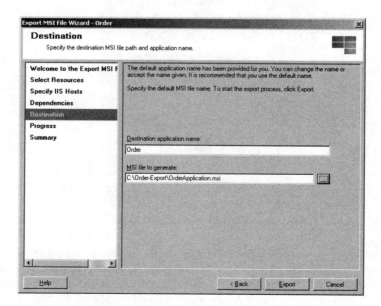

Figure 7-5. *The Destination page of the Export MSI Wizard*

9. Click Export to generate the MSI package.

10. The wizard displays the progress of the export operation, and then shows a summary screen when it has completed, as shown in Figure 7-6. The summary includes a list of steps necessary to import the application into a new environment (see Recipe 7-2), along with a link to the log file of the export operation. Click Finish to close the wizard.

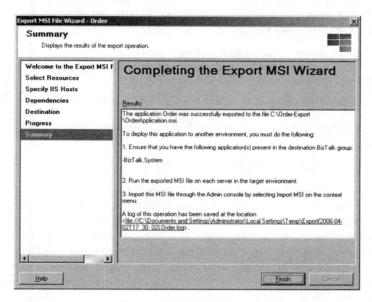

Figure 7-6. *The Summary page of the Export MSI Wizard*

How It Works

While exporting applications is an easy way to migrate solution artifacts between environments, it is important to note what is not included in exported MSI packages. Configuration values you have made in the BTSNTSvc.exe.config file are not exported. If one of your artifacts relies on a custom configuration value existing in this file, you must use another mechanism (manual or otherwise) to add that same configuration value to the target environment.

■**Note** In general, only those artifacts that are specific to an application are exported. This means that BizTalk group configurations (performance values or adapter settings, for example) and Business Activity Monitor (BAM) artifacts are not included in the exported MSI package.

You should be careful with regard to security when exporting applications. Depending on your solution, your MSI package may contain sensitive information (such as passwords) and should be appropriately secured. One consideration is the use of passwords in port bindings. Passwords are removed from all bindings that you export directly from an application (as we did in our example). If you want to persist passwords in a binding file, you must create a binding file with the passwords in it, and then add the binding file to the application as a file resource.

You should also pay attention to access rights on resources added to your application. All permissions on files and folders are removed during the export process. For web directory resources, the security settings in place at the time of export are written to the MSI package.

In addition to using the Export MSI File Wizard, you can access the same functionality via the BTSTask ExportApp command-line utility. This utility accepts the following parameters, which mimic the steps taken in the wizard:

- ApplicationName: The name of the BizTalk application to export.

- Package: Path and file name of the MSI package to export.

- ResourceSpec: Path and file name of the resource specification XML file.

- Server: SQL Server hosting the BizTalk Management database housing the application to export.

- Database: Name of the BizTalk Management database.

In our recipe's example, the exported Order application includes relatively few artifacts—just two BizTalk assemblies and their bindings. Using the Export MSI File Wizard is simple and straightforward. It produces a single file that can be used to import the Order application into the test environment. On a larger project, it is likely that your application will have many more artifacts, including BizTalk assemblies, bindings, policies, and folder structures such as virtual directories and input/output folder hierarchies. Additionally, you might need to migrate only a subset of an application to a new environment. Using the BizTalk Administration Console, you can export application subsets, bindings, and policies.

Exporting Application Subsets

Exporting applications allows for all artifacts (or a subset of artifacts) associated with an application to be exported into an MSI package. All of the artifacts you select during the export process will be packaged into a single MSI file, which you can use to install your application to a different BizTalk environment.

In addition to exporting an entire application, you can use the Select Resources page to specify a subset of artifacts to export. Let's extend the solution one step further in the project life cycle to see how this functionality might be useful. Suppose that after testing the Order application in the test environment, you find and fix an error in the Troubleshooting assembly. In order to apply your fix to the test environment, you need to export only the modified artifacts. Step through the Export MSI File Wizard a second time, and select only the Troubleshooting assembly on the Select Resources page. This produces an MSI package that includes only the selected assembly, which can be used to reimport the modified artifact in the test environment.

Exporting Bindings

Exporting bindings allows for bindings associated with an application to be exported into an XML file. Bindings are the links between your physical environment (for example, a specific MSMQ queue or web service URI) and your logical environment (for example, an orchestration receive port). You can export bindings for an entire BizTalk group or a specific BizTalk application or assembly.

You can use either the Export Bindings Wizard (right-click the appropriate application in the BizTalk Administration Console and select Export ➤ Bindings) or the BTSTask ExportBindings command-line utility to export bindings. See Recipe 7-6 for details on how to export bindings.

Exporting Policies

Exporting policies allows for Business Rule Engine policies associated with a BizTalk group (all policies in your BizTalk environment's Business Rule Engine database) or application to be exported into an XML file. Take the following steps to export policies for your BizTalk application:

1. Right-click the appropriate application in the BizTalk Administration Console and select Export ➤ Policies. This launches the Export Policies Wizard.

2. Select the policies and vocabularies you need to export, and specify a path and file name for the exported policy XML file, as shown in Figure 7-7.

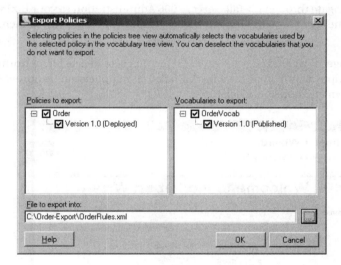

Figure 7-7. *Export Policies Wizard*

3. Click OK to export the policies.

It is recommended that you include all vocabularies contained in the policies you export. This prevents any missing vocabulary issues that can arise when one vocabulary references another.

In addition to using the Export Policies Wizard, you can export bindings using the BTSTask ListApp and ExportApp command-line utilities in combination, as follows:

1. Run the ListApp utility to create an XML file containing all artifacts for the BizTalk group or application for which you need to export policies.

2. Delete all artifacts from the XML file except the policies.

3. Run the ExportApp utility, specifying the updated XML file for the ResourceSpec parameter.

7-2. Importing Applications

Problem

You have completed the build phase of a BizTalk project and need to import your work from the development environment to another environment. You must import the BizTalk application you have been building.

Solution

You can use the BizTalk Administration Console to import a BizTalk application (via an MSI file). The following steps outline the procedure.

1. To open the BizTalk Administration Console, select Start ➤ All Programs ➤ BizTalk Server 2006 ➤ BizTalk Server Administration.

2. In the left pane, navigate through BizTalk Server 2006 Administration to your BizTalk group. Right-click the `Applications` folder and select Import-MSI File. This launches the Import Wizard.

3. On the Welcome page, navigate and select the MSI file that is to be used to perform the import. In this example, we are importing the BizTalk `Order` application (exported in Recipe 7-1), as shown in Figure 7-8. Click Next.

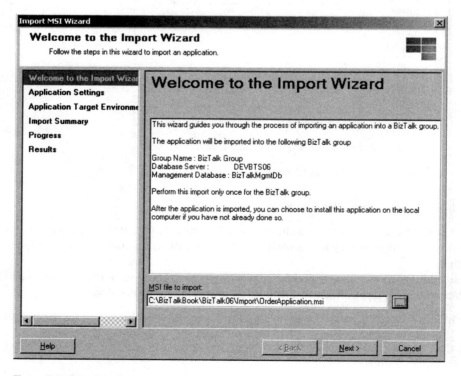

Figure 7-8. *Starting the Import Wizard*

4. On the Application Settings page, verify the settings for your application, references, and resources, as shown in Figure 7-9. In the list of applications available for reference, specify any references your target application has to existing BizTalk application assemblies and artifacts. You can also specify a new application (labeled during the export) or associate with an existing application within your BizTalk Management database. Click Next to continue.

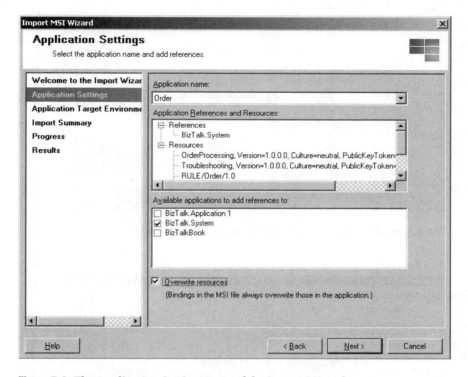

Figure 7-9. *The Application Settings page of the Import Wizard*

5. On the Application Target Environment Settings page, in the Target Staging Environment drop-down list, select the environment to which the application is to be deployed. This option allows for environment-specific considerations. You can partition applications that have been imported with binding-specific settings. By specifying an environment value at this stage, the Import Wizard will apply only to the environment-specific configuration identified during the import process. If you leave the value set to <Default>, the configuration will be applied to all environments.

6. On the Import Summary page, verify the application import information presented, as shown in Figure 7-10. Click Import when you're ready to complete the import process.

7. The wizard displays the progress of the import operation, and then shows a Results page, as shown in Figure 7-11. Verify that the import was successful by checking for errors. You can also view more details of the import by clicking the link to the import operation log. Click Finish to close the wizard.

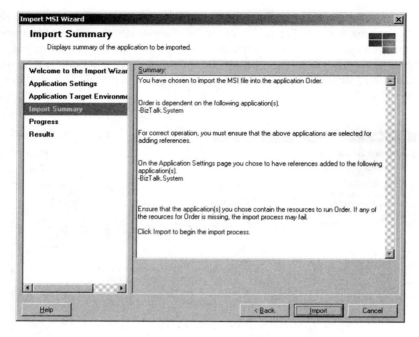

Figure 7-10. *The Import Summary page of the Import Wizard*

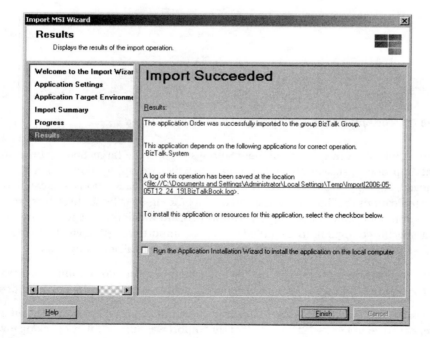

Figure 7-11. *Results page of the Import Wizard*

Figure 7-12 shows the Order application imported in the example added to the Applications node in the BizTalk Administration Console. Once an application has been imported, starting the application will complete the necessary deployment steps.

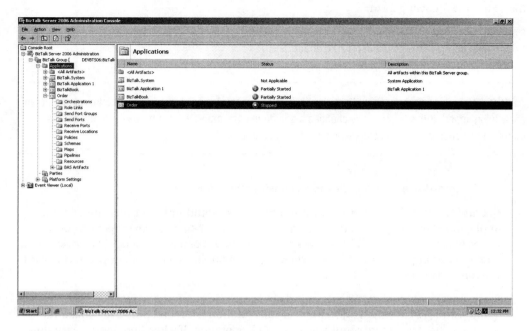

Figure 7-12. *Order application after import*

How It Works

In BizTalk 2006, the import process controls the sequence of shutting down services and provides the administrator with input to control and consider application references and dependencies. In addition, it controls the registering of BizTalk and .NET application artifacts into the Global Assembly Cache (GAC). This eliminates the need for IT users to know the sequence of specific BizTalk deployment steps and perform them manually, leading to faster and easier application deployment cycles.

In this recipe's example, we imported an MSI file, which contains application artifacts. You can also import policies (business rules artifacts) and bindings. Binding information examples could include an address (such as a file or queue location) port information, or specific properties that specify retries, security options, and so on. You could import bindings when the BizTalk solution artifacts already exist and the target requires only binding input/updates for deployment.

■**Note** Importing an MSI file can include both bindings and policies. If these artifacts are specified in the application export process, they will be imported as part of the MSI file import process.

In addition to using the Import MSI File Wizard, you can access the same functionality via the BTSTask ImportApp command-line utility. This option could be useful when performing regular environment promotion activities, fully automated deployments, and so on. The command has the following form:

```
BTSTask ImportApp /Package:value [/Environment:value]    [/ApplicationName:value]
[/Overwrite] [/Server:value] [/Database:value]
```

■**Note** BTSTask commands should not be used in a preprocessing or postprocessing script run during an application import. If this is done, any changes made during the import will not be visible to the scripts; therefore, the success of the deployment cannot be guaranteed.

When importing BizTalk applications, consider the following:

Overwrites: Determine whether the import process should support overwrites. On the Application Settings page of the Import Wizard (Figure 7-9), you can set generic overwrites of BizTalk artifacts. If this check box is selected, existing artifacts will be overwritten on the target import. If this box isn't selected and a duplicate is found, the Import Wizard will raise an error.

Downstream components: Keep in mind downstream components, such as URIs, files, queues, and HTTP URLs. For example, if your solution uses send port URIs, make sure that the URIs exist before running your BizTalk operation. If a location doesn't exist (for example, a receive location), BizTalk may detect this, raise an error to the Windows Event Viewer, and show the application status as partially started. Whenever an application is in the status of partially started, it's a good idea to check the application Windows Event Viewer for failures and information.

Runtime/operational considerations: When deploying to an existing environment, keep in mind runtime considerations. Make sure that users have been notified and usages of running BizTalk processes are known.

Security: By default, BizTalk does not store passwords for binding information unless explicitly referenced within the binding file build process. As a matter of caution, always verify your deployment, and update passwords and access rights appropriately within your BizTalk artifacts.

7-3. Deploying a BizTalk Solution from Visual Studio

Problem

You have developed a BizTalk solution and wish to deploy the solution for testing in your development environment directly from Visual Studio, rather than using other deployment methods.

Solution

Since BizTalk projects compile into .NET assemblies, the deployment process in Visual Studio is similar to deploying other .NET projects. You must first sign the BizTalk assembly before you can add the assembly to the GAC. Then set up the BizTalk project properties, and finally deploy the project. The following steps outline the procedure.

1. To sign a BizTalk assembly, open a Visual Studio Command Prompt (Start ➤ Microsoft Visual Studio 2005 ➤ Visual Studio Tools ➤ Visual Studio Command Prompt), and type the following command:

   ```
   Sn -k "c:\somepath\mykeyname.snk"
   ```

2. Press Enter. If you are successful, the output will show `Key pair successfully written to....`

3. Open the solution you wish to deploy in Visual Studio.

4. For each project in the solution, right-click the project and choose Properties.

5. In the left pane of the Property Pages dialog box, under `Common Properties`, click the `Assembly` node.

6. In the right pane of the Property Pages dialog box, enter the full path/key name for the key you created for this project (in step 1) for the `Assembly Key File` property, as shown in Figure 7-13 (`C:\somepath\mykeyname.snk` in this example).

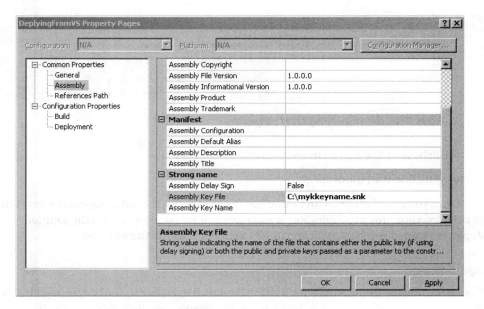

Figure 7-13. *Setting up a strong named key*

7. In the left pane of the Property Pages dialog box, under `Configuration Properties`, click the `Deployment` node.

8. In the right pane of the Property Pages dialog box, enter an application name for the project. Set other properties as desired (see Table 7-1). Figure 7-14 shows a project configured for deployment. Click OK to close the dialog box.

■Note The application name is not required, but it is a best practice to give all projects an application name to facilitate management of the project.

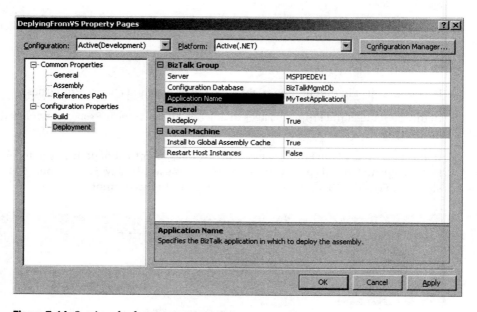

Figure 7-14. *Setting deployment properties*

9. Right-click the project or solution and select Deploy.

10. Bind and start the artifacts.

Once you have bound an orchestration, the binding will be remembered the next time you deploy your project. In addition, if you have multiple projects within the solution, deploying from the solution will deploy all the projects within the solution.

How It Works

Deploying directly from Visual Studio is an alternative to exporting and importing BizTalk applications through the BizTalk Administration Console (see Recipes 8-1 and 8-2).

Within Visual Studio, several deployment properties are available (see Figure 7-14), as described in Table 7-1.

Table 7-1. *Visual Studio Deployment Properties*

Property	Description
Server	Defines the BizTalk deployment server. The local server name is the default setting for this property. If the project is shared across multiple development machines, set this value to localhost.
Configuration Database	Defines the name of the BizTalk configuration database. By default, and unless it was changed, the configuration database name will be BizTalkMgmtDb.
Application Name	Defines the application that will house this BizTalk project. Although leaving this property blank will cause the solution to deploy to the default application, it is a best practice to provide a value for this property.
Redeploy	Defines whether the deployment process will automatically delete the old deployed assembly before deploying the current assembly. This option is very useful, but should be used only within a development environment.
Install to Global Assembly Cache	Controls whether the assembly will be deployed to the GAC as part of the deployment process.
Restart Host Instances	Controls whether to restart the in-process host instance. By default, this property is False. Due to artifact caching during development, it is a best practice to change this setting to True to force the removal of artifacts from the cache. If this property is False, you may notice inconsistent behavior in your solutions, particularly during repeated deployments.

7-4. Enlisting and Starting Send Ports

Problem

You have deployed a solution and need to validate that your send ports are enlisted and started.

Solution

An important step in the deployment of a BizTalk solution is to enlist and start send port messaging artifacts. You can do this from the BizTalk Administration Console, either in isolation or as part of a larger application deployment.

■Note An important prerequisite to enlisting and starting a send port involves configuring the send port to subscribe to BizTalk messages, either via setting a filter on a send port or by binding a send port to a BizTalk orchestration artifact. In both of these instances, a send port has subscription criteria identifying which messages it will consume from BizTalk. For information about binding send ports to an orchestration, refer to Recipe 7-6.

The following steps outline the procedure for starting and enlisting send ports using the BizTalk Administration Console.

1. To open the BizTalk Administration Console, select Start ➤ All Programs ➤ BizTalk Server 2006 ➤ BizTalk Server Administration.

2. In the left pane, navigate through BizTalk Server 2006 Administration to your BizTalk group, expand the `Applications` folder where your send port resides, and select the `Send Ports` node.

3. Right-click your send port and select Enlist, as shown in Figure 7-15. The send port will move from the unenlisted to the stopped state.

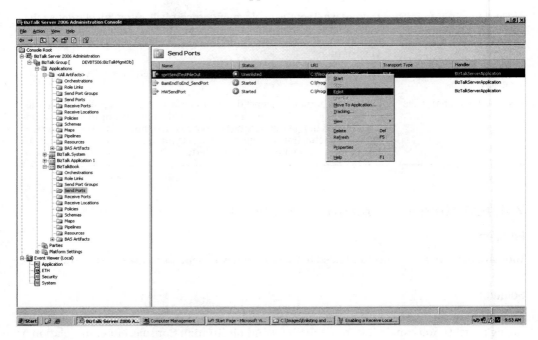

Figure 7-15. *Enlisting a send port*

4. Right-click your send port again and select Start, as shown in Figure 7-16. Your send port should now be started and enlisted.

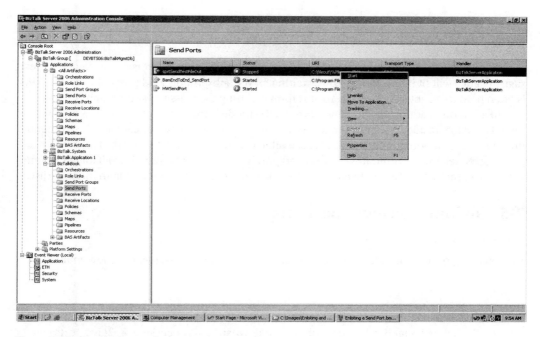

Figure 7-16. *Starting a send port*

How It Works

In this recipe's solution, we demonstrated how to enlist and start send ports via the BizTalk Administration Console. You can also enlist and start send ports via the BizTalk Server Explorer within the Visual Studio development environment. Typically, a developer may find it convenient to manage send ports from the BizTalk Explorer, while a system administrator might need to work only within the confines of the BizTalk Administration Console.

Enlisting and starting are two mutually exclusive states on a send port. Enlistment sets up the port and ensures that it is recognized and properly bound. Starting the port has it begin listening for the trigger that will cause it to execute. These are two logical mandatory steps to enable a BizTalk solution to be deployed.

■**Note** In this example, we demonstrated the explicit steps of enlisting and starting for demonstration purposes only. A send port can also be explicitly started from an unenlisted state. This enhancement is aimed at simplifying the administration process and the steps involved to complete the enlisting/starting task.

Enlisting a port enables a subscription in the BizTalk MessageBox. If a send port is not enlisted, a message published to the MessageBox will not be subscribed to by the send port. If a subscriber is not found (the message had only the send port as the intended subscriber), a BizTalk error would be thrown, indicating that a matching subscription could not be found and the message instance would be suspended, but resumable in the MessageBox. (In previous versions of the product, this would have caused the message instance to be suspended but not resumable.)

If a message is published to the BizTalk MessageBox and a send port is not started, the message instance will sit in the MessageBox, waiting for the subscribing send port to be started. This is often hard to troubleshoot, as no error is thrown during the message-submission process.

In addition to administering send ports via the product tool set, BizTalk also has an object model available to allow programmatic administration via Windows Management Instrumentation (WMI). Send port administration is accessible via the base class `Microsoft.BizTalk.ExplorerOM.SendPort`. Within this class, a send port has a variety of methods available (for example, `ChangeSendPortStatus()`). Refer to the BizTalk product documentation for an inclusive list.

7-5. Enabling Receive Locations

Problem

You have deployed a solution and want to validate that your receive locations are enabled.

Solution

A receive location is the entry point into a receive port for pipeline processing and submission into the BizTalk MessageBox for subscribers and downstream processing. Receive ports can have multiple receive locations belonging to them. To allow messages to be received and consumed, you should enable a receive location.

■**Note** For a receive location to be enabled, make sure that the receive location has been associated with a receive handler and pipeline. The receive handler determines the security context (file access permissions) under which a receive location operates.

To enable a receive location, follow these steps:

1. To open the BizTalk Administration Console, select Start ➤ All Programs ➤ BizTalk Server 2006 ➤ BizTalk Server Administration.

2. In the left pane, navigate through BizTalk Server 2006 Administration to your BizTalk group, expand the `Applications` folder where your receive location resides, and select the `Receive Locations` node.

3. Right-click your receive location and select Enable, as shown in Figure 7-17.

■**Note** Multiple receive locations can be enabled by holding down the Shift key as you select the target receive locations. Then right-click and select Enable from the context menu.

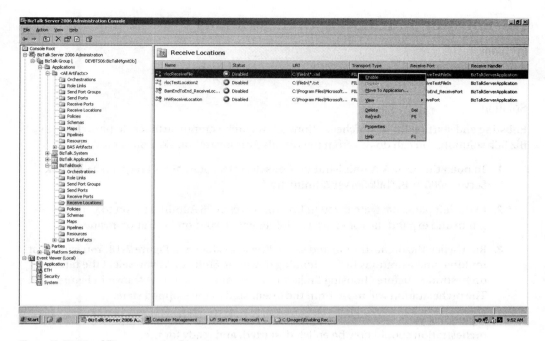

Figure 7-17. *Enabling a receive location*

How It Works

Enabling a receive location is an important deployment activity. If a receive location is not enabled, a message will reside in the physical adapter's transport receive location, and it will not be consumed by BizTalk. For example, the message could be a file in a folder for the file adapter or a message in an MSMQ queue for the MSMQ adapter.

A common problem when initially deploying and verifying receive locations is often security access and file permissions. When enabling a receive location, it is a good idea to check the Windows Event Viewer to ensure no errors are raised by BizTalk. Common errors with receive locations are often security-related. Always check to ensure your receive location has been granted permission to the security credentials associated with the receive port's receive handler or the receive port itself.

■**Note** BizTalk now provides a much friendlier way of dealing with intermittent receive location problems. As an enhancement, once a receive location has been enabled, intermittent transport problems (for example, security or network access) will not disable the receive location. Previous product versions required intervention to enable the receive location. However, note that once a receive location is explicitly disabled, it must also be explicitly enabled to allow the receive location to function correctly.

7-6. Enlisting and Starting Orchestrations

Problem

You need to validate that your orchestrations are enlisted and started.

Solution

Enlisting and starting BizTalk orchestrations allows orchestration artifacts to participate in a BizTalk solution. You can do this from the BizTalk Administration Console, as follows:

1. To open the BizTalk Administration Console, select Start ➤ All Programs ➤ BizTalk Server 2006 ➤ BizTalk Server Administration.

2. In the left pane, navigate through BizTalk Server 2006 Administration to your BizTalk group and expand the Applications folder where your orchestration resides.

3. Right-click the orchestration and select Enlist, as shown in Figure 7-18. You can enlist multiple orchestrations by first holding down the Shift key as you select the target orchestration before choosing Enlist from the context menu, as shown in Figure 7-19. The orchestration will move from the unenlisted to the stopped state.

4. Right-click your orchestration again and select Start, as shown in Figure 7-20. Your orchestration should now be enlisted, started, and ready for use.

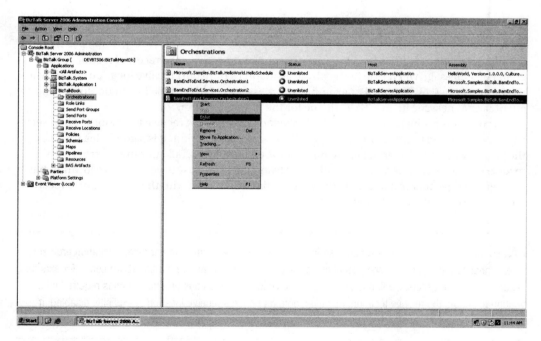

Figure 7-18. *Enlisting an orchestration*

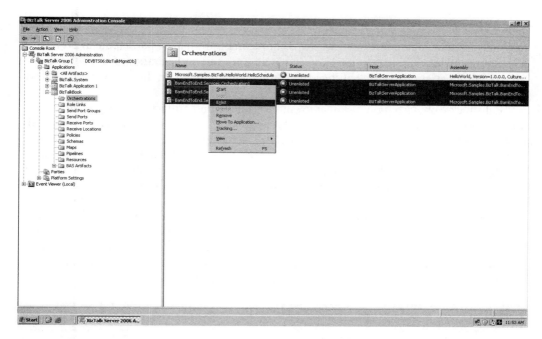

Figure 7-19. *Enlisting multiple orchestrations*

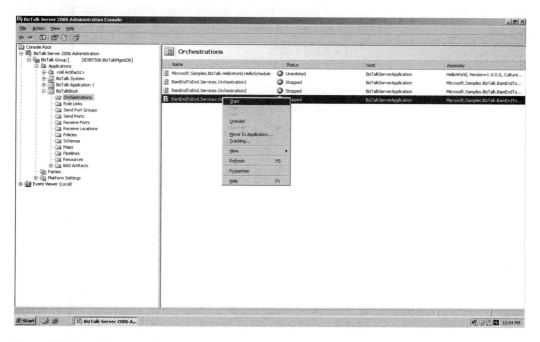

Figure 7-20. *Starting an orchestration*

How It Works

Enlisting and starting BizTalk orchestrations allows orchestrations to participate in BizTalk messaging and processing solutions. You can enlist and start orchestrations from either the BizTalk Administration Console or the Visual Studio environment. In this recipe's solution, we demonstrated using the BizTalk Administration Console.

Enlisting an orchestration is similar to enlisting a send port artifact. Enlisting an orchestration allows it to set up subscriptions with the MessageBox so it can receive messages published to it. In essence, enlisting holistically in the BizTalk product gives BizTalk artifacts (send ports and orchestrations) the ability to subscribe to the MessageBox for desired message contexts. Starting an orchestration allows an orchestration to physically consume and process a message.

Two important prerequisites to allow an orchestration to be started and enlisted are orchestration binding and host binding. Only orchestrations that have been bound can be enlisted; that is, an orchestration's port must be bound to a solution's physical send/receive port before enlisting. All orchestration ports must be bound to a physical host. If you attempt to enlist or start an orchestration when a host has not been bound, an error will occur, indicating that the enlisting has failed, as shown in Figure 7-21. In addition, an orchestration's configuration cannot be unbound when in an enlisted or started state.

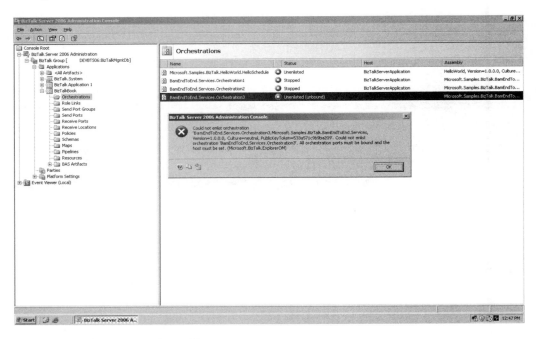

Figure 7-21. *Enlisting an unbound host*

It's also worth noting that entire BizTalk applications can be started and stopped. This activity ensures that all BizTalk artifacts under an application are enlisted, started, enabled, and ready (depending on the artifact), without any knowledge required by the user. Figure 7-22 shows starting a BizTalk application.

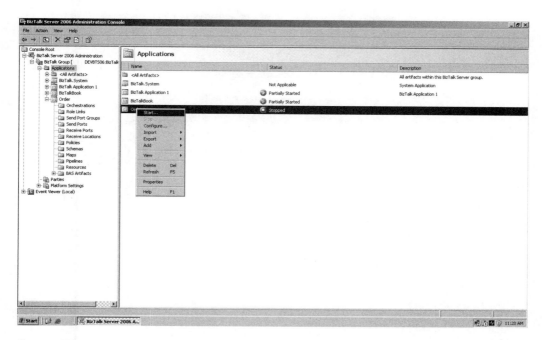

Figure 7-22. *Starting an entire BizTalk application*

CHAPTER 8

■ ■ ■

Administration and Operations

Integration solutions play a key role in many organizations' technology offerings. While much time and effort are typically spent on the actual implementation of these solutions, administration and maintenance tasks are often treated as a "second-class citizens." This reality can have costly consequences, as downtime of integration points can have large financial impacts on businesses.

In order to help make administration and operation more efficient, a number of enhancements have been built into BizTalk Server 2006. The BizTalk Administration Console includes two new pieces of key functionality: the Group Hub page and application views. The Group Hub page exposes information for a single BizTalk Server, providing a view into the health of the server and allowing for troubleshooting and triage of issues. Specifically, the Group Hub page provides the following:

- Queries for work in progress and suspended items (service instances and messages)

- The ability to perform bulk operations (terminate, suspend, or resume) on service instances

- The ability to build and save custom queries to return information on service instances and messages

The application views expose information for a single BizTalk Server application. An application is a new concept within BizTalk Server 2006, and is a logical grouping of BizTalk artifacts. By grouping artifacts, applications allow them to be managed as a single unit as opposed to individual items. Applications can be started and stopped, which starts and stops all the underlying artifacts, such as orchestrations, receive locations, and send ports. When an application is started or stopped, the individual artifacts are started or stopped in the correct order, accounting for all interdependencies. Applications also facilitate a number of deployment-related tasks, such as importing and exporting. For information about deploying BizTalk Server solutions, see Chapter 7.

The other tool used in administering BizTalk Server environments is Health and Activity Tracking (HAT). HAT facilitates troubleshooting of service instances and messages. It provides debugging capabilities, allowing breakpoints to be set on orchestration shapes. Once an orchestration instance has hit a breakpoint, it can be resumed in debug mode and stepped through in a sequential fashion. HAT also provides the ability to query both in-process and archived items in BizTalk Server. In addition to supplying a number of predefined queries, such as "all messages received in the past day" and the "most recent 100 service instances," HAT allows you to create your own queries. You can find messages by using schema, property, and port information pertaining to the instance you need to locate. You can also create your own message and service instance queries using the Query Builder tool, which assists in the creation of SQL queries that extract information from the BizTalk databases.

This chapter focuses on the use of the administration tools within BizTalk Administration Console and HAT, and how to ensure a well-managed BizTalk environment and a streamlined troubleshooting process.

8-1. Troubleshooting Suspended Services

Problem

Your integration solution has encountered an error, and you must determine what caused the fault.

Solution

The primary tool BizTalk Server provides for troubleshooting is the BizTalk Administrator Console. This tool helps you to identify why errors occur in an integration solution and to determine the best way to fix them.

Often, the event log gives the first indication an error has occurred in BizTalk, especially during the development stages of an integration project. BizTalk Server writes errors to the application event log each time it suspends a service instance. The error event contains helpful information on when, why, and where the fault happened. You can view errors posted to the event log by BizTalk Server through the BizTalk Administrator Console, which includes the Event Viewer MMC snap-in.

Occasionally, the event log will have enough information to determine what action needs to be taken to fix the error (server name not specified on the SMTP adapter, for example), but often, further troubleshooting is necessary. To obtain more detailed information about the fault, you can use the BizTalk Administrator Console's Group Hub page, which provides a number of ways to search for suspended service instances.

The following steps outline a procedure for troubleshooting a suspended service.

1. To open the BizTalk Administration Console, select Start ➤ All Programs ➤ BizTalk Server 2006 ➤ BizTalk Server Administration.

2. Expand the Event Viewer folder in the left pane and select Application. You should see an error event relating to the service instance that was suspended. This event is flagged with a BizTalk-related source, such as BizTalk Server 2006 or XLANG/s.

3. To obtain more detailed information about the event, expand the BizTalk Server 2006 Administration folder in the left pane and select your BizTalk group. This opens the Group Hub page.

4. Click the Suspended service instances link in the Suspended Items section. Clicking this link launches a query window, as shown in Figure 8-1.

■**Note** The Group Hub page also provides filtered views of suspended service instances, including resumable service instances; nonresumable service instances; suspended MSMQT messages; and suspended service instances grouped by application, error code, service name, and URI.

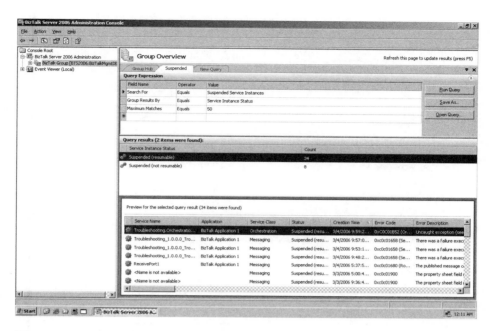

Figure 8-1. *Suspended service instances query*

5. Order the query results on the Creation Time column by clicking the column header. You can compare the creation date with the timestamp of the error event log entry to determine if they relate to one another.

6. Once you have found the appropriate suspended service instance in the query results list, double-click the row to launch the Service Details dialog box, as shown in Figure 8-2. The General tab of this dialog box includes high-level information regarding the suspended instance, including the BizTalk component that encountered the error, the service's status, and the instance ID. Knowing the particular component that encountered the error is a valuable and significant piece to the troubleshooting puzzle, as it assists in narrowing down where the fault occurred. In our example, we see that the error occurred in `Orchestration_1`, an artifact within the `Troubleshooting` project.

7. Click the Error Information tab. As shown in Figure 8-3, this tab displays the text of the exception that the suspended service instance encountered, which is the same as what is written to the application event log. The error text usually includes key stack information, indicating at what level the fault occurred and how it was "bubbled up" through BizTalk. In our example, we see that a `MissingPropertyException` was thrown when BizTalk attempted to retrieve the `SMTP.Subject` message property. We also see in which orchestration the exception occurred (`Troubleshooting.Orchestration_1`) and the specific shape that contained the faulty code (`Expression_1`).

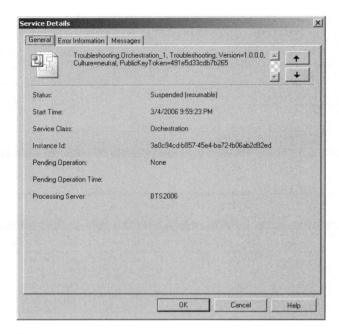

Figure 8-2. *General tab of the Service Details dialog box*

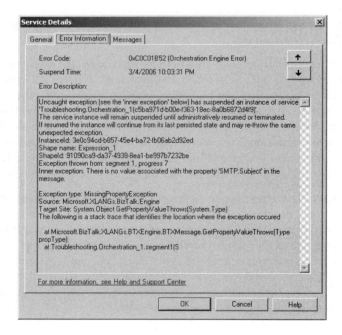

Figure 8-3. *Error Information tab of the Service Details dialog box*

8. Click the Messages tab. As shown in Figure 8-4, the Messages tab displays a list of all messages related to the suspended service instance. From this tab, you can save the suspended message to a file for further inspection, turn on tracking for the message, or view additional details of the message (right-click the message for these capabilities).

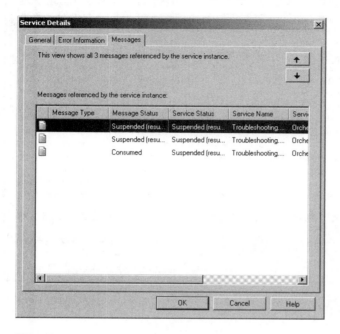

Figure 8-4. *Messages tab of the Service Details dialog box*

9. Double-click one of the messages and select the Context section, as shown in Figure 8-5. This view displays the context of the suspended message, which can be especially helpful when troubleshooting. Particularly, it alerts you to what properties the message had when it was suspended and which were promoted. In our example, we see that there is no promoted property for SMTP.Subject on the message.

You now have sufficient information to locate and fix the error. By opening the Troubleshooting.Orchestration_1 artifact, you find the exception-producing line of code in the Expression_1 shape:

```
SMTPSubject = Message(SMTP.Subject);
```

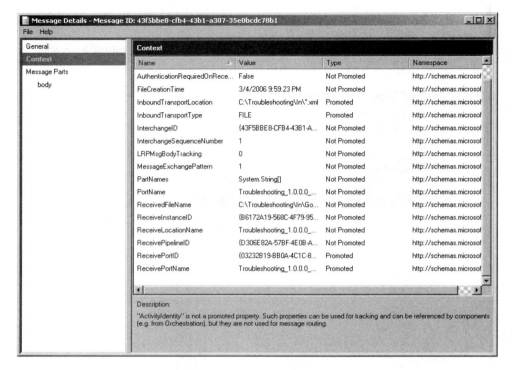

Figure 8-5. *Context section of Message Details*

How It Works

When errors occur in your integration solutions, BizTalk typically suspends the service instance encountering the error. *Service* is a generic term used to describe an area of BizTalk processing, such as orchestration, messaging, or adapter. *Service instance* refers to a specific instance of the orchestration, messaging, or adapter component. The troubleshooting tools of BizTalk are primarily used by system/solution administrators, and are not typically used (in a production environment) by developers or testers.

Finding the particular suspended service instance you are troubleshooting is the first step in solving the issue. In this recipe's solution, we compared the timing of event log errors and suspended services to find a specific instance. This technique of timestamp comparison would not work well if you were troubleshooting a long-running service instance (in which case, the creation time of the instance and the time of the error may be significantly different). While our solution used a simple way of locating the suspended instance, more-advanced methods can be useful, especially in production, heavy-load, or long-running environments.

In most cases, exceptions that are thrown from BizTalk (and the corresponding event log error) include the instance and/or message ID. You can use these IDs to locate a suspended service instance. In our solution, the event log error indicated an instance ID of 3e0c94cd-b857-45e4-ba72-fb06ab2d92ed. Within the suspended service instance query view in the BizTalk Administration Console, add the Service Instance ID column to the query results grid by taking the following steps:

1. Right-click any column header and select Add/Remove Columns. This launches the Add/Remove Columns dialog box.

2. Add the Service Instance ID field to the list of displayed columns, as shown in Figure 8-6, and then click OK.

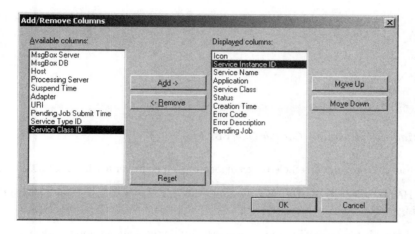

Figure 8-6. *Adding a column to the query results*

3. Sort the query results by the Service Instance ID column.

4. Scroll down until you find the appropriate suspended service instance ID.

The BizTalk Administration Console also allows you to create your own queries to find suspended service instances. Right-click your BizTalk group in the left pane and select Query Tasks ➤ New Query to create a new query, as shown in Figure 8-7. A number of fields are available for queries, including Creation Time, Error Code, and Service Class. Additionally, you can save and retrieve custom queries for future troubleshooting needs.

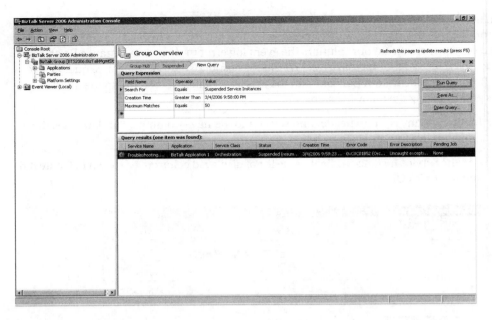

Figure 8-7. *BizTalk Administration Console Query Builder*

The HAT tool also provides an efficient way of locating a specific service instance ID, as follows:

1. Open HAT by selecting Start ➤ All Programs ➤ BizTalk Server 2006 ➤ Health and Activity Tracking.

2. Select Reporting ➤ Query Builder. The Query Builder tool allows you to select and view service instances within your BizTalk environment.

3. Drag and drop the appropriate items from the SQL Views pane to the SQL Query pane, building a query to return our service instance ID. A completed version of the query and associated results are shown in Figure 8-8.

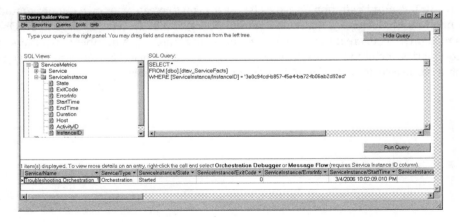

Figure 8-8. *HAT Query Builder*

■Note In the SQL Views pane, the root-level items (ServiceMetrics, for example) are views within the BizTalk Tracking database, and the child items (InstanceID, for example) are columns contained within the views.

In our scenario, the suspended service instance is an orchestration. HAT allows you to view which steps an orchestration completed prior to being suspended by right-clicking the query result record and selecting Orchestration Debugger (see Recipe 8-5).

■Note While HAT provides debugging and message location utilities, it does not directly allow common administrative tasks such as resuming service instances. The BizTalk Administrative Console should be used for these activities.

Once you have found your suspended service instance, the details that BizTalk Server tracks against the suspended instance provide a solid starting point for determining the best way to fix the issue. In general, you should use generic problem-solving skills when troubleshooting BizTalk errors: break down the problem into its component parts and use the tools at your disposal to evaluate the fault using a bottom-up approach. Using the BizTalk Administrative Console and HAT in combination allows you to break down complex solutions into manageable parts and troubleshoot the specific component encountering the error.

8-2. Finding a Message

Problem

You have deployed a BizTalk solution and need to troubleshoot exceptions occurring within your solution. You have already identified and enabled tracking for specific messages. You need to find the tracked messages to identify the exception.

Solution

The following instructions outline the steps required to find a message in BizTalk based on a specific message type in the BizTalk HAT tool. We assume that the outbound send port on your solution and the promoted properties within the message have tracking enabled. For more information on tracking, refer to Recipe 8-6.

1. To open HAT, select Start ➤ All Programs ➤ Microsoft BizTalk Server 2006 ➤ Health and Activity Tracking.

2. From the HAT menu, select Reporting ➤ Find Message. The Find Message View window appears, as shown in Figure 8-9.

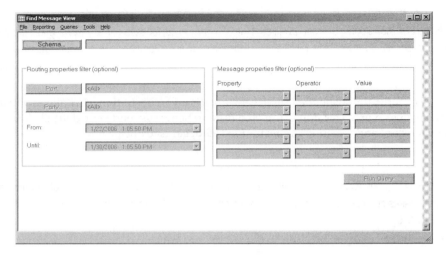

Figure 8-9. *Find Message View window in HAT*

3. Click the Schema button. In the Schema Selection dialog box, choose the appropriate schema target namespace (`http://SQLAdapterStoredProcedure` in this example) and schema root name (`Customer_Request` in this example), as shown in Figure 8-10. The unique combination of a schema namespace and root node name defines the message type. Click OK after making your selection.

■**Note** When defining the message type to find, you will only be able to select from a list of typed messages. Messages processed in orchestrations as `System.XML.XMLDocument` objects will not appear within the list of schemas.

Schema Selection

Select a schema to search for:

Target Name Space	Schema Root Name
http://BizTalk_Server_BAM_Test_Project.schTestMessage	Customer
http://SQLAdapterStoredProcedure	Customer_Request
http://SQLAdapterStoredProcedure.schCustomer	Customer
http://SQLAdapterUpdategram	Customer_Request
http://SQLReceiveAdapter	Customer_Response
urn:BamEndToEnd.Services.Schema1	Schema1
urn:BamEndToEnd.Services.Schema3	Schema3

OK   Cancel

Figure 8-10. *Schema Selection dialog box*

4. In the Find Message View window, define additional search criteria for the query, as follows:

   - Port: By default, messages from all ports display in the query results. You may filter on a specific port by clicking the Port button and choosing from the list of ports. You may select a single logical or physical port for filtering.

   - Party: By default, messages from all parties display in the query results. You may filter on a specific party by clicking the Party button and choosing from the list of parties. You may select a single party for filtering.

   - From: The From parameter allows sorting by a specific date range. The default value in the From field is seven days prior to current date in which the search is occurring. For example, if the Find Message View window is opened on 1/29/2007, the From field will display 1/22/2007 by default. The time is not adjustable and defaults to the current machine time in which the Find Message View opens.

   - Until: The Until parameter allows sorting by a specific date range. The default value in the Until field is one day past the current date in which the search is occurring. For example, if the Find Message View window is opened on 1/29/2007, the Until field will display 1/30/2007 by default. The time is also adjustable by selecting the individual hour, minute, or second and typing in the value desired.

   - Property: You can specify up to five promoted properties as part of the search criteria. Only promoted properties deployed in a property schema are displayed in the property list. Distinguished properties are not selectable as part of the search criteria. The promoted properties will not appear within the search criteria window until you have enabled tracking for the promoted properties and verified that a message has been processed. Property fields allow you to search based on a value range. If you use the LIKE or NOT LIKE keyword, you can implement SQL wildcards for partial word matching in your searches.

5. After selecting the appropriate criteria, click the Run Query button to execute the query. The result set without promoted properties will resemble Figure 8-11. If you included a promoted property as part of the search criteria, the result set will resemble Figure 8-12. In the example in Figure 8-12, notice the use of the SQL wildcard character % to facilitate a partial word match.

■Note Promoted properties will be displayed as a column in the result set and populated with data as long as the properties are tracked (see Recipe 8-6). If tracking is not enabled, then promoted properties will have no data displayed in the promoted properties columns.

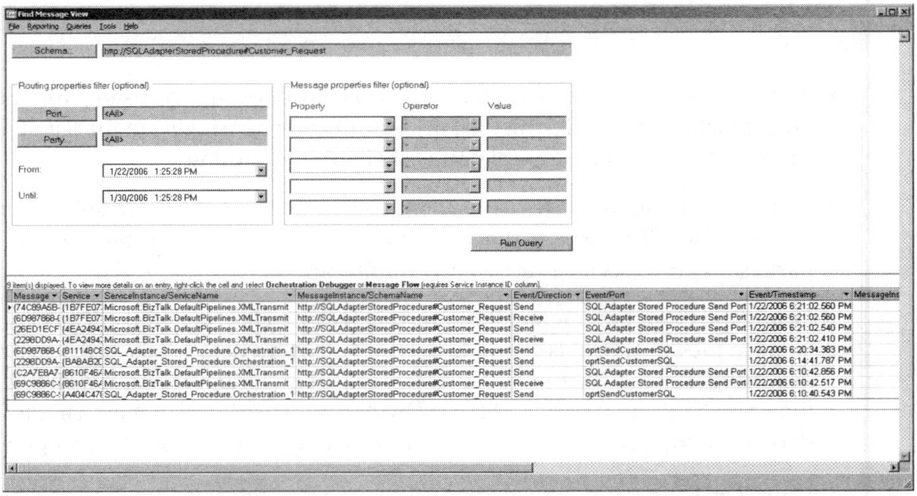

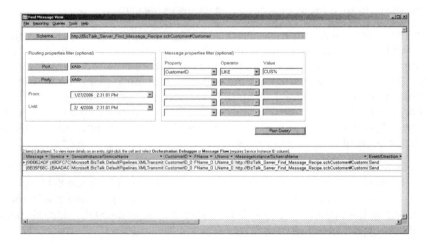

Figure 8-11. *Completed Find Message query without promoted properties*

Figure 8-12. *Completed Find Message query with promoted properties*

How It Works

The HAT tool offers an excellent capability for finding messages that your BizTalk solution processes or has processed. The Find Message View window is useful in almost every BizTalk solution, as long as the messages implement a namespace and root node.

The following are key considerations to remember when searching for messages:

- Only promoted properties that exist in a property schema can be used as part of the search criteria.

- If you are using the LIKE or NOT LIKE keyword, you can use the SQL wildcard character for searches using partial word matches.

- You must enable the tracking of promoted properties within the BizTalk Administration Console before you can access those properties as part of your find message query (see Recipe 8-6).

The BizTalk Administration Console offers similar message-searching capabilities to the HAT tool. However, the BizTalk Administration Console search facility operates only on messages that BizTalk is currently processing or has suspended; it does not show messages that have been processed. HAT shows both messages that BizTalk is currently processing and those that it has processed.

8-3. Resubmitting Messages

Problem

Your integration solution has encountered an error, and you need to resubmit the messages that have been affected by the fault.

Solution

The BizTalk Administrator Console allows you to resume service instances and resubmit their associated messages. You can locate the suspended service instance (which will contain the suspended message) that you need to resume, and then choose to resume it, as follows:

1. Open the BizTalk Administration Console by selecting Start ➤ All Programs ➤ BizTalk Server 2006 ➤ BizTalk Server Administration.

2. Expand the BizTalk Server 2006 Administration folder in the left pane and select your BizTalk group. This opens the Group Hub page.

3. Click the Resumable link in the Suspended Items section. This launches a query window displaying all suspended service instances in your BizTalk environment that can be resumed.

4. If you are unsure if a particular suspended service instance contains the message you need to resubmit, right-click the instance record in the results pane and select Show Messages. This displays a list of messages referenced by the service instance, allowing you to drill down further into the message details and interrogate the actual message, its context, and the flow the message took prior to suspension.

5. When you have located the service instance you need to resume, right-click the record in the results pane and select Resume Instance, as shown in Figure 8-13. In addition to resuming single suspended service instances, you can also resume multiple instances by holding down the Ctrl key and selecting multiple rows in the results pane. To resume all instances, right-click the header record in the results pane and select Resume Instances, as shown in Figure 8-14.

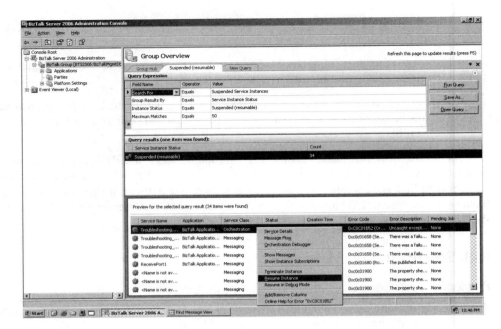

Figure 8-13. *Resuming a single suspended instance*

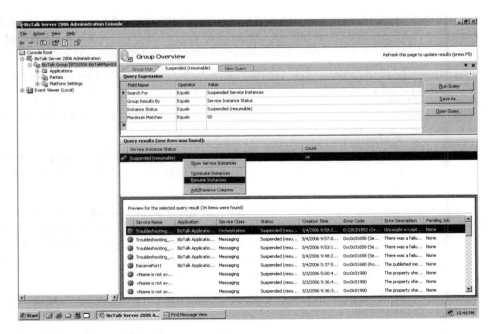

Figure 8-14. *Resuming all suspended instances*

How It Works

BizTalk errors can be caused by a number of faults, including hardware or network failure, or errors during pipeline or adapter processing. When errors occur in your integration solutions, BizTalk typically suspends the service instance that encountered the error (see Recipe 8-1 for details on troubleshooting suspended services). Services are areas of BizTalk processing—such as orchestration, messaging, or adapter—and service instances are specific instances of the orchestration, messaging, or adapter component. A service instance may contain one or more suspended messages. BizTalk differentiates between two basic types of suspension events: resumable (the service instance can be restarted) and nonresumable (the instance cannot be restarted).

Finding the service instance that contains the message you want to resubmit is critical. A number of methods for searching for suspended instances are provided by BizTalk, including those described in this recipe's solution, as well as those outlined in Recipes 8-1 and 8-2.

If you know that you must resubmit a message that was suspended in a specific orchestration, here is a quick way to search for service instances:

1. Within the BizTalk Administrator Console, expand the navigation tree in the left pane down to the appropriate application and click the Orchestrations folder.

2. In the right pane, right-click the appropriate orchestration and select View ➤ Instance Information, as shown in Figure 8-15. This launches a new query of suspended services instances for that particular orchestration.

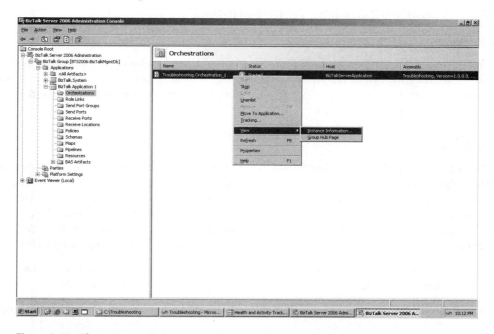

Figure 8-15. *Choosing to view instance information*

In addition to resuming services instances normally, you can also resume service instances in debug mode. Resuming in debug mode will restart the service instance at the last successful persistence point prior to the error. For more information, on debugging service instances, see Recipe 8-5.

BizTalk also provides Windows Management Instrumentation (WMI) methods for resubmitting suspended service instances, such as `MSBTS_ServiceInstance.Resume` and `MSBTS_HostQueue.ResumeServiceInstancesByID`.

Finally, messages can be manually resubmitted. This process involves finding a particular service instance or message via the BizTalk Administrator Console or HAT, saving the message data, and using a resubmit mechanism (such as ports or administrative tools) to resend the message through BizTalk. To save a message, right-click the record (in either the BizTalk Administrator Console or HAT) and select the option for saving the tracked message(s). While this method is generally more time-consuming and task-intensive, it can be particularly helpful when the error is such that it would be significantly difficult to successfully resume a suspended service instance. You should consider the following when manually resubmitting messages:

- Security, with regards to encryption and authentication

- Data privacy and protection for sensitive information

- User error if data is manipulated

8-4. Managing BizTalk Applications

Problem

You have BizTalk solution artifacts that should be grouped together for ease of management and maintenance. Specifically, you would like to group BizTalk Solution components so that you can easily deploy those components to another environment as well as start and stop the components together as a whole.

Solution

You can use a BizTalk application to group and manage BizTalk solution artifacts. As outlined in the following steps, the process involves creating the new application, configuring it, and then adding components. After creating the BizTalk application, you can import BizTalk MSI files and bindings, and also add previously created BizTalk assembly DLLs, scripts, and resources. The instructions in this solution describe the process for adding a BizTalk assembly DLL that contains multiple schemas. See Chapter 7 for details on the MSI export/import process.

1. To open the BizTalk Administration Console, select Start ➤ All Program Files ➤ Microsoft BizTalk Server 2006 ➤ BizTalk Server Administration Console.

2. In the left pane, right-click the `Applications` folder and choose New ➤ Application. This launches the Application Properties dialog box, as shown in Figure 8-16.

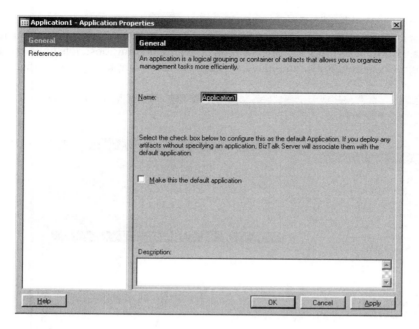

Figure 8-16. *Application Properties dialog box*

3. In the Application Properties dialog box, make the following settings, and then click the OK button to create the new BizTalk application.

- Enter the name of the application that you are creating.

- Specify if this application is the default application. Identifying your application as the default application is significant when deploying new BizTalk artifacts from Visual Studio. Unless you specify an application in Visual Studio, your BizTalk artifact deploys to the default BizTalk application. A BizTalk artifact that does not specify a deployment application name will be grouped in your newly created default application.

- Identify any application references. Identifying application references allows you to share resources across applications. For example, if you have a common set of shared schemas, maps, or pipelines, you can specify them as part of an application reference and not need to make multiple copies of those components for each BizTalk application.

4. After the application is created, verify that the artifacts have been bound appropriately. Right-click the application and choose Start.

■**Note** When you start a BizTalk application, you have the choice of enlisting and starting all orchestrations, send ports, send port groups, receive locations, host instances, and resuming suspended instances.

5. To configure your application, from the BizTalk 2006 Administration Console, right-click it and choose Configure. You will be presented with a Configure Application dialog box, as shown in Figure 8-17. Here, you can configure binding, host, role links, and messaging/port settings for your application. Click OK after completing your configuration.

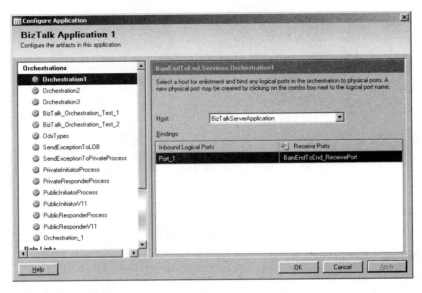

Figure 8-17. *Configure Application dialog box*

6. From the newly created application, right-click and choose Add ➤ BizTalk Assemblies. This launches the Add Resources dialog box, as shown in Figure 8-18.

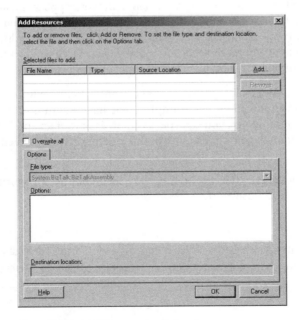

Figure 8-18. *Add Resources dialog box*

7. Click the Add button to identify the assemblies to add to the BizTalk application. You can add assemblies (BizTalk or custom), scripts, bindings, COM objects, and other objects to your BizTalk application. This dialog box includes the following settings:

- Overwrite all: This flag indicates whether to overwrite an existing resource that exists in the Management database with the resource specified in the application. If you do not specify this flag and you have a resource that contains the same name, the process will fail when trying to add the object.

- Options: Depending on the type of resource being added, you have different options. For example, if you are adding an assembly to your project, you also have the option to add the assembly to the Global Assembly Cache (GAC), make the resource visible to COM, and register the component as a serviced component. Figure 8-19 demonstrates the result of adding a standard assembly to a BizTalk application.

- Dependencies: You will receive a list of dependencies if you choose to add an assembly (BizTalk or custom) to your BizTalk application.

- Destination location: The location or path where the resource file will be copied when the application is installed. You may specify an absolute, a relative, or a UNC path. The default path copies the resource file to the application installation folder.

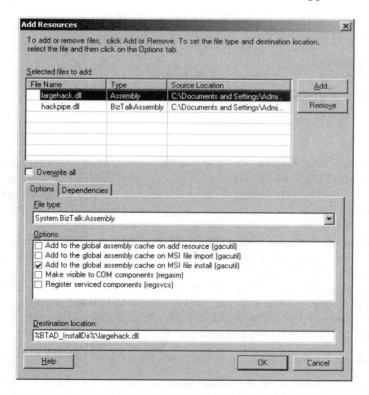

Figure 8-19. *Adding an assembly to a BizTalk application*

8. When you have selected the resources to add to you BizTalk application, click the OK button. Figure 8-20 shows an example of a BizTalk application with a schema resource added. Notice that BizTalk automatically manages the placement of the resource into the correct folder location within the BizTalk application.

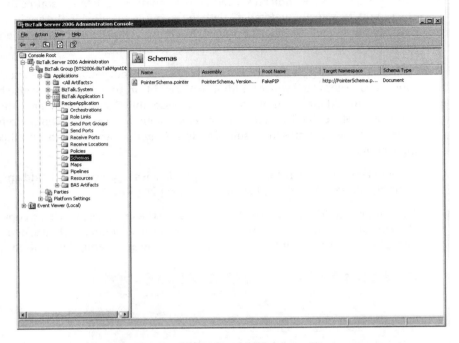

Figure 8-20. *Schema resource added to an application*

How It Works

BizTalk applications represent a powerful concept in organizing BizTalk artifacts into logical groupings. You can group like or related artifacts together in a BizTalk application. Once BizTalk artifacts are grouped logically, it is possible to export the application to another BizTalk environment. The concept of applications simplifies management, troubleshooting, and deployment of BizTalk artifacts.

The monitoring tools that are included in the BizTalk Administration Console take advantage of the BizTalk application concept. Multiple BizTalk solutions can now be managed through logical application groupings.

BizTalk 2006 is set up with a default application container under which all BizTalk artifacts are deployed to by default. When you upgrade a previously created BizTalk solution, the artifacts will initially be placed in the default application. Additionally, in the following situations, BizTalk artifacts will be placed in the default application:

- When you deploy BizTalk artifacts from Visual Studio without specifying an application

- When you use BTSDeploy to deploy BizTalk artifacts (because this tool was created for a previous version of BizTalk)

- When you use BTSTask without specifying an application name

> **Note** If you perform automated deployment, make sure to use the BTSTask tool versus the deprecated BTSDeploy tool. With BTSTask, you can specify the application under which your BizTalk artifacts are deployed. If you continue to use the BTSDeploy tool, your BizTalk artifacts will be deployed to the default BizTalk application.

Consider using a separate BizTalk application in the following situations:

- When sharing BizTalk assemblies across multiple applications. In this situation, group BizTalk assemblies in a separate application.

- When sharing a deployed website. The best approach here is to implement the shared website in a separate application. When uninstalling a BizTalk application that contains a website, the virtual directory of that website will be removed even if it is currently being used. Any other application sharing that website will encounter exceptions if that website is removed.

- When sharing a policy across multiple applications. In this situation, create a separate application for that policy. When you stop a BizTalk application that includes a policy, the policy is undeployed. If another application is referring to the undeployed policy, you will encounter exceptions.

You can move artifacts between BizTalk applications in the same BizTalk group by selecting an application resource, right-clicking, and choosing Move To Application from the context menu. This will launch the Move to Application dialog box, where you can choose a new BizTalk application. If you need to move artifacts to another BizTalk application in a different BizTalk group, you must export the artifact and then import it into the other BizTalk group's application.

8-5. Debugging Orchestrations

Problem

You need to debug a BizTalk orchestration.

Solution

You can use BizTalk's Orchestration Debugger, available through the HAT tool, which can be configured on any currently active or dehydrated orchestration. The Orchestration Debugger allows you to set breakpoints on any shape in an orchestration. Once an instance of an orchestration executes and encounters one of these breakpoints, it will go into a wait state in the BizTalk MessageBox, allowing a developer or administrator to manually step through the orchestration.

> **Note** A dehydrated orchestration is an orchestration that has been removed from memory and persisted to SQL Server while it waits for its next action to occur, such as receiving a document. Upon this next action, the orchestration is returned to memory in the exact state prior to dehydration, and processing continues. This ability to dehydrate/rehydrate allows BizTalk Server to better utilize server resources.

This solution will work with a sample orchestration that receives a message and moves through a series of steps, as shown in Figure 8-21.

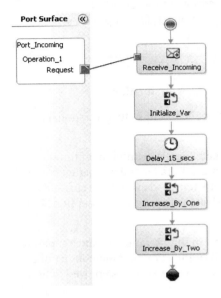

Figure 8-21. *Sample orchestration for debugging example*

The sample orchestration uses several Expression shapes to increase the value of an integer. Additionally, it has a Delay shape, which will pause the orchestration for a short period of time. The following steps demonstrate setting a breakpoint and stepping through the orchestration.

1. Make sure that an instance of the orchestration is either currently running or has been previously run. An instance of the orchestration must execute before the Orchestration Debugger can be set to debug it.

2. Open HAT by selecting Start ➤ All Programs ➤ BizTalk Server 2006 ➤ Health and Activity Tracking.

3. Open the Queries menu and select one of the options that will return at least one instance of the orchestration to be debugged in the results list.

■**Note** You can find running instances by using the BizTalk Administration Console. Select an orchestration from a BizTalk application, right-click it, and select Tracking to view the instance information.

---

4. Right-click the instance of the orchestration to debug and select Orchestration Debugger, as shown in Figure 8-22. The Orchestration Debugger window will open. The full orchestration will appear with a pane on the left showing a list of tracked events, as shown in Figure 8-23.

Figure 8-22. *Accessing the Orchestration Debugger (in HAT)*

■**Note** Large orchestrations can take longer to load. Occasionally, with smaller development machines and larger orchestrations, you may need to wait for a while before the Orchestration Debugger window actually opens.

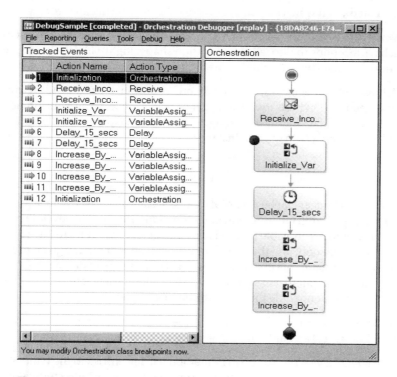

Figure 8-23. *Orchestration Debugger window*

5. To set a breakpoint, right-click any shape and select Set Breakpoint on Class.

6. Step through the orchestration by clicking tracked events in the left pane.

7. At any time, select Debug ➤ Attach. A new pane will open and display the values of all variables at the given stage of the orchestration. This allows for a full view into the state of the process. You'll notice a number of debugging actions are available on the Debug menu.

■**Note** You can attach only to orchestrations that have not completed. If this is the first time that the orchestration has executed, it will likely have already completed. You may need to start a new instance before the orchestration will pause on a breakpoint that has been set.

---

8. Click through the tracked events in the left pane to see which steps have executed by highlighting the corresponding orchestration shapes in the right pane. The color green indicates input to a shape, and blue indicates an exit from a shape. This will aid in determining which paths have been followed (in the case of Decide and Parallel Action shapes), how many times they may have executed (for instance, how many times a loop has executed), and which step in the process may be causing an error.

9. If desired, step into a child orchestration by clicking the event in the Tracked Events pane, which corresponds to the Call Orchestration shape. Right-click the event and select the option to step into the child orchestration.

10. Once all debugging has been completed on an orchestration, make sure to clear all breakpoints. Open the Orchestration Debugger on an instance of the same orchestration (any instance will do) and select Debug ➤ Clear All Breakpoints on Class (this can be done only when not attached to an instance).

How It Works

While the Orchestration Debugger can be a helpful tool, especially in cases where an orchestration is deployed in a production environment and is encountering errors, developers often need a much more rapid and controllable method for debugging. It is helpful to have logging in development and in production, and the ability to turn it on and off for any given process at any given time should be available. Several techniques enable this type of debugging.

For example, using two standard .NET lines of code will allow a view into what is happening in an orchestration without opening the Orchestration Debugger:

```
System.Diagnostics.EventLog.WriteEntry("Demo","Value: " + strValue);
System.Diagnostics.Trace.WriteLine("Value: " + strValue, "Demo");
```

The System.Diagnostic.EventLog.WriteEntry method will log entries to the Windows Event Viewer. To view this logged event, open the Control Panel, select Administrative Tools, and double-click Event Viewer. Events will be logged to the application log, and you'll need to refresh the display to see results as they are written.

■**Note** The user that runs the orchestration (whatever the Host User has been configured to be) must have rights to write to the Event Viewer to use the `System.Diagnostic.EventLog.WriteEntry` method.

The `System.Diagnostics.Trace.WriteLine` method will allow all of the trace outputs to be read by attaching to the main BizTalk executable and monitoring in Visual Studio. Use the following steps to do that monitoring:

1. In Visual Studio, select Debug ➤ Attach to Process.

2. In the window that opens, find `BTNTSvc.exe` and highlight it. Click the Attach button.

3. Run an instance of the orchestration. Trace information will be made available in the Output window in Visual Studio.

One way to use the `System.Diagnostic` methods for debugging/tracing in orchestrations is to wrap the logging code in an `If` statement, and create a `TraceFlag` that can be set in a configuration file, such as the `BTSNTSvc.exe.config` file in the root BizTalk `Program Files` folder. Here is an entry you could add to the `BTNTSvc.exe.config` file:

```
<add key=" TraceFlag" value="true"/>
```

Listing 8-1 demonstrates how to retrieve the `TraceFlag` and, based on its value, log information.

Listing 8-1. *Configurable Trace Flag*

```
// set the trace flag based on a value stored in the BizTalk Config File
blnTraceFlag = System.Convert.ToBoolean(System.Configuration.
ConfigurationSettings.AppSettings.Get("TraceFlag"));

// set the source to something unique for this orchestration
strSource = "DebugDemoOrchestration";

// Trace
if(blnTraceFlag == true){
strValue = System.Convert.ToString(intValue);
System.Diagnostics.EventLog.WriteEntry(strSource,"Value: " + strValue);
System.Diagnostics.Trace.WriteLine("Value: " + strValue, strSource);
}
```

When using this approach, keep tracing information separate in the orchestration from other functionality, and label it appropriately. You can do this by dedicating an Expression shape to a single trace event and naming it `Trace`, as shown in the example in Figure 8-24.

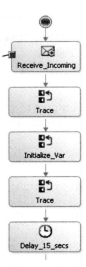

Figure 8-24. *Expression shapes for tracing*

One of the most helpful ways to debug is to see the actual XML of a message, especially before and after mapping. This can be done by setting a variable of type System.Xml.XmlDocument equal to an orchestration message, and then tracing the value of this variable, as shown in Listing 8-2.

Listing 8-2. *Tracing XML*

```
// set the xmlDoc variable equal to the message to be traced.
// msgOrch is an orchestration message
xmlDoc = new System.Xml.XmlDocument();
xmlDoc = msgOrch;
System.Diagnostics.EventLog.WriteEntry(strSource,"Value: " + xmlDoc.OuterXml);
System.Diagnostics.Trace.WriteLine("Value: " + xmlDoc.OuterXml, strSource);
```

■**Note** A maximum size of 32KB can be written to the Windows Event Viewer. Often, XML messages will exceed this size. If a string longer than 32KB is written, an exception will be thrown, and the orchestration will terminate (unless appropriate exception handling is implemented). There is no limitation to the size when using the Trace.WriteLine method.

8-6. Tracking Messages

Problem

You want to be able to view the contents of messages that have arrived in a given BizTalk solution, to monitor messages and actions that have been processed through ports and orchestrations.

Solution

The ability to monitor orchestration activity and access message contents and flow is known as *tracking messages*. BizTalk allows tracking to be set at a number of different levels. This solution describes how to configure tracking so that messages can be saved in their entirety and viewed in any text editor. You can configure tracking using the BizTalk Administration Console, and then access the tracked messages using the HAT tool.

Configure Tracking

The following steps outline the procedure to configure tracking on receive and send ports on any orchestrations where messages need to be tracked.

1. To open the BizTalk Administration Console, select Start ➤ All Programs ➤ BizTalk Server 2006 ➤ BizTalk Server Administration.

2. Expand the tree in the left pane until the BizTalk application that contains the solution on which you want to configure tracking is visible, and then click the `Receive Ports` folder.

3. In the right pane, right-click the receive port that is to be configured for tracking and select Tracking, as shown in Figure 8-25.

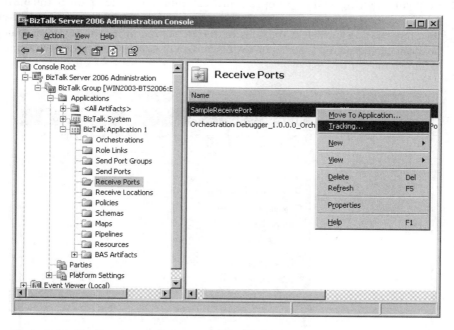

Figure 8-25. *Configuring tracking within the BizTalk Administration Console*

4. In the Tracking Options dialog box, set the desired options for tracking. The settings are generic across one-way and two-way ports.

   • Request Message Before Port Processing: Request messages exist in one-way and two-way ports. Checking this value will track the message prior to being processed by the port (processing includes any pipelines or maps that may be on the port).

■**Note** A message is a request if the message is initiated by the port/orchestration. A message is a response if the port/orchestration is receiving it from an external source.

- Request Message After Port Processing: Checking this value will track the message after being processed by the port (processing includes any pipelines or maps that may be on the port).

- Response Message Before Port Processing: Response messages exist on two-way ports only. Checking this value will track the message prior to being processed by the port (processing includes any pipelines or maps that may be on the port).

- Response Message After Port Processing: Checking this value will track the message after being processed by the port (processing includes any pipelines or maps that may be on the port).

5. If desired, configure tracking for send ports. Right-click the send port, select Tracking, and choose options in the Tracking Options dialog box.

6. Configure tracking on the appropriate orchestrations. In the left pane of the BizTalk Administration Console, click the Orchestrations folder. In the right pane, right-click the orchestration and select Tracking. In the Orchestration Tracking Options dialog box, you can configure tracking on events and on messages within the orchestration, as shown in Figure 8-26.

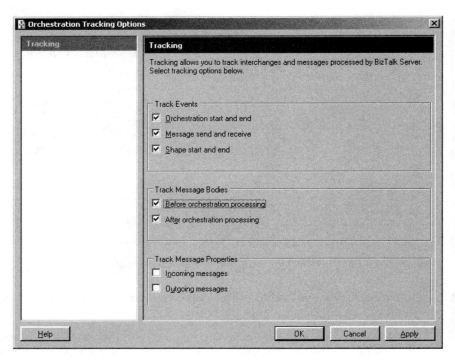

Figure 8-26. *Orchestration Tracking Options dialog box*

Access Tracked Messages

After you have configured tracking through the BizTalk Administration Console, access the tracked messages via HAT, as follows:

1. Drop a message on the appropriate receive location to instantiate the orchestration.

2. Open HAT by selecting Start ➤ All Programs ➤ BizTalk Server 2006 ➤ Health and Activity Tracking.

3. Open the Queries menu and run a query that will return results consisting of an instance of the orchestration or send/receive ports that were instantiated after setting up tracking (instances that may have run prior to tracking will have been set up with the default tracking). A typical query to run would be Recent Service Instances. Alternatively, open BizTalk Administration Console, right-click an orchestration within a BizTalk application, and select View Instance Information.

4. Right-click the orchestration shown in the query results and select Save All Tracked Messages.

5. In the dialog box that appears, select a location to save the messages, as shown in Figure 8-27.

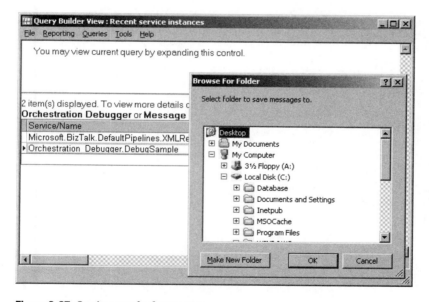

Figure 8-27. *Saving tracked messages*

Depending on the complexity of the orchestration, the number of send and receive ports, and the level of tracking configured, there may be a few or a large number of messages written out to the directory specified. A combination of system messages and XML messages will have been tracked.

How It Works

There is a direct relation between the level of tracking configured for a given solution and the size of the underlying BizTalk databases. For solutions with high levels of tracking and a high volume of message transactions, the databases can grow at a quick rate. An intelligent approach to traditional SQL database management is required, especially as it pertains to table truncation and data backups.

■■■

CHAPTER 9

Business Activity Monitoring

BizTalk *implementations* can be generally defined as business processes, and *business processes* generally create metrics and data, which are needed for reporting purposes. The ability to rapidly generate and access such metrics and reports about business processes is essential to many parties, including managers, developers, and integration partners. One of the core components of BizTalk Server 2006 is the Business Activity Monitor (BAM) framework, which allows you to create, deploy, and view information about running or previously run processes. BAM implementations publish the metrics and reports and make them available to users through custom interfaces, which are updated in near real time as data progresses through the system. This chapter will introduce the steps necessary to build, deploy, and access BAM implementations.

A business process within BizTalk consists of the combination of all the pipelines, ports, orchestrations, maps, and other components needed for the successful completion of a specific task or set of tasks. You can trace the full life cycle—from the moment a document arrives through all the steps of processing to the ultimate delivery of any documents—using the tools available through the BAM framework. Business analysts and developers must work together to define which steps in the business process are important to track and how these steps will be reported to users.

BAM is tied directly to the central BizTalk engine (that is, processes and databases) through OLAP *cubes*. These cubes are created automatically when a developer deploys a BAM report and profile, typically by using a combination of Microsoft Excel pivot tables and the BizTalk Tracking Profile Editor. Once all the BizTalk components are deployed and a running instance of an orchestration is executing, all defined steps of the flow will be subscribed to via the OLAP cubes and published via BAM components to the user. Users can access the published data via the Web, SharePoint, Excel spreadsheets, or applications that have been customized to display the information.

The recipes in this chapter include detailed information about working with standard BAM development and deployments, working with the BAM API, and viewing information available via the BAM engine.

9-1. Creating BAM Activities and Views

Problem

You have business users requesting metrics, visibility, and business data from the execution of a deployed BizTalk solution and the associated artifacts. The business users are interested when any of the BizTalk processes execute the following steps: process begins, process ends, or process encounters exceptions. The business users are also interested in the following attributes of the messages consumed by the BizTalk processes: the transaction ID and transaction type.

Solution

This recipe outlines how to use Excel to create a BAM workbook that tracks milestones and business data for reporting. This recipe addresses the four categories of steps required in creating a BAM solution. Each category of steps plays an integral role in developing a useful, rich, and powerful BAM solution:

- Creating the BAM activity workbook

- Outlining the BAM view

- Identifying aggregations, dimensions, and measures

- Constructing the pivot table

■**Note** This recipe does not address how to use the Orchestration Designer for business analysts or the Tracking Profile Editor. Please see Recipe 9-7 for information about how to use the Tracking Profile Editor.

Create the BAM Activity Workbook

BAM *activities* identify the milestones and tracking data an individual is interested in tracking. *Milestones* are the steps in an activity that are measured in time, and *tracking data* is the key data points in a process you are interested in tracking (such as a customer ID or name).

   This category of steps outlines how to create a BAM activity in Excel. The activity defined in this recipe includes milestones that indicate when a process begins, ends, and encounters an exception. Additionally, the following steps outline how to create tracking data that captures the transaction ID and transaction type.

   1. Create a new Excel workbook, select the BAM menu item, and choose BAM Activity. Choosing the BAM activity will launch the Business Activity Monitoring Activity Definition Wizard.

■**Note** If the BAM menu item does not appear in the menu, then verify that the Business Activity Monitoring Excel add-in is enabled (for example, select Tools ➤ Add-Ins ➤ Business Activity Monitoring).

---

   2. In the Business Activity Monitoring Activity Definition Wizard, click the New Activity button to create a new activity. Name the new activity **Process Activity**.

   3. Create the items listed in Table 9-1 for your activity, and click the OK button to complete the Business Activity Monitoring Activity Definition Wizard. The completed activity should resemble Figure 9-1.

Table 9-1. *Activity Milestones and Key Tracking Data Items*

ID	Milestone/KPI	Item Type	Data Type	Description
1	Begin	Business Milestone	Date Time	Identifies the date/time a process begins
2	EndSuccess	Business Milestone	Date Time	Identifies the date/time a process successfully ends
3	Exception	Business Milestone	Date Time	Identifies the date/time a process exception occurs
4	Transaction Id	Business Data – Text	Text (50)	Identifies the ID of the transaction being processed
5	Transaction Type	Business Data – Text	Text (50)	Identifies the type of the transaction being processed

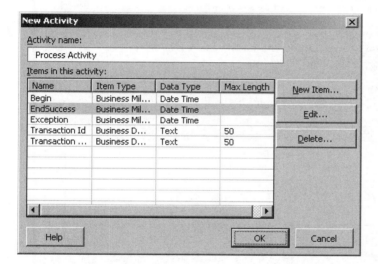

Figure 9-1. *New Activity dialog box*

   4. Click the OK button twice to complete the wizard and create a BAM view.

Outline the BAM View

A BAM view is a representation of the milestones and business data tracked in one or more activities. A view may comprise multiple activities or multiple milestones from a single activity and can contain tracked data or milestones as well as provide aggregations or summaries of the tracked milestones and business data. Creating a BAM view is a necessary step because it defines which tracked milestones and business data to report. Typically, different views are created to show multiple audiences different aspects of the same tracked data.

   This category of steps demonstrates how to outline your view and display tracked data items and milestones. The view created in this recipe summarizes how many processes execute successfully versus how many processes encounter an exception.

1. When the Business Activity Monitoring View Creation Wizard begins, click the Next button twice to advance the wizard.

■**Note** If the wizard does not start, then launch the wizard by selecting BAM ➤ BAM View Excel.

---

2. Name the view **Process View**, and select the Select All Activities box. The Business Activity Monitoring View Creation Wizard will resemble Figure 9-2. Click the Next button to advance the wizard.

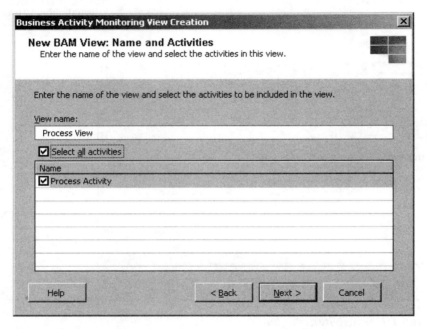

Figure 9-2. *Business Activity Monitoring View Creation Wizard*

3. On the New BAM View: View Items page of the Business Activity Monitoring View Creation Wizard, select the Select All Items box to add all the milestones and business data to the new view. Click the Next button to advance the wizard.

4. Click the New Group button to create a Group item, and select the box next to the milestones listed in Table 9-2. Figure 9-3 demonstrates the milestones to select.

■**Note** The Group milestone allows related milestones to be treated as a single milestone. In this example, grouping the EndSuccess and Exception milestones is useful to indicate the completion of the process regardless of whether it completed successfully or failed.

Table 9-2. *Business Milestone Group*

Business Milestone Alias	Name	Activity
End	EndSuccess	ProcessActivity
End	Exception	ProcessActivity

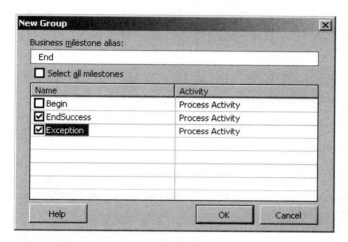

Figure 9-3. *New business milestone group*

5. Create a New Duration item with the parameters listed in Table 9-3 to record the total process execution time. Figure 9-4 demonstrates the New Duration creation dialog box.

■**Note** A duration calculates the time between two business milestones and is useful when reporting the time elapsed between two milestones is important. In this sample, the duration will display the time elapsed for the process execution from the beginning of the process to the End milestone group created earlier.

Table 9-3. *Duration Properties*

Duration Name	Start Milestone	End Milestone	Time Resolution
ProcessDuration	Begin (Process Activity)	End (Process Activity)	Day

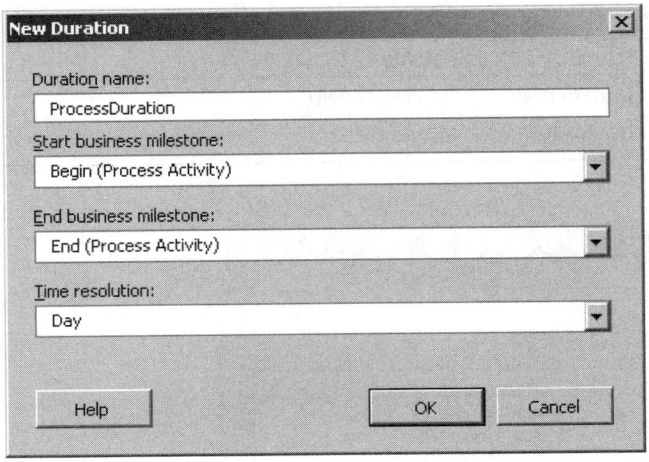

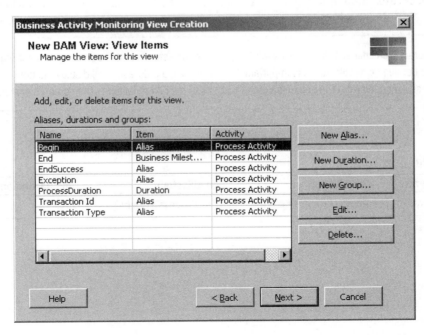

Figure 9-4. *New Duration dialog box*

6. The completed Business Activity Monitoring View Creation Wizard should resemble Figure 9-5. Click the Next button to advance the wizard and create aggregations, dimensions, and measures.

Note All names used for aliases, durations, groups, dimensions, and measures must be unique for a single view.

Figure 9-5. *Completing the Business Activity Monitoring View Creation Wizard*

Identify Aggregations, Dimensions, and Measures

Aggregations, dimensions, and measures in your BAM solution provide rich functionality for deriving computations and information based on the tracked data and milestones. This category of steps is not required; however, it adds richness to a BAM solution. After completing this category of steps, you must also complete the steps outlined in the "Construct the Pivot Table" section to organize the derived results.

1. Create a new progress dimension, and name it **ActivityProgress**.

Note A *progress dimension* defines milestones and stages for a process. A progress dimension allows you to display how many processes are at an existing status at a given time. In this example, a progress dimension will display how many processes are in the middle of execution, how many encountered an exception, or how many processed without an exception. Table 9-4 lists the milestones and stages created in this example.

Table 9-4. *Progress Dimension Items*

ID	Milestone Name	Description
1	Started	The process begins as soon as a message is received. Started is a milestone, and each progress dimension must contain a milestone.
1	Processing	Processing is a transient stage and indicates a transition from when the process started to when it completes.
1	Completed	Completed is a milestone indicating the process has successfully completed.
1	Failed	Failed is a milestone indicating the process has failed to complete because of an exception.

Note When defining a progress dimension, you must define the steps in your process and the transitions between the steps. Milestones define the steps, and stages define the transitions between milestones. Each progress dimension must begin with a milestone.

---

2. The following instructions detail how to create the items listed Table 9-4:

   a. Click the New Milestone button to launch the New Progress Milestone dialog box. Create a new milestone, name it **Started**, and make it refer to the business milestone called Begin (Process Activity).

   b. Click the New Stage button to launch the New Progress Stage dialog box. Create a new stage named **Processing**, and make it refer to the business milestone called Begin (Process Activity). You will not be able to select the milestone because the wizard automatically selects the milestone.

    c. Click the New Milestone button to launch the New Progress Milestone dialog box. Create a new Milestone named **Completed**, and make it refer to the business milestone called EndSuccess (Process Activity).

    d. Click the New Milestone button to launch the New Progress Milestone dialog box. Create a new Milestone named **Failed**, and make it refer to the business milestone called Exception (Process Activity).

    e. Figure 9-6 demonstrates the completed progress dimension. Click the OK button to complete the New Dimension dialog box.

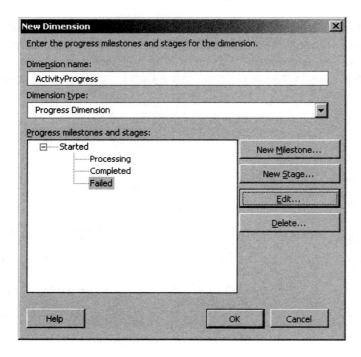

Figure 9-6. *Finishing the progress dimension*

3. Create a new measure with the properties listed in Table 9-5. A new measure will provide a count of processes currently executing. Click OK to complete the New Measure dialog box. Figure 9-7 demonstrates the New Measure dialog box.

Table 9-5. *Measure Properties*

Measure Name	Base Data Item	Aggregation Type
Count	Process Activity	Count

■**Note** You must select Count as an aggregation type before you can select Process Activity as the base date item.

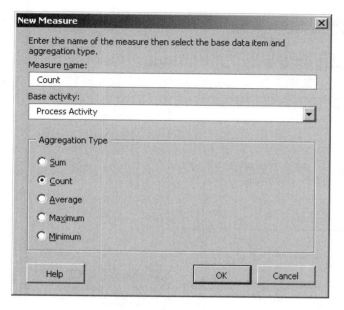

Figure 9-7. *Creating a new measure*

4. Click the Next button to complete the New BAM View: Aggregation Dimension and Measures page of the wizard.

5. Review the contents of the New BAM View: Summary page of the Business Activity Monitoring View Creation Wizard. Click the Next button, and finally click the Finish button to complete the wizard.

Note At this point you have successfully created a BAM activity and view (including aggregations, measures, and dimensions). The next step is to complete the pivot table layout for the BAM view.

Construct the Pivot Table

This final category of steps demonstrates how to lay out the computed items created in the earlier category of steps. If you did not complete the previous category of steps, then you will not be presented with the option of creating a pivot table. The pivot table created in this recipe appears in the BAM portal and is the representation of the data for the user. An Excel pivot table allows you to lay out worksheet data in a grid to analyze trends over data as well as perform data aggregations. In this scenario, the progress dimension previously created is organized in the pivot table alongside the count measure also previously created.

After completing the Business Activity Monitoring View Creation Wizard, you will have a workbook with an empty pivot table that resembles Figure 9-8. The image displays the empty Pivot Table report and the Pivot Table Field List window. Data items from the Pivot Table Field List window are organized in the Pivot Table report.

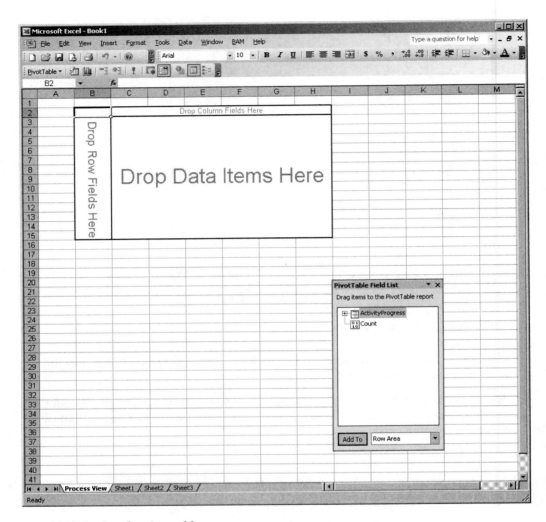

Figure 9-8. *Viewing the pivot table*

1. In Excel, drag the ActivityProgress dimension from the Pivot Table Field List window onto the Drop Row Fields Here section of the pivot table.

■**Note** If the pivot table field list is not visible, right-click the PivotTable report, and choose Show Field List.

---

2. From the Pivot Table Field List window, drag the Count item to the Drop Data Items Here section of the pivot table. The pivot table should resemble Figure 9-9.

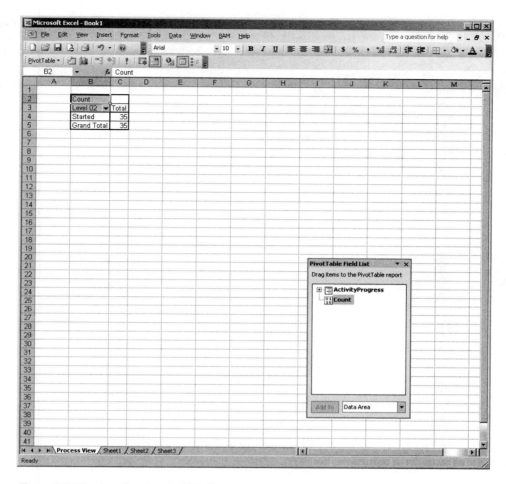

Figure 9-9. *Viewing the pivot table's data items*

3. This step demonstrates how to expand the progress dimension to see all the defined stages and milestones. Double-click the Started milestone to expand and see the stages and milestones within the progress dimension. The completed pivot table will resemble Figure 9-10.

Note If you receive an error message, then verify that you clicked inside the Started milestone cell first before double-clicking the started milestone.

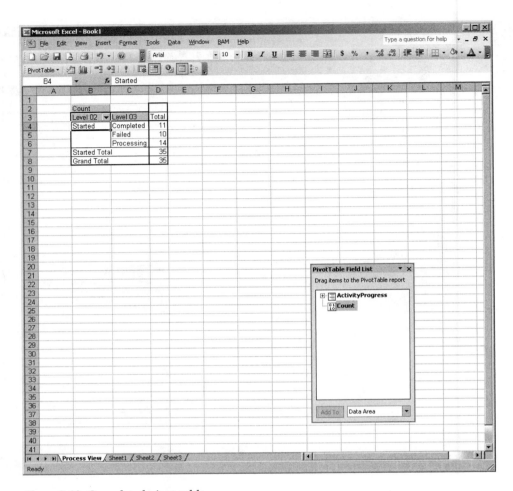

Figure 9-10. *Completed pivot table*

4. Mark the pivot table as a real-time aggregation by clicking the Real-Time Aggregation button in the pivot table toolbar. Figure 9-11 displays the Real-Time Aggregation button.

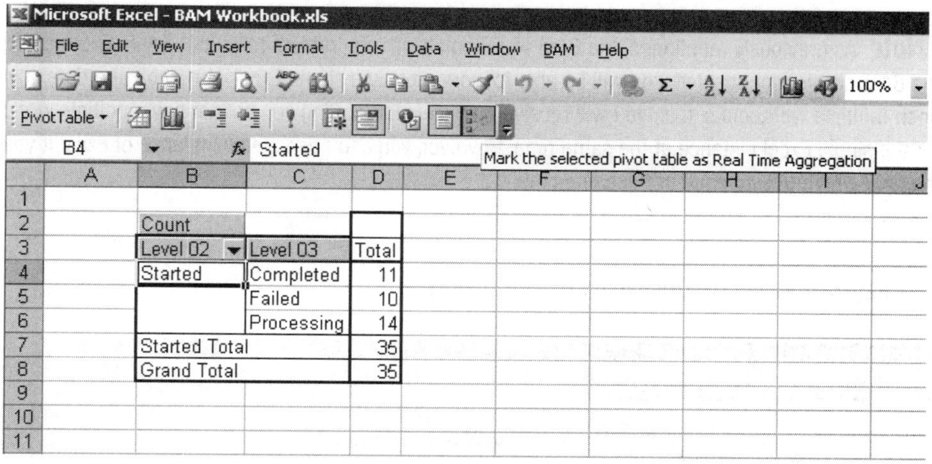

Figure 9-11. *Real-Time Aggregation button*

5. Save the workbook as `C:\BAMWorkbook\BAMWorkbook.xls`.

How It Works

BAM is a flexible framework to expose key metrics about business processes modeled within BizTalk. Creating a BAM solution using the BizTalk tool set is a straightforward process requiring little custom development. As outlined earlier, creating and deploying a BAM solution requires four basic categories of steps.

Create the BAM Activity Workbook

The first category of steps in creating a BAM solution is defining the structure for recording data about a BizTalk process. The structure for recording process data is created in an Excel workbook via the BAM add-in tool. The workbook captures key performance indicators or milestones as defined by the user as well as defines how a user views the milestones. Keep in mind that the Excel workbook is independent from any of the BizTalk solution artifacts and serves only as a container for recording information and computing aggregations.

Using the BAM Excel workbook removes the need for the user to have familiarity with the physical BizTalk solution artifacts. In actuality, the user may be more interested in a logical process implemented through multiple BizTalk artifacts versus the specifics for a single artifact. Consider when you tell someone about a trip you have taken. Do you relay the highlights of the trip or all the travel details (such as flight number, gas station fill-ups, and so on)? The BAM workbook allows the user to specify the BizTalk process highlights to monitor.

■Note As previously mentioned, the BAM workbook is an integrated add-in tool within Excel. If you have the BAM add-in tool enabled, you will be able to work on only a single Excel workbook at a time. If you try to open multiple workbooks, then you will receive an Excel alert stating you cannot have multiple workbooks for the single Excel instance at the same time. However, you can open a new instance of Excel if you need multiple workbooks opened at the same time.

Figure 9-12 shows the Excel exception alert.

Figure 9-12. *Workbook alert message*

After creating the BAM workbook, the next step is to identify the key data items, milestones, or key performance indicators implemented through data aggregations. Again, keep in mind that the milestones are logical markers and are not tied directly to physical BizTalk artifacts. For example, a milestone could signify the start or completion of a process. After creating the milestone and deploying the workbook, you map the multiple BizTalk artifacts to that milestone or data item. A BAM activity is a reference to a group or collection of milestones or data items and can span multiple BizTalk artifacts. Table 9-6 describes the four types of items that can be created in a BAM activity. Please review the "Considerations" section of this recipe for additional information about relating multiple activities and grouping of activity items.

Table 9-6. *BAM Activity Items*

Milestone	Name	Description
1	Business Data – Milestone	Placeholder for a date/time marker. Use this type of milestone when interested when an event occurred.
2	Business Data – Text	Placeholder for a text type of data item. Use this type of milestone when reporting a specific textual value piece of data (such as a promoted property) that is a textual value.
3	Business Data – Integer	Placeholder for an integer type of data item. Use this type of milestone when reporting a specific number piece of data (such as a transaction ID).
4	Business Data – Decimal	Placeholder for a decimal type of data item. Use this type of milestone when reporting a specific piece of data requiring decimal precision (such as a dollar amount).

Outline the BAM View

After defining the BAM activity structure and necessary milestones, the next step is creating the view that will represent the tracked data items and milestones. The BAM view is a representation of the milestones and business data defined in a single activity or multiple activities. Views can contain both data and computed aggregations based on the data.

The BAM view also facilitates the creation of data aggregations. If you have distinct audiences interested in different data aggregations or representations of activity milestones, then using a BAM view to represent those views is advantageous. Additionally, you can restrict BAM views to specific audiences in order to restrict the viewing of sensitive data or milestones. You can create a BAM view in one of two ways: as part of the Business Activity Monitoring View Creation Wizard or from the BAM add-in menu.

An optional task in creating a BAM view involves creating the necessary alias, duration, and group view items. These items are not required but offer extended desirable functionality to a BAM view. Consider view items as computed milestones that show the grouping of items or time durations between two milestones. Table 9-7 describes each view item.

Table 9-7. *BAM Computation Milestones*

ID	Name	Description
1	Alias	Allows the referencing of a previously created milestone.
2	Duration	Allows the monitoring of a span of time between two date/time milestones. For example, if you have a milestone for when a process begins and a milestone for when a process completes, you can create a duration milestone to report the time difference between the two milestones. The duration milestone will report on the following time scale (day, hour, minute, or second).
3	Group	Creates a new milestone for grouping of milestones into a single point in time. For example, if you have a milestone indicating when a process completes successfully or when a process fails, you could create a group milestone that indicates a process finished and group the process completes and process fails milestones. The composite or grouped milestone would identify when a process completed regardless of whether it completed or failed. Another common use is in the situation that you have a process that could fail at multiple points and you want to group all failures into a single process failed milestone.

Identify Aggregations, Dimensions, and Measures

Also optional when creating a BAM view is the inclusion of aggregations, dimensions, and measures based on the milestones and data items tracked. In this example, you created a measure to track the count of processes. Additionally, you created a progress dimension to show the progress of the process as it executes. These items are not required but offer additional flexibility to a BAM view.

Construct the Pivot Table

The final category of steps involves laying out the items of your view into a pivot table for reporting. In this recipe, you created a pivot table that displays the progress of your solution and aggregations of that process through a progress dimension, aggregations, and measures.

Considerations

Two items are worth mentioning for consideration when creating a BAM view. If you have an interest in categorizing multiple milestones into a single group, then you should look at using activity grouping. Additionally, if you have an interest in logically relating two activities, then you should review the "Related Activities" section of this recipe.

Activity Grouping

Considering the milestones to be included in an activity and considering the scope of the activity can be challenging. A single activity can reference multiple activities; however, it may also make sense (depending on the level of detail) to create a single activity with the necessary milestones. Again, imagine a trip with multiple legs and side trips containing many details. If the user is interested in many details about the overall trip as well as the individual legs of the trip, then it may make sense to create multiple activities to represent the trip as a whole as well as the individual trip legs. Alternatively, if the user is interested only in the trip highlights, then it may make sense to create a single activity with those highlights for the entire trip (including trip legs).

In the recipe sample, milestones indicate when a process begins, ends, encounters an exception, and defines data characteristics about the processed transaction. Typically, these milestones include enough information for a user interested in a high-level view about the health of a business process.

Related Activities

In this example, you created a single activity to report on the behavior of a business process. If you create a solution that has multiple related processes, then you may need to create and relate multiple activities. Creating related activities is also necessary in situations where you have a process that involves a looping structure (such as an orchestration with a loop). In the situation where you have a loop structure in an orchestration, you would create one activity for the orchestration and an additional activity for the events occurring within the loop. The physical act of relating activities occurs in the Tracking Profile Editor (or via code).

■**Note** When creating related activities, verify that the activities are included in the same BAM view. Additionally, verify that a shared attribute (for example, MessageID) relates the two activities.

Summary

BAM is a powerful extensible architecture that facilitates the sharing of key metrics and process milestones. This recipe outlined the basics of creating a BizTalk activity and view and demonstrated how to create relationships between activities and employ computed milestones via view items.

9-2. Deploying BAM Activities and Views

Problem

You have created a BAM activity and view within an BAM Excel workbook and must deploy the BAM artifacts within your environment.

■**Note** This recipe uses the BAM workbook created in Recipe 9-1 as the basis for the scenario.

Solution

Successfully deploying a BAM activity and view involves a number of steps, typically performed by a few different users. After a business analyst creates the BAM activity and view within the BAM Excel workbook, an administrator deploys the artifacts to the BizTalk environment. The first set of steps to use the BAM Management Utility to deploy the activity and view defined in the BAM Excel workbook is as follows:

1. Open a command prompt by navigating to Start ➤ Run, typing **CMD**, and clicking OK.

2. Navigate to the folder containing the BAM Management Utility by typing the following line at the command prompt, and pressing Enter:

   ```
   cd "C:\Program Files\Microsoft BizTalk Server 2006\Tracking\"
   ```

3. Use the deploy-all command to deploy the BAM activity and view defined in your BAM Excel workbook. For this solution, type the following line at the prompt, and hit Enter:

   ```
   bm deploy-all -DefinitionFile:"C:\BAMWorkbook\BAMWorkbook.xls"
   ```

   The status of the deploy operation appears in the console, as shown in Figure 9-13.

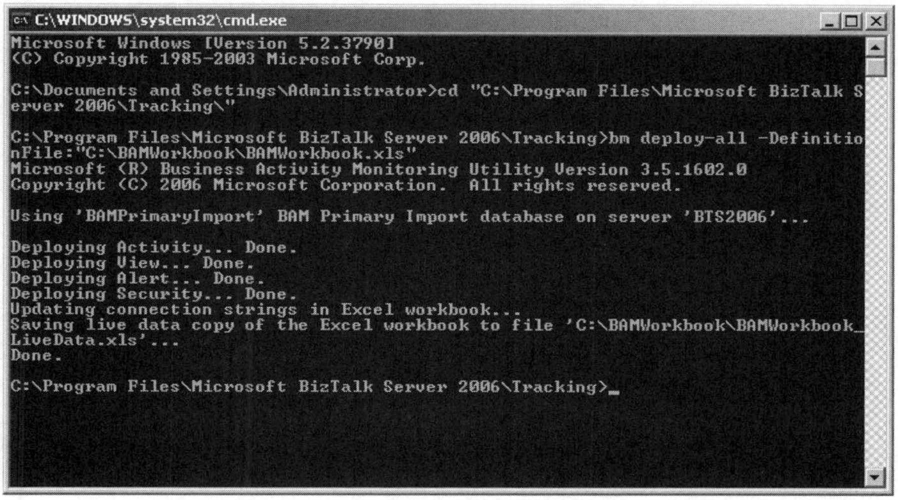

Figure 9-13. *Deploying the BAM Excel workbook*

The next set of steps is for either a developer or an administrator to use the Tracking Profile Editor to define and deploy the mappings between the activities defined in the BAM Excel workbook and actual BizTalk artifacts, such as orchestrations and schemas. (BizTalk Server 2006 also allows pure messaging solutions to feed BAM.)

4. Open the Tracking Profile Editor by navigating to Start ➤ Programs ➤ Microsoft BizTalk Server 2006 ➤ Tracking Profile Editor.

5. Import your BAM Excel workbook by clicking the Click Here to Import a BAM Activity Definition link. This link launches the Import BAM Activity Definition dialog box. Select the appropriate activity definition from the list. In this solution, select the activity definition named Process Activity, as shown in Figure 9-14.

Figure 9-14. *Import BAM Activity Definition dialog box*

6. Select the BizTalk artifacts you need to map the activity definitions to by clicking the Click Here to Select an Event Source link. This link launches the Select Event Source Parent Assembly dialog box. Select the appropriate BizTalk assembly containing the artifacts you will map to the activity definitions; in this solution, select the assembly named BAMProject, as shown in Figure 9-15. Click Next to proceed.

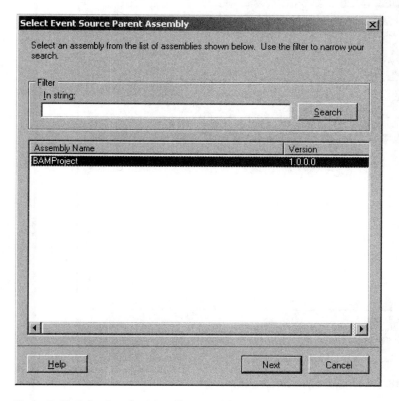

Figure 9-15. *Selecting the BizTalk assembly*

■**Note** The list of assemblies contains all those BizTalk assemblies that have been deployed within your BizTalk environment.

---

7. In the Select Orchestration dialog box displayed next, select the orchestration containing the workflow and the links to the schemas that define the activity definitions. In this solution, select the orchestration named BAMProject.Process, as shown in Figure 9-16. Click OK.

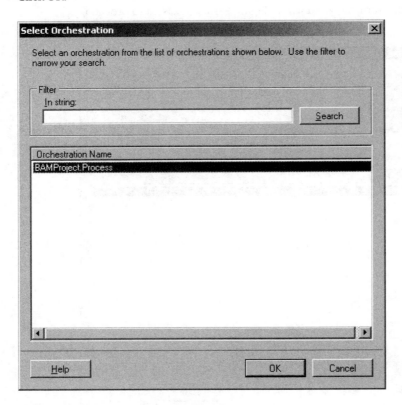

Figure 9-16. *Selecting the BizTalk orchestration*

8. Now map the orchestration steps in the right pane to the activity definition milestones in the left pane. Drag and drop the orchestration shapes to the activity definition milestones, as outlined in Table 9-8. Figure 9-17 shows how the Tracking Profile Editor looks after the orchestration steps have been mapped to the activity definition milestones.

Table 9-8. *Activity Definition Milestone Mapping*

Activity Definition Milestone	Orchestration Step (Shape)
Begin	Begin Process (Receive Shape)
EndSuccess	End Process (Send Shape)
Exception	Failure (Expression Shape)

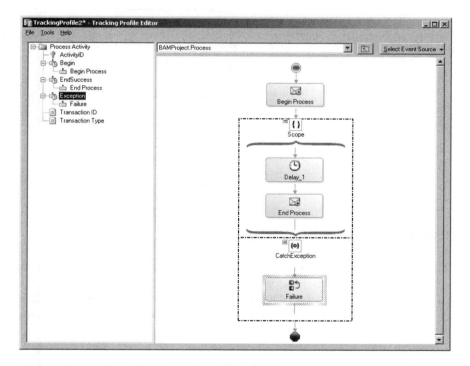

Figure 9-17. *Activity definition milestone mapping*

9. Next, map the appropriate schema fields to the activity definition business data. Since the message containing the schema data fields you need to map is received by the Begin Process shape in the orchestration, right-click this shape, and select Message Payload Schema, as shown in Figure 9-18.

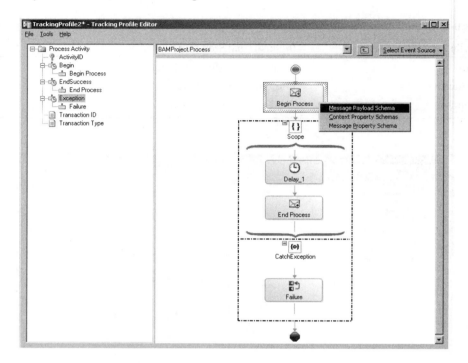

Figure 9-18. *Selecting the BizTalk schema*

10. Map the appropriate schema fields in the right pane to the activity definition business data fields in the left pane. Drag and drop the schema fields to the activity definition business data fields as outlined in Table 9-9. Figure 9-19 shows how the Tracking Profile Editor looks after the orchestration steps and business data have been mapped to the activity definition milestones.

Table 9-9. *Activity Definition Business Data Mapping*

Activity Definition Business Data	Schema Field
Transaction ID	ID
Transaction Type	Type

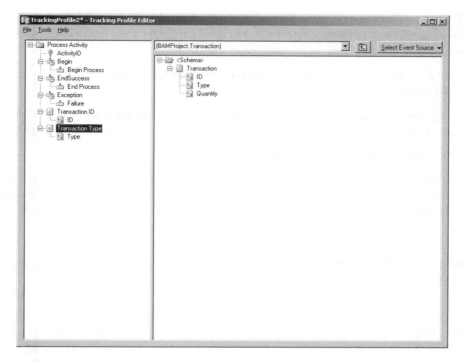

Figure 9-19. *Activity definition business data mapping*

11. Save the tracking profile by selecting File ➤ Save. Save the file as `C:\BAMWorkbook\ BAMTrackingProfile.btt`.

12. Deploy the tracking profile by selecting Tools ➤ Apply Tracking Profile. Click OK to confirm the successful deployment of the tracking profile.

How It Works

Deploying BAM activities and views involves two BizTalk tools: the BAM Management Utility and the Tracking Profile Editor. The BAM Management Utility is a command-line tool used for managing your BAM environment. It includes a number of commands, but the one we'll focus on is `deploy-all`. The `deploy-all` command takes the following parameters:

`DefinitionFile`: Path and file name of the BAM Excel workbook (or the exported XML file that can be generated from the BAM Excel workbook) containing the activities to deploy.

`Server`: Name of the server to which to deploy the activities. If this parameter is not specified, the local server is used.

`Database`: Name of the database to which to deploy the activities. If this parameter is not specified, the `BAMPrimaryImport` database is used.

This command reads the BAM Excel workbook specified in the `DefinitionFile` parameter and creates SQL Server database artifacts based on the activities and view defined in the spreadsheet. Specifically, this command creates the following:

- Tables within the BAM primary import database for capturing activity data in the live BizTalk environment.

- SQL Server Integration Services packages for transferring data between the live BizTalk databases and the SQL Server Analysis Services cubes.

- SQL Server Analysis Services OLAP cubes.

- A live data copy of the Excel workbook in the same folder as the original spreadsheet. Use the live data workbook to view up-to-date data within BizTalk Server after completing the deployment steps (including those involving the Tracking Profile Editor).

■**Note** The BAM Management Utility has no update capabilities for BAM artifacts. You must first remove the old artifacts and then deploy the updated ones.

See Recipe 9-1 for further information about how to use the BAM Excel workbook.

Use the Tracking Profile Editor to map the activities defined by the business analyst in the BAM Excel workbook to actual BizTalk artifacts such as orchestration shapes and schema data fields. This task is absolutely critical in ensuring that the deployed BAM artifacts communicate the appropriate information. Although it is common to have a developer or administrator perform this task, this user should have a strong understanding of the business process. Applying the tracking profile places the hooks into the BizTalk Server environment used to record the necessary milestones and data fields, which map to the activities defined by the business analyst. The Tracking Profile Editor in BizTalk Server 2006 also provides new functionality to feed BAM via pure-messaging scenarios (those that do not use orchestrations). To access schemas directly, click the Select Event Source drop-down list, and click Select Messaging Payload. This launches the Select Event Source Parent Assembly dialog box. Select the appropriate BizTalk assembly and then the appropriate schema.

Once the deployment steps have executed, you can see the activity data either through the live data copy of the BAM Excel workbook or through the BAM portal. See Recipe 9-3 for further information about how to use the BAM portal.

9-3. Using the BAM Portal

Problem

You need to create a solution that will track your company's business processes, compile the data into key performance indicators (KPIs), and develop a portal to display the information to executives. You have already created and deployed activities and views from a BAM worksheet to define and track the key performance indicators, and you would now like to consume that data from a portal.

Solution

Once you have developed and deployed BAM activities to track your KPIs, you may now consume the data from an ASP.NET portal without writing any code. You can accomplish this by utilizing out-of-the-box BizTalk reporting capabilities through the BAM portal. The BAM portal is a web-based portal built from ASP.NET that allows you to view and query cubed data created within the BAM framework. This recipe will cover three primary activities within the BAM portal:

- Accessing the BAM portal
- Performing an activity search
- Viewing aggregations

Accessing the BAM Portal

Take the following steps to access the BAM portal:

1. Deploy BAM activities and views.

■**Note** Please see the additional BAM recipes in this chapter for further information about how to accomplish this task. If you do not have any activities and views deployed, you will not be able to view information in the portal.

---

2. Open the portal by navigating to Start ➤ All Programs ➤ Microsoft BizTalk Server 2006 ➤ BAM Portal Web Site.

3. Once you have opened the portal, you will notice three primary panes: the header frame at the top, the view frame to the left, and the content frame to the right. If you have deployed activities and views, they will be available under the MyViews tree.

Performing an Activity Search

BAM activities capture business processes milestones and business data at a specific point in time. An activity search allows you to define, save, open, and execute queries to retrieve that transactional business data. The activity search page has three main sections, as shown in Table 9-10.

Table 9-10. *Sections of Activity Search Page*

Page Section	Description
Query	This section of the page allows you to define, save, and open queries. Queries let you constrain which activities to return in the results window.
Column Chooser	This section of the page defines which columns to return in the result set.
Results	The section of the page displays the result set retuned by executing the query against the BAM activity data.

To perform an activity search, take the following actions:

1. Under the My Views tree, expand the view that correlates to the view name you have deployed.

2. Expand the Activity Search node, and click a deployed activity. This action will open a query window like the window displayed in Figure 9-20.

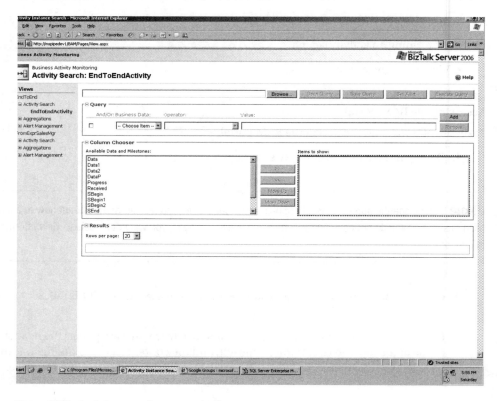

Figure 9-20. *Activity search query window*

3. Within the Query pane, build a query by configuring one or more constraints. To configure a constraint, follow these steps:

   a. Choose a field from the Business Data drop-down list.

   b. Choose an operator from the Operator drop-down list.

   c. Enter a value in the Value text box.

   d. Click the Add button to insert additional constraints.

■**Note** You cannot create complex constraint logic, such as nested constraints. The portal will allow you to add constraints only with simple And/Or relationships. By adding more than one constraint, an additional drop-down list will appear that will allow you to define the constraint relationship.

4. Within the Column Chooser pane, choose one or more columns to display in the Results pane.

5. Click Execute Query. The Results pane will display the query results.

Viewing Aggregations

Activity searches provide transactional business data from a specific point in time, and aggregations provide aggregated business data about a group of processes at a specific point in time. This aggregated data is processed and stored in OLAP cubes and accessed through pivot tables. The Aggregations page has two main sections, as shown in Table 9-11.

Table 9-11. *Sections of the Aggregations Page*

Page Section	Description
Pivot Table View	This section contains a standard pivot table. The table automatically points to the BAM framework and specifically the activities and views you have deployed.
Chart View	This section contains the chart view that displays, in chart form, the data filtering configured in the pivot table. It is also possible to change the chart view to any chart available through the office framework.

To view an aggregation, take the following actions in the BAM portal:

1. Under the My Views tree, expand the view that correlates to the deployed view name.

2. Expand the Aggregations node, and click a deployed pivot table. This action will open a window like the one displayed in Figure 9-21.

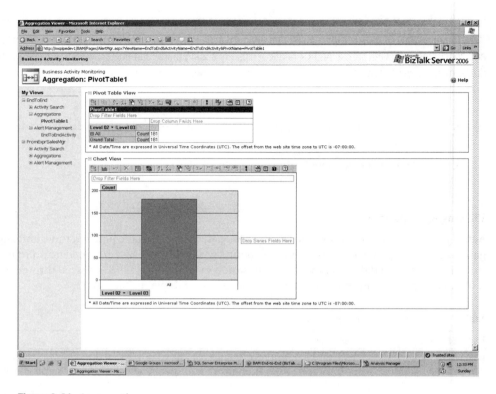

Figure 9-21. *Aggregations page*

■**Caution** If the BAM portal displays the "Safety settings on this machine prohibit accessing a data source on another domain" error in the pivot table, you need to change your security settings for Internet Explorer. Open the security settings by selecting the Tools ➤ Internet Options menu in Internet Explorer. Next, select the Security tab, and then click the Custom button. Once you are prompted with the Security Settings dialog box, locate the Miscellaneous heading, and select the Enable option for the Access Data Sources Across Domains choice. Finally, you will receive an error if no data exists in the cube.

---

3. From the pivot table View toolbar, click the Field Chooser icon. This will display a list of fields available with your BAM view.

4. Drag one or more total or detail fields to the center of the pivot table.

5. Next, drag one or more column fields to the column section of the pivot table.

6. Close the Pivot Table Field List control. Figure 9-22 shows what the pivot table with data should look like.

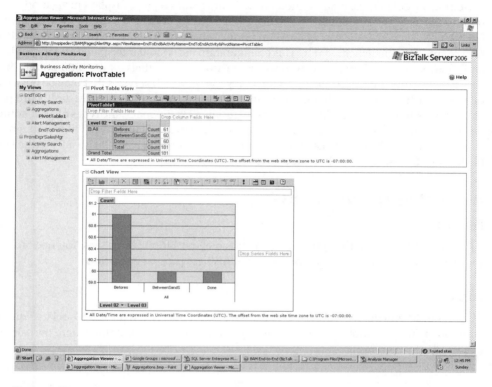

Figure 9-22. *Aggregations view*

■**Note** The pivot table is a powerful tool, and this recipe does not go into the many features it provides. You should spend some time researching what this tool can provide and how to use it to its full potential.

How It Works

The BAM portal is a new feature in BizTalk 2006 that facilitates the rapid consumption of business transactional and aggregated data, without writing any code. The portal is self-configuring, easy to set up, and provides rich data retrieval capabilities. This recipe has provided a high-level understanding of what you can do with the portal, but it has an additional powerful feature, BAM alerts. BAM alerts allow you to configure and receive alerts related to specific changes in business data. Recipe 9-4 covers this feature.

The BAM portal is easy to configure and provides several areas of configuration: the look and feel of the main or dashboard page, the web.config file, and Network Load Balancing (NLB) clustering. By default, the main dashboard, or Getting Started page, displays navigation instructions to the user. The content for the main dashboard page is located in the MainPageContent.htm file, which is located in the root of the BAM portal website folder and can be altered. Another area of configuration is web.config. This configuration file is similar to standard web.config files and allows you to configure security as well as environment settings for the BAM portal. The web.config setting highlights include referencing the BAM web services that may be hosted on different machines in a distributed environment, referencing a different main dashboard page file, culture support, and service timeout configuration. Additionally, the types of alert notifications are customizable in web.config. Finally, BAM fully supports high availability through clustering and can be scaled like other web applications through NLB. Please refer to the help file for specific instructions about how to change these settings.

9-4. Setting Up BAM Alerts

Problem

You have to set up BAM to capture data analysis on your BizTalk processes. You need to monitor these processes and set up alerts based on business process conditions.

Solution

BizTalk's BAM tool enables alerts to be set up based on business data and associated query conditions. In this sample, you will be setting a BAM alert on a condition where the sales price of a good is less than $1.

■**Note** BAM alerts rely on the creation of a BAM view deployment. For further information about deploying a BAM solution, please refer to Recipe 9-2.

The following steps show how to create a BAM alert:

1. Open the BAM portal by navigating to Start ➤ All Programs ➤ BizTalk Server 2006 ➤ BAM Portal Website.

2. On the portal home page, select the BAM view in the left pane.

■**Note** The portal will display all the deployed BAM views. Alerts are set up per BAM view.

---

3. Click the Activity Search link; Figure 9-23 shows the Activity Search page.

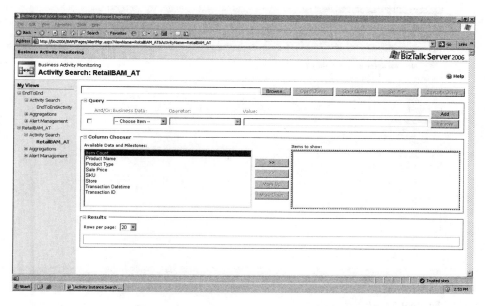

Figure 9-23. *Activity search*

4. Select your search criteria for the activity, and click Set Alert.

■**Note** It might be a good idea to execute the query first to provide a sanity check on the query results. You can set up an alert before or after query execution.

---

5. The Alert Details screen will now display. At this screen, enter the details for your alert:

Name: Enter the name of the alert.

Message: Describe the message that should be displayed when the alert is fired.

Priority: Assign relative priority. This would be used as a priority identifier within your solution.

Alert Security: Allow this alert to be seen and used by other users.

6. Click Save Alert to save the alert details, as shown in Figure 9-24.

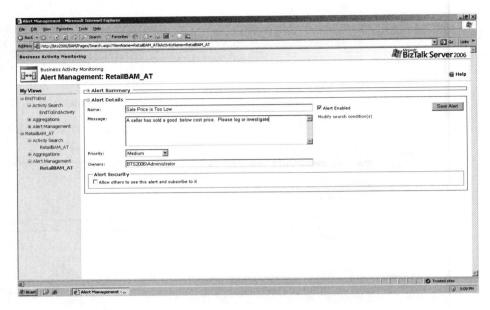

Figure 9-24. *Alert details*

7. Next, you must set up a subscriber to identify who should be notified and when the alert is fired, so click the Add Subscriber button. The Add Subscriber dialog box appears, as shown in Figure 9-25.

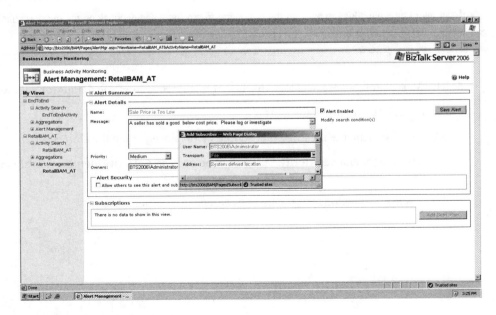

Figure 9-25. *Add Subscriber dialog box*

8. In the Add Subscriber dialog box, select the transport option for the alert. In BAM alerting, you can set up subscribers for either an email address or a file location.

9. Click the Save button to complete the subscriber setup.

10. This completes the subscriber setup. Now to review your newly created alert and subscription, click the Alert Management node under your view. On this page, you can view a list of alerts and associated alert and subscription detail, as shown in Figure 9-26.

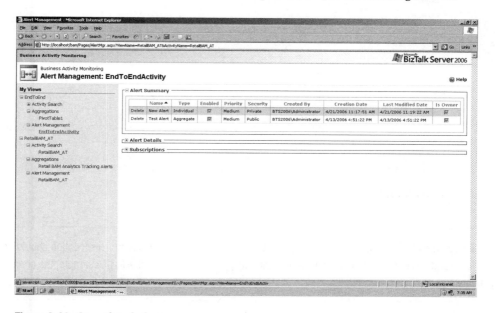

Figure 9-26. *Completed alert*

11. Finally, review that your subscription works. In this sample, you set up a subscription for a file location. Run your business process with data that will cause the alert to fire. When this occurs, an alert should be found in the alert location, as shown in Figure 9-27.

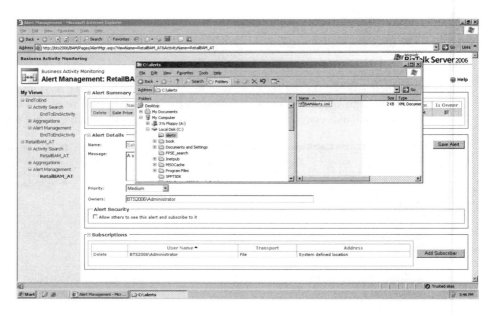

Figure 9-27. *BAM alert*

■**Note** The alert location is a static location, set up during BizTalk installation. This location should be shared and assigned with appropriate Active Directory permissions/security. In this sample, the share location was \\localhost\alerts.

How It Works

BAM is a powerful tool in BizTalk that allows a solution that you can configure to monitor data passed through BizTalk without performing large amounts of custom development. BAM is based on SQL Server Reporting Services, and events are fundamentally triggered via SQL Server Notification Services.

You must consider these prerequisites to successfully enable a BAM deployment:

Infrastructure: Ensure your SQL Server environment and Windows server security configuration are all in working order. This can be problematic and a necessary step in ensuring a secure environment.

BAM workbook: A BAM workbook with associated activities must be deployed in order to access BAM activity searches, aggregations, and associated alerts in the BAM portal.

Tracking Profile Editor: You must deploy a Tracking Profile Editor to see queries and alerts within the BAM portal.

BAM alerts location: You must specify a location to drop file alerts during installation/setup.

You can configure BAM alerts for aggregate or individual data conditions. You can create an alert initially or modify one after creation. An alert can be fired based on a condition of a row of data or as a condition of a summary of data (aggregate). To enable this, you have to set up individual data conditions by setting the alert in the activity search page (demonstrated in this sample) and set up aggregate alerts via acting on the pivot table on the Aggregations tab. Figure 9-28 shows this step.

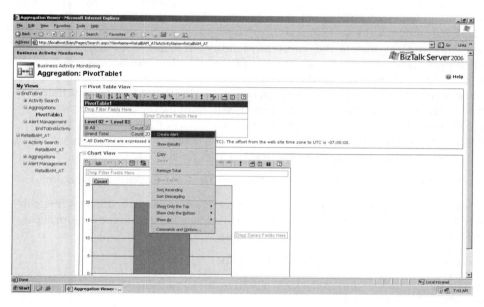

Figure 9-28. *BAM alert*

You can set subscribers for BAM alerts via two transport mechanisms:

Email: Any valid email address or group alias, such as someone@apress.com. A link to the alert detail will be provided in the email body.

File: Alerts will be dropped to the file location specified during product install.

A receive location can be set up to allow consumption back into the BizTalk process for further examination and process action. In addition, aggregate alerts can have threshold limits set to ensure that subscribers are not saturated with repeated messages.

When deploying alerts, it is important to remember the testing aspects and notification success. If a file alert cannot be published as a result of incorrect setup, the alert can be lost. An error will be indicated in the application event log. However, the alert instance itself cannot be salvaged.

9-5. Using the BAM Interceptor

Problem

You want to send custom events to BAM and be able to track these events as if they were published by a core BizTalk component (such as an orchestration).

Solution

The BAM Interceptor is part of the API that is available to interact with BAM from a .NET code base (BizTalk or otherwise). The Interceptor is used primarily by the core BizTalk components, such as orchestrations and pipelines, but can be tied to custom code by a developer. By calling the Interceptor and the associated API methods, you have full control over when and what is sent to deployed and tracked BAM instances.

When orchestrations execute, they constantly send events to the BAM Interceptor. Events that are being subscribed to (tracked events, set in the BAM Tracking Profile Editor) will be saved, and all others will be ignored. When external components to the orchestration are called (such as referenced assemblies), however, they do not log to BAM, and events that occur can be inferred only by the surrounding events sent from the orchestration.

This solution will walk through the sample that is included in the BizTalk SDK. You can find the SDK project files at `Microsoft BizTalk Server 2006\SDK\ Samples\BAM\BamApiSample`.

You must go through several key steps to interface with the BAM Interceptor:

1. Create and deploy a BAM definition, and import it into the Tracking Profile Editor.

2. Create an Interceptor instance, which can be used to interface with the BAM Interceptor. This contains the configuration needed to associate the data in the custom event being fired with the event in the BAM definition.

3. Implement the code to call the BAM Interceptor.

The first thing to do is to import the BAM definition and understand how it corresponds to the rest of the files in the SDK:

1. Run the `Setup.bat` file. This will install the components.

2. Open the BizTalk Tracking Profile Editor. Click File, and then select Import BAM Activity Definition. Assuming the BAM definition has been deployed successfully, the option to select BAMApiPo will be available, as shown in Figure 9-29.

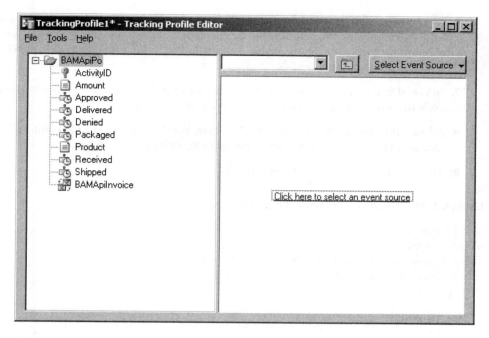

Figure 9-29. *Tracking Profile Editor*

During the setup process, two console applications are compiled. One of them is the InterceptorConfig.exe file, which takes a series of inputs to determine how to map data logged to the Interceptor to the BAM definition. The second is the BAMApiSample.exe file, which references the output of the InterceptorConfig.exe file to determine how to push data to the BAM Interceptor.

3. Open the BAMApiSample.sln file.

4. First examine the InterceptorConfig.cs file to observe how it creates the binary file, which will be referenced by BAMApiSample. It creates an Interceptor instance, which is a binary file containing the information needed to map the values to the definition. The XPaths are in reference to the document, which is statically created within BAMApiSample.

An example of the mapping between the definition and BAMApiSample is as follows:

```
locNewInvoice [in BAMApiSample] = Received
    Event [in Tracking Editor]
@PoID [inBAMApiSample] = xpath in xml
    document to InvoiceID [in Tracking Editor]
```

5. Open the PurchaseOrder_config.xml document to see all the mappings as configured by InterceptorConfig.exe. You can change these values; however, you also have to change the document in BAMApiSample to match the new values.

6. Assume for a moment that the only fields in the Tracking Profile Editor are Start and End. By simplifying the definition and the creation of the binary reference file, the solution becomes more manageable. Use the following steps to create an Interceptor instance based on the simplified definition.

7. In Visual Studio, create a new Visual C# Console Application project. This will allow code to be written that will produce the Interceptor instance.

8. Add a reference to the `Microsoft.BizTalk.Bam.EventObservation.dll` assembly. This is located in the `Tracking` directory of the main BizTalk installation path.

9. The code in `Main` will look as shown in Listing 9-1.

Listing 9-1. *Main Function to Create Binary File*

```csharp
using System;
using System.IO;
using System.Runtime.Serialization.Formatters.Binary;
using Microsoft.BizTalk.Bam.EventObservation;
// etc.

static void Main(string[] args)
{
// the following creates a new instance based on the definition that
// has been deployed to Tracking.  If BAMApiPo does not exist as a valid
// deployed definition, this code will fail.
ActivityInterceptorConfiguration interceptorConfig = new  ➥
    ActivityInterceptorConfiguration("BAMApiPo");

// registrations map the name of the tracked event to the
// name that is in the binary file/Interceptor code.
interceptorConfig.RegisterDataExtraction("Start","StartSample","");
interceptorConfig.RegisterDataExtraction("End","EndSample","");

// this is the indicator for when the Interceptor is to start and stop
// listening for events.  @ID is an XPath to where to locate the ID
// in the document passed in (see code for calling Interceptor, below)
interceptorConfig.RegisterStartNew("StartSample", "@ID");
interceptorConfig.RegisterEnd("EndSample");

// Create the Interceptor bin file
BAMInterceptor interceptor = new BAMInterceptor();
interceptorConfig.UpdateInterceptor(interceptor);

// write the file out
BinaryFormatter format = new BinaryFormatter();
Stream file = File.Create("BAMApiSample.bin");
format.Serialize(file, interceptor);
file.Close();
}
```

10. Build the solution. Run the executable. This will write out a binary file, which can now be referenced by the code to call the interceptor.

11. Additionally, an XML document could be generated, which would look like the following (this is not a required step):

```
<TraceInterceptorConfiguration xmlns:xsd="http://www.w3.org/2001/XMLSchema"➥
    xmlns:xsi="http://www.w3.org/2001/XMLSchema-instance">
 <TrackPoint Type="Start">
  <Location xsi:type="xsd:string">StartSample</Location>
  <ExtractionInfo xsi:type="xsd:string">@ID</ExtractionInfo>
 </TrackPoint>
 <TrackPoint Type="End">
  <Location xsi:type="xsd:string">EndSample</Location>
 </TrackPoint>
</TraceInterceptorConfiguration>
```

12. Now open the BAMApiSample.cs file to observe how it is structured. The key items to look at are as follows:

The class MainApp: This class contains the main function that constructs the XML document and event stream that will be used to call the BAM Interceptor.

The class DataExtractor: This class contains the extractor that returns the data within a given node of the XML document based on the XPath passed as a parameter. The XPath comes directly from the binary configuration file created by the InterceptorConfig.exe file.

The #If *Interceptor statements*: All statements within these directives call the BAM Interceptor.

The following code is directly from one of the SDK's #If Interceptor directives. It shows how the binary file is loaded and how the OnStep method in the BAM Interceptor is called. In this case, the dataExtractor contains information about how to extract the data from a given node (with the XPath from the binary file), and locNewPo maps to the Received Activity in the Tracking Profile Editor.

```
BAMInterceptor interceptor=Global.LoadInterceptor("BAMApiPo_interceptor.bin");
interceptor.OnStep(Global.dataExtractor,"locNewPo",xePO,Global.es);
```

How It Works

The previous solution explored how to use the Interceptor API and introduced the concept of interaction with the BAM Interceptor. The functionality of this SDK sample is limited in use with true BizTalk implementations. The most likely use of calling the BAM Interceptor directly would be in the case of a custom assembly, which is called from an orchestration. Modifying the console application (BAMApiSample) to a .NET class is fairly straightforward.

Listing 9-2 shows a simplified approach to the application as a class that can be called directly from an Expression shape.

Listing 9-2. *Interceptor in a .NET Class*

```
class Sample
{
 // the EventStream and DataExtractor tie into Interceptor events
 public static EventStream es=null;
 public static DataExtractor dataExtractor=new DataExtractor();

 public void PassDocument(System.Xml.XmlDocument xmlDoc)
 {
  // instantiate the interceptor by referencing the binary file
  Stream file=File.Open("C:\BAMApiSample.bin", FileMode.Open, FileAccess.Read, ➥
    FileShare.Read);
  BinaryFormatter format=new BinaryFormatter();
  BAMInterceptor interceptor=(BAMInterceptor)format.Deserialize(file);
  file.Close();

  // send an event that will start the tracking
  // xmlDoc is the instance of the document passed in
  interceptor.OnStep(Sample.dataExtractor,"StartSample",xmlDoc,Sample.es);

  // end the tracking
  interceptor.OnStep(Sample.dataExtractor,"EndSample",xmlDoc,Sample.es);
 }

 // add functions for constructing the EventStream and the DataExtractor
}
```

9-6. Creating a BAM Service Request

Problem

You have a deployed BizTalk solution and associated BAM artifacts. You have users viewing the BAM views and associated activities. The user would like additional information about one of the activity line items. Specifically, the user notices the process has terminated with an exception and would like the technical support team to investigate the exception. For this recipe, the sample BizTalk solution and BAM artifacts demonstrated are from the BAMEndToEnd sample project included in the SDK\BAM\Samples folder created with the BizTalk software installation.

Solution

This solution outlines how to use the BAM portal to view an activity line item and issue a technical assistance request for that activity line item. The following instructions assume you have deployed a BizTalk solution and the associated BAM artifacts and that the BizTalk solution has processed transactions. This solution outlines the steps required for creating a technical assistance service request from the BAM portal:

1. From the Start menu, select All Program Files ➤ Microsoft BizTalk Server 2006 ➤ BAM Portal Web Site.

2. Locate the view, and perform the activity search on the activity in which you would like to request technical assistance. Figure 9-30 displays a sample activity search.

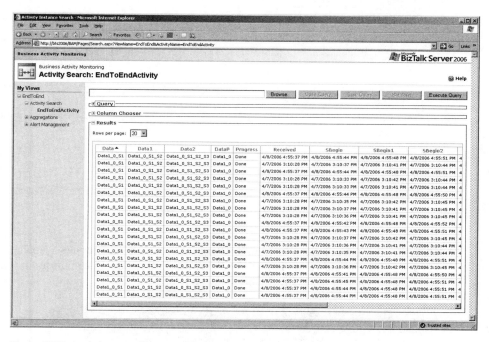

Figure 9-30. *Activity search example*

3. Click the activity line item in which you would like to request technical assistance. The Activity Status screen will display and detail information about the chosen line item as well as the Assistance button. You should see a screen similar to Figure 9-31.

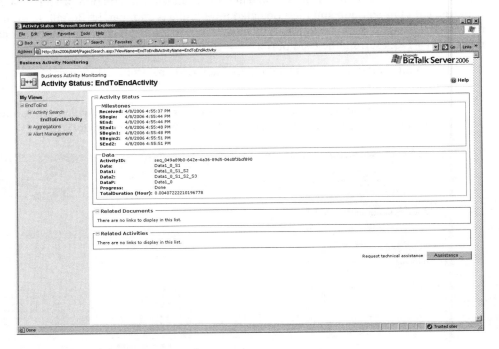

Figure 9-31. *Activity status example*

4. Click the Assistance button to open the Request Technical Assistance – Web Page Dialog dialog box, as shown in Figure 9-32. Enter the appropriate information for the technical request, and click the Send Report button.

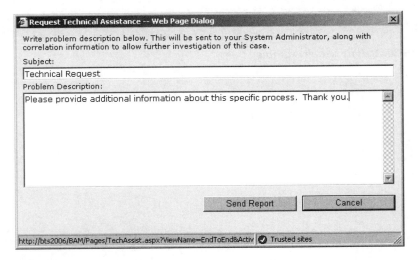

Figure 9-32. *Request Technical Assistance – Web Page Dialog dialog box*

5. Open the Event Viewer to verify that an event log entry has been created for the submitted request. Figure 9-33 demonstrates the generated event log entry for the submitted technical assistance request. The entry will be displayed in the Event Viewer as a success audit.

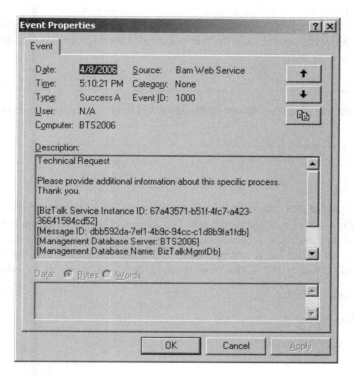

Figure 9-33. *Event Viewer entry*

How It Works

The Request Technical Assistance functionality included with the BAM portal allows the user to request additional information about a specific activity instance without having context to the business artifacts or the team supporting the solution. To take the greatest advantage of the Request Technical Assistance functionality, the support team should implement an automated solution to monitor Event Viewer entries or exceptions (such as the Microsoft Operations Manager). Via an automated tool, the support team could receive an email or perform some automated action once receiving the technical assistance request.

By default, the Request Technical Assistance functionality creates an entry only in the Event Viewer of the BizTalk Server. For more advanced functionality, investigate how to use a tool that monitors the Event Viewer for new events and performs action based on those events.

9-7. Creating a Tracking Profile

Problem

You have deployed a BAM workbook and the associated BizTalk artifacts. You need to map the BizTalk artifacts to the deployed BAM workbook milestones, data items, and key performance indicators. Additionally, you need to save the mapped profile for deployment to other environments.

■**Note** Recipe 9-2 introduced how to use the Tracking Profile Editor; this recipe takes a more in-depth look at how to use it.

Solution

The example reviewed as part of this recipe outlines how to use BizTalk's Tracking Profile Editor to map BizTalk artifacts to an Excel BAM workbook. The following sections outline the category of steps required for creating a tracking profile, mapping BizTalk artifacts to the deployed workbook activities within the Tracking Profile Editor, and finally applying the tracking profile to the deployed BizTalk artifacts. The three main categories of steps are as follows:

- Select the activity and artifacts.

- Map events and data items.

- Save and apply the tracking profile.

Select the Activity and Artifacts

To select the activity and artifacts, follow these specific steps:

1. From the Start menu, open the Tracking Profile Editor by selecting Start ➤ All Programs ➤ Microsoft BizTalk Server 2006 ➤ Tracking Profile Editor. You will see an application screen that looks similar to Figure 9-34.

■**Note** This solution assumes you have deployed a BAM workbook and BizTalk artifacts.

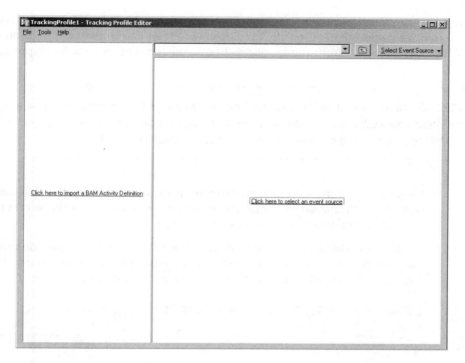

Figure 9-34. *Tracking Profile Editor*

2. Click the Click Here to Import BAM Activity Definition link to load the deployed BAM workbook and associated activity:

   a. A BAM Import Activity dialog box will ask you to choose the activity to use in the Tracking Profile Editor. If you have deployed the BAM workbook created in Recipe 9-1, then choose the Process Activity BAM activity.

   b. Leave the Retrieve the Current Tracking Settings for This Activity Definition box unchecked, and click the OK button to select the activity.

Note If you have already applied a tracking profile to the selected activity, then you can retrieve the results by selecting the Retrieve the Current Tracking Settings for This Activity Definition box.

---

3. Click the Click Here to Select an Event Source to load the BizTalk artifacts that will be used during the mapping activity. Identify the assembly that contains the orchestration to map, and identify the specific orchestration that contains data for mapping.

▪Note In this example, a basic orchestration has been created that performs a message receive and send and that implements a catch block for any exceptions. In this example, the name of the assembly is BizTalk Server BAM Test, and the name of the orchestration is BizTalk_Orchestration_BAM.

---

a. On the Select Event Source Parent Assembly page, locate the assembly that contains the orchestration you would like to map to the activity. Click the Next button to continue and to select the orchestration to map.

b. On the Select Orchestration page, select the name of the orchestration you would like to map to the activity. Click the OK button to complete the Event Source Wizard. Figure 9-35 displays the example with a sample orchestration.

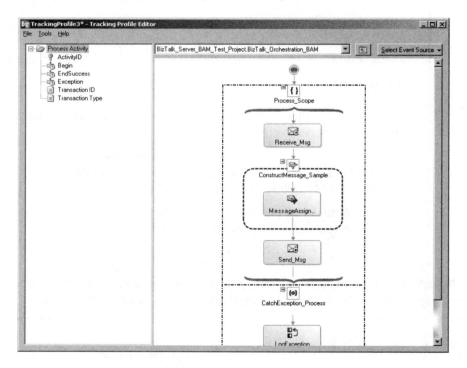

Figure 9-35. *Completed Event Source Wizard*

Map Events and Data Items

To map events and data items, follow these steps:

1. Drag the orchestration shapes to the Activity nodes listed in Table 9-12.

Table 9-12. *Sample Orchestration Step Mapping*

Activity Node	Orchestration Step	Description
Begin	Drag the Receive_Msg shape to the Begin activity node.	Captures the successful receipt of a message, which indicates that the process began successfully
EndSuccess	Drag the Send_Msg shape to the End activity node.	Captures the successful sending of a message, which indicates that the process completed successfully
EndException	Drag the LogException shape to the EndException activity node.	Logs an exception occurred in the process

2. Right-click the Receive_Msg shape, and choose Message Payload Schema.

    a. Expand the <Schema> folder icon, and navigate to the data items that are to be reported in BAM.

    b. Drag each reportable data item to the correct Activity node. Table 9-13 outlines the mapping of sample orchestrations to the deployed BAM activities.

Table 9-13. *Sample Orchestration Data Item Mapping*

Activity Node	Orchestration Step	Description
Transaction ID	Drag the Customer.MessageID node to the Transaction ID node.	MessageID is the unique identifier for the message received.
Transaction Type	Drag the Customer.TransactionType node to the Transaction Type activity node.	Transaction Type is the transaction identifier indicating the type of message received.

Figure 9-36 demonstrates the completed mapping between the sample orchestration and activity.

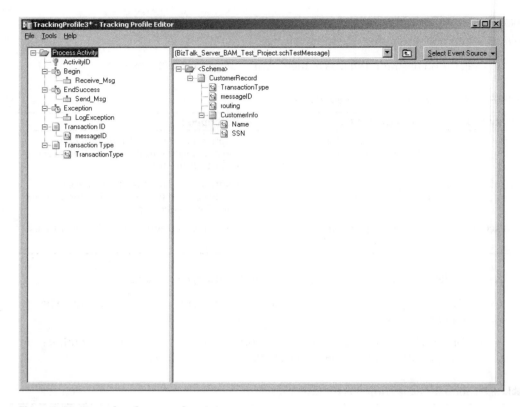

Figure 9-36. *Completed mapped activity*

Save and Apply the Tracking Profile

To save and apply the tracking profile, follow these steps:

1. From the Tools menu, select Apply Tracking Profile. Applying the tracking profile immediately sets the mapping to start recording data the next time the orchestration or process executes.

2. If you plan on deploying the tracking profile in other environments or would like to save a copy of the profile, then choose File ➤ Save As.

How It Works

As mentioned earlier in this chapter, BAM is a powerful tool and architecture for monitoring predetermined milestones and business data. Implementing BAM requires identifying the milestones and business data to report and then mapping those data points to the physical BizTalk solution artifacts. You can map milestones and business data to physical solution artifacts via the Tracking Profile Editor or via the BAM APIs and custom code.

This recipe outlined how to use the BizTalk Tracking Profile Editor to map between a deployed BAM workbook and physical BizTalk solution artifacts. This example outlined a simple scenario involving the mapping of a deployed activity to a single orchestration and data points contained within the message processed by the single orchestration. However, the Tracking Profile Editor can map multiple BizTalk artifacts to a single BizTalk activity or multiple activities. When using the Tracking Profile Editor, keep in mind the three categories of steps that were completed in this recipe, as outlined in the following sections.

Select the Activity and Artifacts

Before mapping an activity to a BizTalk solution artifact, you must choose the activity and the BizTalk artifact(s) that will be mapped. When you open the Tracking Profile Editor, you first select the activity from the list of deployed activities that will be receiving data. Once the activity loads, it will display each of the defined milestones and data items that were previously defined in the activity. The list of the milestones and data items is referred to as the *activity tree*. An activity tree lists the stages and business data items tracked in the deployed activity. When you load an activity in the Tracking Profile Editor, the stages identified in the activity and the business data items appear in the tree.

The basic premise of the Tracking Profile Editor is the ability to map from the deployed activity (which is a conceptual view of a business process) to the physical BizTalk solution. When loading an activity, in the Tracking Profile Editor the activity tree will list all the items created in the deployed activity.

■**Note** In addition to the list of activity items displayed in the activity tree, you can create four additional items. Please review the "Considerations" section of this recipe for more information about the additional items you can create.

After selecting the activity, the next step is to select the BizTalk artifacts that will be contributing data to the items listed in the activity tree.

Map Events and Data Items

The next category of steps involves the physical mapping between the BizTalk artifacts and the activity items listed in the activity tree. You map between a BizTalk artifact and an activity item by dragging the BizTalk artifact to the activity item. After dragging the BizTalk artifact to the activity item tree, the artifact will be listed in the activity tree.

Save and Apply the Tracking Profile

The final category of steps applies the tracking profile to the deployed BizTalk artifacts and allows you to save the tracking profile for deploying in other environments or making adjustments later.

Considerations

Two items worth mentioning for consideration when creating a tracking profile include the activity tree and the concepts of activity continuation and relationships. The activity tree displays the items in the deployed BAM workbook and includes shapes to further extend your solution. Please review the next section for more information about activity tree items. The concepts of activity continuation and relationships are extremely useful if you need to create a reference between two activities and have the reference represented to the user. For more information about activity continuation and relationships, please review the respective sections later in this recipe.

Activity Tree Items

The activity tree typically lists the milestones and data items defined in an activity. However, you can also create four other types of items in the activity tree to further enrich your BAM solution. Table 9-14 outlines the items that are included as part of the deployed activity as well as the additional possible items available in the Tracking Profile Editor to help you map activity items to the solution artifacts.

Table 9-14. *Activity Tree Items*

Tracking Profile Editor Item Icon	Description	Notes
Stage	Automatically created in the activity tree when defining a milestone within an activity. The stages are listed when an activity is loaded.	Orchestration steps are mapped to this shape. Some orchestration steps cannot be mapped to this shape including Termination shapes and any steps included within a Loop shape.
Data Item	Automatically created in the activity tree when defining a data item within an activity. The data items are listed when an activity is loaded.	You can specify data items from messages in orchestrations or pipelines. Additionally, you can specify context property information for those messages.
Activity ID	Uniquely identifies the instance of an activity that has executed and is automatically included within the activity tree.	This value can be user generated and identified from a message. However, the field must be unique because it is a key in a SQL Server table. If no value is mapped in the Tracking Profile Editor, then BAM will automatically generate this value.
Continuation	Inserts a new continuation folder within the activity tree.	Used in conjunction with ContinuationID to allow multiple components to populate the same activity. For example, if Orchestration A depends on Orchestration B and both contribute data to the same activity, then a continuation folder would be created and mapped to a data item in Orchestration A that is carried over to Orchestration B.
ContinuationID	Inserts a new continuation ID folder within the activity tree.	ContinuationID is mapped to the data item in Orchestration B that was passed from Orchestration A.

Tracking Profile Editor Item Icon	Description	Notes
Relationship	Relationship folders are used to imply a relationship between one or more activities.	Relationships are especially useful in relating two activities for a single orchestration. For example, if you have an orchestration with a Loop shape, then the orchestration and the Loop shape must be represented by separate activities. Via the relationship folder, you can create a relationship between the two activities.
Document Reference URL	Allows the linking of a document related to this instance of the activity.	The file name can be mapped from either a schema value or a context property on the message.

Activity Continuation

Activity continuation is the process of taking multiple BizTalk physical artifacts and combining data from those artifacts into a single activity. Combining data is a useful option when a business process spans multiple BizTalk solution artifacts. Think of the process of creating an activity as defining a database table structure with multiple columns representing the containers for the business data and milestones. When a process executes, it creates a new row in the activity database table recording the data as mapped in the Tracking Profile Editor. Multiple BizTalk artifacts reporting data to the same activity results in multiple rows created in the activity database table. For those artifacts to contribute to a single row in the activity, you need a continuation between the artifacts indicating their relationship.

A common business scenario where activity continuation is useful is the scenario of a life cycle of a purchase order. One company sends a purchase order to another company to purchase goods. The entity shipping the goods will typically send a shipment notice after receiving the purchase order. Additionally, the entity shipping the goods will usually send an invoice for payment of the shipped goods. Managing the sending a purchase order and the receipt of a shipment notice and invoice typically involves many BizTalk artifacts. However, it may be useful to have an end-to-end view of the purchase order life cycle (once issued to the receipt of an invoice) versus each artifact reporting independently. With activity continuation, all the artifacts involved in the life cycle of a purchase order can report information to a single activity, allowing for an end-to-end view of the purchase order life cycle.

Consider the following example: Orchestration A processes a message and transmits that message to Orchestration B for processing. When Orchestration B is finished, it sends a response message back to Orchestration A. When Orchestration A receives the response from Orchestration B, it completes processing. Figure 9-37 demonstrates the sample relationship between Orchestration A and B.

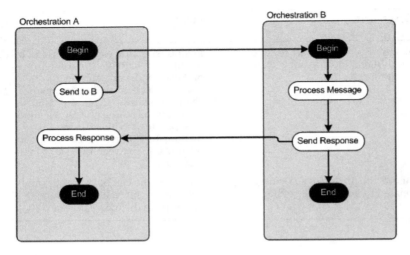

Figure 9-37. *Continuation sample*

Both Orchestration A and Orchestration B can be mapped to the sample activity. However, when the orchestrations execute, two data rows will be created in the activity table to record the information from the orchestrations (one for Orchestration A and one for Orchestration B). If both orchestrations need to contribute data to the same row in the activity, then you must create a continuation in the activity tree to indicate the continuation of activity between Orchestration A and Orchestration B.

The following items are required to create an activity continuation between two orchestrations:

- A data item that relates the two orchestrations (or other BizTalk artifacts). This data item can be an attribute in a message shared between the two orchestrations.

- A continuation folder that specifies the data item in a parent orchestration that relates the two orchestrations.

- A continuation ID folder identifies the data item in the child orchestration that relates the two orchestrations.

■Note The name of continuation folder and the name of continuation ID folder must be identical in the activity tree. For example, if you create a continuation folder with the name of Continuation, then you must create a continuation ID folder with the name of Continuation. You will receive an exception message if the continuation folder and continuation ID folder do not share the same name.

In the Orchestration A and Orchestration B example, the message ID in Orchestration A from the Send shape is mapped to the continuation folder. The same message ID in the Orchestration B Receive shape is mapped to the continuation ID folder. The message ID is the data item that links the two orchestrations and is also the data item in the continuation and continuation ID folders. The BAM end-to-end SDK sample included with the standard BizTalk installation provides a sample implementation of a continuation.

Activity Relationships

Activity relationships are different from activity continuations in that they allow implicit linking between multiple activities. Consider the Orchestration A and Orchestration B example. If both orchestrations represented different business processes, then it may not make sense to have them report to the same activity. If they report to different activities, it may be useful to represent that the activities have a relationship but are disparate. A real-world example of an activity relationship may be how a single purchase order represents multiple shipments. Each activity (purchase order and shipment) is a different activity but is related to the others.

Activity relationships are also necessary when needing to report on BizTalk orchestrations that contain the Loop shape. You can define the parent orchestration as one activity and the looping activity as a separate activity and still accurately report on the activity of the entire process.

When creating activity relationships, you must adhere to the following guidelines:

- Related activities should belong to the same BAM view.

- A relationship item must be created in each activity in the Tracking Profile Editor and must be given the appropriate name of the related activity.

Consider that Activity A reports on the activity in Orchestration A and Activity B reports on the activity in Orchestration B; you would create the relationships activity items listed in Table 9-15.

Table 9-15. *Example Relationship*

Orchestration Name	Activity Name	Relationship Item Name
Orchestration A	Activity A	Activity B
Orchestration B	Activity B	Activity A

After specifying the activity items in each activity, the data item that represents the relationship between the activities must be mapped to each activity item. After creating the relationship item in Activity A, a data item (for example, the message ID) that is shared between the activities would need to be mapped to Activity A. The same data item (that is, the message ID) is then mapped to the ActivityID item of Activity B. Mapping the data item to the ActivityID creates the relationship between the first and second activity.

CHAPTER 10

■ ■ ■

Encore: BizTalk Server 2006

The latest offering from Microsoft in the BizTalk product family is BizTalk Server 2006. The BizTalk Server 2006 product builds upon the powerful development and integration of the BizTalk platform, focusing on a variety of functionality and capability improvements. These include the following:

- Core messaging engine enhancements

- Setup and administration

- Application management and operations and deployment

- Core functionality enhancements to the Business Activity Monitoring (BAM) component

In this chapter, you will be introduced to the latest functionality and associated implementation inputs and considerations. BizTalk Server 2006 is a product release aimed at making integration and business process management easier. We are extremely excited to provide samples of the product's functionality and how it directly achieves the simplification goal across the life cycle of a business process.

10-1. Working with the Flat File Schema Wizard

Problem

You are receiving an order file in flat file format from one of your customers. You would like to use the Flat File Schema Wizard to expedite the creation of an XML schema.

Solution

To demonstrate how to use the Flat File Schema Wizard, we will use the flat file sample shown in Listing 10-1.

Listing 10-1. *File: CustomerSalesOrder.txt*

```
1234567890123456789012345678901234567890123456789123456789012345678 90
ORDER2004-10-24
SoldTo Shauna Marie    1223 Buttercup Lane Seattle      WA 98155
ShipTo Jen Schwinn     3030 Moby Road      Kent         WA 98110
ITEMS,ITEM111-AA|Merlot|1|2.00|Bottle of Wine, ➡
   ITEM111-AB|Cabernet|1|2.00|Bottle of Wine
```

481

■Note For demonstrative purposes, this file is the same format of that specified in Recipe 1-10.

Now, to create the flat file schema using the Flat File Schema Wizard, follow these steps:

1. Open a new BizTalk Server project.

2. Right-click the project, and select Add ➤ New Item.

3. In the Add New Item dialog box, select the Schema Files category, and select the Flat File Schema Wizard template. Click Add. Figure 10-1 demonstrates this step.

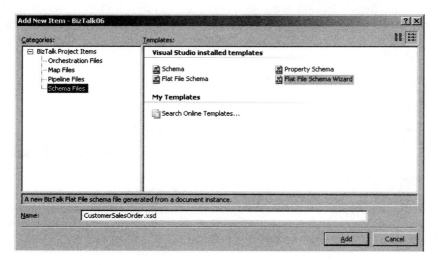

Figure 10-1. *Creating a new flat file schema*

4. On the BizTalk Server Flat File Wizard page, click Next.

5. On the Flat File Schema Information page (shown in Figure 10-2), specify the information that will be used as input to generate the specifics of the desired flat file schema:

   - *Instance File*: Use this to specify where your source instance file is located.

   - *Record Name*: Specify the Root node of the schema you want to create. For this example, enter **CustomerSalesOrder**.

   - *Target Namespace*: Specify the namespace of the schema you'd like to create.

   - *Code Page*: This identifies the encoding format of a file. In this instance, use the default, which is UTF-8 (65001).

   - *Count Positions in Bytes*: This specifies whether positions are calculated by bytes. If this box is not checked, positions will calculated by characters.

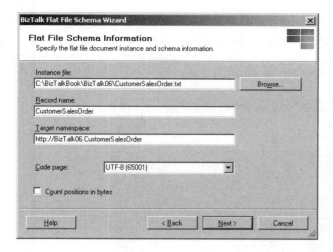

Figure 10-2. *Flat File Schema Information page*

6. Click Next.

7. On the Select Document Data page, specify the data contents that will be used to generate the schema. The data contents are based on the instance file specified on the Flat File Schema Information page. Highlight the contents of the file that will be used to define the document data, as shown in Figure 10-3.

■Note The number bar at the top of the source data is included for reference only and is not part of the document data. Do not select this as part of specifying document data.

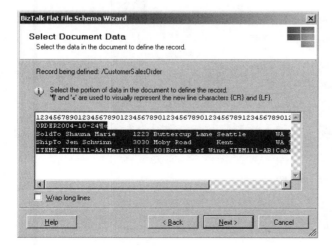

Figure 10-3. *Source Document Data page*

8. Click Next.

9. Now define the record format. In this example, the record is delimited by a carriage return and a line feed, as shown by the record identifier ORDER2004-10-24. Select the By Delimiter Symbol radio button, as shown in Figure 10-4.

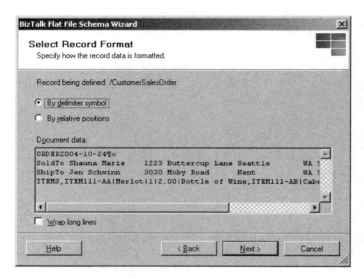

Figure 10-4. *Selecting the record format*

10. Click Next.

11. Now specify the properties of the record (as shown in Figure 10-5). This step will define the makeup of the record to represent CustomerSalesOrder:

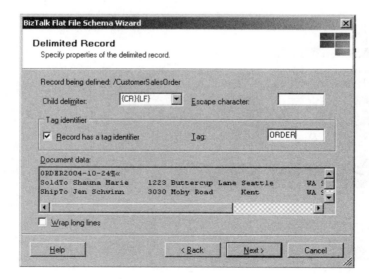

Figure 10-5. *Specifying the properties of the delimited record*

    a. Specify the child delimiter. Given that the record is defined by delimiter, select the child delimiter {CR}{LF}.

    b. Select the Record Has a Tag Identifier box. In this example, the tag identifier will be ORDER.

■Note ORDER is the identifier based on it being the text identifier that is specified in the source record. This text will be searched for to identify the continuation or creation of a new record.

---

12. Click Next.

13. Now specify the properties of the child elements for the record (as shown in Figure 10-6). This step will identify the makeup of the elements for `CustomerSalesOrder`. Using the grid on the Child Elements page, define the record's child elements. In this example, set the values shown in Table 10-1.

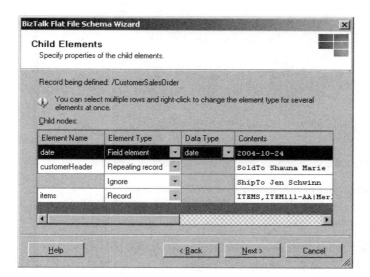

Figure 10-6. *Specifying the properties of the record's child elements*

Table 10-1. *Child Element Properties*

Element Name	Element Type	Data Type
date	Field Element	Date
customerHeader	Repeating Record	
	Ignore	
items	Record	

Note Observe that the customer ShipTo information is ignored because the record is the same structure as the customer SoldTo. Instead, the customer Header can be modeled using the Repeating Record element type.

---

14. Click Next.

15. On the Schema View page, the fundamental structure of the CustomerSalesOrder schema appears. Now, you'll define the individual characteristics of the child records of the schema. Figure 10-7 shows the page showing the schema structure.

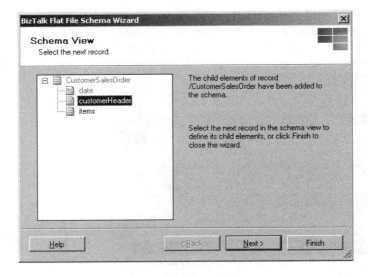

Figure 10-7. *Schema view of the* CustomerSalesOrder *schema*

16. Select the customerHeader element. Click Next to continue.

17. On the Select Document Data page, select the data that will be used to define the customerHeader record by ensuring the first line is selected, as shown in Figure 10-8.

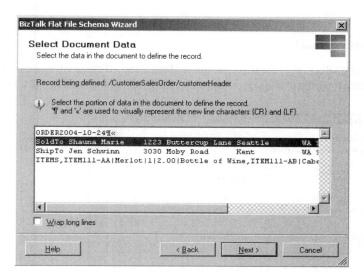

Figure 10-8. *Document data—customer header*

18. Click Next.

19. Now you will select the record format for the customer header. In this example, select the By Relative Positions radio button, as shown in Figure 10-9.

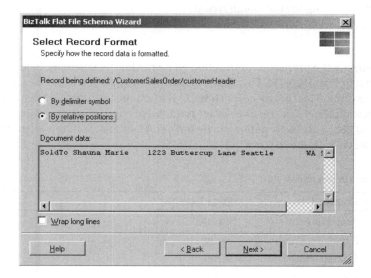

Figure 10-9. *Record format—customer header*

20. Click Next.

21. The wizard will give a visual representation of the record's element positions.

  a. Use this tool by selecting the starting position of each record element. You can do this by clicking the mouse at each element's starting point, as shown in Figure 10-10.

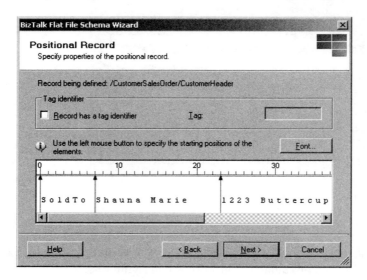

Figure 10-10. *Specifying the positional record*

22. Click Next.

23. Next, you will specify the properties of the child elements for the customer header record (as shown in Figure 10-11). This step will identify the makeup of the elements for CustomerSalesOrder/customerHeader. These XML elements are derived from the positional representation of the record elements on the previous page. So, using the grid on the Child Elements page, define the record's child elements. In this example, set the values shown in Table 10-2.

Table 10-2. *Child Element Properties*

Element Name	Element Type	Data Type
customerType	Field Element	string
fullName	Field Element	string
street	Field Element	string
city	Field Element	string
state	Field Element	string
postal	Field Element	string

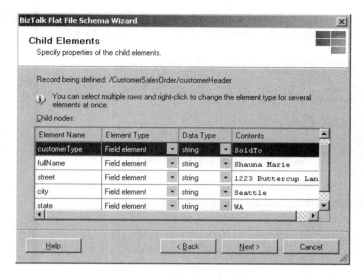

Figure 10-11. *Specifying the properties of the record's child elements*

24. Click Next.

25. On the Schema View page, the CustomerSalesOrder schema appears with an updated customerHeader structure, as shown in Figure 10-12. Next, you'll define the characteristics of the items record, so click Next.

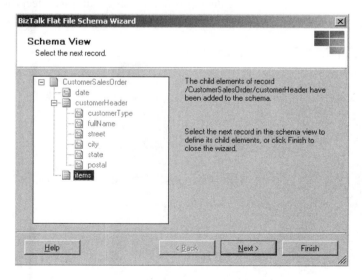

Figure 10-12. *Schema view of CustomerSalesOrder*

26. On the Select Document Data page, select the data that will be used to define the items record. Ensure the items data line is selected, as shown in Figure 10-13.

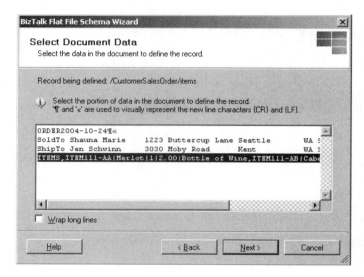

Figure 10-13. *Document data—items*

27. Click Next.

28. Now you will select the record format for the items data. In this example, select the By Delimiter Symbol radio button, as shown in Figure 10-14.

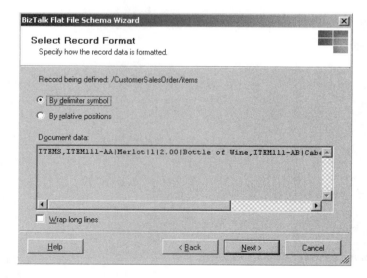

Figure 10-14. *Record format—items*

29. Click Next.

30. Now you will specify the properties of the items record (as shown in Figure 10-15). This step will define the makeup of the record to represent CustomerSalesOrder/items:

    a. Specify the child delimiter. Given that the record is defined by a comma delimiter, select the , child delimiter.

    b. Check the Record Has a Tag Identifier box. In this example, the tag identifier will be ITEMS.

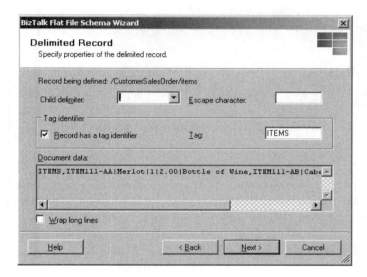

Figure 10-15. *Properties of the delimited record—items*

31. Click Next.

32. You will now specify the properties of the child elements for the items record (as shown in Figure 10-16). This step will identify the makeup of the elements for the CustomerSalesOrder/items that are derived from the delimiter specified on the previous page. Using the grid in the Child Elements page, define the items record's child elements. In this example, set the values shown in Table 10-3.

Table 10-3. *Child Element Properties—Items*

Element Name	Element Type	Data Type
items	Repeating Record	
	Ignore	

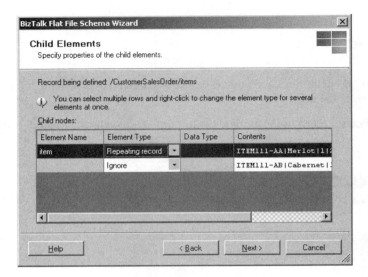

Figure 10-16. *Specifying properties of the items record's child elements*

33. Click Next.

34. On the Schema View page, the structure of the CustomerSalesOrder schema is updated. Now, you can define the individual characteristics of the items record's child elements. Figure 10-17 shows the page with the schema structure.

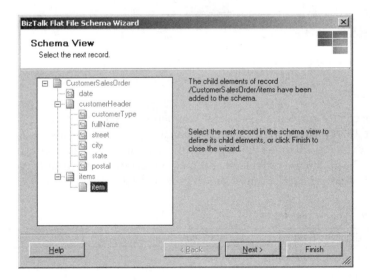

Figure 10-17. *Schema view of the CustomerSalesOrder schema*

35. Make sure the item element is selected. Click Next to continue.

36. On the Select Document Data page, select the data that will be used to define the item record. Ensure the items line is selected, as shown in Figure 10-18.

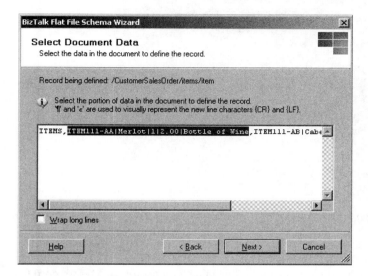

Figure 10-18. *Document data—items data*

37. Click Next.

38. Now, select the record format for the items data. This example will use delimited, so select the By Delimiter Symbol radio button, and click Next.

39. Next, you will specify the properties of the items data elements. This step will define the makeup of the data elements to represent CustomerSalesOrder/items. You'll now specify the child delimiter: given that the record is defined by the pipe delimiter (|), select the child delimiter |, as shown in Figure 10-19.

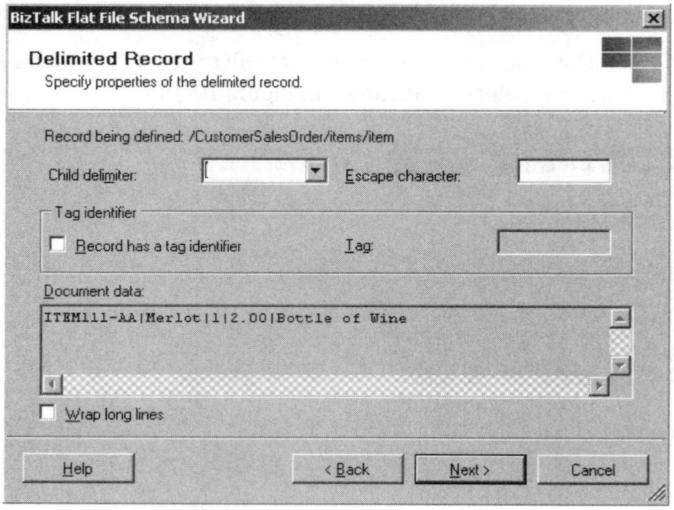

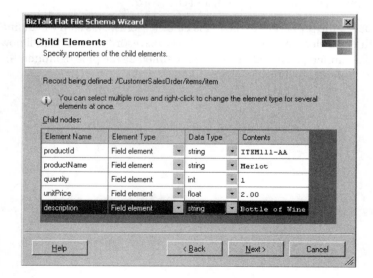

Figure 10-19. *Properties of the delimited record—items data*

40. Click Next.

41. Now you will specify the properties of the child elements for the items record (as shown in Figure 10-20). This step will identify the makeup of the elements for the CustomerSalesOrder/items/item and are derived from the delimited specification. Using the grid on the Child Elements page, define the record's child elements. In this example, set the values as shown in Table 10-4.

Figure 10-20. *Specifying the properties of the record item's child elements*

Table 10-4. *Child Element Properties*

Element Name	Element Type	Data Type
productId	Field Element	string
productName	Field Element	string
quantity	Field Element	int
unitPrice	Field Element	float
description	Field Element	string

42. Click Next.

43. This completes the creation of the schema, so click Finish to complete the schema. Figure 10-21 shows the finished product.

44. To test, right-click the newly created schema in your Solution Explorer, and click Validate.

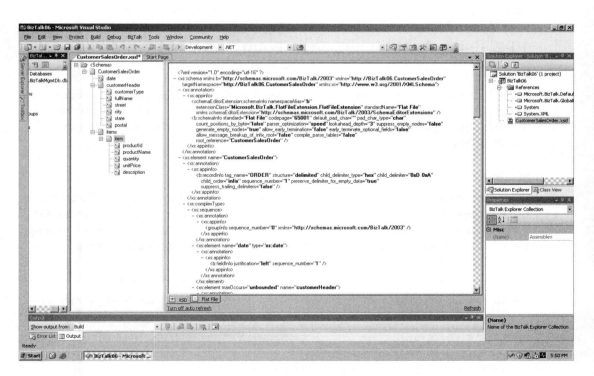

Figure 10-21. *The finished schema*

How It Works

In this recipe, we demonstrated how to use the Flat File Schema Wizard. To recap the scenario, you used the wizard to create a fairly complex illustration of a flat file to XML schema creation using different positional and delimited flat file references at the record, line, and field levels. The tool allows a developer to reverse engineer a schema based on a sample flat file instance.

Not demonstrated in this example but a common consideration when working with flat files is the usage of escape characters. You can accommodate escape characters when defining the properties at the record, line, or field level.

The Flat File Schema Wizard makes the process of defining schemas simpler, because the user sees the schema being modeled through the process and, in addition, is not exposed to the complexity of the schema syntax.

As helpful as the tool might be, it is still important to understand what the requirements are for the schema and how specifically the file will be implemented. Given this, you should spend some design time trying to understand exactly what the schema will do and how this relates to other processes (such as other interfaces and other trading partners).

10-2. Using the Windows SharePoint Services Adapter

Problem

You want BizTalk to send messages to a Windows SharePoint Services (WSS) form library, where a user can approve an expense report. Approving the expense requires subjective judgment, and a person must make the approval decision. BizTalk receives the approved reports to begin the expense approval.

Solution

This example demonstrates how to send and receive messages from a WSS form library with BizTalk. The example in this case is an expense report. The WSS form library exposes the XML information to a user with an InfoPath form. The user can accept the expense report, causing BizTalk to pick up the approved expense report and forward it for further processing.

■**Note** This solution requires both InfoPath and Windows SharePoint Services. Windows SharePoint Services is part of Windows Server 2003.

Begin this example by creating the expense report schema:

1. Create a new BizTalk project.

2. Add a new schema to the BizTalk project.

3. Define a schema to represent expense report information. Figure 10-22 depicts an example schema. For more information about creating BizTalk schemas, please see Recipe 1-1.

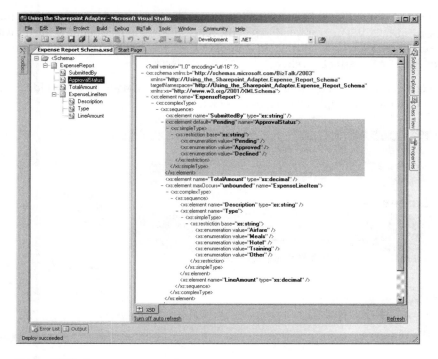

Figure 10-22. *Expense report schema*

4. Build and deploy the BizTalk project containing the expense report schema.

Create the InfoPath form template. Accomplish this outside the BizTalk tool set, with the InfoPath Office application. InfoPath is a powerful tool with many capabilities outside this book's focus. Nonetheless, this example outlines the steps to create a simple InfoPath form to demonstrate BizTalk's capabilities:

1. Open Microsoft Office InfoPath 2003.

2. In the Fill Out a Form dialog box that appears, select Design a Form.

3. In the Design a Form toolbar, select New from XML Document or Schema.

4. In the Data Source Wizard, browse to the location of the expense report schema, click Next, and then click Finish.

5. Select controls in the toolbar. Specifically, drag a Section control onto the design surface. When prompted, select the root element of the expense report schema.

6. Select a data source in the toolbar. Drag the top-level data elements from the expense report schema. This example places the expense submitter, the total expense amount, and the approval status fields in the section control.

7. Select controls in the toolbar. Specifically, drag a Repeating Section control onto the design surface. When prompted, select the repeating element containing the individual expense report line items. In this example, the line items are contained in the repeating `ExpenseLineItem` element.

8. Select a data source in the toolbar. When complete, the InfoPath form should appear similar to the form depicted in Figure 10-23.

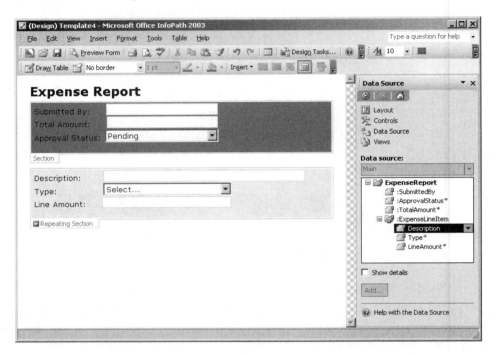

Figure 10-23. *InfoPath expense approval form*

9. Select File ➤ Publish to begin the Publishing Wizard, and click Next.

10. When asked where you would like to save the form, select To a SharePoint Form Library, and then click Next.

11. Select the option Create a New Form Library, and click Next.

12. Enter the URL of the WSS website, and click Next.

13. Enter a description, such as **Expense Report Approval**, and click Next.

14. Add the Approval Status, Submitted By, and Total Amount fields in the expense report schema to the list of columns to display in the form library, and click Finish.

15. When prompted, select the option to open the form library after the wizard creates it.

After publishing the form to the WSS form library, give the BizTalk host identity permissions to access it:

1. Open the Computer Management console from the Administrative Tools program group, and add the BizTalk host identity to the SharePoint Enabled Hosts windows group. This group is a local machine group by default.

2. Open the WSS site, and select Site Settings from the top navigation menu.

3. Under the Administration options, click the Manage Users link.

4. On the Manage Users page, click the Add Users button.

5. Type the name of the BizTalk host instance identity in the Users box, and select the Contributor site group. Click Next and then Finish to complete granting the BizTalk account permissions to the WSS site.

6. Restart IIS and the BizTalk host instance to ensure the permissions changes take effect.

After configuring the security of the WSS form library and WSS adapter, add a send port to deliver the expense report message:

1. Open the BizTalk Server 2006 Administration Console, and expand the BizTalk Application 1 default application.

2. Right-click the Send Ports folder, and select New ➤ Static One-Way Send Port.

3. Select the Windows SharePoint Services transport type, and click the Configure button to open the Windows SharePoint Services Transport Properties dialog box.

4. Under the General properties, set the destination folder URL to the name of the form library, which is Expense Report Approval in this example.

5. Under the General properties, set the Filename property to Expense Report-%MessageID%.xml. The %MessageID% macro appends a unique GUID to the end of each message sent to the WSS form library.

6. Under the General properties, set the SharePoint site URL to the location of the WSS site. This example specifies http://localhost.

7. When configured, the properties should appear as depicted in Figure 10-24.

Figure 10-24. *Configured Windows SharePoint services properties*

8. Bind the send port or create a filter expression as appropriate to define when BizTalk sends messages to the WSS form library.

9. Test the send port configuration by submitting a message conforming to the expense report schema. The expense report will appear in the form library as shown in Figure 10-25.

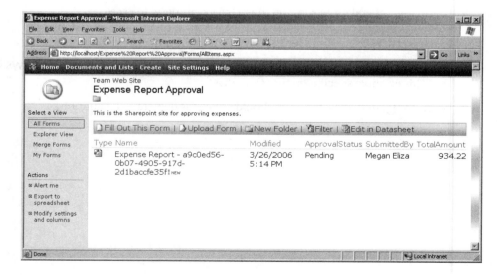

Figure 10-25. *Expense report in the form library*

Now that BizTalk is able to send the expense reports to the WSS form library, you need to add a receive location to pick up the accepted expense reports. The first step is to create a view in the WSS form library to display only the approved expense reports:

1. While viewing the form library, select Modify Settings and Columns from the left navigation pane.

2. Scroll to the bottom of the Customize Expense Report Approval page, and click the Create a New View link.

3. Select Standard view, and enter **Approved Expense Reports** to name the new view.

4. Under the Filter section, select the option Show Items Only When the Following Is True. Specify these conditions: ApprovalStatus, is equal to, and Approved, as shown in Figure 10-26. Click OK to create the view.

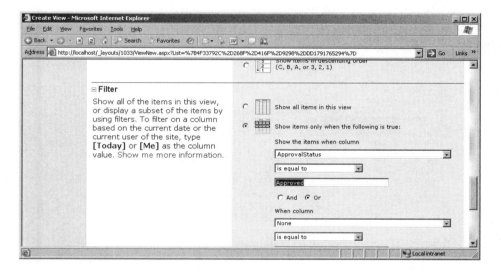

Figure 10-26. *Specifying filter criteria*

Now that the Approved Expense Reports view displays only approved expense reports, create a receive location to grab messages presented in the view:

1. Return to the BizTalk Server 2006 Administration Console.

2. Under the BizTalk Application 1 application, right-click the Receive Ports folder, and select New ➤ One-Way Receive Port.

3. Add a receive location to the new receive port, and specify the Windows SharePoint Services transport type.

4. Click the Configure button to open the Windows SharePoint Services Transport Properties dialog box.

5. Under the General properties, set the SharePoint site URL to the location of the WSS site. This example specifies `http://localhost`.

6. Under the General properties, set the source document library URL to the form library name. This example specifies Expense Report Approval.

7. Under the General properties, set the view name to the view that displays only approved expense reports. The `View Name` property in this example is `Approved Expense Reports`. The adapter properties should now appear as depicted in Figure 10-27.

Figure 10-27. *Receive location configuration*

8. Enable the receive location to start monitoring the WSS form library for approved expense reports.

After configuring the receive location to receive the approved expense reports from the WSS form library, demonstrate that the example is working correctly by approving an expense report:

1. Open the WSS form library, and select the name of the pending expense report. Figure 10-25 displays this existing expense report. Select Open when prompted to open the InfoPath form.

2. Change the approval status to Approved, as shown in Figure 10-28. Then save and close the InfoPath form.

3. After a few minutes, verify that the expense report no longer exists in the WSS form library. BizTalk has detected the new message in the `Approved Expense Reports` view and received the message.

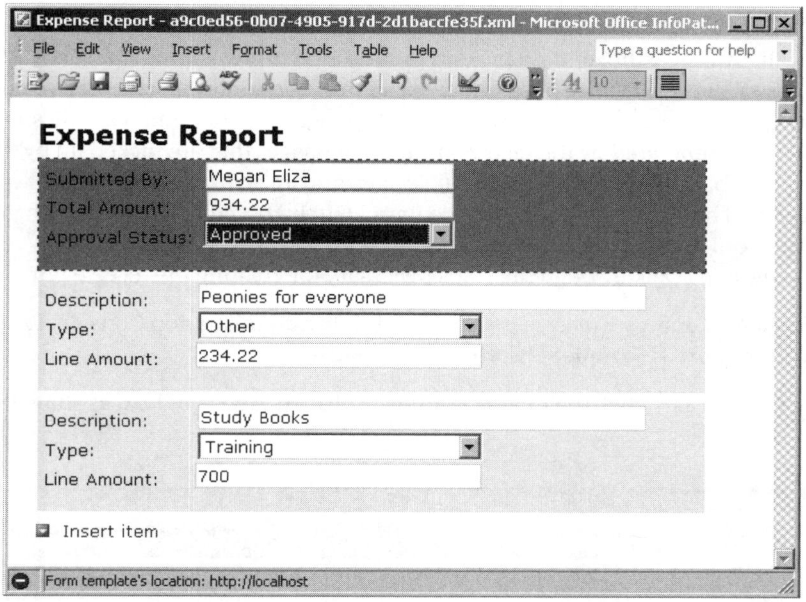

Figure 10-28. *Approving the expense report*

How It Works

Information workers are a new breed of business professionals. They are technology-savvy and depend on information to make their critical business decisions. Windows SharePoint Services delivers the information these demanding users need when and where they need it. It is an important piece of the Microsoft platform that will become more important with the advent of future innovations such as Microsoft Office 2007.

The legacy of enterprise integration technologies has primarily focused on facilitating computer-to-computer integration. With BizTalk 2006, Microsoft has introduced the Windows SharePoint Services adapter to make BizTalk a valuable tool in meeting information workers' demands.

The Windows SharePoint Services adapter also facilitates integration decisions that BizTalk cannot make automatically. Some decisions about how BizTalk should process information are simply too subjective, and human judgment must determine the outcome. The Windows SharePoint Services adapter provides one avenue for solving this problem, using WSS to display the known information, and capturing the result.

10-3. Subscribing to Suspended Messages

Problem

A message fails at some point in your BizTalk 2006 solution (such as a receive port, map, or orchestration) and ends up as a suspended message on the BizTalk MessageBox. You want to be able to subscribe to these suspended messages and route them to a file drop.

Solution

This solution will introduce the method needed to subscribe to suspended messages by demonstrating how to use a receive port/filtered send port combination. The receive port will listen for messages of a certain type to arrive on the MessageBox. The send port will subscribe to all error messages generated by the receive port. All messages that are picked up by the receive port will fail because of not having a subscriber, and an error message will be written to the MessageBox. These messages will then be immediately routed to the send port, and a file will be written out to a specified file location.

The following steps walk through the steps necessary for creating the receive port:

1. Creating a new one-way receive port in the BizTalk Administration Console. Enter the name of this port as **SampleSubscribeToSuspended**.

2. On the General Tab, click the Enable Routing for Failed Messages box, as shown in Figure 10-29.

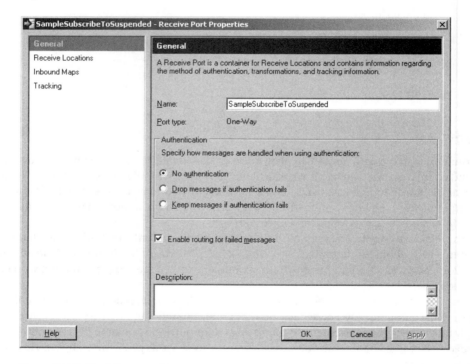

Figure 10-29. *Enabling routing*

3. On the Receive Locations tab, add a receive location to the port. Give a valid file path for the address of this location (such as C:\drop).

■Note When creating a receive port within the BizTalk Explorer in Visual Studio .NET, there is no way to set the `Enable Routing for Failed Messages` flag. You must do this through the BizTalk Administration Console.

---

4. Click OK. The receive port has been successfully configured and created.

5. Right-click the receive location, and enable it.

The following steps walk through the steps necessary for the send port. You can set up additional subscribers—for instance, an orchestration—to allow for more complex processing. In this solution, the send port will simply write the suspended message out to a file drop. For any properties not listed in the following steps, keep the default values.

1. Create a new one-way send port in the BizTalk Administration Console. Enter the name of this port as **SampleSuspendedToFile**.

2. On the General tab, set Transport Type to File, and enter a valid file path to which to write outgoing files. Set `Send Pipeline` to `PassThruTransmit`.

3. On the Filters tab, click the Property drop-down list, and select `ErrorReport.ReceivePortName`. Set the value equal to the name of the receive port created in the earlier steps (`SampleSubscribeToSuspended`). Do not use quotes.

4. Click OK. You have successfully configured and created the send port.

5. Do not enlist or start the send port at this time. At this point the solution is complete— aside from the enlistment of the send port. Dropping a file on the receive location will cause the receive port to throw an exception and log to the Event Viewer—there is no subscriber. The error message has been routed to the MessageBox, but there is no subscriber for it either.

6. Now enlist and start the send port. The receive location will fail to find a subscriber. This time, however, the error will be routed to the send port, and the message will be written out to the send port file location.

How It Works

A number of properties are available on the `ErrorReport` object. This solution worked with one of these, `ReceivePortName`. Building a more complex solution using an orchestration will allow access to all the remaining properties. For example, assume that instead of a send port subscribing to the `ErrorReport` as shown in this solution, you have an orchestration with a receive port. The orchestration will receive the message, and you can then access the `ErrorReport` properties in an Expression shape, as shown in Figure 10-30.

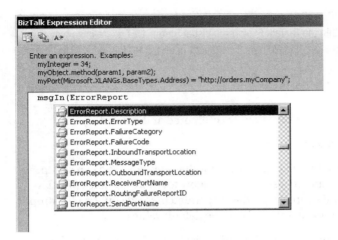

Figure 10-30. *Accessing the* ErrorReport *properties*

10-4. Using the POP3 Adapter

Problem

You need to receive an email message from a Post Office Protocol 3 (POP3) Internet email server.

Solution

This example configures a BizTalk receive location using the POP3 adapter to receive an email message. The steps to accomplish this are as follows:

1. Open the BizTalk Server 2006 Administration Console, and expand the BizTalk Application 1 default application.

2. Under the BizTalk Application 1 application, right-click the Receive Ports folder, and select New ➤ One-Way Receive Port.

3. Add a receive location to the new receive port, and specify the POP3 transport type.

4. Click the Configure button to open the POP3 Transport Properties dialog box.

5. In the POP3 Server configuration section, enter the name of the POP3 Internet mail server where BizTalk will receive messages, as shown in Figure 10-31.

6. Under the security configuration section, select the appropriate value for the authentication scheme setting for the POP3 mail server. Table 10-5 describes the authentication scheme choices.

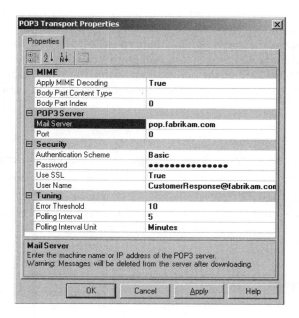

Figure 10-31. *POP3 receive location properties*

Table 10-5. *Authentication Schemes*

Authentication Type	Description
Basic	BizTalk passes the username and password to the POP3 mail server in clear text. Set the Use SSL property to True when using this option to protect the password confidentiality.
Digest	BizTalk computes a hash value of the username and password to send to the POP3 mail server. While this option obfuscates the credentials, set Use SSL to True to prevent a more sophisticated attempt to determine the credentials.
SPA	Secure Password Authentication (SPA) uses Windows credentials to authenticate with the POP3 mail server. Specify the username in the format <domain>\<username>, or <machine name>\<username> if using a local account. Set Use SSL to True to prevent exposing email messages while receiving them from the POP3 mail server

7. Specify the User Name property value. Some POP3 mail servers require the domain information, shown as CustomerResponse@fabrikam.com in Figure 10-31.

8. Select the Password property, and click the ellipsis to expose the password control. Enter the password for the username specified.

BizTalk will now detect and receive messages sent to the CustomerResponse@Fabrikam.com email address.

How It Works

The POP3 adapter can also receive email messages with a Multipurpose Internet Mail Extensions (MIME). A MIME message can contain multiple parts, and BizTalk can detect which of these parts to treat as the message body based on the part position within the MIME message or based on content type. The POP3 adapter can also receive message encrypted and signed with the S/MIME protocol.

■**Note** The POP3 adapter can only receive email messages. To send messages via email, use the SMTP adapter.

The POP3 adapter also promotes information about the email shown in Table 10-6 into message context. Filter expressions in an orchestration or send port can use these values.

Table 10-6. *POP3 Message Properties*

Property	Description
From	The email address of the message sender
To	The email address where the message was sent
ReplyTo	The reply to address specified by the message sender
CC	Email addresses of recipients copied on the message
Subject	The email subject
Date	The date when the mail server received the message
DispositionNotificationTo	The disposition notification recipient address of the email message
Headers	Contains all email message headers

10-5. Calling Pipelines from Within an Orchestration

Problem

You are developing an orchestration and need to use pipeline-processing stages within the workflow. Specifically, you need to validate a document and batch multiple messages into a single interchange. You want the orchestration to be efficient, minimizing the interactions between the orchestration and the MessageBox database.

Solution

BizTalk Server 2006 exposes a programmatic interface into pipelines, allowing you to call both receive and send pipelines directly from orchestrations. Your orchestration has the following steps, as shown in Figure 10-32:

1. Receive an order message in an industry-standard format.

2. Transform the message to a canonical version of the order schema.

3. Send the canonical order message to an external application for processing.

4. Receive a status message from the external application indicating the success or failure of the message processing.

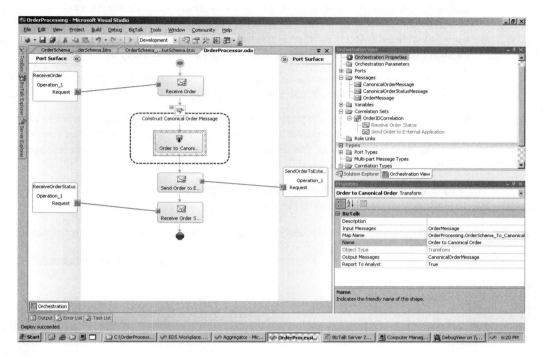

Figure 10-32. *Order processing orchestration—baseline*

In addition to the orchestration, you have also created a receive pipeline to validate the canonical order schema, an envelope, and a send pipeline to batch the canonical order and order response documents into a single interchange.

Open your orchestration in Visual Studio, and perform the following steps to implement the pipeline calls:

1. From the Toolbox, drag the following shapes onto the orchestration design surface (as shown in Figure 10-33):

   a. Drag a Scope shape named `Execute Receive Pipeline` directly below the `Construct Canonical Order Message` shape, and set the `Transaction Type` property to `Atomic`.

■**Note** The orchestration's `Transaction Type` property must be set to `Long Running` in order for it to hold an Atomic Scope shape.

---

b. Drag an Expression shape named `Execute Receive Pipeline` inside the Scope shape added in the previous step.

c. Drag a Construct Message shape named `Construct Validated Message` directly below the `Execute Receive Pipeline` Expression shape (also inside the `Execute Receive Pipeline` Scope shape), and set the `Messages Constructed` property to a message defined by your validating schema—in this solution, a message named `CanonicalOrderValidatedMessage` defined by the canonical order schema.

d. Drag a Message Assignment shape named `Assign Validated Message` inside the construct message shape added in the previous step.

e. Drag a Construct Message shape named `Construct Batched Message` directly below the `Receive Order Status` receive shape, and set the `Messages Constructed` property to an XML message—in this solution, a message named `BatchedOrderMessage` of type `System.Xml.XmlDocument`.

f. Drag a Message Assignment shape named Assign Batched Message inside the construct message shape added in the previous step.

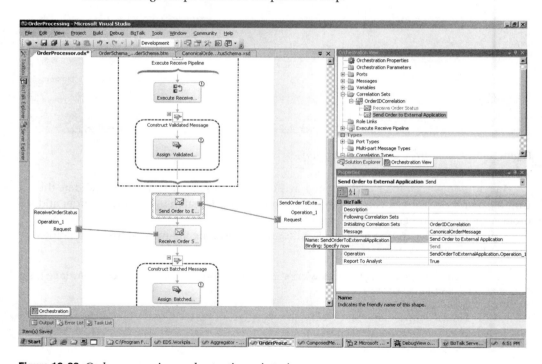

Figure 10-33. *Order processing orchestration—interim*

2. Add a reference in your BizTalk project to the `Microsoft.XLANGs.Pipeline.dll` (found in the root BizTalk installation folder), which holds the classes required for calling pipelines from orchestrations.

3. Create a new variable named ValidatePipelineOutput of type Microsoft.XLANGs.Pipeline. ReceivePipelineOutputMessages in the Execute Receive Pipeline Scope shape. This variable will hold the validated output of the call to the receive pipeline, containing the validated canonical order message.

4. Add the following code to the Execute Receive Pipeline Expression shape in order to call the appropriate receive pipeline:

```
ValidatePipelineOutput = Microsoft.XLANGs ➡
    .Pipeline.XLANGPipelineManager.ExecuteReceivePipeline ➡
    (typeof(OrderProcessing.ValidateCanonical ➡
    OrderSchemaReceivePipeline), ➡
    CanonicalOrderMessage);
```

5. Add the following code to the Assign Validated Message shape in order to extract the validated canonical order message:

```
CanonicalOrderValidatedMessage = null;
ValidatePipelineOutput.MoveNext();
ValidatePipelineOutput.GetCurrent(CanonicalOrderValidatedMessage);
```

Note To handle multiple output messages from a receive pipeline (when using an envelope for message debatching, for example), you may need to use a loop in order to iterate through the message collection and handle each appropriately.

---

6. Create a new variable named BatchingPipelineInput of type Microsoft.XLANGs.Pipeline. SendPipelineInputMessages. This variable will hold the output of the call to the send pipeline, containing the batched order messages.

7. Add the following code to the Assign Flat File Message shape in order to call the appropriate send pipeline (BatchedOrderMessages is a BizTalk message of type System.XML. XmlDocument and is used to hold the output of the ExecuteSendPipeline method call):

```
BatchedOrderMessages = null;
BatchingPipelineInput.Add(CanonicalOrderValidatedMessage);
BatchingPipelineInput.Add(CanonicalOrderStatusMessage);
Microsoft.XLANGs.Pipeline.XLANGPipelineManager.ExecuteSendPipeline
(typeof(OrderProcessing.BatchOrderAndStatusMessagesSendPipeline), ➡
    BatchingPipelineInput, BatchedOrderMessages);
```

8. Build and deploy the solution.

How It Works

This solution shows how to leverage pipeline processing directly from orchestrations—a feature new to BizTalk Server 2006 and one many of us wished was present in BizTalk Server 2004. In the past, one common workaround to this would be to send a message from an orchestration to the MessageBox database and then receive that same message in the orchestration. By making a round-trip to the MessageBox, a developer could leverage pipeline processing.

The `Microsoft.XLANGs.Pipeline.XLANGPipelineManager` class eliminates the need for round-tripping by exposing an API for calling pipelines programmatically.

■**Note** To use this class, you must add a reference in your BizTalk project to the `Microsoft.XLANGs. Pipeline` assembly.

In this scenario, you needed to use both a receive pipeline and a send pipeline. The receive pipeline allows you to validate a message that you create in the orchestration. You call the receive pipeline via the `ExecuteReceivePipeline` method, which has the following signature:

- Type: The fully qualified type of the receive pipeline you need to call. You format this parameter as `typeof(FullyQualifiedNameOfReceivePipeline)`. You can easily find the fully qualified type name of your receive pipeline by clicking the pipeline file in the Solution Explorer and viewing the `Fully Qualified Name` property, as shown in Figure 10-34.

- `XLANGMessage`: The XLANG Message object you need to pass into the receive pipeline.

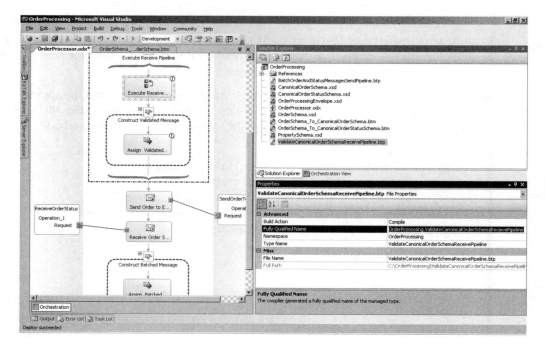

Figure 10-34. *Finding the fully qualified name*

This method returns an instance of the `Microsoft.XLANGs.Pipeline.`
`ReceivePipelineOutputMessages` class, which contains an enumeration of output messages
from the receive pipeline. In this solution, the pipeline produces a single message, and you are
able to easily extract the message by using the `MoveNext` and `GetCurrent` methods of the class.
If multiple messages could be returned by the receive pipeline, you would need to loop
through the `ReceivePipelineOutputMessages` object to extract each message. You can
accomplish this by using a Loop shape configured with `ValidatePipelineOutput.MoveNext()`
as the expression and an Assign Message shape configured with `ValidatePipelineOutput.`
`GetCurrent(CanonicalOrderValidatedMessage);` as the expression.

■Note You must place the code (usually contained within an Expression shape) that calls the receive pipeline
in an Atomic Scope shape because the `ReceivePipelineOutputMessages` class is not serializeable and cannot be persisted to the MessageBox.

The send pipeline batches multiple messages within the orchestration into a single interchange.
You call the send pipeline via the `ExecuteSendPipeline` method, which has the following signature:

- Type: The fully qualified type of the send pipeline you need to call. You format this
  parameter as `typeof(FullyQualifiedNameOfSendPipeline)`.

- `SendPipelineInputMessage`: The collection of messages you need to pass into the send
  pipeline.

- `XLANGMessage`: The XLANG Message object you will receive as output from the send
  pipeline.

■Note You must place the code that calls the send pipeline in a Message Assignment shape because the
`ExecuteSendPipeline` method constructs the `XLANGMessage` it passes as an output parameter.

Although calling pipelines from an orchestration generally results in the same functionality
and processing as when they are executed via BizTalk messaging objects, you need to be aware of
some differences. One of the most important discrepancies is the input and output XLANG Message objects that are passed to `ExecuteReceivePipeline` and `ExecuteSendPipeline`, respectively.
Although XLANG Message objects allow you define them as being of any type (`XmlDocument`,
`String`, `DateTime`, and so on), the XLANG Message instances you pass to the pipeline execute
methods must be XML documents. This means that the XLANG Message objects should be
defined by either the `System.Xml.XmlDocument` type or an XML schema to ensure consistent
behavior. This limitation is because the pipeline execution methods treat their XLANG Message
parameters as `XmlDocument` objects. Although it is possible to use a different type to define your
XLANG Message objects (such as `System.String`), it is advised you do so with caution and careful
consideration and validate that any data written to the message is in XML format.

■Note One shortcoming of this limitation is that it is not straightforward to call a send pipeline that assembles an XML document into flat file format, because the flat file string is returned as an XmlDocument object but likely does not conform to XML.

Another difference to be aware of is how tracking and monitoring data is handled. When calling pipelines from an orchestration, pipeline components leveraging the BAM Interceptor API are not supported, and the assembler/disassembler stages do not process tracking information. Additionally, transactional pipeline components are not supported when called from orchestrations.

Exception Handling

Any errors occurring in pipelines called from orchestrations cause an XLANGPipelineManagerException exception object to be thrown. Messages are not suspended, as they would be if the pipeline were executed by a messaging object (receive location or send port). This exception object can be handled via a catch exception block, which is configured on a Scope shape within an orchestration. Once the exception is caught, the exception's properties can be interrogated and the event handled appropriately.

Using an invalid document (using a character in the Identifier element, which expects an integer value) in this solution produces the following error:

```
There was a failure executing pipeline "OrderProcessing.ValidateCanonicalOrderSchema ➡
    ReceivePipeline".
Error details: ➡
    "The 'Identifier' element has an invalid value according to its data type.".

Exception type: XLANGPipelineManagerException
Source: Microsoft.XLANGs.Pipeline
Target Site: Microsoft.XLANGs.Pipeline.ReceivePipelineOutputMessages ExecutePipeline ➡
    (Microsoft.BizTalk.PipelineOM.ReceivePipeline, Microsoft. ➡
    XLANGs.BaseTypes.XLANGMessage)
```

As you can see, the exception thrown has a type of XLANGPipelineManagerException, and the description indicates the specific validation failure.

10-6. Resuming Inbound Message Processing

Problem

BizTalk has encountered an error and suspended the processing of an inbound message. You need to fix the error and resume message processing to receive it successfully.

Solution

This example demonstrates the resumable inbound message-processing capabilities of BizTalk 2006. BizTalk initially receives a message that has no recipients. In the publish/subscribe architecture of the MessageBox, the error message will indicate that BizTalk cannot find a subscriber to the message. After creating the appropriate subscription, this example resumes processing and successfully delivers the message.

This example highlights an important change between BizTalk 2004 and BizTalk 2006. BizTalk 2006 supports resumable inbound interchange processing. BizTalk suspends the message while receiving it, and the administrator can resume the message after fixing the configuration error. With BizTalk 2004 certain adapters such as the File adapter would discard the message after failing to find a subscriber to it and lose the message. Other adapters would receive a failure code from BizTalk and leave the original message intact.

Begin by creating the receive port and receive location that will accept the message:

1. Open the BizTalk Server 2006 Administration Console by selecting Start ➤ All Programs ➤ Microsoft BizTalk Server 2006 ➤ BizTalk Server Administration.

2. In the left pane of the BizTalk Server 2006 Administration Console, go to the default BizTalk Application 1, and right-click the `Receive Ports` folder. Select New ➤ One-Way Receive Port from the context menu.

3. Enter **SuspendedMessagesExampleIn** for the name of the new receive port.

4. Add a receive location to the receive port, using the default `PassThroughReceive` pipeline. For more information about creating a receive port, please see Recipe 3-1.

5. Using the File transport type, specify `C:\SuspendedMessagesExample\In` as the receive folder. Create the folders if necessary.

6. Grant the BizTalk Application Users group full control to the `C:\SuspendedMessagesExample` folder.

7. Enable the receive location.

BizTalk can now receive messages, but the administrator has not specified where BizTalk should deliver the messages. BizTalk will raise an error to the event log and suspend messages received through the `SuspendedMessagesExampleIn` receive port. Follow these steps:

1. Place an XML file in the `C:\SuspendedMessagesExample\In` folder.

2. In the left tree view of the BizTalk Server 2006 Administration Console, select the BizTalk group to display the group overview in the right pane. Press the F5 key to refresh the Group Overview page. Note that there is one resumable suspended message, as shown in Figure 10-35.

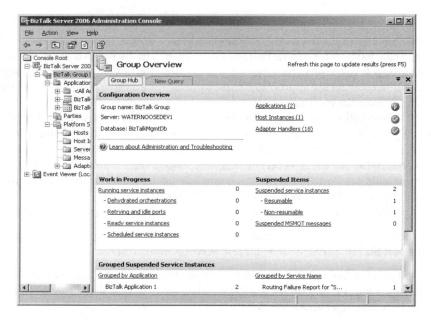

Figure 10-35. *Suspended a message in the group overview*

3. Click the Suspended Service Instances link to open the Suspended tab. Note that the Suspended tab displays one resumable suspended service instance, as shown in Figure 10-36.

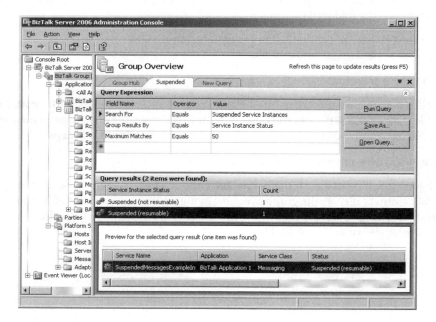

Figure 10-36. *Resumable service instance*

Now that there is a suspended message in BizTalk, create a send port to deliver the message and resume message processing:

1. In the BizTalk Server 2006 Administration Console, navigate to the BizTalk Application 1, right-click the Send Ports folder, and select New ➤ Static One-Way Send Port from the context menu.

2. Enter **SuspendedMessagesExampleOut** for the name of the send port, and configure the File adapter to deliver messages to the C:\SuspendedMessagesExample\Out folder. Create the folder if necessary. Use the default PassThruTransmit send pipeline.

3. In the left pane of the SuspendedMessagesExampleOut – Send Port Properties dialog box, select Filters.

4. Define a filter where BTS.ReceivePortName equals SuspendedMessagesExampleIn, as shown in Figure 10-37. This will create a subscription for all messages received through the SuspendedMessagesExampleIn receive port.

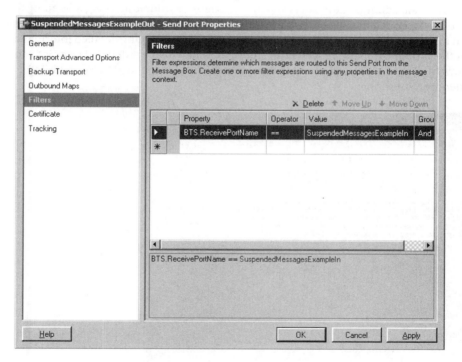

Figure 10-37. *Defining a message subscription*

5. Enlist and start the SuspendedMessagesExampleOut send port.

6. On the Group Overview page of the BizTalk Server 2006 Administration Console, return to the Suspended tab.

7. Select the Suspended (Resumable) query results to display the suspended SuspendedMessagesExampleIn service instance.

8. Right-click the suspended service instance, and select Resume Instance from the context menu. Click Yes when prompted to confirm. If the Resume Instance option is not available, verify that the selected service instance's status is Suspended (Resumable) under the query results.

9. Verify that BizTalk successfully delivered the XML message to the C:\SuspendedMessagesExample\Out folder.

How It Works

The resumable inbound message–processing capabilities of BizTalk 2006 reflect the improved administrative capabilities over BizTalk 2004. For additional information about the improved suspended message troubleshooting capabilities of BizTalk 2006, please see Recipe 8-1.

The BizTalk administrator can also perform extensive troubleshooting to identify the cause of a suspended message. Double-clicking the Suspended (resumable) service instance shown in Figure 10-36 opens a Service Details dialog box containing detailed information about the suspended message. The Error Information tab displays detailed error information as shown in Figure 10-38, indicating that the message was suspended because BizTalk could not identify a subscriber.

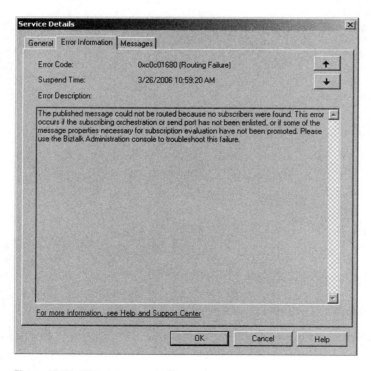

Figure 10-38. *Viewing error information*

The Messages tab displays all the messages in the suspended service instance. Double-clicking a message opens the Message Details dialog box. Select Context in the left pane of the Message Details dialog box to display the message's context properties, as shown in Figure 10-39. BizTalk can use the Promoted context properties to identify the subscriber of a message.

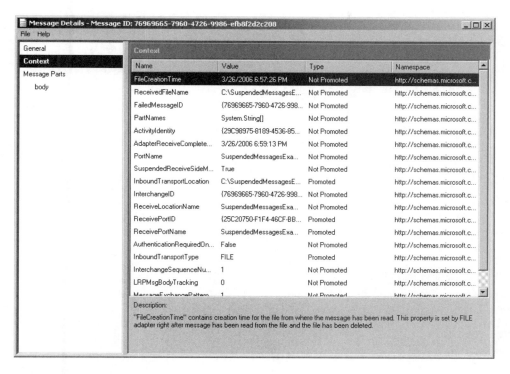

Figure 10-39. *Message context properties*

Back on the Suspended tab of the BizTalk Server 2006 Administration Console, the BizTalk administrator can right-click a suspended message and navigate the Troubleshoot Routing Failure submenu to identify the cause of a routing failure.

Although most suspended messages in BizTalk 2006 are resumable, in some situations BizTalk cannot resume message processing. One example is when BizTalk uses order delivery messages in the same order BizTalk receives them. In this situation, resuming a message would also deliver it out of order, so BizTalk prevents resuming the message.

Index

FIND IT FAST

with the Apress *SuperIndex*™

Quickly Find Out What the Experts Know

Leading by innovation, Apress now offers you its *SuperIndex*™, a turbocharged companion to the fine index in this book. The Apress *SuperIndex*™ is a keyword and phrase-enabled search tool that lets you search through the entire Apress library. Powered by dtSearch™, it delivers results instantly.

Instead of paging through a book or a PDF, you can electronically access the topic of your choice from a vast array of Apress titles. The Apress *SuperIndex*™ is the perfect tool to find critical snippets of code or an obscure reference. The Apress *SuperIndex*™ enables all users to harness essential information and data from the best minds in technology.

No registration is required, and the Apress *SuperIndex*™ is free to use.

❶ Thorough and comprehensive searches of over 300 titles

❷ No registration required

❸ Instantaneous results

❹ A single destination to find what you need

❺ Engineered for speed and accuracy

❻ Will spare your time, application, and anxiety level

Search now: *http://superindex.apress.com*

You Need the Companion eBook